THE OREGON QUESTION

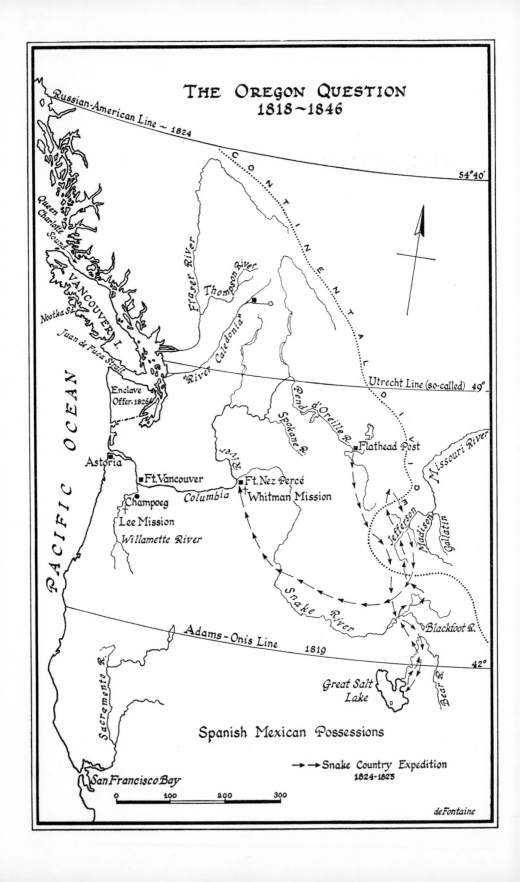

THE OREGON QUESTION
1818~1846

Russian-American Line ~ 1824

54°40'

CONTINENTAL

Fraser River

Thompson River

Queen
Charlotte
Sound

VANCOUVER I.

Nootka Sd.

Juan de Fuca Strait

"River Caledonia"

Utrecht Line (so-called) 49°

Enclave
Offer 1826

PACIFIC OCEAN

Pend d'Oreille R.

Spokane R.

Flathead Post

Missouri River

DIVIDE

Astoria

Ft.Vancouver

River

Ft.Nez Percé
Whitman Mission

Champoeg

Columbia

Jefferson

Madison

Gallatin

Lee Mission

Willamette River

Snake River

Blackfoot R.

Adams-Onís Line   1819

42°

Sacramento R.

Great Salt
Lake

Bear R.

Spanish Mexican Possessions

→ → Snake Country Expedition
1824-1825

San Francisco Bay

0   100   200   300

deFontaine

THE OREGON QUESTION

Essays in Anglo-American Diplomacy and Politics

FREDERICK MERK

THE BELKNAP PRESS OF
HARVARD UNIVERSITY PRESS

CAMBRIDGE, MASSACHUSETTS · 1967

To

L.B.M.

K.L.M.F.

F.B.M.

CONTENTS

CONTENTS

viii

INTRODUCTION

AMONG THE continents of the world the North American is unique in one respect. All its principal states are transcontinental. The United States, Canada, and Mexico each has frontage on two oceans, a circumstance of obvious significance in world history. The United States and Canada acquired their adjacent Pacific frontage at the same time and by the same treaty—the Oregon Treaty of 1846. This agreement and the diplomacy by which it was achieved have more than passing significance, therefore, for each of them.

A long series of disagreements and crises preceded the treaty. The disagreements—exhibited in repeated unsuccessful negotiations —became part of the final crisis. They must be understood if the treaty is to be understood. They were a product of forces reaching back to the early years of American nationality.

One of the forces was curiosity in regard to the geography of that far country—scientific interest, if you will. This led to exploration. The earliest exploration was maritime and was directed in part, at least, to the age-old question whether a passage could be found at the northern end of the North American land-mass which would permit intercourse between the Pacific and Atlantic oceans. This was a force for exploration as late as the 1790's. It was mentioned in the directions to Captain George Vancouver for his famous exploring expedition to the Northwest Coast.

Overland exploration by way of British North America and of the United States was likewise a result of scientific interest. The overland journey of Alexander Mackenzie from Lake Athabasca to the Pacific shore in 1792–93 was motivated largely by such interest. So was the Lewis and Clark expedition which Jefferson sent to the Columbia a decade later. Jefferson was not moved at all by territorial acquisitiveness in sending out the expedition. Indeed, he was opposed to acquiring any trans-Rocky Mountain territory for fear of what the acquisition would do to American democracy. It would fasten colonialism onto the structure of the United States.

Colonialism was a disease of monarchy. It would be fatal to American democracy if the virus took hold. This was a sentiment general among Jeffersonians, and it became general later among Whigs.

One force generating national rivalries in the Oregon Country was the fur trade. This served as a stimulus to exploration. It moved Alexander Mackenzie in part. It also sent British maritime adventurers to the Nootka Sound region and into the Nootka Sound crisis. Robert Gray, the American discoverer of the mouth of the Columbia, who gave the United States its first claim to the Oregon Country, was a fur trader. So was John Jacob Astor, who founded Astoria.

Fur traders were generators of diplomatic tensions. They kept the British Foreign Office busy in the early stages of the Oregon controversy as will appear in these essays. They influenced British Oregon policy and kept the issue unsettled. The British government was a monarchy, much interested in the profits of colonialism. It did not scruple to employ methods which a democracy would not tolerate. One of these was the creation of colonizing corporations armed with monopolistic privileges, such as were given the British East India Company and the Hudson's Bay Company. As early as 1821 Parliament gave the Hudson's Bay Company a monopoly of all British trade rights in the Oregon Country. The Company became a power against which American individual enterprise could not compete, as was pointed out by Caleb Cushing, a leading statesman and diplomat of the United States, in December 1845, in a lead article in the *Democratic Review* entitled "English Politico-Commercial Companies." The article received wide publicity at the time of the final Oregon crisis and aroused indignation against the British in Democratic circles. By virtue of monopolistic practices the Hudson's Bay Company was able to drive American fur traders out of the Oregon Country. It became the colossus of that country under the direction of its Chief Factor, Dr. John McLoughlin. Still, in the end, the Company could not hold the region south of the 49th parallel for the British crown. All this would seem to indicate that the fur trade was not an enduring force in shaping the evolution of the Oregon question.

Missionary enterprise was also a force, though not an enduring one, in shaping the course of that question. It impelled missionaries to come to the Oregon Country to convert the heathen to Christianity. It introduced an idealistic thread into the furry fabric of the problem. Such a thread was not uncommon. It has appeared in the world often in the rivalries of states to uplift the heathen. In Oregon the earliest missionaries were American. In 1834 a group of Methodists, led by Jason Lee and his nephew Daniel, arrived at Fort Vancouver with a view to working among the aborigines of the Flathead country. They decided, however, almost at once to labor in the Willamette, where the outlook was better and protection nearer. They became interested increasingly in material things, indeed, to an extent arousing criticism from their religious supporters in the East. Their glowing reports home of the beauties of the Willamette Valley and its agricultural promise are said to have caught the eye of the restless in the United States who were potential pioneers, and may have induced pioneering to the Oregon Country. But it is true that pioneering to the Oregon Country assumed no significant dimensions until the early 1840's, when farmers in the Middle West had become reduced to despair by the hard times following the panics of 1837 and 1841.

A group of missionaries led by Marcus Whitman and representing the American Board of Commissioners for Foreign Missions arrived in the Nez Percé country of the Walla Walla Valley in 1836. It labored heroically though not wholly successfully with those Indians. The Nez Percés were attracted by the imagery of the Catholic faith, set before them by Canadian missionaries and by the itinerant, Father Pierre De Smet, a St. Louis missionary. A legend was developed later that Marcus Whitman "saved" the Oregon Country by a dramatic "winter ride" across the Great Plains in 1842–43 and by an appeal to Daniel Webster not to give up the country. But this has been disputed by historians and has credit no longer with any of them. The Whitman party was ultimately wiped out in a famous massacre by the Nez Percés.

British missionaries cannot be said to have determined the fate of the Oregon Country either. The earliest of them was an Anglican, Reverend Herbert Beaver, sent to Fort Vancouver in 1836 by the religious-minded in the directorate of the Hudson's Bay Company. He was to serve as chaplain at the Fort Vancouver post and to minister to the surrounding Indians. He was not well suited to missionary labors on a raw fur traders' frontier. He devoted

himself chiefly to his chaplain duties. He took exception to the customs of fur traders at the post, especially to their informal unions
with half breed or full breed Indian women. He thought unions
not sanctified by the law and sacraments of the Anglican church
immoral. They seemed unions in sin even if children resulted. The
white-haired Chief Factor had been living in sin in that way. The
servants of the Hudson's Bay Company residing at the post were
predominantly French Canadians and Catholics, and Dr. McLoughlin had Catholic leanings himself. Controversies over the schooling
of Catholic children at the post arose. Problems arose also because
of the absence of creature comforts at Fort Vancouver. A limited
supply of wine was a major one of these. Differences with
McLoughlin finally led to a physical encounter in which the missionary was knocked down by a blow over the head with a cane
carried by the imperious Chief Factor. This led to a return of the
missionary to England as soon as possible thereafter (1838) and the
publication to the world of accounts of shocking moral conditions
condoned by the Company in Oregon. The result was that the
missionary field at Fort Vancouver was left untilled thereafter by
the Company. It was left to be worked by non-Anglicans. When
the Oregon crisis arrived in 1845–46 no missionary interest in it
was felt in England. More eloquence was heard in Parliament and
in the British press in a fortnight over happenings in the French
protectorate of the island of Tahiti in the South Pacific, where a
British Anglican missionary had been mistreated, than had been
heard regarding Oregon in a quarter century.

Oregon pioneers of American background were a steadily growing power in Oregon affairs at the time of the crisis of 1845–46.
But their contribution to the solution of the crisis was not the simple one ascribed to them in earlier accounts. They did not just take
possession of the region in dispute. The region in dispute was that
which lies between the Columbia River and the 49th parallel—the
so-called "Oregon triangle." The possessors of that triangle in the
critical period were indeed pioneers, but of British origin—servants
of the Hudson's Bay Company and of the Puget Sound Agricultural Company. Their pre-emption of the ground at the core of the
dispute became one of the complications facing the British government in conceding the area to the United States. If Polk had been
content to wait, under Calhoun's prescription of "masterly inac-

tivity," while American pioneers silently and gradually occupied the Oregon Country, the outcome might conceivably have been that Canada would not have acquired frontage on the Pacific. But Polk acted before they could become a decisive factor, even for the area which came to the United States by the treaty.

If the truth must be told, the forces described above were merely marginal in their effects on the outcome of the Oregon dispute. The definitive forces were diplomacy and, related to it, politics in both countries. These are the forces emphasized in these essays. Diplomacy and politics are less fashionable than they once were in explaining the course of international issues, but they did operate at the centers of authority in both Washington and London in 1846, and with effects on the outcome that are measurable by scholarly documentation.

The postulate upon which these essays rest is that diplomacy and politics are summations of interrelated forces at work in society—in national and international society. The two forces were certainly at work in Polk's America. Indeed in the Polk era they seem almost indistinguishable. An observation once made by a clear-sighted observer of American diplomacy and politics, Carl Russell Fish, is to the point here. He noted in his volume, *American Diplomacy:* "By 1815 diplomacy had ceased to shape politics; after 1830 politics began to shape diplomacy." By the time of the Polk administration the shaping of diplomacy by politics was a confirmed habit.

In the extended history of the Oregon dispute six negotiations to partition the vast region were held—the first in 1818, the last in 1846. An early series of three was held in London. The three later ones were held in Washington. Both series are described in chronological order here. The concluding negotiation and the forces shaping it are described in detail in a succession of essays topically arranged.

Of the essays, nine are reprints from scholarly journals. A tenth is a reprint of one of the Harvard Historical Monographs, *Albert Gallatin and the Oregon Problem.* Four of the essays are now printed for the first time. They are Essay Two, "The Oregon Question in 1818," Essay Seven, "Arbitration Only at the Cannon's Mouth!" Essay Twelve, "Sea Power and the Oregon Boundary Settlement," and "Résumé." The "Résumé" is a dovetailing of all the others. The volume is intended to illustrate the principle of multiple causation in history. Each essay is a self-contained unit with a thesis of its own. At the same time each essay advances the narrative of the whole. This form will be found to have merits for the reader. It entails some repetition of factual matter but this has been kept to a minimum.

I am indebted to the publishers of the *American Historical Review*, the *Mississippi Valley Historical Review* (now the *Journal of American History*), and *Agricultural History* for permission to republish articles originally appearing in them. My greatest indebtedness is to my wife, Dr. Lois Bannister Merk, who in the more recent of these essays has been my collaborator in research and in writing. If errors are found she cannot claim to be guiltless of them for our collaboration has been too close to permit distributing any fault or merit which the essays may have.

F.M.

Cambridge, Massachusetts
May 1966

THE OREGON QUESTION

ESSAY 1 · THE GENESIS OF
THE OREGON QUESTION*

IN THE spring of 1792 two sea captains, sailing a few days distance apart, moved northward on the little known waters of the Northwest coast of North America. They were on voyages destined to be famous in the annals of exploration and diplomacy. One of them was Captain George Vancouver, an officer of the British navy, commanding the sloop of war *Discovery* and the armed tender *Chatham*. He had served an apprenticeship in exploration of the Pacific as a youthful seaman and midshipman under the great Captain James Cook. The other was Captain Robert Gray, a New England trader, commander of the ship *Columbia*. He had been for several years engaged in the traffic of furs on the Northwest coast.

Captain Vancouver had orders from his government to explore and survey the coast of the Pacific Northwest, and particularly to ascertain whether, between the North Pacific and the North Atlantic, there was any navigable passage. He was to determine whether by means of inlets of the Pacific or by large rivers that had communication with lakes in the interior an intercourse could be established between the opposite shores of the North American continent. He was to explore especially the "supposed" strait of Juan de Fuca, said to be situated between the 48th and 49th degrees of north latitude. The discovery of a near communication between any such strait and any river running into or from the Lake of the Woods would be particularly useful.[1] If a navigable passage was not found at the strait of Juan de Fuca or some other southerly inlet, an examination was to be made of Cook's River, the sources of which were to be inquired about from Canadian and British fur traders. But the finding of a communication more to the south-

---

* Reprinted from the *Mississippi Valley Historical Review*, XXXVI (March 1950).

[1] Captain George Vancouver, *A Voyage of Discovery to the North Pacific Ocean, and Round the World*, 3 vols. (London, 1798), I, xviii.

ward, should any such exist, was much preferred, and the search for it was to be given priority.

Exploration was but one of Vancouver's assignments. Diplomacy was another. In 1789 a British merchant, John Meares, who had built a fur trading establishment at Nootka Sound, had been dispossessed of his establishment and of vessels connected with it by a Spanish naval officer acting in enforcement of Spain's claim to sovereignty on the Northwest coast. The seizure had produced an Anglo-Spanish crisis—almost a European war. In the end Spain had been obliged to capitulate. By the Nootka Sound Convention of 1790 she had renounced her claim to exclusive jurisdiction over the Northwest coast; she had compensated Meares for his losses; and had agreed to make formal restitution to a representative of the British crown of the land and buildings that had been seized. Vancouver was the agent chosen by the British government to accept the restitution.

Vancouver had another purpose in coming to the Northwest coast. He had a patriotic resolve to establish British claims of sovereignty in place of those which Spain was relinquishing. It was a resolve that did not appear in his written instructions but became clear enough in his activities as an explorer. On the completion of a portion of his survey he paused in Admiralty Inlet to take formal possession, on behalf of his sovereign, of all the coast line of "New Albion" from the point at which he had begun the survey, in north latitude 39° 20', to the point at which he had then arrived. And at the end of his survey he had a similar ceremony performed covering the coast line from Admiralty Inlet to the farthermost limit in Alaskan waters reached by his expedition. Likewise on his way homeward he induced the King of Owhyee to cede his island to George III.

On his voyage northward Vancouver was brought by favorable winds and fair weather at noon on April 27, 1792, to north latitude 46° 19'. There he observed, outlined against the shore six miles off, an opening or bay south of a conspicuous promontory. Between the opening and his ship lay a line of white breakers, warning of a concealed bar. A description of the opening was in his possession, written by the trader Meares. In 1788 Meares had made a superficial examination of the opening in search of a river that a Spanish explorer, Bruno de Heçeta, reported to have seen there in 1775.

No river had been found by Meares, in token of which he had named the promontory "Cape Disappointment," and the opening south of it "Deception Bay." Vancouver noticed that the sea through which his vessel was passing had changed at this point "from its natural to river coloured water," which, he thought, was "the probable consequence of some streams falling into the bay, or into the ocean to the north of it through the low land."[2]

The combination of two such phenomena as an opening and river-colored water six miles out at sea was suggestive. Normally an explorer would have paused for an investigation. But Vancouver was eager to reach the strait of Juan de Fuca where lay what seemed to him his greatest opportunity as an explorer. The opening he believed to be inaccessible, because of the bar, to a vessel of the burthen of his own. He was swayed in his thinking, perhaps, by the negative findings of Meares. A favorable wind was upon the sea and he decided to make use of it. He dismissed the subject of the opening from his mind with this comment entered upon his record: "Not considering this opening worthy of more attention I continued our pursuit to the N. W. being desirous to embrace the advantages of the now prevailing breeze and pleasant weather, so favorable to our examination of the coast."[3] It was a comment that recorded a missed opportunity, for the opening that he did not deem worthy of more attention was the mouth of the Columbia River.

Two days later a sail was sighted by Vancouver just ahead. It proved to be the ship *Columbia* with Captain Robert Gray in command. The *Columbia* was overhauled, and Gray, who was credited in England with having penetrated the mysterious strait of Juan de Fuca and having emerged from it to the northward in 1789, was eagerly interviewed on behalf of Captain Vancouver. The interview satisfied Vancouver that Gray had not gone far into the strait. Then the two captains parted company, Gray turning his ship southward in the direction from which Vancouver had just come. Sailing close in to shore, for he was seeking Indian villages that might yield a trade in furs, Gray appeared off Cape Disappointment on May 11, 1792, just a fortnight after Vancouver had been there. South of the cape he sighted the opening which

2 *Ibid.*, 209–10.
3 *Ibid.*

Vancouver had deemed not worthy of attention. To him it appeared to be a spacious harbor. He noted the line of white breakers that stretched across the entrance. Turning the prow of his ship into the breakers, an act that seemed madness to at least one of his officers, he rode safely through them, and on the other side found the mouth of the mighty river—mightiest in North America next to the Mississippi—which still bears his ship's name.[4]

This casual discovery, this accident of the fur trade, was an accident of the kind that shapes history. It established for the United States a claim to the whole valley of the Columbia; it built for the republic the foundations of empire. In America it aroused curiously little interest at first. It was a discovery ahead of its generation. The earliest public reference to it seems to have been Vancouver's in his *Voyage of Discovery to the North Pacific Ocean*, printed in 1798.[5] In 1792 the American nation, it should be remembered, was hardly more than three years out of the cradle of the Constitution, and its territory and horizon were still bounded by the river channel of the Mississippi. But the day was to come when Gray's achievement was to be put to full use, when added to such others as the Lewis and Clark expedition, the Astoria venture, the Spanish treaty of 1819, and the migration of the pioneers to the valley of the Willamette, it was to give the United States frontage on the Pacific, it was to convert the republic into a transcontinental power, with ambitions in Hawaii, with outlook toward the Orient, and with interests in the Orient that were to be challenged ultimately at Pearl Harbor.

As for Vancouver, he explored and mapped the coast of the Pacific Northwest from California to Cook's Inlet. He established, in place of information that was spotty, inaccurate, and private, a chart that was detailed, accurate, and public. He devoted to this service two and a half years of arduous labor. In the first year he examined the waters around Vancouver Island, circumnavigating the island for the first time. He discovered Puget Sound, the Gulf of Georgia, and Johnstone Strait. He failed, through a curious

---

[4] The documentary records of this discovery are conveniently gathered in F. W. Howay (ed.), *Voyages of the "Columbia,"* Massachusetts Historical Society *Collections* (Boston), LXXIX (1941); see especially pp. 396–99, 435–38, 483–84. Robert Gray was off the mouth of the Columbia seeking unsuccessfully to enter the river earlier on this voyage, according to an account he gave to Vancouver's officers. See Vancouver, *Voyage of Discovery to the North Pacific Ocean*, I, 215.

[5] Vancouver, *Voyage of Discovery to the North Pacific Ocean*, I, 415.

inability to recognize the coastal evidences of the presence of great streams, to discover the mouth of Fraser River. By the late summer of 1792 he had completed his circuit of Vancouver Island and was back at Nootka Sound for the restitution agreed upon with Spain. While at Nootka he learned of Gray's great river discovery and was shown a chart, drawn by Gray, of the mouth of the Columbia.[6] In the autumn of the year on his way southward to winter quarters he took occasion to verify the discovery. He confirmed his earlier opinion that the bar athwart the opening south of Cape Disappointment could not be crossed by a vessel of the burthen of his own. On this occasion, however, he sent across the *Chatham*, which, under the command of Lieutenant William R. Broughton, entered the Columbia and explored and surveyed it for a distance of a hundred miles from its mouth.

The voyage of Vancouver, judged as a venture in imperialism, was unsuccessful. It failed in its chief empire objectives. The projected ceremony of restitution at Nootka came to no result owing to the fact that Vancouver raised the issue with the Spanish representatives of the precise lot of land to be restored. The Owhyee triumph proved vain, the cession of that island being in the end disapproved by the British government. The exploration of the Northwest coast reinforced merely, it did not create, a British claim to territory. At the mouth of the Columbia the great opportunity of the expedition was passed by, an opportunity that a fortnight later an American was to seize and that the American government was ultimately to convert into a claim to the Pacific Northwest rival to England's.

A contest of exploration, colonization, and diplomacy in the Pacific Northwest followed the discovery of the Columbia. It followed not at once, but as soon as the American people had caught a glimpse of their destiny on the Pacific Ocean. In 1803 the United States acquired the province of Louisiana. By this coup of diplomacy the republic extended its boundaries to the crest of the Rocky Mountains and strengthened, through the principle of contiguity, the claim it had to the territory west of the mountains. In 1805–1806 the Lewis and Clark expedition explored and mapped the middle tributaries of the Columbia and the main river from its junction with the Snake to the sea. In 1811–1812 John Jacob Astor,

[6] *Ibid.*

at the head of the Pacific Fur Company, built Astoria at the mouth of the Columbia and other trade posts on the upper waters of the river. These measures broadened the claim of the United States to the Columbia Valley. They added to American rights arising from Gray's discovery those of contiguity, systematic exploration, and occupation.

In the same period the British also strengthened their claims to the Pacific Northwest. They did so, however, in the area north rather than in the area south of the 49th parallel. In 1793 Alexander Mackenzie crossed the continent to the Pacific Ocean in the northerly latitude of Lake Athabasca, coming out to the sea at Bentinck Inlet. In 1805 Simon Fraser of the North West Company established for the British their first interior trading post west of the Rocky Mountains in what is now British Columbia. In 1808 the same trader and an associate, at the head of an exploring party, descended the turbulent Fraser to its mouth. In the years 1807–1811 David Thompson, the geographer of the North West Company, worked his way down the great northern arm of the Columbia to the river's mouth, where, however, he found, already established, the associates and servants of John Jacob Astor.

The outbreak of the War of 1812 opened a new phase in this competition for empire. At the prompting of the North West Company the British government sent out the sloop of war *Racoon* to capture Astoria. With her a North West Company merchantman sailed to take over the fur business of the Columbia River. The *Racoon* appeared at Astoria in December, 1813, her officers joyfully anticipating a rich war prize. They found Astoria and all its contents already British property. The associates of Astor, realizing that they were helpless in the face of British sea power, had already sold the entire property to local agents of the North West Company. The captain of the *Racoon*, not content to leave well enough alone, made a formal capture by staging at the post a flag lowering ceremony. Astoria as a result became doubly British. Its name was changed, in honor of the British King, to Ft. George, and over it, at the mouth of the river Gray had discovered, was raised the British flag.

The American government, in the meantime, was preparing for peace negotiations. In March, 1814, before the news of the taking of Astoria had reached Washington, the following special instructions were sent to the American peace commissioners in Europe:

Should a treaty be concluded with Great Britain, and a reciprocal restitution of territory be agreed on, you will have it in recollection that the United States had in their possession, at the commencement of the war, a post at the mouth of the river Columbia, which commanded the river, which ought to be comprised in the stipulation, should the possession have been wrested from us during the war. On no pretext can the British Government set up a claim to territory south of the northern boundary of the United States. It is not believed that they have any claim whatever to territory on the Pacific ocean. You will, however, be careful, should a definition of boundary be attempted, not to countenance, in any manner, or in any quarter, a pretension in the British Government to territory south of that line.[7]

This instruction, written by James Monroe, is the first ever prepared by the American government on the Oregon issue. It is therefore of special interest in the history of the evolution of American Oregon policy. Two ideas stand out in it, both rather loosely phrased, which had importance for the future. One is the idea that south of the "northern boundary of the United States" British pretentions were not to be countenanced. The northern boundary of the United States referred to so confidently was that of Louisiana. It was believed to be the 49th parallel and to have been fixed by commissioners appointed by France and England to implement the Treaty of Utrecht of 1713. It had never been actually established. In 1807 an attempt had been made to establish it. The 49th parallel had been designated by commissioners of the United States and England as the line from the Lake of the Woods westward as far as the respective territories of the two states extend in that quarter. But the convention, of which this agreement was part, had failed of ratification. Monroe, however, in 1814 assumed that the 49th parallel was the boundary and his instruction is the germ of later American policy of making this the boundary, also, of the Oregon country. A second idea appearing in the instruction, which was destined to reappear in later years, was the sweeping denial that the British "have any claim whatever to territory on

[7] *American State Papers, Foreign Relations*, 6 vols. (Washington, 1832–1859), III, 731.

the Pacific ocean." This idea, the genesis of "Fifty Four Forty or Fight," was of doubtful historical validity, and in 1814 it comported ill with the military and diplomatic situation of the United States.

At Ghent territorial issues were given precedence over all others. The issues that had caused the war were allowed to be pushed unsettled to one side. The British commissioners at the outset of the negotiations made territorial demands on the United States such as a conquering nation makes upon one defeated and suing for peace. The American commissioners met these demands with a determination to negotiate no peace other than one based on a reciprocal restoration of conquests. The treaty ultimately concluded contained a formula of reciprocal restitution of conquests. The formula was that "All territory, places and possessions whatsoever taken by either party from the other during the war, or which may be taken after the signing of this Treaty, excepting only the Islands hereinafter mentioned [in Passamaquoddy Bay], shall be restored without delay."[8]

In the discussions at Ghent silence was maintained by both sides on the Astoria issue and the related boundary. The Astoria issue was not mentioned at all; the boundary issue was mentioned once, in the protocols, but only for the purpose of being excluded from the boundary proposed to be drawn from the Lake of the Woods westward. The British silence was later explained to the North West Company by Lord Bathurst, the colonial secretary, on the ground "that requiring from the Americans any recognition or guarantee of His Majesty's rights thereto [the Pacific Northwest], might lead to cast doubts upon a title which was sufficiently strong and incontrovertible."[9] The silence of the Americans is to be accounted for by their preference for a general formula of restoration which would include Astoria.

Soon after the Ghent treaty was ratified the American government moved to recover Astoria. Monroe notified the British chargé d'affaires in Washington that measures would be adopted without delay to reoccupy the post. No indication was offered as to what was meant by the term "reoccupy," whether the mere restitution of the American flag over Astoria or something more. Astoria,

---

[8] See *ibid.*, 695–726, 730–48, for documents relating to this negotiation.
[9] See references cited in n. 29.

Monroe wrote, had been taken during the war by a British expedition; it came, therefore, within the stipulation of restitution in the Ghent treaty. The British chargé was asked to furnish the American government a letter addressed to the British naval officer in command in the Pacific Northwest to facilitate the restitution.[10]

To this request the chargé returned a prompt refusal. He based the refusal on three grounds. One was the absence of instructions from his government. Another was the insufficiency of the evidence submitted by the American government to support the claim to restitution. The third was an uncertainty whether any persons whatsoever remained at the site of Astoria. The chargé expressed the belief that the post had been broken up and that all persons in it had been brought away. He suggested that a communication regarding Astoria be sent by the American government direct to the British naval officer in command in that part of the Pacific.[11]

As a preparation for further correspondence on the subject the chargé sent a request for information regarding Astoria to the governor general of Canada. He also wrote home for instructions. From the governor general he received a memorandum, drawn up by Simon M'Gillivray, a partner of the North West Company, in which the argument was made that Astoria did not fall within the formula of the Treaty of Ghent since it had been bought by British subjects, not captured.[12] This memorandum the chargé stowed away, waiting apparently for instructions that were expected from England. But the instructions never arrived.

The Astoria issue vanished, after this brief appearance, from the diplomatic exchanges of the two governments. It remained out of sight from July, 1815, to November, 1817. So long a disappearance is understandable from a British point of view. The British held Astoria and gained from diplomatic inaction the opportunity to make their possession and their control of the river more secure. But for the American silence explanation is necessary, especially after Monroe's announcement that his government would proceed "without delay" to the reoccupation of the post.

The explanation comporting best with the meager information available is the state of the American navy. In any reoccupation of

[10] *A.S.P., F.R.,* IV, 852.
[11] *Ibid.*
[12] The documents here referred to are published in *Oregon Historical Quarterly* (Salem), XX (September, 1919), 254–60.

Astoria the navy would have to participate. The American government intended nothing more adventurous in a reoccupation than a symbolic assertion of right, a formal raising of the flag at the site of Astoria. Yet a national vessel bearing a national officer would have to be sent to the Columbia for the purpose. If the British government agreed to the restitution the presence of an American naval unit would be none the less necessary. The national dignity and the practice of nations would require it. The British government had sent a national vessel to Nootka for the ceremony of restitution in the Nootka Sound affair. That had been the initial purpose of the Vancouver voyage. But the United States had a very slight navy at the end of the War of 1812, and economies were necessary in the use of it owing to the clamor in Congress for a retrenchment in expenditures on the armed services.

Such naval vessels as the government possessed or was building were pre-empted by foreign problems much more urgent than Astoria. One of these was the North African state of Algiers. Algiers had long been exacting tribute from the government of the United States. While the United States was engaged in hostilities with England the Dey of Algiers had ventured to make predatory war on American commerce in the Mediterranean. The neighbors of Algiers—Tunis and Tripoli—had likewise, during the war with England, offended the United States. On March 3, 1815, a fortnight after the Treaty of Ghent had been ratified, Congress authorized hostilities against Algiers. For nearly two years the American navy was occupied in bringing this pirate state, as well as Tunis and Tripoli, to terms.

In Latin America lay another problem. There the Spanish empire was dissolving; its provinces were fighting for their independence. Privateers, which the rebellious states had commissioned to prey on the commerce of Spain, swarmed over the Gulf of Mexico and the Caribbean, capturing and plundering not merely Spanish merchantmen but any others that came within their reach. This freebooting forced the United States to keep units of its navy patrolling the Gulf of Mexico and the Caribbean.

At the same time the relations of the United States and Spain were disturbed over the provinces of West Florida and East Florida. Most of West Florida had been seized piecemeal by the American army prior to and during the War of 1812 on the questionable theory that it formed part of the Louisiana Purchase. After the war the United States not only refused to give up the province but exerted pressure on Spain to part with East Florida as well.

Two projects which the American government contemplated in this period, but put aside, confirm the theory that lack of naval units was responsible for inaction regarding Astoria. One was a project sponsored by Captain David Porter, an American officer, who in the War of 1812 had won renown by carrying the flag of the navy for the first time into the Pacific on a raid against British whalers and merchantmen. In the autumn of 1815, Porter, then one of the commissioners of the navy, wrote President James Madison asking assignment to a voyage of discovery in the Pacific. He urged the advantages to the nation of an exploration of the Northwest coast, and he recommended that the overland approaches to this coast be also examined, the explorers to follow a route different from the one taken by Lewis and Clark. His proposal appears to have won President Madison's interest. His projected voyage would have afforded an opportunity to combine with exploration an assertion of American rights at Astoria. It is said two frigates were selected for this work. Then, however, more urgent naval needs and the dictates of economy intervened and the project was given up.[13]

It was resumed in somewhat different form in the following summer. This time a Connecticut naval officer, Captain Charles Morris, was given the assignment. Morris was ordered to prepare the United States frigate *Congress*, then fitting out at Boston, for an expedition to the Pacific. He was evidently given particular instructions to visit the Columbia, for he at once solicited and received data regarding the river and its trade from a specialist in the trade, William Sturgis, of the Boston firm of Bryant & Sturgis, who had spent many seasons on the Northwest coast.[14] This voyage,

[13] The David Porter letter was published initially in the Washington *National Intelligencer*, January 25, 26, 1821. It was republished in *Niles' Weekly Register* (Baltimore), XX (March 10, 1821), 24–25, and in *Pacific Historical Review* (Berkeley and Los Angeles), IX (March, 1940), 61–65. President James Madison made no reply to Porter's letter that is extant, but orders given by Secretary of the Navy Benjamin W. Crowninshield to the commanding officers of the frigates *Guerrière* and *Java* seem to support the conclusion that provisional assignments were made of these vessels to Porter for his project. See Letters to Officers of Ships of War, XII, Navy Archives of the National Archives (Washington, D.C.).

[14] Benjamin Homans to Charles Morris, August 1, October 11, 1816, Letters to Officers of Ships of War, XIII, Navy Archives of the National Archives; William

also, was subsequently canceled as a result of the affair of the *Firebrand*. The *Firebrand* was a United States schooner that was engaged in patrolling the waters of the Gulf of Mexico. In the late summer of 1816 she was fired upon off the port of Vera Cruz by a Spanish squadron and a member of her crew was killed. In the ensuing national excitement the assignment of the *Congress* to the Pacific was canceled. Morris was ordered instead to cruise the troubled waters of the Mexican gulf.[15]

If the lack of a naval unit was responsible for the American failure to press the Astoria issue, what was the meaning of the notice Monroe sent the British chargé in July, 1815, that the American government, "without delay," would reoccupy Astoria? The meaning was probably the opposite of what was said. The message was probably a mere protective assertion of a right that the Treaty of Ghent gave; a caveat to prevent default of the right during the interval when the American government could not act.[16]

The Astoria venture had been a bold bid for dominion in the Pacific Northwest. It had been, as conceived by Astor, a project to control the trade and destiny of all northwestern America. The fort was to have been the headquarters, or base of operations, of all the plan. Built at the mouth of the Columbia it was to have controlled the interior as well as the coastal trade. It was to have had connection by means of the wide-spreading tributaries of the river, with subsidiary posts in the interior. To those posts the Indians would bring their furs, taking in exchange blankets, guns, trinkets, and rum. River craft would keep Astoria and these posts in communication with each other.

For the maritime trade Astoria would also be the center. It would be a building, refitting, and supply base for coastal craft. The craft would ply up and down the coasts of the Pacific

---

Sturgis to Morris, August 22, 1816, Albert Gallatin Papers (New-York Historical Society, New York). See also "Autobiography of Commodore Charles Morris, U. S. N., United States Naval Institute *Proceedings* (Annapolis), VI (1880), 183–85.

[15] Homans to Crowninshield, October 16, 1816, Private Letters, February 1, 1813–January 20, 1840, Navy Archives of the National Archives; Morris to John Graham, October 24, 1816, Gallatin Papers; *Niles' Weekly Register*, XI (October 12, 19, 26, December 14, 1816), 108, 125–27, 142, 255. The correspondence relating to the affair of the *Firebrand* is to be found in the National Archives under State Department Archives and Navy Archives.

[16] This conclusion seems to be supported by comments of John Quincy Adams in a conversation with Stratford Canning in 1821. See Charles F. Adams (ed.), *Memoirs of John Quincy Adams*, 12 vols. (Philadelphia, 1874–1877), V, 447.

Northwest, as far northward as Russian America, sweeping harbors and inlets clear of furs, and bringing the furs for deposit to Astoria.

To Astoria would come each year from New York City ships of supply, freighted with equipment and trade goods for coastal craft and posts, and also reinforcements of men. By these ships the furs accumulated at Astoria would be transported to Canton, where exchange would be made of the furs for luxuries of the Orient, teas, silks, nankeens, chinaware, and silver. Then the ships would return with rich cargoes to the city of New York, having completed a circumnavigation of the globe. This was to be the pattern of the trade.

Astor realized that rivals would be waiting for him in the Pacific Northwest. Two rivals, in particular, he knew would be there, the North West Company, the British and Canadian group operating out of Montreal, and the Russian American Company, operating out of New Archangel. He proposed to work in peace with rivals of this stature, entering with them into trade agreements. With the North West Company he undertook to make an agreement for dividing or cooperatively exploiting the interior Columbia trade. With the Russian American Company he undertook to come to an agreement for dividing the coastal trade by a delimitation of spheres of influence.

With rivals of lesser stature, particularly with the independent or casual traders frequenting the coast, he would follow a policy less accommodating. He would drive them off by unrelenting competition. These independents were mostly American, Europeans having withdrawn from the coast as a result of the demands the Napoleonic wars made for shipping. The independents were in fierce competition with each other for a steadily declining body of furs. Often they made profits so scant as hardly to justify voyages to this remote part of the world. Some of them found a supplementary source of income in furnishing supplies to the Russian American Company. They had been encouraged to do so by the Russian American Company which had suffered interruption in its regular sources of supply as a result of the European wars. But to the Russian company the independents constituted a problem. On the way to and from New Archangel they took the opportunity to traffic with the natives. They gave the natives rum and firearms for furs, which meant not merely a loss to the company's trade, but a threat to the safety of the company's establishments. The Russian government had made futile protests on this score to the American government.

Astor's plan was to conclude with the Russian American Company a contract of supply in addition to an agreement delimiting spheres of influence. By himself supplying the Russian company he would remove a source of profit from the independent traders and help to drive them from the coast. Astor was in the process of negotiating agreements of this kind with the Russian company when he was interrupted by the War of 1812.

With the fur trade of the Pacific Northwest Astor intended to link that of upper Louisiana. He proposed to establish a series of trading posts extending from the Great Lakes and from St. Louis, by way of the Missouri River to the Rocky Mountains, and thence across the continental divide to the headwaters of the Columbia. He hoped to open up in this way the rich and as yet undeveloped fur resources of the Rocky Mountain region and bring to the support of Astoria the trading strength and experience of Mackinac and St. Louis.[17]

Still another element in Astor's plan was colonization, the occupation of the Pacific Northwest by pioneers of American stock. This was to be a future phase of the project; it was something that would follow the growth of trade. It seemed, however, to the romantically minded Thomas Jefferson, one of Astor's correspondents, the most significant aspect of the plan. In 1813, before news of the fall of Astoria had reached the East, Jefferson wrote Astor from Monticello:

Your favor of October 18th has been duly received, and I learn with great pleasure the progress you have made towards an establishment on Columbia river. I view it as the germ of a great, free and independent empire on that side of our continent, and that liberty and self-government spreading from that as well as this side, will ensure their complete establishment over the whole. It must be still more gratifying to yourself to foresee that your name will be handed down with that of Columbus and Raleigh, as the father of the establishment and founder of such an empire. It would be an afflicting thing indeed, should the English be able to break up the settlement. Their bigotry to the bastard liberty of their own country, and habitual hostility to every degree of freedom in any other, will induce the attempt; they would not lose the

[17] The Astoria project is well described in Kenneth W. Porter, *John Jacob Astor, Business Man*, 2 vols. (Cambridge, 1931), I, Chaps. VII-VIII.

sale of a bale of furs for the freedom of the whole world. But I hope your party will be able to maintain themselves. If they have assiduously cultivated the interests and affections of the natives, these will enable them to defend themselves against the English, and furnish them an asylum even if their fort be lost. I hope, and have no doubt our government will do for its success whatever they have power to do, and especially that at the negotiations for peace, they will provide, by convention with the English, for the safety and independence of that country, and acknowledgment of our right of patronizing them in all cases of injury from foreign nations. . . . While you are doing so much for future generations of men, I sincerely wish you may find a present account in the just profits you are entitled to expect from the enterprise. I will ask of the President permission to read Mr. Stuart's journal. With fervent wishes for a happy issue to this great undertaking, which promises to form a remarkable epoch in the history of mankind, I tender you the assurance of my great esteem and respect.[18]

Such was Astoria—a vision of trade and colonization just as Jamestown had been two centuries earlier—a vision that might lead to empire. It was a project natural to an age when expansionists were hungering for West Florida, East Florida, and Canada. Astor was hardly a man to indulge much in dreams, especially if the pot of gold in them was far off. Yet he seems in this case to have been touched a little by the romanticism of empire that Jefferson had expressed. His empire was shattered by the War of 1812. At the end of the war Astor had to face the question whether he would try to build it up again.

He was two years in arriving at an answer. In September, 1814, he received the news of the sale his partners had made to the North West Company. He regarded the sale, and especially the rate at which the post and its contents had been sold, as a betrayal of his interests. He vowed he would fight to repair the injury as long as he breathed and had a dollar to spend. In March 1815, after the terms of the Treaty of Ghent had been made known, he wrote to a relative in somewhat less determined spirit: "By the peace we shall have a right to Columbia river, & I rather think I shall again engage in that business."[19] In the autumn of the same

[18] Thomas Jefferson to John Jacob Astor, November 9, 1813, Andrew A. Lipscomb and Albert E. Bergh (eds.), *The Writings of Thomas Jefferson*, 20 vols. (Washington, 1903–1904), XIII, 432–34. The Stuart journal mentioned in this letter is that of the Astorian, Robert Stuart, returning from Astoria. It is published in Philip A. Rollins (ed.), *The Discovery of the Oregon Trail* (New York, 1935).
[19] Porter, *John Jacob Astor*, I, 240.

year or the spring of 1816 he informed Albert Gallatin that he would be disposed to try the Columbia River trade again provided he could be assured of the protection of the American flag. A "lieutenant's command would be sufficient," he said, by which he probably meant a platoon of troops to guard a new venture against any British or North West Company interference.[20] Denied an assurance of this kind he arrived at his final decision in the latter half of 1816. The decision was against returning to the Columbia.

Astor never recorded completely his reasons for this decision. Probably he was moved chiefly by business reasons. The trade of the Columbia had proved less rich than he had anticipated. It had netted him, instead of profits, a succession of losses and fatalities culminating in the final disaster of the forced sale. The North West Company, which by 1816 was firmly established on the Columbia, was a notoriously belligerent organization. The reception it would accord him if he returned to the Columbia was indicated by the murderous and ruinous war it was then fighting with the Hudson's Bay Company in Rupert's Land. Sharing with such an antagonist a trade that had proved profitless even when held virtually uncontested can hardly have seemed attractive to Astor. It did not hold a prospect of that "present account" in just profits which Jefferson had agreed should accompany empire building.

Yet, uncertain prospects of profits should not be allowed to appear as the sole basis for deciding such a problem. Astoria was a national interest. It had been so proclaimed to leaders of the federal government by Astor for years. If it was to be relinquished the grounds for doing so must seem public. As the hesitation of Astor regarding a return to the Columbia grew he increasingly stressed as a condition of returning assurances from the federal authorities of military protection. Such assurances were not likely to be given, for military intervention on the Columbia might lead to clashes with England. The wish of Astor for military protection was communicated to President Madison by Gallatin, but seems never to have been given serious consideration. Whether failure to obtain such protection was a real factor in the decision

[20] Washington Irving, *Astoria, or Anecdotes of an Enterprise beyond the Rocky Mountains*, 2 vols. (Philadelphia, 1836), II, Appendix, 268.

of Astor is a question to which no positive answer can be given. Military protection had not seemed essential to Astor in his first venture on the Columbia and none was extended to his rival after the return of peace by the British government.[21]

In 1835, when *Astoria* was being written by Washington Irving, Astor obtained from Albert Gallatin a letter testifying that he had proposed in the autumn of 1815 or the spring of 1816 to return to the Columbia provided he were assured the protection of the American flag. This letter was made public in 1836 as an appendix to *Astoria*.[22]

The result of Astor's decision was that the valley of the Columbia was left where the war had left it, under British control. It remained under the control of the North West Company until 1821; then it passed, as a result of a merger, into the control of the Hudson's Bay Company. It continued, throughout the period of the first three Oregon negotiations, a British sphere of influence, with the result that all attempts at partition failed and the way was prepared for an ultimate Anglo-American crisis.

While Astor was relinquishing the interests of the United States on the Columbia his government was moving toward a reassertion of them. The government had become, by the autumn of 1817, ready to act. Hostilities in the Mediterranean had been brought to a successful conclusion. The navy had been enlarged by new building. The Spanish problem of the Floridas had become, for the time being, less explosive. A cession of the two provinces to the United States was being considered by the Spanish government; the issue was becoming gradually one of terms. The new president, James Monroe, was an expansionist. His secretary of state, John Quincy Adams, was even more so.

In September, 1817, Captain James Biddle was given orders to prepare the sloop of war *Ontario* for a voyage to the Columbia. He was directed to take John B. Prevost, a friend of the President, with him as executive agent. The two, on arrival at the Columbia, were to assert "by some symbolical or appropriate mode

[21] Repeated requests for protection were sent by the North West Company to the British Colonial Office in the summer of 1815 but they produced no result. The letters are to be found in Colonial Office, XLII, 164, British Public Record Office. Excerpts from them are printed in *Oregon Historical Quarterly*, XX (December, 1919), 305–306.

[22] See n. 20.

adapted to the occasion" a claim to sovereignty on behalf of the United States to the valley of the Columbia. They were explicitly directed to limit themselves to peaceful measures. Should an unexpected obstruction to the achievement of their object occur they were not to employ force.[23]

No notice of the *Ontario* project was given the British government, a considerable omission in view of the fact that the valley of the Columbia was controlled by British subjects. The omission may have been a mere accident. It was so explained subsequently both by Adams and by President Monroe to Sir Charles Bagot, the new British minister in Washington. On the other hand, the error may have been deliberate, a reflection of the aggressiveness that Adams had brought to his office. Adams may have considered a notice unnecessary and likely to produce nothing except further delay. A notice had been given two years earlier and had brought, except for an inconclusive note from the British chargé d'affaires, no response from the British government.

The news that the *Ontario* had departed for the Columbia reached Bagot in distorted form from New York. The account was that the captain of the *Ontario* had instructions to seize or destroy the settlements and trade of the North West Company on the Pacific coast. The informant of Bagot was Simon M'Gillivray, a leading partner of the North West Company, who happened to be in New York on a visit at the time and heard the news, perhaps, as a leak from Astor's office.[24] His distortions were a product of misinformation or fear or design.

In alarm Bagot hastily arranged a conference with the American secretary of state. He opened the conference with a discussion of several minor matters. Then "assuming suddenly a very grave air and tone" he confronted Adams with the report he had received and asked for confirmation of it. According to Bagot, Adams was considerably embarrassed.[25] If Adams was, he permitted no sign of it to appear in his reply, and he confessed none to his diary. He denied that the *Ontario* had orders to disturb any British settlement

[23] Homans to James Biddle, September 30, 1817, Private Letters, February 1, 1813–January 20, 1840, Navy Archives of the National Archives; Adams (ed.), *Memoirs of John Quincy Adams*, IV, 11.
[24] Simon M'Gillivray to Charles Bagot, November 15, 1817, Foreign Office, V, 123, British Public Record Office.
[25] Bagot to Lord Castlereagh, December 2, 1817, *ibid.*

whatever. He reminded Bagot that after the Treaty of Ghent a demand for restitution of Astoria had been made to the British representative in Washington, that the answer had been that Astoria had been destroyed by the British force that had taken it, and that no persons had been left there who could make a restitution. Adams declared that the voyage of the *Ontario* had been ordered merely with a view to re-establishing the settlement. This exchange was followed by a brief argument over title, Adams concluding the conference with the observation that "it would be hardly worth the while of Great Britain to have any differences with the United States on account of the occupation of any part of so remote a territory."[26]

Bagot left the conference still disturbed. The Nootka Sound affair of 1790 was in his mind. He was anxious to do nothing that would produce another such crisis. Yet he was suspicious of the intentions of the American government and concerned for the interests of England on the Northwest coast. He sent a hurried secret message to the governor general of Canada suggesting that a warning of the coming of the American warship be carried by overland express to the mouth of the Columbia. What he particularly urged was that the river should be found, when the *Ontario* arrived, actually in the possession of His Majesty's subjects. He contemplated also suggesting to the British admiral at Halifax that a British warship be sent around Cape Horn to anticipate the *Ontario*, if possible, at the Columbia. He made a full report of the affair and of what he had done to his government.[27]

In England where this report arrived early in 1818 conditions were not such as to encourage making an issue of the *Ontario* affair.

---

[26] Adams (ed.), *Memoirs of John Quincy Adams*, IV, 24-25. At a later conference the omission of notice was again discussed and Bagot was again assured that it was accidental. "Mr. Adams informed me," Bagot wrote home, "he had been directed by the President to assure me that the circumstance of the Ontario having been dispatched to the Columbia River without any intimation being given to me of her destination was entirely accidental, that she had received her instructions whilst he was at New York on his tour of the Northern frontier, and that in the pressure of his business there, he had omitted to direct the proper communications to be made to me upon the subject." Bagot to Castlereagh, June 2, 1818, Foreign Office, V, 132. See also Adams (ed.), *Memoirs of John Quincy Adams*, IV, 93-94.

[27] Bagot to John C. Sherbrooke, December 1, 1817, Foreign Office, V, 123; Bagot to Castlereagh, December 2, 1817, *ibid.*; Bagot to Castlereagh, December 3, 1817, Charles Vane (ed.), *Memoirs and Correspondence of Viscount Castlereagh, Second Marquis of Londonderry*, 12 vols. (London, 1850-1853), XI, 388-89.

The country was in the grip of a heavy reaction, following a quarter of a century of European revolution and war. Economic life was profoundly disordered, the national debt was staggering in size. Want was general and the public was in a riotous, almost a rebellious mood. An uneasy peace lay over Europe, the peace imposed by the Congress of Vienna. The age was that of Metternich. England was governed by the Tory party, a party consisting of bitter factions. Lord Liverpool was prime minister, Lord Castlereagh headed the foreign office. George Canning was president of the Board of Control. The foreign office was coveted by Canning. Between him and Castlereagh existed a long-standing feud that had earlier in their careers led to a duel. The policy of the government was repression in domestic affairs and the maintenance of the *status quo* in foreign. Castlereagh sought, wherever possible, to allay international excitements, after the wracking years of the Napoleonic era, by conciliation or the application of sedatives. He described this policy succinctly in a dispatch sent to Bagot, by coincidence, while first reports of the departure of the *Ontario* were disturbing that minister in Washington. "The avowed & true Policy of Great Britain is, in the existing state of the World to appease controversy, & to secure if possible for all states a long interval of Repose."[28]

The problem of Astoria was reviewed by the British cabinet as soon as the news of the turn it had taken reached London. The primary question before the cabinet was, probably, whether a restoration of the flag of the United States was required by the provisions of the Treaty of Ghent. The North West Company had developed the theory that the post did not fall within the treaty's provisions, inasmuch as it had been acquired by purchase, not capture. That theory had the approval in 1815 of Lord Bathurst, the colonial secretary, if the testimony of Simon M'Gillivray is accepted.[29] The weakness in the theory lay in the formal seizure that had been made of Astoria by the efficient captain of the *Racoon*. Of that seizure Castlereagh was aware. It was referred to in the letter M'Gillivray had written Bagot regarding the *Ontario* departure, and which Bagot had transmitted to Castlereagh with

---

[28] Castlereagh to Bagot, November 10, 1817, Foreign Office, CXV, 29.

[29] "Statement relative to the Columbia river (1815)," enclosure in M'Gillivray to Bagot, November 15, 1817, *ibid.*, V, 123. The statement is printed in full in *Oregon Historical Quarterly*, XX (September, 1919), 254–60.

his own report of the *Ontario* affair.[30] The discussions in the British cabinet are not recorded. Those on the Astoria problem cannot have been very exciting or prolonged. In 1826 Canning declared he did not know the Astoria problem had been before the cabinet in 1818, though he agreed he must, as a member of the cabinet, have given his approval to the solution reached.[31]

The solution reached was that the United States was entitled, under the terms of the Treaty of Ghent, to the same position on the Columbia that it had formerly held. It was therefore entitled to a restoration of Astoria. This was a recognition that Astoria had been taken by capture during the war. The restitution was to be safeguarded, however, so that it would not become a recognition by England of American title on the Columbia. It was to be accompanied by adequate reservations.

Regarding the failure of the American government to give notice of the mission of the *Ontario*, the decision of the cabinet was to accept the assurances of the secretary of state that the captain of the vessel had no belligerent instructions. Castlereagh was authorized to take measures to avert the danger of an armed clash on the Columbia. The Admiralty, at Castlereagh's request, sent directions to its commanding officer on the Chile station to take steps to facilitate a peaceful restitution of the post to the United States. The North West Company was given directions by Lord Bathurst of the same character. The company's representative on the Columbia was authorized to take an official part in the restitution.

Regarding the underlying issue of sovereignty on the Columbia

---

[30] M'Gillivray to Bagot, November 15, 1817; Bagot to Castlereagh, December 2, 1817, Foreign Office, V, 123.

[31] George Canning to Lord Liverpool, July 7, 1826, Edward J. Stapleton (ed.), *Some Official Correspondence of George Canning*, 2 vols. (London, 1887), II, 71–75. In the partition negotiation of 1818 the British plenipotentiaries intimated that the British cabinet did not know, when it ordered the restoration of the American flag to Astoria, that the post had been acquired by the North West Company through purchase. This intimation was given in the absence of Castlereagh. It seems difficult to reconcile with the fact that in 1815 Lord Bathurst knew that the North West Company had acquired the post by purchase and that Castlereagh had in his possession at the time of the cabinet decision M'Gillivray's memorandum describing the acquisition as a purchase. The memorandum had come to the Foreign Office as an enclosure in the Bagot dispatch in which the *Ontario* affair was reported. See document marked "1 London, 1818. Substance of what passed at the fourth conference not entered on the Protocol," Gallatin Papers. The report which Captain William Black made to the British Admiralty of the ceremony of taking possession at Astoria is published in *Oregon Historical Quarterly*, XVII (June, 1916), 147–48.

the decision reached was to offer to submit the question for settlement to commissioners chosen by the two states. Like offers were to
be made regarding two other controversial issues, the undetermined
boundary between the Lake of the Woods and the Rocky Mountains, and damages for the loss of American slaves carried off by
British forces after the signing of the Treaty of Ghent. Recourse
to commissioners was to be, in each case, a first step to a settlement.
If it failed the questions were to be referred for arbitration to a
friendly sovereign.[32]

These were the cabinet's decisions. They were conciliatory
decisions, a reflection of Castlereagh's general policy of tranquil-
ization. They reflected his personal wish to clear away the Anglo-
American controversies and ill will that he had inherited from
Canning's and Wellesley's preceding years in the foreign office.[33]
Out of the decisions developed a correspondence between the two
governments that was to lead, in the summer of 1818, to a general
negotiation in London for the settlement of all outstanding Anglo-
American controversies. In the meantime, as soon as the decisions
were reached, Castlereagh held a conference with the minister of
the United States. He expressed regret at the failure of the American government to give notice of the mission of the *Ontario*,
pointed out the danger that the omission had created, and described
the measures which the British government had taken to preserve
peace.[34]

The return of the American flag to Astoria, delayed for two
and a half years for lack of means to hold a ceremony, was now
effected with a multiplication of ceremony. The *Ontario* arrived
at Valparaiso, in Chile, early in 1818. Prevost, the American
agent busied himself there for five months with duties assigned
to him by the State Department. He and Captain Biddle became

---

[32] *A.S.P., F.R.*, IV, 853. See also Castlereagh to Bagot, February 4, 1818 (two
dispatches), Foreign Office, V, 129. Excerpts from one of these dispatches are
printed in *Oregon Historical Quarterly*, XX (December, 1919), 317–18.

[33] Joseph Schafer in "The British Attitude Toward the Oregon Question, 1815–
1846," *American Historical Review* (New York), XVI (January, 1911), 283–85,
has characterized the policy reflected in these decisions as a "baiting" policy. He
is suspicious of Castlereagh's purposes, more so, the writer is inclined to think,
than the facts warrant. Dr. Schafer wrote before the appearance of the two notable
volumes of Charles K. Webster, *The Foreign Policy of Castlereagh, 1815–1822*
(London, 1925), *The Foreign Policy of Castlereagh, 1812–1815* (London, 1931),
which properly assess Castlereagh's policy.

[34] See references cited in n. 32.

involved in misunderstandings, which led the latter in 1818 to depart for the Columbia River in the *Ontario* without his colleague. Biddle reached Cape Disappointment on August 19. He deemed it not prudent to cross the bar. Instead, he anchored on the ocean side and proceeded in with three boats manned by fifty officers and men. On the river's north bank, in the presence of his crew and a group of puzzled Chinook Indians, he took possession of the country. He turned up a sod of soil, and, with flag flying, to the accompaniment of three cheers, nailed upon a tree a leaden plate on which were cut the words:

TAKEN POSSESSION OF, IN THE NAME AND ON THE BEHALF OF THE UNITED STATES BY CAPTAIN JAMES BIDDLE, COMMANDING THE UNITED STATES SHIP ONTARIO, COLUMBIA RIVER, AUGUST, 1818.

The plate soon disappeared, probably into the possession of the Chinooks, to whom lead, abandoned in the wilderness, must have seemed an invitation to appropriation. Biddle's flotilla next moved upstream twenty miles and across to Ft. George, where the North West Company traders were encountered. Biddle disclosed to them nothing as to his purposes, keeping his men separated from them as a means of avoiding friction. He turned at Ft. George down stream, repeating on the south shore, at some distance from the post, the ceremony of taking possession. He nailed up on this occasion an inscribed wooden board, his supply of lead having given out. The next day he was once more on the *Ontario*, pointed for the coast of South America.[35]

In the meantime, Prevost in Chile had decided to restage the ceremony. He had met in Santiago Captain Frederick Hickey of H.M.S. *Blossom*. He had learned that Hickey had instructions from his superior on the Chile station to proceed to the Columbia for the purpose of restoring Astoria to any representative of the United States who might be empowered to receive it. Prevost proposed to sail as a passenger with Captain Hickey to the Columbia, which hardly comported with his government's previous ideas of national dignity, but which Captain Hickey cordially accepted. Pre-

[35] The documents relating to this event are printed in *Oregon Historical Quarterly*, III (September, 1902), 310–11; XIX (September, 1918), 180–87; XX (December, 1919), 322–25.

vost and Hickey appeared some months later at Ft. George, where on October 6, 1818, a joint ceremony of restitution was staged. The British flag was lowered; in its stead the American flag was hoisted, to which Captain Hickey fired a British salute. Papers of transfer were signed, by Captain Hickey and the local agent of the North West Company on behalf of England, and by Prevost on behalf of the United States. Soon after the *Blossom* and her guest were again at sea, leaving the North West Company in quiet possession of the post and the trade of the river.[36]

A strange haphazardness marked these important proceedings. On the American side a succession of accidental or unplanned steps were taken. The departure of the *Ontario* without the giving of any notice was, if the earnest testimony of Adams and Monroe is to be believed, one of them. The decision of Captain Biddle and Prevost to separate in Chile was another. A third was the accidental establishing of contact between the American and the British agent in Chile.

On the British side accidents of a more serious nature occurred. The most important of them, from the point of view of permanent results, were failures to make adequate reservation of British title in the return of Astoria to the United States. Castlereagh had given Bagot the following instructions on the subject of reservations:

> You will observe . . . that whilst this Government is not disposed to contest with the American Gov't the point of possession as it stood in the Columbia River at the moment of rupture, they are not prepared to admit the validity of the title of the Gov't of the U. States to this settlement. In signifying therefore to Mr. Adams the full acquiescence of your Gov't in the reoccupation of the limited position which the U. States held in that River at the breaking out of the war, you will, at the same time assert in suitable terms the claim of Great Britain to that Territory upon which the American settlement must be considered as an encroachment.[37]

What form the making of the reservation was to take was not specified in the instruction. Possibly it was supposed Bagot would

---

[36] The documents relating to this event are printed *ibid.*, XIX (December, 1918), 271–82; and in *House Documents*, No. 112, pp. 13–19, 17 Cong., 1 Sess. Thomas H. Benton pointed out in a partisan speech in Congress attacking Adams soon after these documents were published that Prevost had been brought to the mouth of the Columbia in a British warship. See *Annals of Congress*, 17 Cong., 2 Sess., 246.

[37] Castlereagh to Bagot, February 4, 1818, Foreign Office, V, 129.

know without being told. Bagot, however, seems to have given the question of form not much thought. He arranged an interview with Adams at which he reported the cabinet's decisions, the gist of which had already been sent to Adams by the American minister in London. He made the required reservations of British title in announcing the intended restitution of Astoria. He did it orally. He left with Adams no written reservation, then or thereafter. In reporting his interview home he noted that Adams had taken the reservation in good part and had declared that the American government put very little value on the post of Astoria.[38] Adams' good humor and his depreciation of the value of the post might well have put the Briton on his guard. It did not. Bagot left the interview blissfully unaware that in failing to leave a written reservation he had made a damaging error of omission.

A reservation in any diplomatic act, such as the Fort George restitution, is comparable to a reservation in a treaty. It should be made in accordance with the principles and usages that govern treaty reservations. It should be in documentary form so that its terms may not thereafter become the subject of dispute. It should be registered when the diplomatic act takes place with the government against which it is to operate. Unless it is so registered the government against which it is to operate has no opportunity of halting the proceeding, or of formally declaring its counterunderstanding of the nature of the act. These principles were in 1818 established in British and in American diplomatic practice. Their careful observance was especially necessary in an act which the British government realized might become the subject of future dispute and which involved the fate of a vast area. These principles were not carefully observed by the British minister in Washington.

Even more unguarded were the British agents on the Columbia who executed the actual restoration. They had for their guidance instructions which Lord Bathurst, secretary of state for war and the colonies, had issued to the partners or agents of the North West Company residing on the Columbia. Bathurst's instructions declared it to be the pleasure of the Prince Regent that due facility should be given to the reoccupation of the Columbia River settlement by officers of the United States, "without, however,

[38] Bagot to Castlereagh, June 2, 1818, *ibid.,* 132.

admitting the right of that Government to the possession in question."[39] The reserving clause in the instructions was not clear. It seemed to require merely that no admission of American title be made. It gave no order that any reservation of British title should be made. The result was that in drawing up the restoration act the British agents, though scrupulously refraining from recognizing American title, made no reservation of British title. The paper they signed was an unconditional restoration, and it was accompanied by not even a verbal reservation.[40] On both sides of the continent a failure thus occurred on the part of British agents to register proof of reservation of British title.

The failure at Fort George—the more critical failure of the two—was late in becoming known to the governments of the United States and England. The act of restoration was signed on October 6, 1818. It arrived in Washington, in the report of Prevost, on July 17, 1819. The British copy arrived in London similarly late. In the meantime, in the summer and autumn of 1818 the first Anglo-American negotiation for the partition of the Oregon country took place in London. In this negotiation the effect of the restoration was already discernible, though only faintly, in the attitude of the British government. The full effect, including the effect of the failure to implement the reservation of British title, was to become evident in later negotiations.

In the 1818 negotiation the American plenipotentiaries proposed that the line of partition between the American and British claims be the 49th parallel from the "Stony" Mountains to the sea. The British offered no partition line. They hinted, merely, that the line of the 49th parallel to the Columbia River and thence the channel of the river to the sea would be a more convenient boundary. The hint must have had the sanction of Castlereagh. It was, perhaps, the first reluctantly admitted effect of the decision of restoration taken nine months earlier—a half concealed confession that by the very act of restitution, even though guarded, as was still

[39] This instruction was a copy virtually of a letter written by Castlereagh to Bathurst on the subject of the restitution. It did not differ from Castlereagh's original except in the arrangement of clauses and other unessentials. The reservation clause is identical in the two documents. See for the Bathurst instruction, Colonial Office, XLIII, 56, p. 148; for the Castlereagh letter, *Oregon Historical Quarterly*, XX (December, 1919), 317–19.

[40] *House Documents*, No. 112, pp. 17–18, 17 Cong., 1 Sess.

supposed, by reservations of title, Britain had weakened her Columbia River position. The hinted offer was coldly received by the American plenipotentiaries, and the negotiation of 1818 ended in a mere agreement of joint occupation.

In the negotiation of 1823–24 the American government possessed the knowledge, received since the 1818 negotiation, of the British failure to reserve title in any form at the Fort George restoration. It also had the will to exploit the error. To Adams the congenial task fell. In drawing up instructions for the American plenipotentiary, he referred contentedly to the restoration that had been made in 1818. He dismissed the oral reservation Bagot had made at the time as a "vague intimation" of British claims. He wrote:

> Previous to the restoration [in the Fort George act] of the settlement at the mouth of the Columbia river in 1818, . . . some disposition was manifested by Sir Charles Bagot . . . to dispute the *right* of the United States to that establishment; and some vague intimation was given of British claims on the Northwest Coast. The restoration of the place, and the convention of 1818, were considered as a final disposal of Mr. Bagot's objections.[41]

In the course of the 1823–1824 negotiation the British altered the position they had taken in the negotiation of 1818. They definitely offered what they had earlier merely hinted at. They offered the line of the 49th parallel to an intersection with the Columbia and thence the channel of the river to the sea. They were induced to do this possibly in part by the fact that the United States had strengthened its position in the meantime by the acquisition of the claims of Spain on the Northwest coast. But the British knew by now also that the Astoria restoration had been made without effective reservations. The Americans rejected the British offer and the negotiation ended in failure.

In the next negotiation, that of 1826–1827, a more prominent notice was taken of the restoration errors. George Canning was then the British foreign secretary. He had little of the conciliatory temper, especially toward the United States, that Lord Castlereagh had shown. Before the opening of the negotiation he complained to Lord Liverpool, the prime minister, that the restoration of Astoria on any terms in 1818 had been "absolutely unjustifiable."

[41] *A.S.P., F.R.,* V, 791–93.

He argued that Astoria had not been taken by British arms in the War of 1812; it had been bought, and lay, therefore, outside the bounds of the treaty of peace. He was refurbishing the old North West Company thesis. He was aware of the failure of British agents to make proper reservation, either in Washington or at Fort George, of British title. He lamented these errors in private.[42] In an argument, drawn up for the American plenipotentiary, however, he put up a bold front. He reproduced copies of the instructions Castlereagh had given Bagot and that Bathurst had given the British agents on the Columbia. He pointed out that the Castlereagh reservations had been registered verbally with the American government. These reservations, he concluded, put the nature of the restoration at Fort George "in too clear a light to require further observation."[43]

The American plenipotentiary in the negotiation was Albert Gallatin. With quiet competence he demolished the Canning position. He pointed out that British representatives in 1818 had registered no written reservations of British title of any kind with the American government in making the restoration. He observed that the instructions which Canning had reproduced were mere communications between the British government and its officers, with which the United States could have no concern. Regarding Bagot's verbal reservation, he pointed out that no evidence had been offered as to how it had been received, or whether the American government had consented to accept a qualified restitution. The only written document affecting the restitution in the possession of the United States, Gallatin concluded, was the act of restoration itself, as signed at Fort George, "which contains no exception, reservation, or protest, whatever."[44]

The remarks of Canning on reading this letter are not recorded. He writhed, doubtless, to think that the government of which he had throughout this period been a member had been caught by another of the Yankee tricks for which the diplomacy of the United States was famous. He had been irritated with the American government for its unilateral announcement of the Monroe Doctrine

---

[42] Edward J. Stapleton (ed.), *Some Official Correspondence of George Canning*, II, 72–73.
[43] *A.S.P., F.R.*, VI, 665.
[44] *Ibid.*, 670.

in 1823. He had other grievances against the American government. The negotiation of 1826–1827 ended in no partition agreement, and the Oregon question was left to be decided in the heat of the crisis years of 1845–1846.

In British, and also in American diplomacy, Astoria was a symbol. It symbolized to the British government that side of the valley of the Columbia where the post lay—the river's whole southern watershed. Its restoration to the United States was a recognition, despite British intentions and protestations to the contrary, of American tenure in all that area. After the restoration the British government was never again able seriously to contest the American position south of the river. Even Canning, in the partition negotiation of 1826, found it necessary to abandon the south side,[45] and to make his point of departure the channel of the river. The American government had gained reinforcement for its position on the south side by acquiring the rights of Spain there in 1819–1821. That side was thereafter virtually American soil. The only objectives remaining to be won in the Oregon country were to formalize south-side tenure and to acquire the relatively small but important triangle of territory north of the river to the 49th parallel. These objectives the Oregon Treaty of 1846 gained. Thus the treaty of that year is the capstone of an edifice, the foundation stones of which were American claims, made solid by the mortar of British errors of procedure in the Astoria restoration of 1818.

[45] In the winter of 1824–1825, at the request of Canning, the Hudson's Bay Company abandoned Fort George on the south side of the Columbia and, in its place, built as a base, Fort Vancouver on the north side. The letter of Governor J. H. Pelly of the Hudson's Bay Company to Canning, announcing the shift, is a valuable reflection of the reoriented British policy. It reads in part: "In compliance with a wish expressed by you at our last interview, Governor Simpson, when at the Columbia, abandoned Fort George on the South side of the River and formed a new Establishment on the North side, about 75 miles from the mouth of the River, at a place called by Lt. Broughton Belle Vue point. Governor Simpson named the new Establishment 'Fort Vancouver' in order to identify our Claim to the Soil and Trade with Lt. Broughton's discovery and Survey." Pelly to Canning, December 9, 1825, Frederick Merk (ed.), *Fur Trade and Empire: George Simpson's Journal* (Cambridge, 1931), 257–58.

ESSAY 2 · THE OREGON QUESTION IN 1818

IN THE era of uneasy peace following the close of the War of 1812 the British minister in Washington, Charles Bagot, sent a disquieting dispatch to his government. He reported on December 2, 1817, that an American warship, the "Ontario," had sailed for the mouth of the Columbia River to regain possession of the post of Astoria, captured by the British during the war. The warship had gone without notice to Bagot, though the British flag flew over the post. An immediate demand for an explanation had been made by Bagot to John Quincy Adams, the American Secretary of State. Adams' explanation had been that repossession was to be no more than ceremonial, was not to be effected by force, and was to be limited to the site of Astoria. The reason given for the unannounced departure was that already on July 23, 1815, an announcement of American intention to re-occupy the post under the provisions of the Treaty of Ghent had been sent the British chargé in Washington and had brought no response other than that the post had probably been dismantled and its personnel taken away. The omission of a new notice had been a mere oversight by the President.

Enclosed with Bagot's dispatch was a copy of a letter the minister had received from Simon M'Gillivray, a principal partner of the North West Company. M'Gillivray had ferreted out the news of the "Ontario's" mission in New York and had described it in sensational terms. Its intention, M'Gillivray asserted, was to seize and destroy the establishments and trade of the North West Company on the Columbia. M'Gillivray wrote further that Astoria had not been embraced in the provision of the peace treaty of 1814 for reciprocal restoration of conquests made in the war. Astoria had come to the North West Company not by conquest but by purchase from Astor's agents.[1]

The Bagot dispatch arrived in London early in January 1818. It found the Foreign Office unprepared with an Oregon policy.

[1] Charles Bagot to Lord Castlereagh, Dec. 2, 1817, Foreign Office 5: 123, British Public Record Office; see also Essay 1.

The dispatch jolted it into the formulation of a policy. The one formulated was conciliatory, reflecting difficult conditions prevailing in England. The nation had recently emerged from a quarter century of almost continual war. It was exhausted; its economy was disordered; unemployment was widespread; the distressed were in a riotous, almost rebellious mood. An uneasy peace hung over Europe. The policy of the cabinet was to maintain the *status quo* and to reduce international tensions. Lord Castlereagh, the Secretary for Foreign Affairs, was, by instinct, a conciliator. His approach to American problems was in sharp contrast with that of his immediate predecessors in the Foreign Office.

The response Castlereagh made to the "Ontario" affair was to accept the assurances of Adams that the vessel had sailed on a peaceful mission and that the failure to give notice had been an oversight. He accepted the American view that the mutual restoration provision of the Ghent treaty did cover the case of Astoria. He persuaded the cabinet of this, and orders went out to British representatives in the Pacific Northwest and at Washington to cooperate with American representatives in a ceremony restoring the post to its prewar status.

But restoring the post to its prewar status would be restoring discord. It would be recreating a problem of undetermined and disputed sovereignty not merely for Astoria but for the whole area which the post represented. That problem Castlereagh wanted to resolve. He thought it could best be resolved by an arbitration, an arbitration that would lead either to a delimitation of claims in the Oregon Country, or to a line of partition. He obtained from the cabinet authority to submit an offer of arbitration to the American government, and sent it to Washington at the same time that he sent his orders for the restoration of Astoria.

Another territorial issue Castlereagh wanted to resolve was the so-called "Northwest boundary" question. This was the question of a boundary to be drawn from the Lake of the Woods to the Rocky Mountains—separating British Rupert's Land from the Louisiana Purchase area of the United States. It had been an issue ever since the purchase was made from France in 1803. It had withstood all direct negotiations. Castlereagh proposed to settle it by arbitration. He had in mind a single arbitration for both territorial issues, one that would draw a line from the Pacific Coast across the Oregon

Country to the continental divide, and thence across the Great Plains to the northwesternmost point of the Lake of the Woods, where it would meet the line of the peace treaty of 1783.[2]

Castlereagh was offering here to carry to completion the work of pacification which had been left unfinished at Ghent. There a series of arbitrations of territorial issues had been agreed to, which related only to eastern controversies. What Castlereagh proposed in 1818 was to extend the concept to western issues left unresolved at Ghent. But his proposal was of a design so sweeping as almost to be of a different order. At Ghent what had been agreed to was the solution by arbitration of issues of disjointed eastern segments of boundary. What Castlereagh proposed was to solve by arbitration issues of boundary of vast western provinces. His vision, articulated with that of Ghent, was truly magnificent in scope—arbitrations extending from the Pacific to the Atlantic and freeing from the hazards of future Anglo-American boundary clashes a continental wilderness.

In Castlereagh's plan still another issue was to be referred to arbitration. In the Treaty of Ghent the British had agreed that slaves were not to be carried off from the United States by British forces withdrawing after the peace. But the naval forces withdrawing from Chesapeake Bay had nevertheless carried off slaves in large numbers. The British government, relying on a technicality, had refused indemnity to the owners. The American government had proposed arbitration, which the British had declined. Castlereagh now proposed to accept arbitration, but tied his acceptance to an acceptance by the American government of his two boundary arbitration proposals. He offered the American government what a later generation would have called a "package."

Arbitration was an established mode of resolving boundary disputes in Anglo-American relations. It had its beginnings in the Jay Treaty of 1794 in which a boundary issue and two others, which had proved resistant to direct negotiations, had been referred to arbitral commissions. In this respect the treaty had been a pioneering achievement. It had restored a mode of resolving disputes which, though as ancient as the Greek city states, had fallen into disuse. The treaty had ushered in the modern era of international arbitrations. In the Ghent treaty the two nations had authorized

2 Lord Castlereagh to Charles Bagot, Feb. 4, 1818, F.O., 5: 129.

wholesale arbitrations. They had applied it to four boundary issues. The four were to go, in the first instance, to arbitral commissions; if not settled there, to a friendly sovereign or state. Every matured issue on the long line of boundary from the Atlantic Ocean to the Lake of the Woods was to go to some sort of arbitral decision. As one of the Ghent commissioners, Adams had shown full willingness to rely on such procedures.[3]

In 1818, however, Adams viewed the western arbitration proposals of Castlereagh with suspicion. He would have been willing to accept the slave arbitration offer had it been made separately. But he wanted nothing of the boundary arbitrations. On July 28, 1818 he instructed Richard Rush, the American minister in London, to decline both the western proposals and spelled out the reasons. The reasons were a lack of confidence in territorial arbitrations, even of those not yet implemented to which he had agreed at Ghent. He wrote of these:

> The expedient, itself, of submitting questions of territorial rights and boundaries in discussion between two nations to the decision of a third was unusual, if not entirely new, and, should the contingency [of implementing them] occur, will probably encounter difficulties of execution not foreseen at the time when the stipulation was made of resorting to it. The subjects in controversy are of a nature too intricate and complicated, requiring on the part of the arbitrator a patience of investigation and research, historical, political, legal, geographical, and astronomical, for which it is impossible to conceive that the sovereign of a great Empire could *personally* bestow the time.[4]

The sovereign of a great empire whom both parties at Ghent had intended to ask to serve as arbitrator, according to Adams, was the Emperor of Russia. He was a person in whose impartiality and integrity both parties had confidence. He was, also, Adams considered, well disposed to the United States. The Emperor would be able to bestow time personally to the slave issue, where his assigned task would be mere construing of a paragraph in the Ghent treaty and inspecting a short statement of the facts of the case— a statement to which both parties would have agreed in advance.

---

[3] Hunter Miller, ed., *Treaties of the United States* (Washington, 1931), II, 245–274, 574–582.

[4] John Q. Adams to Albert Gallatin and Richard Rush, July 28, 1818, *American State Papers, Foreign Relations* (Washington, 1832–1859), IV, 375–378. The underscoring is Adams'.

But the Emperor, Adams wrote, was obviously not the person to serve as arbitrator in the Oregon dispute. He had territorial ambitions in Oregon of his own. And to designate some other arbitrator for that task in whom both parties would have confidence so strong and clear that they would give cordial acquiescence to an award he would make, "might," Adams observed, "be difficult."

Furthermore, the modes of the proposed arbitrations (modeled on those of the Ghent treaty) seemed to Adams objectionable—reference initially to a joint arbitral commission and, in case of failure, to a friendly sovereign or state. All this seemed to him too cumbersome, too costly of time and money, and too uncertain of result. He made no mention of the fact that this was the pattern he himself had helped to establish.

Adams was troubled, also, by the linking in the Castlereagh plan of the two western arbitrations. He thought he detected in this a maneuver on the part of Castlereagh to win from the United States by one sweeping operation, behind the screen of an arbitration, a valuable portion of its claim to the Oregon shore and a prize yet more valuable at the heart of America—the right to share again in the navigation of the Mississippi River. Great Britain had possessed full contact with the river prior to the War of the American Revolution. Her diplomats had supposed she had retained some vestige of this in the peace settlement made at the end of the war. On the Mitchell map, used at the peace conference, the river was pictured as taking its rise north and west of the Lake of the Woods. When, after the peace, this representation was found to have been a cartographic error, and the truth became known that the river rose well to the south of the Lake of the Woods, and that British North America no longer had any access via the interior to the Gulf of Mexico, British diplomats had been inconsolable. They had sought, before and after Louisiana became part of the United States, to regain some sort of access to the river, some semblance of the old position. They had failed. By 1807 they seemed to have reconciled themselves to the failure. They had agreed to a boundary running from the Lake of the Woods due west on the line of the 49th parallel toward the Rocky Mountains. When that agreement failed of ratification in the United States, they had shown some willingness to renew it. At Ghent they had reluctantly given up the fight to regain navigation rights on the river.

Nevertheless Adams believed in 1818 that he could see in Castlereagh's linking of the two territorial arbitration proposals the same old lure of the river. He believed Castlereagh's scheme would be, if an arbitration were accepted, to persuade the arbitrator somehow to fix a hinge on the coast of Oregon well to the south of the 49th parallel, and then swing a line from it inland on such a parallel of latitude as would bring it out on the Mississippi River, on the vital channel, before it turned northward to a junction with the established boundary at the Lake of the Woods.

One other objection, applying more particularly to the Oregon proposal, seemed to Adams to stand in the way of the Castlereagh offer. There was nothing in the Oregon area worth the great labors of an arbitration. This point was driven home with more than his usual forcefulness:

But the delineation of an unsettled boundary across the western deserts of this continent, the title to establishments on the Pacific ocean, where the arbitrator himself is not without his pretensions, and where, save pretensions, there is no object to any party worth contending for —to create burdensome commissions and to make solemn references to a foreign sovereign for these, appears scarcely to be necessary, if altogether justifiable.[5]

This shrugging off of the vast Oregon province as a desert where, save pretensions, there was no object to any party worth contending for, may have surprised Rush. Or, it may have caused him, as a diplomat, merely to lift his eyebrows. This was not the appraisal Adams was accustomed to make of any territorial pretension or claim of the United States. He was already then known in government circles in Washington as an extreme expansionist. In an earlier instruction to Rush to mollify Castlereagh concerning the "Ontario" affair, he had indicated a strong desire for Oregon, though starting off with a slighting reference to Astoria:

In suggesting these ideas [concerning the "Ontario"] to Lord Castlereagh, rather in conversation than in any more formal manner, it may be proper to remark the minuteness of the present interests, either to Great Britain or to the United States, involved in this concern; and the unwillingness, for that reason, of this Government to include it among the objects of serious discussion with them. At the same time you might give him to understand, though not unless in a manner to

5 *Ibid.*, 375–378.

avoid every thing offensive in the suggestion, that, from the nature of things, if in the course of future events it should ever *become* an object of serious importance to the United States, it can scarcely be supposed that Great Britain would find it useful or advisable to resist their claim to possession by systematic opposition. If the United States leave her in undisturbed enjoyment of all her holds upon Europe, Asia, and Africa, with all her actual possessions in this hemisphere, we may very fairly expect that she will not think it consistent either with a wise or a friendly policy to watch with eyes of jealousy and alarm every possibility of extension to our natural dominion in North America, which she can have no solid interest to prevent, until all possibility of her preventing it shall have vanished.[6]

This letter had probably prepared Rush for Adams' later characterization of the Oregon Country as an arid waste with no object in it "worth contending for." It had made understandable to Rush that the desert concept was for diplomatic uses, that it was to be brought casually into conversations in London with the right people, that it was meant to start currents of thinking which in a direct Oregon negotiation, to come afterwards, might carry the negotiation forward to a termination pleasing to the American government.

In addition to the reasons given for declining an Oregon arbitration, Adams had one which was not communicated. It was that he was already engaged in a strenuous negotiation with the Spanish minister in Washington which he thought might end in an American acquisition of all, or the greater part, of Spain's rights and claims in the Oregon Country. This negotiation had begun soon after Adams took office as Secretary of State. It had been directed at first to issues that were old—a cession by Spain to the United States of East Florida, a relinquishment by her of title to West Florida, part of which had already been seized by the United States, a line of delimitation in the West which would mark off American Louisiana from the territories and claims of Spain, and damage claims of various sorts against Spain which the United States had accumulated.

Among these issues the one with the possibilities of greatest exploitation in territorial terms was the line of delimitation in the West. Its possibilities Adams and his chief, Monroe, had discerned early, how early is not determinable, though probably in February 1818. The two conceived the idea of a delimiting line that would

[6] *Ibid.*, 853–854. The underscoring is Adams'.

do something more than separate the Louisiana Purchase from New Spain, one that would turn due westward to the Pacific after rising ladder fashion from the Gulf of Mexico to the source of the Arkansas River, and, in turning, hand over Spain's claims in the Oregon Country to the United States.[7]

In the middle of July 1818 this idea was carried into a program of action. It was broached to the startled and fuming minister of the Spanish government in Washington, Luis de Onís. A map was sent him via an intermediary on which appeared a line of demarcation that rose from the Gulf of Mexico up the Trinity River to its source, moved thence irregularly to the source of the Rio Grande, and there turned due west to the Pacific. Thus, well before July 28 when the Castlereagh arbitration proposals were refused, Adams and Monroe were setting in motion a plan of negotiation to acquire Spain's rights in the Oregon Country.[8]

The Spanish negotiation was not expected to come to an early end. It opened with relations strained as a result of an invasion of the Floridas by an army under Andrew Jackson. With the army still in northern Florida the Spanish government was loath to go forward with the negotiation. But it relented before long. It had learned from the Florida invasion that it was friendless in Europe. It saw its empire dissolving in Latin America. It was beset by mortal fears of what would happen if the negotiation broke off—fears of a new adventure in East Florida that would constitute its complete and final seizure, fears of an invasion of Texas to which the United States had a shadowy claim, fears of a recognition by the United States of the revolted Latin American colonies, fears of the use to which the unsettled damage claims of the United States would be put. To these fears Spain finally succumbed. On February 22, 1819, her minister in Washington signed the Adams-Onís Treaty. By one of its provisions she ceded to the United States all her rights and claims in the Pacific Northwest north of the 42nd parallel. What she ceded was about what Adams had anticipated in 1818 when he declined Castlereagh's arbitration proposals.

In declining those proposals Adams had a counter proposal to make. It was that the two governments enter a direct negotiation.

[7] Samuel F. Bemis, *John Quincy Adams and the Foundations of American Foreign Policy* (New York, 1949), 310.

[8] Charles F. Adams, ed., *Memoirs of John Quincy Adams* (Philadelphia, 1874–1877), IV, 110.

The direct negotiation should range over all the issues dividing the two countries. Adams had in mind, besides the two territorial issues, the slave compensation issue; regulation of the commerce which the United States carried on with Great Britain and with the British colonies in North America and in the West Indies; maritime rights, especially impressment; and the old issue of American participation in the fisheries of the territorial waters of British North America. Adams was confident Castlereagh would agree to a direct negotiation since the commercial convention of 1815, which the British valued as did the Americans, was about to expire. Adams gave all the necessary instructions for a general negotiation in the same letter to Rush in which he gave his reasons for declining the arbitration proposals. He also arranged for an additional plenipotentiary to join Rush in London. The reinforcement was to be Albert Gallatin, the American minister in Paris, who was an expert on all these problems. He had already been alerted to be ready for a request to come to London, if Castlereagh agreed to the counter proposal. He was soon in London.

In the ensuing negotiation of 1818 the British linked the "Northwest boundary" issue with the Oregon issue, as Castlereagh had done in his arbitration proposals. They not only kept the issues linked in discussion but proposed that the American government by treaty extend to British subjects the free navigation of the Mississippi and give access from selected points in British North America, through American territory, to the river. They thus confirmed Adams' suspicions as to Castlereagh's arbitration proposals. But the British did not persist in linking the two boundary issues, and their access proposal may have been in part a *quid pro quo* for privileges the Americans were asking in the British North Atlantic fisheries. When the British were firmly told that American instructions gave no authority for an arrangement bringing British North America back into contact with the Mississippi, they dropped the matter. Then they joined the Americans in a Northwest boundary agreement, which was a revival of the abortive 1807 agreement. A line was drawn from the northwesternmost corner of the Lake of the Woods due south to the 49th parallel and thence due west to the crest of the Rocky Mountains. That issue was at last set to rest.

On the Oregon issue the negotiators made less progress. They were powerless to dispose of it with finality. They were confronted by the fact that claims of respectable standing to the Oregon Country were possessed by Russia and Spain which could not be ignored. They were free to delimit only the claims of their own countries against each other. Even this they found they could not accomplish.

At the outset Gallatin, as spokesman for the Americans, made a proposal of major importance. It was to delimit the Anglo-American claims by a line drawn along the 49th parallel to the Pacific.[9] That proposal was coldly received. It was objected to on grounds of convenience and of British rights. On grounds of convenience two objections were made to it. One was that the line would sever rivers. The severed ones were not named, but they were the Columbia, on which were establishments of the North West Company, and the "Caledonia," which had appeared on a map published by the Company shortly before the conference. The Caledonia proved later to have been a mythical river, a creation of the North West Company.[10]

A second British objection to the 49° line was that it would intersect the "Gulf of Georgia." This, by its discoverer's definition, was the body of waters cradling Vancouver Island and including Puget Sound. The "Gulf" would be severed by the 49° line and, in such manner, that the entrance to it—the Strait of Juan de Fuca—would fall wholly on the American side.

To quiet as many of these objections as he could Gallatin unofficially suggested a concession. It was that the 49° line, after having crossed the waters of the Columbia, deviate so far southwardly as to leave within the British claim the whole watershed of the Gulf of Georgia.[11] This extraordinary proposal did not impress the British, who, on their part, offered nothing except an intimation that they might be content with the line of the 49th parallel to the Columbia and thence the river to the sea. No treaty of delimitation proved possible. Something less was accepted—a joint occupation of the Oregon Country for a period of ten years.

[9] Gallatin and Rush to Adams, Oct. 20, 1818, *A.S.P., F.R.*, IV, 381.
[10] See Essay 3.
[11] *Ibid.*

Partition negotiations are normally carried on in the manner of Levantine bargaining. The individual who opens the bargaining asks for much more than he has any expectation of getting. He establishes a margin for subsequent concessions. The margin is ample, indeed, is often outrageous, and is then drawn on cautiously in return for equivalent concessions. The trading goes on leisurely until some deal emerges which is acceptable to both sides and is concluded. This is the age-old method of diplomatic negotiation. To it the Americans in the first Oregon negotiation seem not at all to have conformed.

At the outset they proposed the line of the 49th parallel. If this was something conceived of as a final objective they retained no bargaining margin at all in proposing it immediately, at least none on the mainland. On Vancouver Island they retained a little margin, which, however, Gallatin compromised by his unofficial proposal. In later Oregon negotiations American plenipotentiaries came to the bargaining table with their portfolios exhausted. The initial offer of 1818 was repeated as an *ultimatum* in the summer of 1845. It had become a threat to peace. This poses for the historian the question why an offer, so short-sighted, was made at the outset by a diplomat of Gallatin's skill and experience.

For an answer the historian turns to the instructions given the plenipotentiaries in 1818. He expects to find there directions as to objectives to be gained, values to be guarded, tactics to be employed, limits to be set to concessions. What he finds are reasons for declining an arbitration, among them the worthlessness of the thing to be arbitrated. The instructions produce the impression that Adams became engrossed in a negative case against arbitration to the extent of slighting the direct negotiation. He was very positive in discussing the issue of the "Northwest boundary." He warned there against British eagerness to recover contact with the Mississippi and stressed British willingness in 1807 to take the line of 49° as the boundary. He declared at that point, where direction was hardly needed any longer, that south of 49° the British "can have no valid claim upon this continent."[12] But west of the mountains, in the Oregon Country, where advice was most needed, he gave least. He left the negotiators, as Gallatin evidently felt, discretion in bargaining.

[12] Adams to Gallatin and Rush, July 28, 1818, *A.S.P., F.R.*, IV, 377.

The question as to the negotiation is really two: Why was the 49° line named in the instruction, and why was it proposed so promptly in the negotiation? As to the instruction, it was based on an American conviction that a line at 49° already existed as a boundary separating British North America west of the Lake of the Woods from the possessions of the United States. The line was believed to have been drawn under the terms of the Treaty of Utrecht of 1713, separating British and French possessions west of the Lake of the Woods. The reality of such a line was more than a tradition. It was attested to by maps, European and American, and was credited by such American statesmen as Adams, Gallatin, Rush, Monroe, Madison, and Thomas Hart Benton. Some American statesmen and cartographers, including Benton, believed it had been extended even to the Pacific.[13] That no such line had ever been established was shown, in the closing stages of the Oregon controversy, to have been the case. Yet in 1807 Monroe had relied on it in the Northwest boundary negotiation in proposing to the British the line of 49°, and he had done so again in instructing the American peace commissioners at Ghent. He had warned them that if an Oregon partition were to be attempted they must be careful "not to countenance, in any manner, or in any quarter, a pretension in the British Government to territory south of that line."[14] Gallatin had been one of the peace commissioners so instructed at Ghent, and he probably felt in 1818 that an Oregon line of delimitation at 49° would be satisfactory to his government.

But the real question is not what would have been a satisfactory boundary. It is what Gallatin had in mind in making an opening proposal. If he believed that the line of 49° would be a satisfactory boundary why did he not, as a means of obtaining it propose first a line at 50° or 51°? Why did he come so promptly to 49°? He never explained this to his government and was never asked to do so.

His explanation could have taken the form of an appraisal of American claims to the Oregon Country in terms of priority of discovery. On these grounds American claims to the valley of the Columbia, especially to the portion of it south of the line of 49°,

---

[13] *A.S.P., F.R.,* III, 90; Adams, ed., *Memoirs of John Quincy Adams,* IV, 235. A good brief account is Jesse S. Reeves, *American Diplomacy under Tyler and Polk* (Baltimore, 1907), 194–198.
[14] *A.S.P., F.R.,* III, 731.

were strong. They were supported by the discoveries of Captain Robert Gray and of the Lewis and Clark expedition, all solidified later by the settlement made at Astoria in 1811–12. But they did not compare favorably, north of 49°, with the claims of the British. British claims were supported there by the explorations of Captain James Cook, the activity of the Nootka traders, the great survey of George Vancouver, and the discoveries of Alexander Mackenzie, of Simon Fraser, and of David Thompson. They were buttressed by the triumph of William Pitt over Spain in the Nootka Sound affair of 1790, in which, at the risk of war, British rights in the Oregon Country had been upheld as against Spanish claims of exclusive sovereignty. It would have been a feat of audacity for even a John Quincy Adams to propose, in the face of this record, a line at 50° or 51°. To Gallatin it would have seemed a maneuver so transparently a sham as to be self-defeating. Gallatin seems to have felt some diffidence about defending even a line at 49°. At least he and Rush gave that impression to their British opposites.[15]

Another defense Gallatin could have offered for his prompt proposal of the line was a belief common in Jeffersonian circles that the Oregon Country was destined to become a separate republic, attached neither to the United States nor to Great Britain. The Oregon Country was considered by Jefferson and his followers too distant from the United States to become a state of the Union, and too American in its future population to consent to remain a British colony. That view Monroe also adhered to. If the whole Pacific Northwest was to become a self-governing republic, any line of delimitation drawn across it would not be of perpetual significance.

Gallatin could have defended his prompt proposal of 49° also on the practical ground that it would leave adequate bargaining margin for the prime objective of American diplomacy in the Oregon Country. In 1818 the prime objective was the Columbia River in the opinion of every well-informed American. The river was the central transportation system, the life's artery, the Mississippi of the Oregon Country. It was an outlet to the sea for the vast interior of that country. The river would have been left safe even under the unofficial offer of a line departing from the 49th

[15] Frederick J. Robinson and Henry Goulburn to Castlereagh, Sept. 26, 1818, F.O., 5: 138.

parallel and going out to sea via the watershed between the river and the Gulf of Georgia. As for the Gulf of Georgia, its harbors were of limited usefulness. Begirt by mountain ranges and unconnected by navigable rivers with the interior, they could serve only as naval bases. They were expendible in the interest of obtaining an agreement.

This reconstruction of Gallatin's thought rests partly on conjecture. The report made by him and Rush of the negotiation was brief and gave little attention to tactics.[16] But the two central ideas in the analysis here suggested were imbedded firmly and tenaciously in Gallatin's thinking as shown in his later writing. In 1826, when he was asked by Adams, then President, to undertake a new Oregon negotiation, he strove with earnestness to obtain authorization to repeat his unofficial Gulf offer, and was much troubled in spirit when it was denied him. As late as 1846 he publicly predicted in his famous *Letters on the Oregon Question* that some day the Oregon Country would become an independent republic.[17]

If his instructions in the 1818 negotiation had been sufficiently clear and restrictive he would loyally have adhered to them. He was a diplomat of high sense of responsibility to his government.[18] In the absence of sufficiently clear instructions he appears to have permitted his own views to shape the tactics of the negotiation. He permitted the proposal of 49° to be an introductory rather than an ultimate offer, confident that he had preserved the necessary bargaining margin for the watershed line between the Columbia and the Gulf of Georgia, which he appears to have conceived of as the final line.

In 1823, for a second time, the two governments undertook to delimit their Oregon claims. They opened a new negotiation in London. The British foreign secretary was then George Canning. Adams was still American Secretary of State; Rush was minister to London. On this occasion Adams prepared instructions suffi-

---

[16] Rush kept a journal of the negotiation which throws little light on the question of tactics. The journal is among the Albert Gallatin Papers in the New-York Historical Society.

[17] Albert Gallatin, *Letters on the Oregon Question* (Washington, 1846), No. 5. See also Essay 5.

[18] In the discussion of this negotiation in Bradford Perkins, *Castlereagh and Adams* (Berkeley, 1964), 268, the opinion is expressed that the American negotiators violated their instructions in departing from the line of the 49th parallel. The truth is the instructions were too vague and general to be thus violated.

ciently specific. He directed Rush to propose the 51st parallel as
the initial American bid and later, if necessary, the 49th, a reliance
on standard bargaining procedures. He instilled in Rush, however,
no determination to use a first bid as a means of extracting concessions from the British. He imposed no conditions on a return
to the 49th parallel.

In tactical position Adams was stronger in 1823 than he had
been in 1818. He had acquired by the Spanish treaty all the claims
of Spain north of the 42nd parallel. He had strengthened American
claims where strength was most needed—in the Straits region and
farther north. He was not disposed to underestimate his treaty. On
the day it was signed he exulted over its importance and his own
part in bringing it to pass to the extent of several pages in his diary.
He wrote that Spain's acknowledgment of the American line to
the Pacific marked a new "epocha" in our history; and that he, and
he alone, was responsible for the initial proposal of it in the
negotiation.[19]

Yet, in preparing for the 1823 negotiation in London, he made
singularly unaggressive use of the Spanish treaty. In directing Rush
to propose the 51st parallel as the boundary he did not refer to the
treaty at all. He wrote:

> I mention the latitude of 51°, as the bound within which we are
> willing to limit the future settlement of the United States, because it
> is not to be doubted that the Columbia river branches as far north as
> 51°, although it is most probably not the Tacoutche Tesse [Fraser] of
> MacKenzie. As, however, the line already runs in latitude 49° to the
> Stony Mountains, should it be earnestly insisted upon by Great Britain,
> we will consent to carry it in continuance on the same parallel to the
> sea.[20]

Rush, on his part, manifested no greater determination in the
negotiation than had appeared in his instruction. At the outset he
proposed the 51° line, defending it in terms of American discoveries and the acquisition of Spanish claims. But in short order,
and without having exacted any equivalent in concessions, he
dropped back to the line of 49°. He was there when the negotiation
ended. He had not turned the Spanish treaty to account.

The British were also in their 1818 position, with one exception.
In 1818 they had merely intimated a willingness to adopt as the

---

[19] Adams, ed., *Memoirs of John Quincy Adams*, IV, 274–276.
[20] Adams to Rush, July 22, 1823, *A.S.P., F.R.,* V, 448.

boundary the 49th parallel to the Columbia, and thence along the Columbia to the sea. Now they actually made that proposal. These respective offers remained unchanged until the time of the Polk crisis, except for an unacceptable British offer in the negotiation of 1826–27.[21]

In retrospect the initial 1818 partition offer of the Americans was surprisingly modest. It was the more so as coming from such an engrosser as Adams. It was destined to become an embarrassment to later expansionists. What is more, it became an embarrassment to later moderates interested in preserving peace, who, because of it, were hesitant to accept British proposals of arbitration.[22] The offer had taken its inspiration from what proved to be a myth.[23] The British rejection of it took inspiration from what proved to be also a myth, or the equivalent of one—an inflated estimate of the value of the Columbia as a connection with the continental interior, a myth sedulously kept alive by fur-trading companies for whatever profit it gave them. The two myths established a pattern of negotiation that was carried forward by the agreement of joint occupation. The pattern was of an unresolved controversy. When the time came to resolve it a quarter of a century later, the controversy itself had become so transformed by advances in science and transportation as to be a menace to peace.

[21] See for this proposal ch. vi of Essay 5. The Spanish treaty seems to have profited the United States little in the negotiation of 1826–27. It was minimized by Gallatin himself in the opening stages of that negotiation, as reported by his opposites, though it was used in his written argument later. The Spanish treaty was weak in any case as a prop to American claims. One weakness was that Spanish exploration was not followed by effective settlement north of 42°. Another was "that we ourselves disregarded it as long as it was for our interest to do so, & that it is inconsistent with all our other grounds of title." Edward Everett to A. H. Everett, April 8, 1846, Edward Everett Papers, Massachusetts Historical Society. Another weakness was the impairment of the Spanish claim by the Nootka Sound Convention of 1790. According to Edward Everett "Aberdeen uniformly evinced a very low opinion of the exclusive rights of Spain in the unsettled portions of the continent. This, as you are aware, is an hereditary element in British colonial politics." Everett to Abel P. Upshur, Dec. 2, 1843, Edward Everett Papers, M.H.S. For the use made of the Spanish treaty by Calhoun and Buchanan, see *Sen. Docs.*, 29 Cong., 1 Sess. (1845–46), No. 1, pp. 146–153, 163–192. The exuberant estimate by Adams of the importance of his treaty in its Pacific terms thus needs revision. The same is true of historical studies which have accepted this estimate at its face value. See Philip C. Brooks, "The Pacific Coast's First International Boundary Delineation, 1816–1819," *Pacific Historical Review*, III (March 1934), 62; and Bemis, *John Quincy Adams and the Foundations of American Foreign Policy*, ch. 16.

[22] See Essay 7.

[23] See above, p. 41 and below, pp. 395–396.

ESSAY 3 · THE GHOST RIVER CALEDONIA IN THE OREGON NEGOTIATION OF 1818*

IN THE closing days of a negotiation in London in 1818 a strange offer was made to the British government by representatives of the American government. It was made confidentially. It was rejected by the British government. It was lost from public sight for one hundred and thirty years thereafter until it was exhumed from the private papers of one of the American negotiators. The offer was to partition the Pacific Northwest by a line that would leave the whole of Puget Sound, Admiralty Inlet, and the Georgian Strait, together with all the territory that is drained by them, on the British North American side of the boundary.

The conference at which the offer was made had been called for the purpose of effecting a general settlement of Anglo-American controversies. It was a peace conference in a sense, intended to quiet issues that had led to the War of 1812 or that had grown out of the war and that had not been settled by the Treaty of Ghent. Its agenda included the items of commercial relations, especially the commerce between the United States and the British West Indies; the North Atlantic fisheries; impressment; compensation for slaves carried off by British troops at the end of the war in contravention of the peace treaty; and two territorial problems in the West—the boundary from the Lake of the Woods to the Rocky Mountains, and a conflict of claims in the Pacific Northwest.

The conflict of claims in the Pacific Northwest was one of the newer and less urgent problems of the conference. It was a problem that the war had brought to crystallization. Before the war the United States and England had been rivals in exploration and trade in this distant area, but they had not recognized to each other that they were rivals as to territory. The war had, however, brought this rivalry into the open. Early in the fighting a British war vessel

* Reprinted from the *American Historical Review*, LV (April 1950).

was sent to seize Astoria. Its captain, on arrival, finding the post and its contents in the possession of the British North West Company through a purchase from John Jacob Astor's partners, had nevertheless made a formal seizure by staging a flag-lowering ceremony. After the war the American government had demanded that, in accordance with the Treaty of Ghent, the flag be restored. The demand had been agreed to by the British government, with reservations. The result of the seizure and of the negotiations for the restoration was that an issue of sovereignty in the Pacific Northwest was squarely raised, which meant, under the circumstances, a partition problem.

At the conference the plenipotentiaries of the United States were Albert Gallatin and Richard Rush. Gallatin was the head of the mission, and the logical man for the place. One of the ablest American diplomats of his generation, or of any generation, he had become an expert on the problems of the conference from having wrestled with them at Ghent and at the negotiation, held immediately thereafter, which led to the commercial convention of 1815. He had a special competence in the problems of the Pacific Northwest. He had been a member of the Jefferson government which had sent out the Lewis and Clark expedition. He had been in close touch with John Jacob Astor while the Astoria enterprise was unfolding, and he had guarded American Astoria interests at the peace negotiation of 1814.

Richard Rush, the associate of Gallatin, was the resident American minister in London. He was a man of high competence but young in years and in diplomatic experience. He was thus overshadowed in the negotiation by his older colleague, who had once been his chief in the Treasury Department. At the end of the conference, in a document sent to President Monroe, he indicated the part he had taken in the negotiation by a comment that was a mixture of sensitiveness regarding the position he had occupied and admiration for his colleague: "I should add that the discussions on our side were conducted almost exclusively by Mr. Gallatin. Being at the head of the mission, to lead was his privilege, nor could I complain of his using it freely, while he used it so well."[1]

[1] "Notes of the joint negociation at London in 1818—from the unofficial journal of one of the plenipotentiaries" (Richard Rush), James Monroe Papers (Library of Congress), XXVI, fols. 4800–4825. This is a document of fifty-two pages consist-

The British delegation consisted of Frederick John Robinson and Henry Goulburn. Both were capable men. Robinson was president of the Board of Trade and a member of the British cabinet. His special province in the negotiation was the problem of commerce. Goulburn was undersecretary of state in the Colonial Office. He was probably the moving spirit in that office, Lord Bathurst, its chief and his personal friend, not being overindustrious. At the conference Goulburn was charged more especially with territorial and boundary issues. In 1814 he had been a member of the British peace delegation at Ghent, where he had first encountered Gallatin. He had been conspicuous at Ghent for his eagerness to impose a punitive peace on the United States and had been bitterly disappointed with the inconclusive treaty which he had ultimately had to sign. He was the voice at the conference of the North West Company,[2] the aggressive British and Canadian fur-trade group that had acquired Astoria during the war and had continued after the return of peace to control from it the trade and territory of the valley of the Columbia.

The Pacific Northwest partition problem was linked at the conference with that of the boundary east of the mountains. It was so linked as soon as the problem was taken up at the second session. The linking was at the suggestion of the British, who hoped to derive from it advantage east of the mountains. It was acceptable to the Americans, who hoped to derive from it advantage west of the mountains.[3]

The first partition offer was made by the Americans. It was an offer to run the 49th parallel as the boundary from the Lake of the Woods westward to the Pacific Ocean. In American government

---

ing chiefly of excerpts from the Rush Journal referred to in note 5 below. See also *ibid.*, XXVII, fols., 4904, 4907. Rush did not disclose the gulf offer to Monroe in these "Notes."

[2] In the *Oregon Historical Quarterly*, XX (1919), 306-30, are published letters which the North West Company sent Goulburn prior to and during the War of 1812.

[3] *American State Papers, Foreign Relations* (Washington, 1832–1859), IV, 381. The British strategy in linking the two issues is analyzed in an article by Joseph Schafer, "British Attitude toward the Oregon Question," in *American Historical Review*, XVI (January, 1911), 277–87. In this article Castlereagh's Oregon policy is characterized by Dr. Schafer as a "baiting" policy. The article was written before the studies by C. K. Webster had demonstrated that the policy of Castlereagh toward the United States after 1815 was essentially conciliatory. See Charles K. Webster, *Foreign Policy of Castlereagh, 1815–1822* (London, 1925).

circles the 49th parallel was believed to be the old northern boundary of Louisiana.[4] It was believed to have become so by agreement
of the commissioners appointed by England and France to implement the Treaty of Utrecht of 1713. It had been named, in the
Anglo-American negotiation of 1806–1807, as the boundary from
the Lake of the Woods "westward as far as the respective territories of the parties extend in that quarter." But because this agreement was part of a convention which in other parts had been
unacceptable to Jefferson, the whole had been rejected. The proposal of Gallatin and Rush was to revive the 1807 line and extend it
to the Pacific.

To this proposal the British plenipotentiaries replied by inquiring
whether the United States claimed the country west of the Stony
(*i.e.*, Rocky) Mountains as part of the Louisiana Purchase. The
question led to an argument over claims. The Americans, as recorded by Rush in his journal of the negotiations,[5] stated "that the
U.S. claimed the Country west of the Stony Mountains both as
part of Louisiana and also by right of discovery of and settlement
on the Columbia river. They admitted that other nations might
have claims in that quarter, that all of them were vague, but that
G.B. could have none whatever south of the 49th degree of
latitude."[6]

The British answered with arguments of British discoveries and
economic interests in the Pacific Northwest and the rights, derived
from them. They also made the argument of convenience. Rush
recorded:

It was observed by the B. Plen. that independent of any question of
right that boundary [the 49th parallel] was very inconvenient as it
intersected the rivers west of the Stony mountains, that a river (meaning it is presumed the Columbia river) would be a much more convenient boundary, that the access for vessels to the mouth of the
Columbia river was indispensible for the exportation of the furs pur-

[4] Gallatin and Rush to Adams, Oct. 20, 1818, *A.S.P., F.R.*, IV, 381; *Writings of
Thomas Jefferson* (Washington, 1903–1904), XV, 93–94.
[5] The Journal is among the Albert Gallatin Papers in the New-York Historical
Society. It appears there in two volumes marked "1, London 1818" and "2, London
1818, British Negotiation (16 Oct. 1818–19 Jan. 1819)." Initially the property of
Rush, it was acquired by Gallatin at some later time, probably when he undertook
the London negotiation of 1826–27. It will be referred to hereafter as Rush
Journal.
[6] *Ibid.*, 1, see under Aug. 29, 1818.

chased in the interior parts of the Country, that the North West Company had formed several establishments on the Columbia river south of the 49th degree of latitude, and that that parallel [the 49th] would fall so far north as to intersect the internal sound called Gulf of Georgia, and leave its entrance north of Cape Flattery exclusively within the U.S. The American Plen. observed on the subject of the settlements that at the time of the war taking place, there was none on the Columbia river but that formed by the Amer., which having been captured must be restored, and that all the establishments of the North West Company were made during and in consequence of the war.[7]

It was ominous that in this discussion waterways were so promptly found to be elements of importance in the partition problem. Waterways are traditional disturbers of partition conferences, and the two named by the British as lying in the path of the 49th parallel—the Gulf of Georgia and the Columbia River— were elements of contention not merely in this negotiation but in four others before an agreement could be made regarding them. The Gulf of Georgia is an arm of the sea that lies between the southern end of Vancouver Island and the mainland. It is a composite of waters. On modern maps it has given way to the names of its components, Strait of Georgia, Admiralty Inlet, and Puget Sound. The whole of it, together with the Strait of Juan de Fuca, one of its outlets to the ocean, would have become, if the proposed American line of the 49th parallel to the ocean had been agreed to by the British, the possession of the United States.

These waters were associated in British minds with triumphs of the empire in diplomacy, discovery, and trade. The Strait of Juan de Fuca was associated with the Nootka affair of 1790, in which the Pitt government had maintained British rights on the Northwest coast as against the claims of Spain to exclusive sovereignty in the face of the danger of a general European war. The waters of the Gulf of Georgia were associated with the name of Captain George Vancouver of the British navy, who had explored and surveyed them on the historic voyage of 1792, when he had come to the Pacific coast to receive restitution from Spain for the Nootka seizures.

The Columbia River, especially the harbor at its mouth, was regarded by the British government as of even greater value than the Gulf of Georgia and as the greatest single territorial asset in the

[7] *Ibid.*

Pacific Northwest. The British government was persuaded by the North West Company that a continued free access to the river was indispensable to the company's successful prosecution of the fur trade of the interior. The limit, therefore, of the territorial concessions the British government was willing to make was that hinted at during the first discussion with Gallatin and Rush—the territory south of the lower Columbia River. The north side the British government was resolved to hold.

But the American government was resolved not to yield the north side. The whole lower river was associated by the American government with American exploits of exploration and colonization. The harbor at the mouth Robert Gray had discovered and the name had been conferred by him. From the interior the river had been first explored by the Lewis and Clark expedition. The lower river had been first colonized by the Pacific Fur Company of New York, which had built Astoria near the mouth and posts subsidiary to it upstream. Between the rights claimed by the Americans on these grounds, and those claimed by the British, no easy adjustment was possible, and the negotiators at that session found none.

At the next session the Americans presented formally for the record the proposal they had made of the line of the 49th parallel to the Pacific. To it they attached, in deference to Spain, which had considerable claims to this coast, a reservation that the partition line merely defined the claims of the United States and England and did not prejudice the rights of other powers. The Americans further proposed that each contracting power reserve for its inhabitants freedom to engage in the trade of that part of the country which the dividing line allotted to the other, and freedom of navigation for its nationals, on the rivers or their branches intersected by the line, from the sources of the branches intersected to the Pacific Ocean.[8]

To this proposal the British, at the fourth session, replied with a counterproposal. For the area between the Lake of the Woods and the Rocky Mountains they accepted the line of the 49th parallel as the boundary. For the area west of the Rocky Mountains they segregated a portion—the portion between the 45th and 49th parallels—as a region to be jointly occupied. This region, with its

[8] *A.S.P., F.R.*, IV, 383–84.

harbors, bays, rivers and creeks, was to be open for the indefinite future to the nationals of both powers for purposes of trade and commerce. Neither power was to exercise there against the other any sovereign or territorial authority, nor construe it to the prejudice of the rights of other powers. Concerning the territory which lay to the north and to the south of the segregated portion the British proposal was silent.[9]

This offer represented a hardening on the part of the British. They had, in the first discussion, at least hinted that the Columbia River would be a convenient boundary. They now offered no boundary, realizing that an offer of the Columbia River line would be rejected. Instead, for that part of the contested territory which was the very core of the American claim and which contained the vital north and south banks of the lower Columbia, they offered a joint occupation of indefinite duration.

In a forthright statement the Americans rejected the proposal:

> That portion of the article which relates to the country west of the Stony mountains cannot be agreed to in its present shape. The American plenipotentiaries cannot consent to throw in a common stock that part only of the country to which the United States deny the claim of Great Britain, and which lies within the same latitudes as their own territories east of the Stony mountains; thus, also implying the exclusion of their citizens from the trade on the northwest coast of America, (north of 49°) which they have enjoyed without interruption for a number of years, and as early as the British.
>
> Nor are they authorized to agree to expressions implying a renunciation of territorial sovereignty, although perfectly disposed not to insist on an extension of the line of demarcation to that country.[10]

The Americans in turn offered either that the article on the area west of the mountains be altogether omitted, or that it be changed so that all of the region claimed or held by either power there be covered by the joint occupancy.

The second of these alternatives proved acceptable to the British. They drew up a rephrased article which declared all the territory claimed by either power west of the mountains open to the nationals of both powers for purposes of trade and commerce.[11]

[9] *Ibid.*, p. 391.
[10] *Ibid.*, p. 392.
[11] *Ibid.*, p. 395.

By now, however, Gallatin had developed doubts of the advisability, from an American point of view, of agreeing to any joint occupation that would be of indefinite duration. The aggressiveness and turbulence of the North West Company, which dominated the valley of the Columbia, was notorious, and Gallatin had evidently come to fear that the company, behind the screen of an agreement of joint occupation that was without limit of time, would be able to convert the Pacific Northwest into a permanent British hunting preserve. On October 16, three days before the scheduled date of the next session of the conference, he sought out Goulburn and proposed that the joint occupation be limited to ten years.

The conversation that ensued, of which Rush kept the following memorandum, reveals not merely the direction of Gallatin's thought, but the hapless state of the negotiation:

Mr. Gallatin adverting to the boundary article, said that they had already informed the Brit. Plen. that they could not agree to the proposed arrangement respecting the country westward of the Stony Mountains without an express reservation of the claims to it of either party, but he would add, that on closer investigation of the provisions as stated in the last British project, it appeared to him that they would have the effect of shutting up the country forever to any settlement, or if ever it became settled by Americans those provisions would be incompatible with the exercise of a territorial jurisdiction. In fact, being of a commercial nature, they ought to be temporary; and at all events, if every other subject of the negotiation was left undecided the American Plen. could not agree to this article with a provision making perpetual the arrangement above mentioned. Mr. Goulburn observed that the first part of the article that fixed the boundary as far as the Stony Mountains was to the advantage of America. Mr. Gallatin said that it was always expedient to arrange a subject which had been contested, but no other advantage accrued to the U. States from that part of the article. The boundary thus recognized was theirs of right, and considering in what quarter it lay, could never be altered by the British. Mr. Goulburn having observed that, in that case they would agree only on the slaves article and on the renewal of the [commercial] convention of 1815, Mr. Gallatin said that in that case it did not appear to him worth while to agree to the slaves article, which amounted to nothing. . . . There would be nothing left but the renewal of the [commercial] convention, and he regretted that the negotiation had been opened at all, as Mr. Rush had been authorized to agree to that renewal by itself. . . .[12]

[12] Rush Journal, 2, see under Oct. 16, 1818.

It was evident from this exchange that the conference was at the point of failure. It had reached agreement on little of its agenda. It had been working under auspices that were none too favorable. The people of England and the United States still nursed animosities against each other that were of old standing and that the war had heightened. The two governments would have found it difficult, even if they had wished, to make to each other the mutual concessions necessary to settle their differences. No careful preparation had been made for the conference either by Lord Castlereagh, the British secretary for foreign affairs, or by J. Q. Adams, the American secretary of state. The conference had been hastily called with little preliminary canvassing of the possibilities of success. Lord Castlereagh, who wished the negotiation to succeed, had started the sessions off in a spirit of mutual good will. He had striven within the British cabinet to smooth the path of the negotiators.[13] But he had apparently found among the majority of his colleagues little interest in his own desire for conciliation, and it is doubtful that he would have been able to bring the conference to success even if he had remained in London to watch over it. Early in the deliberations of the conference he was called away to attend the meeting of the European congress at Aix-la-Chapelle. In his absence the bargaining broke down. By October 16 it had reached the impasse that the Gallatin-Goulburn conversation revealed. The closing date of the negotiation was, moreover, near at hand. The American negotiators were under instructions to have the results of their labors in Washington by the third Monday in November, when Congress would assemble.

It was under these circumstances that the American plenipotentiaries, in the hope of rescuing at least the boundary from the bog of failure, on October 19 made their final offer of a line of partition. They made the offer unofficially and confidentially. They did not permit it to appear on the protocol of the negotiation. It is recorded, so far as is known, only in the private journal kept by Rush. The circumstances of the offer, its nature, and the reception given to it by the British, are described by Rush as follows:

The British Plen. then said that the determination of the American Plen. not to sign the boundary article if the arrangement respecting the

13 *A.S.P., F.R.*, IV, 373–79. See also John Harvey Powell, *Richard Rush* (Philadelphia, 1942), p. 123.

territory west of the Stony mountains was made perpetual, had sup-
prised [*sic*] them as apparently inconsistent with what had heretofore
passed on the subject, and a limitation in that respect not having been
suggested in the amendments proposed at the 6th conference. The
Amer. Plen. acknowledged that the proposal of a limitation had been
at that time omitted, but they reminded the Brit. Plen. that when the
first American article was delivered, the commercial arrangement was
limited to such provisions as might without inconvenience be perpetual
and connected with a permanent demarcation of the boundary line in
that quarter; and that they had expressly stated that with respect to
other commercial arrangements, intended principally for the convenience of the British North West traders who had formed establishments within the American claims, they were disposed to agree to them
but only for a limited time. The ultimate object of America was to fix
the boundary and to make agricultural and permanent settlements. That
of G.B. did not seem to go beyond a trade with the natives. She would
have no motive therefore to come to an arrangement for the boundary,
if that for the trade was made perpetual. The Amer. Plen. on a thorough
examination of the article proposed by the Brit. Plen. had become
satisfied of this and that their agreeing to it would either be tantamount
to a renunciation on the part of the U.S. to their claim to the territory,
or be followed by collisions on that subject. If the British Plen. were
disposed to fix the line, they [the Americans] would modify their first
proposal so that, after having (along the parallel of 49° north latitude)
crossed all the waters of the Columbia river, that line should deviate so
far southwardly as to leave within the British claim all the waters
emptying in the sound called the Gulf of Georgia. If the line could
not at this time be agreed on, they would propose either to make no
commercial arrangement with respect to the territory west of the Stony
mountains, or to limit that arrangement to a period of ten years. If
neither of these proposals was acceded to, although the recognition of
the boundary line by G.B. along the parallel of 49° as far as the Stony
mountains was desirable, they would not purchase it by an acquiescence
to the permanent commercial arrangement proposed for the country
west of those mountains, and they must decline signing the article
altogether. The British Plen. said that they were not prepared to agree
to a permanent boundary line, that even by making the Columbia river
the line, which the American Plen. had said they could not agree to,
many of the North West Company's settlements situated on the left
bank of the river would be given up; that they thought however a
temporary arrangement preferable to none, and that they would agree
to the limitation proposed. It was then agreed that the arrangt. (for the
country west of the Stony Mountains) should be thrown in a distinct
article, which was drawn & agreed on.[14]

[14] Rush Journal, 2, see under Oct. 19, 1818. The offer is dismissed by Bradford
Perkins in his *Castlereagh and Adams* (Berkeley, 1964), 267–68, as of no signifi-

The conference was now virtually over. It adjourned the day after the joint occupation agreement was reached. Its achievements consisted of the joint occupation article, the boundary between the Lake of the Woods and the Stony Mountains, an article on commerce, one on the fisheries, and one on the issue of the captured slaves. These achievements were more nominal than real. The joint occupation article was a mere postponement of a settlement; the boundary between the Lake of the Woods and the Stony Mountains was a reaffirmation in more precise terms of the unratified 1807 line; the article on commerce was a renewal of the commercial convention of 1815, already agreed to before the conference; the fisheries article was a compromise; that on the captured slaves was an agreement to accept the decision of a friendly sovereign. These agreements were ratified by the two governments. The joint occupation agreement was renewed in 1827 for an indefinite period and remained the covenant of the Oregon Country until it was replaced by the partition treaty of 1846.

As for the final American boundary offer, made in the vain hope of averting a joint occupation, it was not precise. It was an offer of all the waters entering the Gulf of Georgia without a definition of what that term meant. The historian seeking a definition is obliged to turn to Vancouver, who named the gulf in 1792, and whose narrative and charts, published in 1798,[15] were still in 1818 the

---

cance. It did not appear in a report submitted by the British plenipotentiaries to the Foreign Office, and Perkins conjectures that Gallatin had made the offer so unobtrusively and noncommittally that he was not understood. Such an explanation is hardly credible. If Gallatin was not understood, a request for clarification could easily have been made, and Gallatin was not normally lacking in lucidity.

Omission of the offer from the report made by the British is explainable on more solid grounds. The offer was unofficial and confidential. On the official protocol of the negotiation it had, of course, no place. Neither could it be decently mentioned in a formal report. A lack of interest in the offer is the best explanation, doubtless, of failure to report it. The British had hoped for an offer at the mouth of the Columbia, which would have assured their fur traders access to the interior of the Oregon Country. This was the region where American claims were strongest and British weakest. Gallatin's offer in the Gulf region was where American claims were weakest and British claims strongest. His concession may well have seemed a gesture without meaning. Only later, in the crisis of 1845–46, when the Gulf region had assumed importance, could such an American offer have significance, worthy of recall by British opponents of a settlement at 49°. It is to be noted that opposition to a settlement at this line had to be overcome in the Peel ministry, and that Goulburn and Robinson were members of that ministry.

[15] Captain George Vancouver, *Voyage of Discovery to the North Pacific Ocean and Round the World* (London, 1798).

standard authority on that coast. Vancouver had used more than ordinary care in naming and defining the gulf, for this had been part of a ceremony of establishing a claim for his country and of doing honor to his sovereign, George III. He had planned the ceremony to take place on the birthday anniversary of the king. With a detachment of men he landed on the shores of Admiralty Inlet on June 4, 1792, and to the accompaniment of a royal salute from his vessels, he had taken possession of the coast he had been exploring up to the straits of Juan de Fuca:

likewise all the coasts, islands, etc. within the said straits, as well on the northern as on the southern shores; together with those situated in the interior sea we had discovered, extending from the said straits, in various directions, between the northwest, north, east, and southern quarters; which interior sea I have honored with the name of "*THE GULF OF GEORGIA*," and the continent binding the said gulph, and extending southward to the 45th degree of north latitude with that of *NEW GEORGIA*, in honor of His present Majesty.[16]

On the charts of Vancouver[17] the name, "Gulf of Georgia," appeared in letters of a size which indicate an intention to make it apply to the whole pocket of water lying at an angle to De Fuca Strait, "between the northwest, north, east, and southern quarters." The name is stopped short of Admiralty Inlet and Puget Sound, but this was merely to avoid an overlapping of lettering.

The Gulf of Georgia, thus defined, is rich in harbors. Its southernmost arm, Puget Sound, is especially so. Puget Sound is a veritable cluster of harbors hanging from the stem of the Strait of Juan de Fuca. The harbors are of unusual excellence—commodious, deep, and well located. Because they lie far inland they are safe from the storms and swells of the Pacific Ocean. In the Pacific Northwest the only harbors that have much commercial value in their natural state are those that lie inland, such as the ones in Puget Sound or the Bay of San Francisco. The harbors that front on the open ocean are bar harbors, unsafe, unless improved at high cost, for large vessels to enter or to leave, and exposed to the full blast of ocean winds. The quality of the harbors in Puget Sound is evident from a glance at the names of the ports that have grown up about them—Seattle, Tacoma, Olympia, Everett, and Bellingham.

[16] *Ibid.*, I, 289.
[17] The Gulf of Georgia is shown on two sections of Vancouver's charts.

In 1818 the only good harbors on the Pacific side of the continent to which the United States had any defensible claim were the gulf harbors south of 49°. The harbor at the mouth of the Columbia, to which the United States had a strong claim, was a bar harbor. San Francisco Bay was at that time the virtually undisputed possession of Spain. Under the proposal of Gallatin and Rush all the harbors in the gulf would have been given up to the British.

The United States would also have given up territory that lies south of the 49th parallel—all the territory draining west from the Cascade divide and north from the Columbia River divide into the gulf. That territory includes several river valleys, the Skagit, Stilaquamish, and Snohomish, and the entire basin holding Puget Sound. It includes Mt. Rainier National Park. If the offer of Gallatin and Rush had been accepted, the railroad passes that today admit the Northern Pacific, the Great Northern, and the Milwaukee roads through the Cascades into the Pacific Northwest would lie astride an international boundary.

An offer such as this constitutes a problem. Why was it made by diplomats of ability and experience? An answer is not found in the instructions prepared for the negotiation by Adams.[18] The Adams instructions are in themselves something of a problem. They make no specification of any boundary line that is to be the limit of American concession west of the mountains. East of the mountains they do specify a limit—the limit of the 49th parallel. They roundly declare, however, in the section devoted to the boundary east of the mountains that south of the 49th parallel the British "can have no valid claim upon this continent."[19] To the problem of the offer no answer is found, either, in the private papers of Gallatin, Rush, and Adams, which in so far as they are available give only the offer itself.

In seeking the answer the best procedure is to begin in areas of familiar fact. It is a familiar fact that the American government considered the valley of the Columbia River south of the 49th parallel the greatest territorial prize in the Pacific Northwest. This prize its negotiators were intent on winning, so intent that they were willing to give up, in order to gain it, the Gulf of Georgia and the territory that it drains.

[18] The instructions are printed in *A.S.P., F.R.*, IV, 376–78.
[19] *Ibid.*, p. 377.

To the Gulf of Georgia and its drainage basin the United States in 1818 had no very strong claim, certainly not as strong a claim as that held by England. The American claim was based chiefly on a voyage Captain Robert Gray, the discoverer of the mouth of the Columbia, had made up the Strait of Juan de Fuca prior to Vancouver's exploration. But Gray could not be shown to have sailed far up the strait, and his achievement was hardly a counterweight to the claim acquired by England through Vancouver's careful exploration and systematic survey of the gulf itself. Nor was the American government in a position, in 1818, to cite, in reinforcement of its own rights north of the Columbia River watershed, rights acquired from Spain. These rights were not acquired until 1821. In 1818, moreover, no rights north of the divide could be based safely on grounds of contiguity. The territory that the United States owned east of the Rockies was not yet recognized by England to extend to the 49th parallel. The northern boundary was one of the problems of the conference.

Gallatin and Rush were apparently conscious of the comparative weakness of the American claim north of the Columbia River divide. At least they created the impression on the British that they were. When, at the time of proposing the 49th parallel, they gave in support of the American claim arguments all of which were Columbia River arguments except the one of Gray's voyage up the strait, the British in their analysis of the case to their government reported that they thought they observed in the Americans "a disposition not to insist pertinaciously on the pretensions which were advanced in their projet of an article."[20]

In 1818, moreover, Americans considered the harbors in the Gulf of Georgia to be less than major stakes of diplomacy. They thought of these harbors as potential naval stations or local ports, but not much more. The gulf harbors have no natural means of communication with any hinterland in territory south of the 49th parallel. They have at their service no mighty river such as the Columbia, which, bar-obstructed though it was, was expected to create in the Pacific Northwest a second New Orleans. Ultimately some of these harbors did become major ports. They developed into entrepôts of a world-wide commerce. They became so largely because

[20] Robinson and Goulburn to Castlereagh, Sept. 26, 1818, in Public Record Office, Foreign Office, series 5: 138.

railroads gave them overland connection with a continental interior. But in 1818 railroads were a development still in the future. No one dreamed of the impact they would make on modern life.

In the minds of Gallatin and Rush there was another consideration, perhaps the decisive one, in inducing the gulf offer. It was a belief that a river of considerable magnitude flowing into the gulf would be severed by a boundary line drawn along the 49th parallel. This was a problem which the British had raised in general terms as soon as the Americans made their 49th parallel proposal. The objection of the British had been that rivers flowing into the Pacific would be severed by that line, "rivers" meaning the Columbia and, evidently, one flowing into the Gulf of Georgia. Unless this issue could be compromised no agreement of partition was in sight.

It is now known that no rivers of magnitude flow into the Gulf of Georgia south of the 49th parallel. One major river, the Fraser, does have a gulf outlet, but it lies wholly north of the 49th parallel, as was already known in 1818. Several rivers of secondary size flow into the gulf south of 49°. Their outlet, character, and course were in 1818 virtually unknown. The region adjoining the gulf was then an unexplored wilderness.

One river of great magnitude was believed, however, to rise at the north and to enter the gulf south of 49°. This was the river Caledonia, pictured in impressive length on a recently published map. It was pictured as equaling the Fraser in magnitude, with sources nearly as far north as those of the Fraser, and with an outlet —a forked outlet—far southward, in the latitude of Whidbey's Island, about 48° 40'. The Caledonia was a grossly distorted version of the Skagit River, a minor stream that enters the gulf by a forked outlet south of 49°.

The map on which this river was revealed to the world was a large, folded inlay in a pamphlet published in London in 1817. The pamphlet bore the title *Notice Respecting the Boundary between His Majesty's Possessions in North America and the United States.*[21] It, and its map, were propaganda prepared by the North West Company for the purpose of influencing government policy on two issues then up for decision—the location of the boundary between

[21] This pamphlet is in the Library of Congress and in the Harvard University Library.

the Lake of the Woods and the Pacific Ocean and the ending of the violent trade war which the North West Company and the Hudson's Bay Company were fighting.

The pamphlet was anonymous, but in the text the author gave sufficient information concerning himself to permit him to be identified. He was Simon M'Gillivray,[22] brother of the leading partner of the North West Company and himself a partner. He was the North West Company's agent in its dealings with the government. He had long concerned himself with the problem of the boundary between the Lake of the Woods and the Pacific Ocean. He had served as a witness in London before the negotiators of the abortive boundary agreement of 1807. He was the company's London specialist in the management of the fur trade of the Pacific Northwest. He had directed, prior to and during the War of 1812, the company's successful campaign against Astor in the Columbia valley. He had represented the company's Columbia River interests before the Colonial Office and the Foreign Office during the negotiation of the Treaty of Ghent. After the signature of the treaty he had developed the thesis that Astoria did not need to be restored to the United States under the treaty terms, the post having been acquired by the North West Company through purchase, not capture.[23] In 1817, while on a visit to New York City, he had learned that the United States sloop of war *Ontario* had been sent to the mouth of the Columbia to assert American rights to Astoria under the treaty. He had raised an alarm with the British minister in Washington and with the governor general in Canada,[24] the consequences of which were a minor diplomatic crisis in London

[22] On the title page the statement is made that the pamphlet is intended to accompany the *Narrative of Occurrences in the Indian Countries of North America.* Simon M'Gillivray was the author of the latter work. The author also refers (p. 5) to having been present at discussions of the boundary problem in the Anglo-American negotiation of 1806–1807. He refers to having had in his possession at the time an original map by David Thompson of the country between the Lake of the Woods and the source of the Mississippi, which he was asked to bring to the negotiation. The Library of Congress ascribes the authorship of the pamphlet to Simon M'Gillivray.

[23] See "Statement relative to the Columbia river and adjoining Territory on the Western coast of the Continent of North America [1815]" in M'Gillivray to Bagot, Nov. 15, 1817, F.O. 5: 123. The "Statement" is printed in full in *Oregon Hist. Quar.,* XX, 254–60.

[24] M'Gillivray to Bagot, Nov. 15, 1817, F.O. 5: 123.

and the subsequent agreement by Lord Castlereagh to restore the American flag to Astoria.

In the *Notice Respecting the Boundary*, M'Gillivray undertook to expose the designs, which, in his opinion, the United States had on the region between the Lake of the Woods and the Pacific Ocean. He made use for this purpose of a map which had appeared in 1816 in the United States, published by the well-known Philadelphia map maker, John Melish.[25] The Melish map was believed in diplomatic circles in Europe and in America, and by M'Gillivray, to be an exhibit of the territorial ambitions of the American government and to be actually government inspired.[26] It fairly exuded American expansionism. It laid down without comment as the boundary from the Lake of the Woods to the Pacific shore a line at about 49° 40′, a straight westward projection from the northernmost tip of the Lake of the Woods. Louisiana was outlined by a colored border. It extended northward to the divide between the Missouri and the Saskatchewan at about 52°. It extended westward beyond the Rocky Mountains to the shores of the Pacific. Within Louisiana appeared, neatly included, the Bay of San Francisco. In the area between the Rocky Mountains and the Pacific Ocean there was printed, as a concession to cartographic accuracy, in inconspicuous type, the sentence: "The Limits of Louisiana in this quarter are undefined."[27] The map seemed to M'Gillivray to demonstrate completely the thesis of the territorial aggressiveness of the American government. It was made a feature of the text of his pamphlet and, in addition, its boundary line at 49° 40′ was superimposed on his own map as a warning to the British public. On his own map the Caledonia River appeared, flung across the path of the 49th parallel.

[25] John Melish, *Map of the United States* (1816).

[26] Of the Melish map the Spanish minister to the United States wrote to his government that it was "prepared at the order of this [United States] Government to sustain its pretensions." Philip C. Brooks, *Diplomacy and the Borderlands* (Berkeley, 1939), pp. 142, 215-19.

[27] Thomas Jefferson, to whom Melish sent a copy of his map, wrote a number of corrections in a letter of acknowledgment: "On the waters of the Pacific, we can found no claim in right of Louisiana. If we claim that country at all, it must be on Astor's settlement near the mouth of the Columbia, and the principle of the *jus gentium* of America, that when a civilized nation takes possession of the mouth of a river in new country, that possession is considered as including all its waters." See *Writings of Thomas Jefferson*, XV, 93-94.

The appearance of a mysterious river of the magnitude of the Caledonia on a map in a pamphlet of this type raises a question. Was the river a mere error of cartography or a stratagem of propaganda designed to block a boundary settlement unfavorable to the interests of the North West Company? The question is more easily raised than answered. An answer cannot even be given to the question whether M'Gillivray was the compiler of the map he published. Into a map of a region as little explored as was the region adjacent to the Gulf of Georgia genuine errors creep easily enough. The forked outlet of the mysterious river may mean that it was a confusion of the Fraser. Or it may mean that it was a confusion of the Skagit, of whose lower course fur traders may have had some knowledge. The upper course of the Caledonia is comparable to the great eastern confluent of the Fraser, Thompson River. On the upper Caledonia a North West Company fort is shown, which could be none other than Kamloops of the Thompson.

Yet the Thompson was well known, in North West Company circles, to be a tributary of the Fraser. It was clearly so shown on the great manuscript map of David Thompson, completed in 1813–14, which hung on the walls of the North West Company headquarters at Fort William.[28] And on M'Gillivray's map the Fraser appears in place, with a full complement of tributaries and an outlet into the gulf in a location that is correct. It is clear that M'Gillivray feared that his government might consent to a division of the Oregon Country at the line of the 49th parallel. He had some inkling that such a division was under consideration from having been a witness at the abortive boundary negotiation of 1806–1807. He professed to fear that his government might adopt even the line of the Melish map at 49° 40′.[29] His pamphlet was designed to stiffen British resistance to any line that would interfere with the activities of his company in the lower Columbia valley. His purpose would

[28] The Thompson map is published in *David Thompson's Narrative of His Explorations in Western America*, ed. by Joseph B. Tyrrell (Toronto, 1916), map pocket; also in *New Light on the Early History of the Greater Northwest*, ed. by Elliott Coues (New York, 1897), III, map pocket. The existence and the accuracy of this map were well known to M'Gillivray. That the Fraser was sometimes called the "New Caledonia," was reported in 1824 by Governor Simpson of the Hudson's Bay Company. See Frederick Merk, ed., *Fur Trade and Empire: George Simpson's Journal* (Cambridge, Mass., 1931), pp. 73, 116.

[29] M'Gillivray, *Notice Respecting the Boundary*, p. 8.

undoubtedly be served by the appearance on a map of a great river, thrown across the path of the 49th parallel, and the conjecture may not be unwarranted that the Caledonia River sprang from his mind to meet this purpose.

Whatever the genesis of the Caledonia River, the fact that such a river had appeared on a North West Company map was enough to give it authenticity in the eyes of cartographers. The North West Company was the most competent authority in the world on the geography of that part of North America. The genuineness of the river was accepted without question during the negotiation of 1818, and for seven or eight years thereafter. Aaron Arrowsmith, the greatest of the English map makers of his day, on his *Map exhibiting all the New Discoveries in the Interior Parts of North America*, in the edition marked, "1795 Additions to 1811. 1818,"[30] reproduced the Caledonia River just as it had appeared on the M'Gillivray map. Other English cartographers, as well as French, Belgian, and American, in publications of later date did the same.[31] It is likely that besides the M'Gillivray map the revised Arrowsmith edition of 1818 was available in London in the autumn of 1818 when the Gallatin-Rush proposal was made.

If the Caledonia River was a stratagem designed to add to the difficulties of a boundary settlement at the line of the 49th parallel, it was a success. It increased the determination of the British against that line, and it induced Gallatin and Rush to offer to deflect that line sufficiently southward, after the waters of the Columbia had been passed, to leave a crucial area south of 49° within British territory. In diplomacy a concession once offered is a commitment. It is a commitment even if offered informally and rejected offhand

[30] The 1818 edition of this map may be found in the William L. Clements Library and in the Henry E. Huntington Library. I am under obligation to the staffs of these libraries, also to W. L. G. Joerg of the National Archives and to Lloyd A. Brown of the Peabody Institute of Baltimore for aid in the making of this study.

[31] See map by "Le Chev^r Lapie Géographe," in *Nouvelles Annales des Voyages, de La Géographie, de L'Histoire*, X (1821), p. 5; James Wyld, *Map of North America*, June 1, 1823; H. S. Tanner, *Map of North America*, improved to 1825; Hippolyte Ode, *Atlas Universel de Géographie* (Bruxelles, 1827). The unreality of the Caledonia River was revealed first to the Hudson's Bay Company at the end of 1824 by the trader, James MacMillan, who had been sent by Governor Simpson to explore the lower course of the Fraser. The information he gave was relayed to the British government in December, 1825. See Merk, *Fur Trade and Empire*, 113-17, 248-50. See also, 19 Cong. 1 sess., *House Report* No. 35, p. 24. The river disappeared from Arrowsmith maps thereafter.

in an unsuccessful negotiation. The gulf offer was such a commitment. It could not, since it was informally made, be honorably recorded by the British nor openly exploited by them in later negotiations. And it was not. But it was probably stored in the memories of the British negotiators, Robinson and Goulburn, and these two were still, in the years of the Oregon crisis, high in the service of the British government. In the meantime it was an element in American deliberations.

In 1826 the American and British governments undertook a new general negotiation in London for the settlement of their differences. They had been unable to reach an agreement in the intervening negotiation held in 1823–24. Gallatin was invited to undertake the new mission and agreed to become resident minister in London for the purpose. Before his departure he visited Washington to discuss the agenda issues with Clay, the Secretary of State, and with John Q. Adams, the President. The boundary west of the mountains was again to be one of the issues. Realizing that the gulf offer, made in 1818, would be remembered in Foreign Office circles in London, Gallatin suggested to Clay that authority be given him to renew it. He wished authority for an even wider offer. The United States, he wrote Clay, could "abandon without inconvenience our right to the strip of land watered by the Caledonia river, & the other smaller streams that empty into the Gulf of Georgia or streights of Fuca,"[32] if in return the British government could be induced to give up all the valley of the Columbia lying south of 49°. The proposal to abandon the streams that enter into the "streights of Fuca" was new.

On returning from his Washington conferences Gallatin gathered information, in the city of New York, regarding the territory which would be abandoned by the United States if his suggestions were adopted. The person to whom he turned was Ramsay Crooks, an agent of Astor, who had been upon the Columbia in 1812 as a partner in the Astoria enterprise. Crooks was perhaps the best informed American regarding the lower Columbia valley within reach. But regarding the area north of the divide of the Columbia he could hardly have had first-hand information. He had been at Astoria only seven weeks in 1812, much of the

[32] Gallatin to Clay, June 19, 1826, England Dispatches, XXXIII, U. S. Department of State, National Archives.

time recovering from an exhausting overland journey to the Columbia, and he had never been in the region adjacent to the Gulf of Georgia. From him Gallatin learned that:

> The country north & west of the Columbia extending north to the 49th degree of latitude and west to the sea is extremely worthless; along the sea shore rocky & poor, with little other timber than pine and hemlock, farther inland sandy and destitute of timber, a very small portion of the whole fit for cultivation, and in the meanwhile affording hardly any furs.[33]

By this information Gallatin was strengthened, as he wrote Clay in forwarding it, in the belief that the United States could abandon the northern region "without inconvenience."[34]

If Clay was persuaded by Gallatin, not so the President. The President was ever, especially as regards Britain, a less accommodating spirit than Gallatin. The instructions sent Gallatin were to hold out for the line of the 49th parallel to the Pacific Ocean. "This is our ultimatum, and you may so announce it. We can consent to no other line more favorable to Great Britain."[35] South of that line no concessions were to be made save those of navigation on the Columbia and any of its branches that the line might intersect.

Gallatin protested against the restrictiveness of these and his other instructions both to the President and to Clay. He had been told by the President while the question of his acceptance of the mission was still under discussion that he might write his own instructions. Of this he reminded the President: "Without taking literally what you said . . . I understood that it was intended to leave me sufficient latitude and discretion to enable me to avail myself of circumstances and to give every chance of success to the mission."[36] To Clay Gallatin wrote in greater detail.

> The parallel of the 49th degree of North latitude will intersect the Caledonia river a short distance above its mouth, leaving the mouth to the United States, and almost the whole course of the river to Great Britain. This renders it improbable that she will accede to our proposed

---

[33] *Ibid.* Readers acquainted with the country described here will be surprised at the characterization of it as "destitute of timber." It was a vast forest of Douglas fir and red cedar, and it still is, in large stretches, especially in the Olympic Mountains.

[34] *Ibid.*

[35] Clay to Gallatin, June 19, 1826, *A.S.P., F.R.*, VI, 644–45.

[36] Gallatin to Adams, June 20, 1826, *Writings of Albert Gallatin*, ed. by Henry Adams (Philadelphia, 1879), II, 307.

line without modification. A deviation not greater than what may be sufficient to give them the mouth of that river would be of no importance to the United States, and might facilitate an arrangement. The two Governments being in some degree committed by the respective rejection of the line proposed by each, the pride of both may be saved by a small alteration of the line; and this consideration is in practice not to be altogether disregarded.[37]

But the President was adamant. At his direction a letter was sent by Clay to Gallatin in which the comment was made on the information derived from Crooks that it added little to what was previously possessed. The letter continued:

If the land on the Northwest Coast, between the mouth of the Columbia River and the parallel of 49 be bad, and, therefore, we should lose but little in relinquishing it, the same [consideration] will apply to the British. The President cannot consent to vary the line proposed in your instructions.[38]

A second, half-angry letter of protest was sent by Gallatin to the President to no avail.[39] He was obliged to depart for London shorn of the authority to make any territorial concessions to the British south of 49°.

The restrictions thus imposed on Gallatin proved less hampering in the subsequent negotiation than had been anticipated by him. The gap between himself and the British negotiators on the boundary was so wide that a renewal of the offer of 1818, even in the expanded form which he had proposed to Clay, would clearly have

---

[37] Gallatin to Clay, June 29, 1826, *ibid.*, p. 312.

[38] Clay to Gallatin, June 23, 1826, *A.S.P., F.R.*, VI, 646.

[39] Gallatin to Adams, June 30, 1826, *Writings of Albert Gallatin*, II, 319. See also Adams to Clay, July 5, 1826, Henry Clay Papers, Library of Congress, VII, 1104. The President was inflexible on the issue partly because he was himself not free to agree to concessions. He and Clay were beset in Congress by an opposition as virulent as any American president has ever faced—the followers of Jackson. An agreement on his part to any territorial concession to the hated British would have been used to his destruction and Clay's. This the President later wrote Gallatin, after he had been informed that no boundary agreement on the basis of the 49th parallel could be obtained from the British. The President wrote: "One inch of ground yielded on the North-West coast, one step backward from the claim to the navigation of the St. Lawrence, one hairsbreadth of compromise upon the article of impressment, would be certain to meet the reprobation of the Senate. In this temper of the parties, all we can hope to accomplish will be to adjourn controversies which we cannot adjust, and say to Britain, as the Abbe Bernis said to Cardinal Fleuri, *"Monseigneur, j'attendrai."* See *Writings of Albert Gallatin*, II, 368.

been unavailing. George Canning, head of the British Foreign Office in 1826–27, believed that a valuable commerce would some day develop between the Pacific Northwest and China, of which the British settlements on the Columbia would become the center.[40] He was determined that the British hold on at least the north bank of the Columbia should be retained. The Hudson's Bay Company, successor to the North West Company, was a power in the government. The company insisted that it could not maintain the position it had built up for Britain in the Pacific Northwest if the Columbia River passed entirely under American control.[41] Canning was no conciliator of the United States. On his death in 1827 he was characterized by J. Q. Adams, with some degree of truth, as "an implacable and rancorous enemy of the United States."[42] He was annoyed with the American government because of the unilateral announcement it had made of the Monroe Doctrine in 1823, and because of the congressional publication in 1826, while the Oregon negotiation in London was in progress, of the aggressive report of the Baylies Committee.[43] The negotiation resulted, therefore, in no other Oregon agreement than the renewal of the joint occupation for an indefinite period subject to its termination on a year's notice by either party.

For a decade and a half after that agreement was ratified (in 1828) no new Oregon negotiation was undertaken. The partition issue, and its adjunct, the offer of 1818, remained dormant in the diplomacy of the two states. Elsewhere, however, dynamic forces were keeping the issue alive. American pioneers moved in increasing numbers to Oregon; American expansionists, in and out of Congress, demanded the whole Oregon Country, and in 1844 they

[40] Canning to Liverpool, June 24, 1826, *Some Official Correspondence of George Canning*, ed. by Edward J. Stapleton (London, 1887), II, 62. On July 7, 1826, Canning wrote to Liverpool, "We cannot yet enter into this trade, on account of the monopoly of the E. I. Cy. But ten years hence that monopoly will cease; and though at that period neither you nor I shall be where we are to answer for our deeds, I should not like to leave my name affixed to an instrument by which England would have foregone the advantages of an immense direct intercourse between China and what may be, if we resolve not to yield them up, her boundless establishments on the N.W. Coast of America." *Ibid.*, p. 74.

[41] Simpson to Addington, Jan. 5, 1826, in Merk, *Fur Trade and Empire*, pp. 261–66.

[42] *Memoirs of John Quincy Adams*, ed. by Charles F. Adams, 12 vols. (Philadelphia, 1874–1877), VII, 328.

[43] Gallatin to Clay, Nov. 27, 1826, *Writings of Albert Gallatin*, II, 342–44. The Baylies Report is in 19 Cong. 1 sess., *House Report* No. 35.

elected their candidate President. By 1845 the issue had reached the crisis stage in Anglo-American relations and had become a menace to peace.

At the same time the conceptions shaping the Oregon issue were undergoing important change. The value of the Columbia valley was being reassessed. In the area north of the Columbia River the Hudson's Bay Company still held complete control. But it no longer drew much profit from the fur catch. It no longer clutched the lower Columbia with the old determination. It had shifted its base from the north bank of the river to Vancouver Island as a means of removing its valuable stores from the reach of the hostile pioneers south of the river.[44] A more realistic view was being taken both in England and in the United States regarding the value of the harbor at the mouth of the Columbia, and the potentialities of the river as a route of communication with the interior. The harbors in the Gulf of Georgia were also being reappraised. Their great potentialities were coming to be recognized by Americans in the new railroad age.[45] The American claim to a share in these harbors had, in the meantime, been strengthened by two treaties. One of these had transferred Spain's rights north of 42° to the United States; the other, with England, had reinforced American rights of contiguity to the region of the harbors by establishing the 49th parallel as the boundary east of the Rocky Mountains.

In England new conditions shaped the partition issue. The government was faced with the disruptive problem of the repeal of the Corn Laws as a result of crop failure in Ireland. It was eager to avoid the danger of a clash with the United States over the Oregon issue. The secretary for foreign affairs was Lord Aberdeen, a lover of peace, eager especially for amicable relations with the United States. As early as 1843 he had become persuaded by the American minister in England that a reasonable partition line would be the 49th parallel to the Strait of Georgia and from that point the channel of the strait and of Juan de Fuca Strait to the sea.[46]

But opposition to this concession had been made in the cabinet

---

[44] See Essay 8.

[45] The role of these harbors in Oregon diplomacy is described in Essays 5 and 9. A more detailed account is the valuable study of Norman A. Graebner, *Empire on the Pacific* (New York, 1955), ch. 2.

[46] Aberdeen to Pakenham, March 4, and Pakenham to Aberdeen, March 28, 1844, Aberdeen Mss., British Museum.

by Peel, the Prime Minister. Peel wished Aberdeen to propose, instead of concession, arbitration of the Oregon issue, even though it was expected this would be rejected by the American government. Peel would have replied to American bluster by sending a British warship to the mouth of the Columbia.[47] While such division of counsel tied the cabinet the crisis heightened.

On an important issue in foreign policy a British prime minister does not lightly put himself at the head of an opposition to the wishes of his secretary for foreign affairs. Why was it that on this issue Peel put himself at the head of an opposition to Aberdeen? The answer is probably in part the fear of partisan clamor that would be raised in Parliament if the government made to the United States concessions of territory and position which for more than a quarter of a century successive British governments had refused. Yet Peel was not a person to be deterred by fear of partisan clamor from a course of action he earnestly believed to be right. He must have had doubts that the concessions which Aberdeen wished to make to the United States were justifiable.

In Peel's cabinet happened to be the plenipotentiaries of the old negotiation of 1818, Goulburn and Robinson, the opposites of Gallatin and Rush. Goulburn was Peel's chancellor of the exchequer. He was Peel's closest personal friend. Robinson was a peer. As Viscount Goderich he had briefly been Prime Minister of England. In 1844 he was Earl of Ripon and president of the Board of Control for India. Doubtless these two took an active part in the cabinet discussions on the Oregon issue in 1844–45.

How they stood on the difference between Peel and Aberdeen the records of the period do not reveal. There are no formal records of cabinet discussions; neither Goulburn's correspondence nor Ripon's sheds light on the problem. The probability is, however, that the two disclosed to the cabinet the offer, not recorded in British government documents, which Gallatin and Rush had made in 1818; that as a result Peel and his colleagues became aroused over the extent of the surrender which the British government was being asked by Aberdeen to make; and that this accounted, at least in part, for Peel's unwillingness to agree to Aberdeen's proposals.

Eventually Peel and the cabinet were converted to Aberdeen's views. They became persuaded that the lower Columbia was an

[47] Peel to Aberdeen, Sept. 28, 1844, Peel Mss., British Museum.

overvalued highway, the cession of which would not be a major loss to the empire; that the Hudson's Bay Company could be provided for, in a treaty ceding the river, by special provisions protecting its river navigation rights; that the harbors in the Gulf of Georgia could, without serious sacrifice to England, be divided by a partition line drawn along the 49th parallel to the gulf and thence, via the strait, to the sea. Fears of partisan clamor Aberdeen was able to relieve by a campaign of education carried on under his secret direction by agents in the columns of the British press. When the climax of the Oregon crisis was reached in 1845–46 Aberdeen was able to make the offer to the American government of the line of the 49th parallel to the gulf. He was able to send to Washington a treaty *projet* in which all the gulf harbors on the mainland which Gallatin and Rush had once offered to give up, were accorded to the United States. By the American Senate this *projet* was ratified without a change in the summer of 1846. Then, at last, the spell was exorcised that Simon M'Gillivray had cast over the Oregon issue when, in 1817, he published the map exhibiting the ghost river Caledonia.

ESSAY 4 · SNAKE COUNTRY EXPEDITION, 1824–25*

AN EPISODE OF FUR TRADE AND EMPIRE

THE Hudson's Bay Company in 1821 embarked upon its second great adventure in imperialism. The first had been the wresting from France of Rupert's Land. In the second the goal was the Oregon Country. For such an adventure the company had the advantage of giant size. It bestrode the northern half of the continent like a colossus. It had actual ownership of Rupert's Land, the mighty drainage basin of Hudson Bay. By virtue of a government license of 1821 it had a trade monopoly of all the territory extending from Rupert's Land to the crest of the Rocky Mountains. As a result of another license of the same year it had a monopoly of British trade rights over all the Oregon Country. By virtue of a merger closing a war with the North West Company in 1821 it owned every trading post in Oregon and the influence these gave over the Indians. Its field force was a veritable army, reinforced and reinvigorated by the 1821 merger and commanded, in George Simpson, by an administrative genius. Its capital was a sum limited only by its means of producing profits. A formidable power was this to measure strength with the scattered American adventurers, based at St. Louis, who competed for the trade of the Oregon Country.

The sphere of empire-building of the Company in theory was all the country from California to Alaska and from the Rocky Mountains to the sea. But actually the field was much narrower. In 1818 and in 1823–24 the British government had offered to yield to the United States as much of the Oregon Country as lay south of a line drawn along the forty-ninth parallel from the Rocky Mountains to an intersection with the Columbia River, and thence down the channel of that stream to the sea. These offers, enlarged

* Reprinted from the *Mississippi Valley Historical Review*, XXI (June 1934).

somewhat in 1826, the American government rejected. They left the British government in theory uncommitted. "But," as Lord Aberdeen later observed, "it is obvious that a proposition of this kind once made, must always involve the practical difficulty of subsequently assuming any less extensive basis of negotiation."[1] From the company's sphere of empire-building the territory south of the Columbia was thus in effect removed. Similarly removed was the territory north of the forty-ninth parallel, which in the partition negotiations the American government had offered to yield. The territory left in actual controversy and the area of Hudson's Bay Company opportunity was thus the triangle that lies between the Columbia River and the forty-ninth parallel. This was valuable chiefly for its water appendages. The majestic Columbia flows at its base; the harbors inside Juan de Fuca Strait cluster about its apex. In any diplomatic play for it, control of its trade was likely to be a trump card. That card the Hudson's Bay Company had to hold.

In extending empire the Hudson's Bay Company, like other British trade-carriers of the flag, had to make a profit. Profit was an obligation owed to stockholders. In the Oregon Country opportunities for profit were uneven. New Caledonia, the northern half of the province, was still in 1821 on the advent of the Hudson's Bay Company a rich fur field despite a long history of exploitation. But the southern half of the province, embracing the valley of the lower Columbia, was an area of annual trade losses. It had netted the North West Company, prior to 1821, four successive annual deficits and another followed in 1822. The Snake Country also seemed a "forlorn hope." So discouraging was the trade prospect in these two areas that, notwithstanding the obligations implied in its exclusive license, the Hudson's Bay Company in 1822–24 actually contemplated abandoning them and withdrawing northward to New Caledonia.[2]

To George Simpson, governor of the territories of the company, such counsels of discouragement were but a challenge. In the autumn of 1824, immediately after the completion of his first great task of clearing Rupert's Land of the wreckage left by the North

[1] Aberdeen to Pakenham, December 28, 1843. Public Record Office, F.O. 115: 83.
[2] See Frederick Merk (ed.), *Fur Trade and Empire: George Simpson's Journal* (Cambridge, 1931), xxiv, 175.

West Company trade-war, he appeared in the valley of the Columbia. He discovered in a swift tour of inspection that the losses of
the Columbia Department had been the result chiefly of local mis-
management and extravagance. He devoted a crowded winter and
spring to reform. The Columbia Department was thoroughly reorganized. Dr. John McLoughlin was made its head. Trade was
reduced to system, efficiency and rigid economy took the place of
laxity and extravagance, aggressive expansion in every direction was
ordered instead of retreat. In the mind of the young governor trade
extension was intimately related to the extension of empire. In the
play for the Oregon triangle he proposed to hold the trump card.

The territorial strategy of the governor was a masterly combination of profit and empire. The contested north side of the Columbia
was to be insulated against American competition. The lost south
side was to be the insulator. The south side was to be relentlessly
exploited, its harvest was to be made at once secure. It was to be
converted into a fur desert, a *cordon sanitaire* protecting the contested northern side against St. Louis intrusion.

Marked in particular for sterilization was the southeastern part
of the Oregon Country facing St. Louis. This was a region of
ill-defined boundaries, much of it still unexplored and of unknown
trapping possibilities. Its nucleus was the valley of the Snake. The
Snake in its more accessible parts in 1824 gave signs of fur depletion,
but beaver was still abundant in its upper tributaries. To the east of
the Snake lay the rich fur country of the upper Missouri, its
treasures of beaver guarded by the implacable Blackfeet. It was not
legally open to British trappers since it was American soil. Hudson's
Bay Company officers had orders from London headquarters not to
poach on it. But such orders were not strictly obeyed. To the south
of the Snake, extending from the valley of the Colorado to the
Sierra Nevadas, lay the unexplored wilderness of the Enclosed
Basin. It was to prove a disappointing fur country. It is a region
of semi-aridity without drainage to the sea; its streams lose themselves in sinks and in lakes of which the waters are salt. On contemporary maps a mysterious lake, Timpanogos or Bonaventura,
was represented to lie in it draining either directly or by way of the
Snake into the Pacific.[3] This region was the possession of the

[3] For a good note on the contemporary maps of this region see H. C. Dale,
Ashley-Smith Explorations (Cleveland, 1918), 102.

Mexican Republic, but it was weakly held. As soon as it appeared on the fur horizon, British and American trappers (those of the Hudson's Bay Company, outfitted at Flathead Post, and those of William H. Ashley, outfitted at St Louis) wandered over it with entire freedom. They were not even aware, along its northern borders, that they were within the feeble sway of Santa Fé or Taos.

The Hudson's Bay Company maintained within the Snake and this adjacent country a trapping party designated the Snake Country Expedition. This was an inheritance from the North West Company. Its commander in North West Company days had been that dauntless captain of trappers, Donald McKenzie.[4] In 1824 a less forceful person had charge of it, a field clerk, later historian, Alexander Ross.[5] Governor Simpson considered Ross unequal to his post, and on arriving in the Columbia supplanted him by a man of greater authority and enterprise—Peter Skene Ogden.

Simpson observed in making the change:

The Snake Country Expedition, has hitherto been considered a forlorn hope, the management of it the most hazardous and disagreeable office in the Indian Country, therefore no Volunteer could be found for it among the Commissioned Gentlemen[6] since Chief Factor McKenzie crossed the Mountain. This important duty should not in my opinion be left to a self sufficient empty headed man like Ross who feels no further interest therein than in as far as it secures to him a Saly of £120 p Annum and whose reports are so full of bombast and marvellous nonsense that it is impossible to get at any information that can be depended on from him. If properly managed no question exists that it would yield handsome profits as we have convincing proof that the country is a rich preserve of Beaver and which for political reasons we should endeavour to destroy as fast as possible. A charge of such consequence I therefore conceived should be in the hands of a Commissioned Gentleman and knowing no one in the country better qualified to do it justice than Mr. Ogden I proposed that he should undertake it and it affords me much pleasure to say that he did so with the utmost readiness.[7]

[4] An account of the Snake Expedition under the command of Donald McKenzie is given in Alexander Ross, *Fur Hunters of the Far West* (London, 1855), I, 182–283. See also below, "Snake Country Expedition Correspondence."

[5] Ross's journal of the Snake Expedition of 1824 is published in *Oregon Historical Society Quarterly* (Portland, 1900—), XIV (1913), 366–88; see also Ross, *Fur Hunters*, II, 1–160.

[6] Refers to the field officers of the Hudson's Bay Company—the chief factors and chief traders.

[7] Merk, *Fur Trade*, 45–46.

The new appointee was a Canadian, a veteran, at the age of thirty, of twelve years in the fur trade. He had served the North West Company as a clerk in the war with the Hudson's Bay Company but with a partisanship so turbulent that in 1821 on the merger of the two companies he had been dropped. He was in London the following year making his peace with the officers of the united company. He owed his success in this effort largely to the intercession of Governor Simpson, who wrote in 1823: "The admission of Black, Ogden & Grant, has given great satisfaction and I feel highly flattered that so much attention has been paid to my recommendation, they will be very useful men and will prove they are worthy of the indulgence that has been shewn them. . . . Ogden has gone to the Columbia and determined to do great things; he does not want for ability."[8] Ogden's gratitude for this reinstatement explains, no doubt, the readiness with which a year later he accepted from Governor Simpson the dangerous captaincy of the Snake Country Expedition.

The Expedition of 1824–25 was a powerful one. Manned and equipped for a hunt of a year it comprised "25 lodges, 2 gentlemen, 2 interpreters, 71 men and lads, 80 guns, 364 beaver traps, 372 horses." "This," observed Alexander Ross, "is the most formidable party that has ever set out for the Snakes."[9]

But the party was less formidable than it appeared. Its personnel was inferior in quality. Too small a percentage of its trappers were *engagés;* too large a percentage were freemen. Freemen were superannuated or rejected company servants, who on dismissal elected to remain as independent trappers in the Far West rather than return to the Red River Colony or to Canada. They were usually half-breeds or Indians,[10] a shiftless and irresponsible class. Of those attached to the Snake Expedition Governor Simpson wrote:

This band of Freemen the very scum of the country and generally outcasts from the Service for misconduct are the most unruly and troublesome gang to deal with in this or perhaps any other part of the World, are under no control & feel their own independence they

[8] *Ibid*, 203.
[9] *Oregon Hist. Quart.*, XIV (1913), 388.
[10] An account by Alexander Ross of the Snake Expedition freemen is in *ibid.*, 369–88, and in Ross, *Fur Hunters*, II, 6–160.

therefore require very superior management to make any thing of them, but I regret to find that Mr. Ross has not that talent and that his presence among them has been attended with little good.[11]

The Snake freeman in 1824 were more than normally restless. A heavy sense of oppression hung upon them. Their improvidence compelled them to purchase their trapping outfits and horses from the Hudson's Bay Company on credit. They were obliged to pay prices under these conditions that were exceedingly high. As an assurance that their accounts would be cleared they were obliged at the end of each hunt to dispose of their furs to the company at a prearranged schedule of rates. The rates were exceedingly low. The returns of trapping under these conditions were slight. Most of the Snake freemen, indeed, in spite of the hazard and hardship of their work, remained year after year indebted to the company.[12] So long as the company was unopposed on the Snake there was no escape from this virtual servitude. Discontent could express itself only in that surly misbehavior on the hunt to which Governor Simpson referred. But on the Expedition of 1824–25 an opportunity presented itself of redress, and the result was the episode which is so graphically described in the documents that follow.[13]

As traveling companions Ogden had with him on his outward journey seven Americans. They were Ashley trappers whom, in the preceding season, Alexander Ross had picked up in the Snake Country and had incautiously permitted to return with him to his base at Flathead Post.[14] Their leader was Jedidiah Smith, one of the greatest of Far Western trappers and explorers. They now were on their way back to the Green River Country to a rendezvous with their compatriots of the Ashley expedition. Their presence was unwelcome to Ogden who attributed the misadventure which befell him to the knowledge they had of his movements.

Ogden had orders from Governor Simpson, after equipping his party, to proceed "direct for the heart of the Snake country towards the Banks of the Spanish River or Rio Colorado pass the Winter & Spring there and hunt their way out by the

[11] Merk, *Fur Trade*, 45.

[12] Alexander Ross on his expedition had to wrestle with this problem. See *Oregon Hist. Quart.*, XIV (1913), 371–72, 376; and Ross, *Fur Hunters*, II, 9–14.

[13] See below, "Snake Country Expedition Correspondence."

[14] Cf. Ross, *Fur Hunters*, II, 127–30; also *Oregon Hist. Quart.*, XIV (1913), 385.

Umpqua and Wilhamet Rivers to Fort George next summer sufficiently early to send the returns home by the Ship."[15] This assignment was over-ambitious, as assignments of the governor were likely to be, and it rested on inadequate knowledge of the country ordered to be crossed. The initial instruction to hunt toward the banks of the Rio Colorado was based on an incorrect conjecture by earlier Snake Expedition leaders that the Colorado is an extension of Bear River, a stream in part unexplored. The instruction as to the journey home was based on the assumption that the Umpqua River has its sources not far to the west of Bear Valley. The order to seek out the upper Umpqua with a party already jaded by an outward march was based on ignorance of the nature of the country in which the Umpqua was supposed to rise.

The expedition set out from Flathead Post on December 20, 1824. For five weeks it proceeded southeast—by the same route probably as the preceding Snake Expedition of Ross—up the Missoula to the Bitterroot, up the Bitterroot to its East Fork and across the continental divide via Gibbon Pass to the sources of the Missouri.[16] The upper Missouri was rich in beaver and buffalo. But hunting in it was hazardous; it was infested by Blackfeet. British trappers venturing into it were, moreover, trespassing on American soil. From the watershed of the Missouri the expedition turned back into the Oregon Country crossing the Bitterroot Mountains, probably by Lemhi Pass, to the waters of Salmon River. The Salmon is separated from the Snake by the Salmon River Mountains, a formidable obstacle to surmount in winter when the passes are choked with snow. Twenty days of labor were required to force a passage. Thence the route ran probably along Big Lost River to the Snake, which was reached in April. From the Snake the route ran up a small tributary, the Blackfoot River, and thence to the Bear, whose lower reaches had never been explored by a Hudson's Bay Company party. At the bend of the Bear Jedidiah Smith and his men took their departure. "They separated from us," writes Ogden, "they in

---

[15] Merk, *Fur Trade*, 46–47. For an amplification of these instructions see *ibid.*, 54–57.
[16] *Ibid.*, 134.

ascending Bear River, and we in descending, and found it discharged into a large Lake of 100 Miles in length."[17]

In this casual reference to a "large Lake of 100 Miles in length" Ogden records his discovery of Great Salt Lake, the inland sea of the Enclosed Basin. Whether he was the first to find it will probably ever remain a question. Tradition has it that James Bridger discovered it in the winter of 1824–25 while camping with a detachment of Ashley trappers in the Cache Valley. That tradition is supported by no documentary evidence other than a letter retailing a conversation of Bridger thirty-two years afterwards.[18] Another Ashley lieutenant, Étienne Provost, is credited with having come upon the lake during the same winter by way of Weber River.[19] These men may well have preceded Ogden to Great Salt Lake by several months. But Ogden's discovery alone is substantiated by direct contemporary proof—the proof of the documents that follow.

From the valley of Great Salt Lake, Ogden proposed to turn westward. His instruction to hunt to the Colorado had been canceled by his discovery that the Bear River is an independent system. His next assignment was to find, in the country west of the Bear, the Umpqua River, and follow it to the Willamette. Had he attempted this search, he would in all probability have led his party to destruction. He was extricated from this fate by a dramatic wilderness episode.

On May 23, 1825 in the Bear Valley a party of Ashley trappers marched unannounced into his camp. They were led by Johnson Gardner. With them returned some of Ogden's erstwhile American travel-guests; also the freemen who had been absent several days. This was no friendly call for the exchange of trapper amenities. A lawless spirit of trade rivalry and national resentment at the activities of the Hudson's Bay Company in the Oregon Country brought Johnson Gardner. He engaged Ogden at once in an extraordinary wilderness dialogue in which the lurking national ambitions behind the Oregon fur trade were dragged into full view. Then the scene shifted to the freemen. At last they had their day. In Gardner they had found the competitive market for lack of

[17] See below, "Snake Country Expedition Correspondence," and frontispiece map.
[18] See J. C. Alter, *James Bridger* (Salt Lake City, 1925), 48–55.
[19] *Ibid.*

which they had been obliged to nurse grievances in impotence for years. And what competition now! For beaver Gardner offered eight times the price established at Flathead Post, and supplies he tendered at rates correspondingly low. In vain Ogden sought to discredit such offers as mere "baits." Twenty-three of his freemen, bearing their debt-laden furs, traps, and horses absconded. They actually attempted, in Gardner's heartening presence, to pillage Ogden's camp.

This sudden blow compelled Odgen to recast his plans for the homeward march. His party was reduced to a minimum of strength; his remaining men were dispirited and fearful. To have ventured westward into an unknown wilderness under these conditions would have been rash. "We have done enough," Ogden wrote, "and suffered also without increasing the load." Even had the party been intact, Ogden felt it would have been impolitic "to have open'd a short cut for the Americans to Fort George."[20]

The course he decided upon was to return to the north. On the upper tributaries of the Snake was promising beaver country, and there also, as he learned, was a camp of friendly Flathead Indians. To Henry's Fork, accordingly, his remaining men trapped their way. From Henry's Fork they crossed a second time to the watershed of the Missouri, probably to the headstreams of Jefferson River. This was an even bolder trespass on American soil than the first. It brought the party quickly to the main Missouri, which was followed northward nearly to the entrance of Marias River. Ogden wished to go on and return later to Flathead Post by his outgoing route of the spring.[21] But Marias Valley was Blackfeet country into which his trappers were unwilling to venture farther and he was obliged to retreat. He came home ultimately down the Snake River and across southern Idaho taking familiar trails that brought him at length in November, 1825, to Fort Nez Percés.[22] He had been almost a year on the hunt.

A journal which he kept of this expedition was sent, as required by his instruction, to London headquarters. There it remained long inaccessible to historians. It was reported misplaced or lost, though

---

[20] See below, "Snake Country Expedition Correspondence."

[21] See "Journal of John Work," in *Washington Hist. Quart.*, V (1914), 101–11.

[22] The later phases of the expedition may be followed from the journal of John Work in *loc. cit.*, 101–15, 259–62.

journals of later Snake Country expeditions of Ogden were found and published. The missing journal was later discovered, when the Company opened its records to its own historian, and was published. It adds valuable and colorful detail to the advance report of the expedition given in the document printed below.[23]

In the absence of the journal the only source of historical knowledge of the expedition for many years was mountain tradition. This gathered about the episode of the transferred furs in a form which prejudice against the Hudson's Bay Company distorted. The furs were said to have been acquired by Gardner with the secret connivance of Ogden. Another version was that they had been found by Ashley's men in cache.[24] Their value was grossly exaggerated. They were estimated to have been worth from $75,000 to $200,000, and to have made Ashley's fortune.[25] Tradition similarly unreliable beclouded Ogden's discovery of Great Salt Lake.[26]

Historical light has slowly penetrated this fog. In 1909 T. C. Elliott brought together, in an introduction to the later Ogden journals, some scattered data on the first expedition, drawn chiefly from the unpublished journal of a clerk in the Columbia Department.[27] More recently the present writer found in the archives of the Hudson's Bay Company the accompanying report of the expedition prepared by Ogden on the march. Written at "East Fork Missouri" as a report of progress, and sent via Spokane House to Fort Vancouver, it summarizes seven of the eleven months of the expedition—the central months and the most significant in picturing the problems of the trade.

A number of related Hudson's Bay Company documents follow this report. In them the two groups of company officers, the field force and the London office, express their reactions to the expedition. To one phase of the expedition, the trespass of Ogden onto the soil of the United States, the reactions of the two groups were widely divergent with an outcome that strikingly illustrates

[23] See E. E. Rich (ed.), *Peter Skene Ogden's Snake Country Journals* 1824–25 and 1825–26 in Hudson's Bay Record Society, XIII (London, 1950), xi–lxxix, 2–93. Also, *Oregon Hist. Quart.*, X (1909), 331; XI (1910), 201, 229, 355, 381.

[24] See Hiram M. Chittenden, *The American Fur Trade of the Far West* (New York, 1902), I, 277–78; Katharine Coman, *Economic Beginnings of the Far West* (New York, 1912), I, 357.

[25] See references in preceding footnote.

[26] Dale, *Ashley-Smith Explorations*, 46–47.

[27] *Oregon Hist. Quart.*, X (1909), 331–35.

the influence of London on the British North-American fur trade in this period.

The company's field force regarded trespassing on the soil of the United States with equanimity. Men immersed in the fur trade yielded easily to the infection of wilderness lawlessness. Half the company's field officers were former North West Company men, who had grown up in a tradition of carelessness as to the international border. Respect for the American restrictive law of 1816 was gradually becoming established in the Great Lakes area by 1824, thanks partly to the vigilance of John Jacob Astor, but in the Far West the older tradition still prevailed.

The highest field officers of the Hudson's Bay Company, Governor Simpson and Dr. McLoughlin, sanctioned Ogden's trespass into the Missouri Valley. They ordered it, in fact. They laid out the outward route of march,[28] and five weeks after Ogden started, he was writing the governor of his operations from the "Sources of the Missouri," a letter which the governor read with every indication of approval.[29] Dr. McLoughlin in 1827 in a letter to Governor Simpson proposed another incursion into this country:

If such a party was sent, they ought to go direct to the Trois Tettons and hunt up that place, then turn North and hunt all the head branches of Missouries in the vicinity of where Mr. Ogden was in Summer 1825; in three years they would do this which would destroy the Inducements the American trappers from the other side have to push to the Head waters of the Columbia and by hunting the Head branches of the Missouries where I state diminish the inducements the Americans might have to equip hunting parties from this side of the Mountains and to interfere with our Saskatchewan trade sooner than they otherwise would.[30]

Such lawlessness, however, found no support in London. The contagion of the wilderness did not extend so far. The influences to which the directors responded were those surrounding and protecting the company's charter and license. The charter was not popular in England. The directors knew they might be required at any moment to answer for their stewardship of it at

[28] The two Snake expeditions preceding Ogden's had trespassed by the same route into the Missouri Valley. See *Oregon Hist. Quart.*, XIV (1913), 377–79; Merk, *Fur Trade*, 289.

[29] *Ibid.*, 134.

[30] *Ibid.*, 289.

the bar of public opinion and of Parliament. They felt unable even to seek redress for Ogden's spoliation, believing it had occurred on the soil of the United States,[31] and would, if known, call forth embarrassing questions at the foreign office. They sent to Governor Simpson and Dr. McLoughlin instead emphatic warning against any future trespassing on the territory of the republic.

We have most particularly to desire that all our officers will in future confine themselves and the Parties entrusted to their charge within the limits of the Company's Territories or the Neutral Ground till the Boundaries of the two Powers are defined, and any inattention to this instruction, on the matter being made known to us, will be attended with our serious displeasure.[32]

This warning was sufficient. Never again did responsible officers of the company tolerate trapping raids into the United States. In this important respect as in others the character of the British fur trade after 1821 was fixed in London. Dr. McLoughlin's proposal of 1827, suggested before he had received the directors' warning, was, needless to say, never acted upon. As for Governor Simpson, he became in regard to trespassing utterly moral. In 1829, in response to a proposal from Joshua Pilcher for the coöperative exploitation of the upper Missouri by the Hudson's Bay Company and the Missouri Fur Company, he wrote:

I am aware that the Country watered by the sources of the Missouri, usually known by the name of the "Black feet Country" is a rich preserve of Beaver, and that a well organized Trading and Trapping Party would in all probability make valuable returns therein (altho' perhaps the most dangerous Service connected with the Indian Trade); would therefore readily entertain your proposition with the attention which its importance merits as regards capital, if a difficulty of a formidable character did not present itself, which is the Territorial rights of the United States Government to that Country. These rights, we as British Subjects cannot infringe openly, and although the protecting Laws of your Government might be successfully evaded by the plan you suggest, still I do not think it would be reputable in the Hon[ble] Hudson's Bay Coy to make use of indirect means to acquire possession of a Trade to which it has no just claim. Under those circumstances

[31] The directors were misled in this respect by the confusing geography of the Enclosed Basin. The spoliation occurred either in the Oregon Country or on Mexican soil. See below, "Snake Country Expedition Correspondence."
[32] *Ibid.*

I cannot fall in with your views and as regards Mr. Ogden he cannot without acting in direct opposition to his instruction cross the height of Land.[33]

An internal problem of the Snake Expedition brought under company review as a result of Ogden's adventures was the freemen trapping tariff. This was part of the general company rate-structure established by the field officers' annual council, subject to the approval of the directors in London. In the period following the merger of 1821, as a reaction to the ruinous extravagance of the preceding trade war, the whole rate structure had been rigorously cut. The Snake Expedition rate, based on the reduced standard of Spokane House,[34] took no account of the extraordinary risks to life and property involved in Snake Country trapping.

For various reasons the oppressive operation of the Snake Country rate remained unnoticed by the higher officers of the company. Reductions in the rate structure as a whole had produced lamentation throughout the company's districts, and in the chorus the protests of the Snake freemen remained unheard. Local officers failed to report the Snake rate as bearing especially hard on the freemen. The unpaid debts of the freemen were attributed to improvidence; their misbehavior and desertion on the hunt, to Indian and half-breed depravity.[35] Spokane House accounts conspired to conceal the truth. In them the returns of expedition and district were blended. Governor Simpson and Dr. McLoughlin on their visit to Spokane House in 1824 were permitted by Ogden, then in charge, to depart without a clear understanding of the nature or gravity of the freemen grievances. Reform was possible under these circumstances only after revolt.

Revolt, however, produced reform promptly. Dr. McLoughlin, on receipt of Ogden's report, ordered the accounts of the expedition brought to Fort Vancouver, and, on the basis of an analysis of them ordered on his own responsibility a sweeping advance in the freeman trapping rates. He made some atonement also for the past. With the consent of Simpson he invited such of the

---

[33] Merk, *Fur Trade*, 307–308; also Chittenden, *American Fur Trade*, I, 155–58.

[34] Spokane House was the post to which the Snake Expedition was attached. Its schedule of prices appears in Merk, *Fur Trade*, 171–74. See also, *ibid.*, 276–77.

[35] For desertions among the freemen of the expedition prior to the wholesale absconding under Ogden see *Oregon Hist. Quart.*, XIV (1913), 385.

deserters as could be reached to return to the expedition with old debts scored off on lenient terms.

The plans of Simpson for the Snake Expedition were, under McLoughlin, successfully carried out. As a commercial venture the expedition ceased to be a "forlorn hope." It became the producer of steady, if not handsome, profits, "at least thirty thousand pounds" in the period between 1824 and 1846. As an instrument of empire it likewise served its purpose. It converted the Snake Country and much adjoining territory, with the support at a later date of several strategically located trade posts, into a fur desert. It helped to sterilize the southern and eastern sides of the Columbia Valley, to insulate the northern side against St. Louis influence. It helped to convert the lower Columbia into a principality of the Hudson's Bay Company, governed until the day of the pioneers by Fort Vancouver and London.

The Snake Country Expedition Correspondence, 1824–1825*

EDITED BY FREDERICK MERK

P.S. Ogden to the Governor, Chief Factors and Chief Traders.[1]
East Fork, Missouri 10 July 1825

In January I addressed you by some . . . giving you an account of our Progress to that date, and I regret now to state that I can not give you as pleasing tidings as I did then, but unfortunately a series of misfortunes has attended us from that time to the present. I shall now endeavour to restate all the particulars, tho' the subject to me is one that I heartily detest. In the Month of February the Blackfeet succeeded in stealing 18 of the Freemens horses, and tho' pursued escaped, 6 days after one of the Iroquois (Louis Kanitogan) was killed by the accidental discharge of his Gun by his Wife. In March we reached the waters of Salmon River and here our Progress for 20 days was at a stand, the snow, ice and weak state of our lean worn out horses preventing us. We however made three different attempts, and in one of these Mr. Kittson with Six Men had a narrow escape from a War party. Fortunately for the former they were on horseback and the latter on foot, otherwise not a Soul would have escaped. On the 20th March we again made another attempt and succeeded in crossing the Mountains, and on the 2d April we reached the main Snake River (South branch of the Columbia the same River Lewis and Clark discovered) which we fortunately found free of ice, but to reach it we had from 3 to 4 feet snow, and many of our horses were lost and the remainder could hardly crawl. We now commenced trapping with tolerable success but of short duration, for on the 5th a War party of Black Indians killed Antoine Benoit while in the act of raising his Traps, took his scalp 16 Beaver and three horses and effected their escape. They were in our power, but unfortunately at the time ignorant of the poor Mans fate. This caused me some trouble to induce the Freemen to continue in the direction I wished. They however consented on leaving the Snake River and ascended Blackfeet River a Small entrance the lower part of which had never before been trapped by our party. Here we were doing well averaging 40 Beaver p diem, but

* Reprinted from the *Mississippi Valley Historical Review*, XXI (June 1934).

[1] Hudson's Bay Company Journal, no. 762 (in Hudson's Bay Company House, London). For the privilege of transcribing and publishing this and the succeeding documents the author is indebted to the governor and committee of the Hudson's Bay Company. The governor, chief factors, and chief traders addressed in this letter are Governor Simpson and his associated field officers. The governor and committee referred to elsewhere in the correspondence are the London governor of the company and the directors. For an account of the relationship of the two sets of officers see Merk, *Fur Trade*, xii–xviii.

again of short duration, for on the 23ᵈ another party of Blood and Piegans Indians, succeeded in again stealing 20 horses from the Freemen. I had often from our starting represented to the Freemen the necessity of guarding their horses at night but in vain, they may as well steal them for if we tie them at night, they will die for want of food, this was a severe blow and many of the Freemen then came forward and expressed their determination of abandoning the Country expressing themselves as follows "to what end do we labour and toil, we are now only at the commencement of the season and already one Man has been killed, and one half of our horses have been stolen." However threats and promises had the desired effect and the 5ᵗʰ May we reach'd Bear River supposed by Mr. Bourdon who visited in 1818 and subsequently Mr. Finan McDonald who were at its Sources to be the Spanish River or Rio Collorado, but it is not, on our reaching this River the 7 Americans who had accompanied us from the Flat head Fort, they separated from us, they in ascending Bear River, and we in descending, and found it discharged into a large Lake of 100 Miles in length . . .² but before I proceed it is necessary to inform you, that on one of the Forks of Bear River we met with a party of Snakes about 40 in number who to the surprise of all were at first very distant and shy, they informed us that a party of Americans had wintered there (50 Men)³ and had returned home early in the Spring, and had not taken many Beaver. Of this from our success we were convinced was the case. We had now nearly Three thousand Beaver and our course had been nearly South East, and my intention was now to take a West course with the hopes both of finding Beaver and discovering the Umqua River. We had now got rid of War tribes from the Saskatchewan and had reached the Utas lands who were represented to be friendly to the Whites, and I was then most sanguine in my hopes of reaching the Columbia by the Umqua River, but only three days after all my hopes were blasted. On the 23 a party of 15 Canadians and Spanjards headed by one Provost and François an Iroquois Chief who deserted from our party two Years since joined us, we were surprized of seeing them, and still more so when they informed me, that the Spanish Settlement where they had received their Supplies was not more than 15 days march with loaded horses This place is called *Taas* distant about 100 miles from *St. Fe*⁴ and is now supplied with goods from Sᵗ. Louis overland in waggons by the Americans. Shortly after the arrival of the above party another of

---

² Here follows an imprecation against Alexander Ross for having permitted the Americans on the preceding hunt to come to Flathead Post.

³ These were Ashley trappers. See Dale, *Ashley-Smith Explorations, passim;* also Alter, *James Bridger, passim.*

⁴ Taos was an outfitting center for the fur trade of the southern Rockies, but not for trappers as far north as Bear Valley. The supplies of Ashley came normally from St. Louis. For the fur trade of the Far Southwest see Joseph J. Hill, "Ewing Young in the Fur Trade of the Far Southwest, 1822–1834," in *Oregon Hist. Quart.,* XXIV (1923), 1–35. See also Merk, *Fur Trade,* 276–77.

25 to 30 Americans headed by one Gardner and a Spanjard with 15 of our trappers who had been absent about two days also made their appearance; they encamped within 100 yards of our Camp and hoisted the American Flag, and proclaimed to all that they were in the United States Territories and were all Free indebted or engaged, it was now night and nothing more transpired, the ensuing morning Gardner came to my tent and after a few words of no import, he questioned me as follows, do you know in whose Country you are? to which I made answer that I did not, as it was not determined between Great Britain and America to whom *it* belonged, to which he made answer that it was, that it had been ceded to the latter,[5] and as I had no licence to trade or trapp to return from whence I came without delay, to this I replied when we receive orders from the British Government to abandon the Country we shall obey, he then said remain at your peril, he then left my tent and seeing him go in an Iroquois Tent (John Gray) I followed him, on entering this villain Gray said, I must now tell you, that all the Iroquois as well as myself have long wished for an opportunity to join the Americans, and if we did not the last three Years, it was owing to our bad luck in not meeting them, but now we go, and all you can say or do cannot prevent us. During this conversation Gardner was silent, but on going out he said you have had these Men too long in your Service and have most shamefully imposed on them, treating them as *Slaves* selling them Goods at high prices and giving them nothing for their Furs, Gray then said that is all true and alluding to the Gentlemen he had been with in the Columbia, they are says he the greatest villains in the World, and if they were here I would shoot them, but as for you Sir you have dealt fair with us all. We have now been five Years in your Service, the longer we remain the more indebted we become altho' we give 150 Beaver a year, we are now in a free Country and have friends to support us, and go we will, and if every Man in the Camp does not leave you they do not seek their own interest, he then gave orders to raise Camp and in an instant all the Iroquois were in motion and ready to start this example was soon followed by others, a scene of confusion now ensued. Gardner at the head of the Americans accompanied by two of our Iroquois who deserted two years since,[6] advanced to assist and support all who were inclined to desert. It was now that Lazard an Iroquois called out we are greater in number let us fire and pillage them, on saying this he advanced with his Gun cock'd and pointed at me. Old Pierre[7] then seized

[5] The scene of this dialogue may have been north or south of the line separating the Oregon Country from the "Utas" land of the Mexican republic. The two men apparently thought they were north of the line. Whether they were or not, Gardner's assertion that the country had been ceded to the United States was a bluff.

[6] See also *Oregon Hist. Quart.*, XIV (1913), 385.

[7] For Pierre and Lazard, and their escapades in the preceding Snake Expedition, see *ibid.*, 366–85.

two of the Companys horses but finding I was determined not to allow him or others to pillage, finding it sufficiently galling to see them going off with our Furs and enduring the most approbrious terms they could think of, without allowing them to pillage us from both Americans and Iroquois. All this time, with the exception of Mr. Kittson and McKay and two of the engaged Men, and not before the two latter were called, did any one come to my assistance. Thus we were overpower'd by numbers, and the greatest part of these Villains escaped with their Furs, in fact some of them had conveyed theirs in the night to the American camp they then departed.

In the evening Alexander Carson came back and warned me to be on my guard as a plot was forming amongst the Iroquois and some of the Americans to pillage me in the night as I had refused to sell them Tobacco, I then conversed with some of the most trusty Freemen and engaged Men to know if they would assist in defending the Companys property in case of attack and they said we will, we then made every preparation and kept double guard during the night.

25th May at day light I gave orders to raise camp, and had scarcely commenced loading, when Gardner with his party and some Iroquois, but seeing us prepared kept quiet, soon after Mr. Montour and Clement then came forward and informed me, they were going to join the Americans, that they were free and not in debt, I endeavoured to reason with Mr. Montour but all in vain the Company turned me out of doors and have £260 of my money in their hands, which they intend to defraud me of, as they have refused to give me Interest for, but they may keep it now for my debt and Prudhommes which we have contracted in the Columbia, they were immediately surrounded by the Americans who assisted them in loading, and like all villains appeared to exult in their villainy. As we were on the eve of Starting Gardner came forward and said you shall shortly see us in the Columbia and this Fall at the Flat heads and Kootenais, as we are determined you shall no longer remain in our Territory to this I made answer when we receive orders from our own Government we shall but not before, in answer to this he said our Troops will reach the Columbia this Fall and make you, we then separated. I have been so far particular in giving you a true statement of the whole conversation that passed between Gardner and myself and leave you to form your own opinions.

And now Gentlemen permit me to observe situated and circumstanced as I was at the commencement of this unfortunate affair, I cannot but consider it so far fortunate I did not fire, for had I I had not the least doubt all was gone property and Furs, indeed their plan was I should fire first, and assuredly they said and did all they could to make me, but I was fully aware of their Plan and by that means saved what remains; finding myself then with only 20 Trappers left of the party surrounded on all sides by enemies I resolved on returning to the Snake River as allowing I had remained in that quarter to trap it would have been for the Americans, and I seriously apprehended many more of the Trappers would have willingly joined them, indeed the tempting offers made them independent of the low prices they sell their Goods and high rate they pay for their Beaver were too great for them to resist, and altho' I represented to them all the offers were held out as so many *Baits*, still without effect, indeed they were too well convinced of the contrary, as for a Beaver skin they could procure more for than they could with eight from us. I have already observed it was an unfortunate day Mr. Ross consented to allow the 7 Americans to accompany him to the Flatheads, for it was these fellows that guided and accompanied them to our Camp,[8] and the whole party were on their return home to St. Louis and were enduced to return by letters they received from the Iroquois Chiefs, otherwise we should not have seen them. We were also informed by the Americans the cause of the Snakes not being so friendly towards us as formerly, and which I regret to state the Americans too justly attribute to us, last Summer Mr. Ross consented most probably with such villains he had to deal with, he could not prevent them to go and steal the Snakes horses in which they succeeded, 12 of Mr. Ross's party were then absent in quest of Beaver and were with a large Camp of Snakes who were treating them most kindly, but on hearing this they pillaged them of all their horses and Furs, and in the scuffle they killed a Snake chief,[9] shortly after a party of 7 Americans and one of our deserters fall on the Snakes Camp, and the Snakes lost no time in killing them all this also has greatly irritated the Americans against us, and they would most willingly shoot us if they dared. [My course from the Flat heads had been nearly South east, and at this time I considered myself within 10 days march of the Umqua River intending to take a South West Course, but finding myself with only 20 trappers, I was obliged to retrace back my steps and allowing my numbers to have been greater I am not of opinion it would have been good policy in me to have open'd a short cut for the Americans to Fort George, we have done enough and suffered also without increasing the load.][10]

On the 5th June we again reached the main Snake River by a different Route we had taken in the Spring with a little success in Beaver (300) it was here then I proposed to the Freemen to go in the direction of Nez Perces which one half refused as they are determined on returning

[8] Jedidiah Smith, who had a reputation for piety among trappers, does not appear to advantage in this transaction. He figured in an affair of similar sort in the preceding Snake Expedition of Alexander Ross. See Ross, *Fur Hunters*, II, 127-30.

[9] For another account of this episode see *Oregon Hist. Quart.*, XIV (1913) 382, 385; and Ross, *Fur Hunters*, II, 127-29.

[10] The bracketted section is interpolated from a letter written by Ogden a fortnight earlier, almost identical with the one here printed. Ogden refers to it several times below in this "correspondence."

to the Saskatchewan this Fall, they said our losses have been too great in this Country to remain any longer and we pay there 1/3 less than we do here, and large and small Beaver are all taken at 12 Livres each; it is not difficult Gentlemen to command but enforce obedience in the plains when at the mercy of Freemen it is the reverse. On the 7th fortunately two Flathead Indians reached our Camp, and informed me their Camp was in the upperpart of Snake River or at Henrys forks, and as that quarter had been represented to me as rich in Beaver by our party who were there in 1822 and were obliged to leave it from the heavy loss they sustained,[11] I soon resolved on going there as our numbers would be reinforced by the Flatheads and reached it on the 12th and on my arrival at the Camp I received Governor Simpson's letter from Fort George dated in January, and I cannot but regret I did not more fully explained myself in my last Falls letter. At that time from my ignorance and want of information of the Country I was going to and not being aware of the impediments I might meet with, I considered it my duty to request an outfit might have been brought up in the Spring to Fort Nez Perces by the extra Men on their out. I was fully aware of all the advantages resulting from my reaching Fort George in July and would have succeeded, but for the Villains who deserted us. We had again commenced trapping tho' our success was not great, our time was not entirely lost, and the Flatheads were also following our example, but scarcely ten days elapsed when 5 Tents of Americans containing from 30 to 40 Men were discovered, they were coming down the same River we were then trapping; knowing too well from dear bought experience the loss I should sustain if the Freemen were once more to meet with them and the tempting offers they would make the Flatheads I resolved on leaving it and then took a N. W. course, and three days after we fell on a Peigans Camp, who had already trapped two Rivers which had been represented to me as rich, and from the number they had was the case, here also we met with 4 of the Saskatchewan Freemen, and by them I wrote to the Gentlemen of the East side and in case of failure I shall now forward a Copy of this by the way of Spokan.[12] The greater part of the Peigans were bent on remaining in this quarter to trade at the Flatheads, but before we parted at some expence I prevailed with the exception of 15 Tents to return back with their Furs to their own Fort,[13] and these fellows who remained I have secured their Furs about 170 Beaver at a most reason-

[11] Finan McDonald lost five of his men there. See Ross, *Fur Hunters*, II, 54–59.

[12] Glimpses of the communication which Ogden maintained from the Missouri Valley with his associates on the Columbia side are in John Work's journal, *Washington Hist. Quart.*, V (1914), 101–15, 259–62.

[13] The Piegans were a branch of the family of the Siksika to which the Blackfeet and Blood Indians also belonged. Their habitat was the country drained by the three forks of the Missouri and northward to the Marias. Occasionally they traded at Flathead Post. "Their own Fort" was apparently one of the Saskatchewan posts.

able rate, no good will result from any of them remaining in this quarter. Independent of the great chance there is of their seeing the Americans, while in Company with the Flatheads they will do nothing either Party. I am now going towards a place called the three Forks[14] of the Missourie said to be rich in Beaver, also the most dangerous on account of Blackfeet, indeed I am informed the latter is the cause the Beaver have been allowed to remain quiet in that quarter, if we escape without loosing any scalps all agree in one opinion we will find beaver God grant it! The hunts of the Freemen now fully average 100 Beaver each and we have now in the Camp about Three Thousand Beaver not more.

I have now Gentlemen given you all the particulars of the expedition entrusted to my charge, and have once more to regret it has been attended with so many misfortunes.

P. S. Ogden to the Governor, Chief Factors and Chief Traders.[15]

27 June 1825

. . . . On making the great Snake River on my Return, I proposed to the Freemen to proceed towards the Walla Walla Country but in vain, let us proceed to the Kootannies there probably we may remain quiet and unmolested, but in this quarter we never can do any thing but increase our debts, the next day Ten Flat heads reached us, their Camp of 20 Lodges being near I then proposed to them to steer to the quarter Mr McDonald was obliged to abandon from the loss of Five of his Men, to this all assented, and again we began to take a few Beaver, when another party of Americans were discovered trapping and coming from the quarter we were bound to, we then took a more Northerly course and for the last three days have not seen a Beaver, but warriors by hundreds, we have now nearly Three Thousand Beaver, and I have still some hopes of adding another, but realy am at a loss where to stir. You need not anticipate another expedition ensuing Year to this Country, for not a freeman will return, and should they, it would be to join the Americans, there is Gentlemen a wide difference with their prices and ours, they have opened a communication with waggons over land from St Louis to the first Spanish Settlement call'd Taa's where they fit out their Trappers and receive their Furs in return and they say they intend reaching the Columbia also with Waggons not impossible so far as I have seen. Gentlemen I trust you will excuse this scrawl once, if I have not been more particular I trust you will attribute it to my being surrounded by nearly Two hundred Indians and anxiety of mind which I labour under.

[14] Three Forks is the confluence of the Jefferson, Madison, and Gallatin rivers. It lies in southwestern Montana.
[15] Hudson's Bay Company Journal, no. 762.

P. S.

About 40 Peigan Tents appear determined to remain in this quarter, I have done all in my power to send them back, and have been at some expence with them and have still hopes of succeeding; while they remain here the Flatheads will do nothing and cause of trouble, their Furs I have refused to trade, but should I see or apprehend any danger of their falling into the American camp I shall secure them.

In Merk, *Fur Trade and Empire*, 253–55, appears a letter written by Dr. McLoughlin to the field officers of the Hudson's Bay Company on receipt of Ogden's report. In it he estimates that by "the villany of these rascals" [the Snake deserters] the Company has lost three thousands pounds.[16] He cites the Anglo-American convention of joint occupation of 1818, concerning which he comments, "we are justified in resenting to the utmost of our power any attack on our persons and property or any assumption of authority over us by the Americans." If he had a party sufficiently strong to defend itself against the Indians, and sufficiently trustworthy, he would have no hesitation in making an attempt again in that quarter if it was merely for one year to defy the Americans to put their threats in execution and to counteract the evil impression the vaunting words of Mr. Gardner and the desertion of the freemen will have on the Indians and remaining freemen. Ogden's party is, however, too weak and untrustworthy. The *engagés* evinced disgraceful, indeed, criminal neglect of their bounden duty in not supporting Ogden and in permitting the freemen to walk off with furs, horses, and traps, "all of which were certainly our property." No freeman was ever induced to buy a single article, and "they were in debt much against our will and inclinations," and their advances had been made to accommodate them even at the risk of loss to the company by their death.

P. S. Ogden to Governor Simpson.[17]

Ft. Nez Percés   12 Nov. 1825

. . . . I have requested Mr Kittson who is now at Spokan to forward you a sketch of my travels and have to add the Country I have visited

[16] Dr. McLoughlin seems to have included in this estimate the amount of the freemen debts. The furs carried off numbered only 700.
[17] Hudson's Bay Company Journal, no. 762.

is far from being rich in beaver at least on the waters of the Columbia. That part of the Country where my Men deserted so far as we had advanced was rich, but from the Americans coming towards the Columbia waters I have reason to supposing, had we advanced farther in that direction we should have found nothing, and again on the waters of the Missourie so far as I had advanced we were well repaid for our trouble, and so far as I can judge from appearances and from report had we gone farther we should have been well repaid, but my cowardly freemen did not dare advance, it was in the vicinity of Maria River a fork of the Missouri from whence we returned, it was this River that Donald McKenzie Esq[r] the year he wintered at Bow River sent a party to explore[18] but which they did not reach and it is on the said River that the Americans have it in contemplation to make an establishment and if strong enough to cope with the War tribes of the Sascatchewan is the most suitable spot they could have selected and if carried into effect we shall soon loose our Flathead & Cootany trade if we loose nothing more we may deem ourselfes lucky, but from the high opinion they entertain of our success in the Columbia, we may apprehend a visit from them ere long, they are now by parties to be found in all parts of the Snake country, from what I could learn there are three different Fur Companys and S[t] Louis Company with a list of petty Traders who offer and give as high as three to three and a half dollar p lb. for the most indifferent Beaver and goods at a trifling value independent of their wishes our freemen could not resist such tempting terms compared to ours. . . .

My returns amount to Four thousand Beaver,[19] this is certainly far from what we had a *right* to expect—a journal of my travels I have delivered to Chief Factor McLoughlin with a request to forward the same to you.

Governor & Committee to Governor Simpson.[20]

London   2 June 1826

44. The information brought by Capt[n] Hanwell is satisfactory as far as relates to the Trade carried on with the Islands on the Coast and in the Interior excepting that part under the management of Mr. Ogden.

We have repeatedly given directions that all collision with the Americans should be avoided as well as infringements upon their Territory,

---

[18] Donald McKenzie established Chesterfield House at the junction of Bow and Red Deer rivers in 1822. The projected exploration of the Marias would have been a trespass on American soil.

[19] Dr. McLoughlin wrote of these returns: "As to the Snakes though the desertion of twenty three Men was a great Drawback on its Returns, yet you will see by the accounts sent out that its gains are very handsome." Merk, *Fur Trade*, 270.

[20] Hudson's Bay Company, Gen. Letter Book, no. 621.

it appears however by these dispatches that Mr. Ogden must have been to the Southward of the 49° of latitude and to the Eastward of the Rocky Mountains which he should have particularly avoided, for however desirable and important it is to hunt the Snake country to the Westward of the Mountains pending the unexpired term of the Convention between Great Britain and America he should on no account have crossed the Boundary Lines.

Governor & Committee to John McLoughlin.[21]

London   20 Sept. 1826

3. We much regret the unfortunate result of Mr. Ogdens expedition, which appears from his statement to have been occasioned by his having extended it into the territory of the United States on the East side of the Rocky Mountains—this should on no account whatever have been done, as it was never our wish that trapping parties should hunt beyond the neutral ground, which by the Convention of 1818 is to be free to the subjects of Great Britain and the United States for a period of Ten Years. Had the spoliation taken place on the West side of the Mountains on the neutral ground which from the statement of Mr. Ogden appears not to have been the fact, we might have submitted such a case to the Ministers, as might have induced them to seek redress or a restitution of the property from the United States Government, but as the transaction took place on the United States territory, we fear we must be compelled to bear the loss unless you are able to prove distinctly that it occurred on the West side of the Rocky Mountains, and we direct that you will by return of this vessel transmit the most full and particular information you can collect on the subject.

We have most particularly to desire that all our officers will in future confine themselves and the Parties entrusted to their charge within the limits of the Companys Territories or the Neutral Ground till the Boundaries of the two Powers are defined, and any inattention to this instruction, on the matter being made known to us will be attended with our serious displeasure.

11. There can be no objection in the Vessel employed in the coasting trade visiting St. Francisco, Monterey or the Ports of any friendly power where it is likely a profitable trade may be obtained.

Governor & Committee to Governor Simpson.[22]

London   12 March 1827

. . . . We can afford to pay as good a price as the Americans and where there is risk of meeting their parties it is necessary to pay as much

[21] *Ibid.,* no. 621.
[22] *Ibid.*

or something more to avoid the risk of a result similar to that of Mr Ogden. By attempting to make such expeditions too profitable the whole may be lost and it is extremely desirable to hunt as bare as possible all the Country South of the Columbia and West of the Mountains,[23] but the parties must have positive instructions not to cross to the East of the Mountains South of 49 degrees North latitude. In the event of our trapping party falling in with any Americans in the Country common to both, the leader ought to have instructions to endeavor to make an amicable arrangement as to the parts of the Country which each will take to avoid interference, and to be careful to avoid giving just cause for accusing our people of any aggression against the Americans or violence except in a clear case of self defence.

The problem of the freeman trapping rate is discussed by Dr. McLoughlin in a letter to Governor Simpson of March 20, 1827, printed in Merk, *Fur Trade and Empire*, 287. Dr. McLoughlin announces he has increased the freeman rate to ten shillings for every large beaver and half that sum for a cub. No other course was open if any of the freemen were to be retained. The prices formerly charged to freemen for supplies were enormously high, a bad policy in view of the company's precarious tenure in the Snake region and the cause of all the difficulties, disappointments, and losses the Snake Expedition has suffered. Taking the high prices into account and the extraordinary dangers of Snake Country trapping, and the inducements to desertion held out by Americans it is more surprising that any of the freemen remained than that any ran away. The cost to the company of a made beaver on the Expedition of 1824–25, as shown by an analysis which is enclosed, was ten shillings and two pence. Of this amount the freemen received in goods, valued at an advance of 70%, only two shillings. The rest is accounted for by the losses incurred in desertion and by the expense of sending clerks and servants to watch the freemen. It is more effectual to give the increased rate to the freeman, which will secure their fidelity, equip them better and

[23] The strategy of promptly stripping the region south of the Columbia of furs was one on which the executive officers of the Hudson's Bay Company were agreed. The governor and committee in a dispatch of February 23, 1826, after urging a program of conservation of beaver in the company's home territories, concluded, "In the meantime the deficiency might be made up by keeping all the frontier country hunted close, and by trapping expeditions in those countries likely to fall within the Boundary of the United States." Merk, *Fur Trade*, 268. See also *ibid.*, 294–95.

stimulate them to greater exertion; and the money is paid out only after the furs are actually in hand:

[Enclosure][24]

Cost Snake Expedition   1825
     Returns

2485 large parchm^t Beaver	2485
1210 small Beaver	605
27 lbs cuttings	27
24 lbs castorum	24
47 large Land otters	47
	3188

Cost of the furs exclusive
    of River communication expenses   £1383–18–9 or 27,678 shillings

Cost of a made Beaver delivered at the Flatheads fall 1825 amounted to 8/8 and a fraction without debiting them with the expenses of river Communication.

John McLoughlin to Governor Simpson.[25]
                Ft. Vancouver   20 March 1846

. . . . When I came here in 1824 as you know our trade was limited to the waters of the Columbia; we had [not?] seen the Umpqua and the Snake Country had been given up as a hopeless affair by the late N. W. Company. In 1822 Mr Ale^x Ross had been sent there[26] with a party of men, merely with a view of employing them, when you and I came in 1824 you recollect we sent Mr Ogden in charge of the party and the plans were formed and you must recollect how they were followed and the result that at one time thirty eight [?] of Mr Ogdens men left him with their hunts, horses and traps and joined the Americans. But as in 1824 when you were here we could not ascertain how the business was managed or the cause of the misconduct of the Snake men but we believed as was told us it proceeded from their bad disposition, but I ordered the books to be brought to Fort George and saw it proceeded from the bad system in which the business was carried on and charging exhorbitant prices for the supplies to the men; on my own responsibility and contrary to the wish of my colleagues who happened

[24] Hudson's Bay Company Journal, no. 812.
[25] Hudson's Bay Company Journal, no. 1721.
[26] Dr. McLoughlin's memory was faulty at this point. Finan McDonald had charge of the expedition referred to and its date was 1823.

to be present, I altered the whole system and soon changed the state of affairs and instead of abandoning the trade, as was the desire of two of my colleagues wanted me to do and of the opposition gaining ground upon us from year to year as they had done they soon had to withdraw and most certainly the Hudson's Bay Company have cleared in the Snake Country and from the trapping parties from that time to this (I have not the books to state the exact amount) but speak from memory, at least thirty thousand pounds. . . .

ALBERT GALLATIN
AND THE OREGON PROBLEM

A Study in Anglo-American Diplomacy

FIRST PUBLISHED IN 1950

BY HARVARD UNIVERSITY PRESS

ALBERT GALLATIN
AND THE OREGON PROBLEM

A Study in Anglo-American Diplomacy

PREFACE TO THE FIRST EDITION

FOR MORE than thirty years the Oregon question was a generator of tension in Anglo-American relations. From the time of
the taking of Astoria in the War of 1812 to the Oregon Treaty
of 1846 it produced incidents and crises, one after another, mount-
ing in intensity. The earliest incident was the flare-up in England
over the "Ontario" affair of 1817, when a United States sloop-of-
war departed from New York for the mouth of the Columbia,
unannounced to the British, for the purpose of asserting American
sovereignty at the British-held site of Astoria. The second disturbance came in the period 1824–1826, when George Canning, the
British foreign minister, was roused to anger so high by developments in the United States described in this narrative that Albert
Gallatin felt it necessary to warn his government to make preparations for a rupture. The third was the war crisis of 1845–46, stirred
up by the movement into Oregon of American pioneers and by
the resulting American politics of expansionism.

In each of these crises a peacemaker happily appeared on one
side or the other of the ocean to reduce fever and restore health.
In the "Ontario" affair it was Castlereagh; in the disturbance of the
1820's it was Albert Gallatin; in the war crisis of 1845–46 it was
Lord Aberdeen. In each case the peacemaker was able to direct
existing forces of good will and intelligence in the two countries
to the reduction of emotion and the prevention of a rupture.

In this essay I have sought to assess the forces which made for
rupture and those which made for peace in the second of these
periods of tension. I have described them as focused on the negotiation of 1826–27. The negotiation itself, less well known than it
deserves to be, I have dealt with as an illustration of peacemaking
in the process. I have conceived of it as a case study, a chapter in the
history of the greatest problem facing mankind, the maintenance of
peace among nations.

The peacemaker in this negotiation was Albert Gallatin. He succeeded almost singlehanded in rescuing the negotiation from failure and making it the means of lowering tensions. He was largely responsible for the relative quiescence that marked the Oregon issue in the period from 1827 to the end of the 1830's. He was one of the few American diplomats of his day who was respected on both sides of the Atlantic. He was regarded in England in 1826 as the sage of American statesmen. His association with the Oregon problem was as prolonged as the problem itself. He had watched, as a member of Madison's government and as a friend of Astor, the evolution of the Astoria enterprise. He was one of the American commissioners negotiating the Ghent Treaty of 1814, which provided for the restoration of Astoria. He was the principal American plenipotentiary at the conference of 1818, which framed the joint occupation. His services did not end with the conclusion of the negotiation of 1826–27. In 1846, at the height of the Oregon crisis, he published a series of quieting letters on the issue in the *National Intelligencer*, in which he suggested the line of boundary that was ultimately adopted. The letters were a profound influence for peace on that occasion on both sides of the Atlantic.

In these letters he briefly described diplomatists in their ideal character. In so doing he painted his own portrait as it will appear to the reader of these pages: "But, though acting . . . as advocates, diplomatists are essentially ministers of peace whose constant and primary duty is mutually to devise conciliatory means for the adjustment of conflicting pretensions, for the continuance of friendly relations, for preventing war, or for the restoration of peace."

The area that was at stake in the Oregon controversy was an imperial one. It extended from the Rocky Mountains on the east to the Pacific Ocean on the west, and from latitude 42° to 54° 40'. It embraced approximately 450,000 square miles, more than the combined surface of France, Germany, and Czechoslovakia in 1939. The area was destined to have future strategic importance for the United States and Canada. It became an outlet for both of them to the Pacific.

Five unsuccessful negotiations to partition this country took place between the United States and England before the final negotiation in 1846. Three of the five were in an early group, 1818,

1823–24, and 1826–27; two were of date shortly before and during the crisis of 1845–46. In the early negotiations each government began by proposing a line of partition and refusing the offer of the other. This interchange was repeated with little variation as the second negotiation followed the first and the third the second. By the time of the third, the subject of this essay, less than the whole area was in actual controversy. The controversy had been narrowed by the offers to a core—the triangle that lies between the Columbia River at the south and the 49th parallel at the north. This triangle was of importance to each contestant for its water appendages, the Columbia River on the one side and the harbor waters of the straits on the other.

The proposal which the American government made in the first three negotiations, the line of the 49th parallel to the sea, offered a reasonable basis for a settlement. With a slight alteration to avoid severing Vancouver Island and the straits, it was the line ultimately adopted as the boundary. It divided the deep water harbors of the straits as equitably as could be. It projected to the Pacific the boundary established in 1818 east of the mountains. It accorded well with the established claims of the two contesting powers. South of the line the claims of the United States, reënforced by those acquired from Spain, were far better than those of Britain. North of the line those of Britain were far the stronger. The line was the boundary that the finger of nature and the finger of history pointed out for the partition of the Oregon area.

In 1826 it was rejected by Canning. It had been rejected by him earlier. It was rejected in the interests of the transitory needs of the Hudson's Bay Company and the ambitions which Canning had for the British Empire. The rejection meant the storing up of a war crisis for the future, a crisis which was one of a series that Canning's temper and policy created in Anglo-American relations. Happily when the crisis occurred Lord Aberdeen, a statesman of very different temper from Canning, occupied the foreign office. Canning had been, so his critics charged, a statesman of "talents without character." Aberdeen was, preëminently, a statesman of character, and by him the stubborn issue was finally laid to rest.

I wish to make special reference to a work recently published, which briefly traverses the ground I have here covered, Samuel Flagg Bemis, *John Quincy Adams and the Foundations of Amer-*

ican Foreign Policy (New York, 1949). It is not referred to in the text of this essay or in two companion pieces—"The Genesis of the Oregon Question," *Mississippi Valley Historical Review*, XXXVI (1949–50), 583–612, and "The Ghost River Caledonia in the Oregon Negotiation of 1818," *American Historical Review*, LV (1949–50), 530–551, since it appeared after they were all in typescript and the articles in the hands of the publishers. It is a notable contribution to the literature of American diplomatic history and of the Oregon question. Its treatment of the Oregon negotiation of 1826–27 will be found to differ widely from mine. The differences arise to some extent from the fact that we interpret the negotiation through different personalities and philosophies, the nationalist philosophy and tense personality of John Quincy Adams on the one hand, and the internationalist philosophy and urbane personality of Albert Gallatin on the other. The interplay of these great Americans upon each other was as important to the nation and to the world in the Oregon negotiation as it had been earlier at the Ghent peace conference. It was a fortunate country that had two such minds balancing each other on its behalf.

I am under many obligations for help in the making of this study. In England I am under obligations to the staff of the Department of Manuscripts of the British Museum, and especially to H. R. Aldridge, its assistant keeper. I have received special courtesies from the staff of the British Public Record Office in Chancery Lane. I am indebted to the late third Baron Revelstoke for permission to use the Baring papers, then housed in London, and to the sixth Earl of Harewood for information regarding the George Canning papers. In Canada I am under obligation to the staff of the Public Archives at Ottawa for many courtesies, and especially to Dr. Gustave Lanctot, its Director. In the United States I wish to express my obligation to the staff of the Division of Manuscripts and the Division of Maps of the Library of Congress; to the National Archives; the William L. Clements Library; the New-York Historical Society; the Peabody Institute of the City of Baltimore; the Massachusetts Historical Society; and the Harvard University Library. I am indebted to Albert E. Gallatin of New York City for facilitating my entrance into the papers of his ancestor in the New-York Historical Society. The John Quincy Adams papers are not yet generally open to historians, but Henry Adams kindly made on my behalf a search through them for materials on my subject.

My greatest obligation is to my wife, Lois Bannister Merk, who read the manuscript of this book many times with a scholar's care. On almost every page I owe her a debt for keen and constructive criticism and invaluable help in my literary revision.

CONTENTS

ALBERT GALLATIN AND THE OREGON PROBLEM

CHAPTER I · INCEPTION OF THE
LONDON CONFERENCE OF 1826–27

IN APRIL 1826 George Canning produced a stir in the American government by sending a note to the American minister in London. The note was a proposal to reopen the inconclusively ended Oregon negotiation of 1823–24. Canning gave no hint of his reasons for sending the note. In the game of diplomacy he was not the player prematurely to show his hand. But he gave an impression of urgency in the note by declaring that two British plenipotentiaries were ready to begin conferences at once, that they were prepared either to renew an offer which had been made in 1824, or to bring forward another, or to discuss any new offer the American minister might wish to make.[1] When the head of a foreign office thus presses the government of another state to reopen a negotiation that has recently failed, especially if the issue does not require immediate action, he produces a hope that concessions of importance are on the way. Such a hope Canning produced in the American government.

The reasons for the note were two. One was a Hudson's Bay Company need, set forth in a letter which the Governor of the Company had written Canning the preceding December.[2] The other was annoyance felt by Canning over developments in the United States. If the American government had known of these backgrounds of the note it would have been less hopeful than it was of the outcome of a renewed negotiation.

The Hudson's Bay Company was a partner of the crown in the building of the empire in North America. It had become a partner in 1670 when it obtained a grant of land from the crown. The grant was a vast one, the whole drainage basin of Hudson Bay. It extended westward to the crest of the Rocky Mountains, embracing the greater part of what is now Canada. It included not merely rights of soil but exclusive rights of trade. The Company named the grant Rupert's Land, in honor of Prince Rupert, a member of its directorate and a cousin of the King.

[1] Canning to King, April 20, 1826, *American State Papers, Foreign Relations* (Washington, 1832–1859), VI, 645–646.
[2] See pp. 110–111.

But the title of the Company to Rupert's Land was challenged. It was challenged first by the French. This was one of the issues fought over in the century-long Anglo-French duel in North America. In 1763 the duel ended with the expulsion of France from the continent. A new duel, however, followed. The Company's exclusive rights of trade were challenged by independent traders, especially by those organized as the North West Company. For another half century the Company fought the North West Company in a war that was bitter, increasingly violent, and ruinous to both. In 1821, at the behest of the government, the two companies finally, through a merger, made peace. The Hudson's Bay Company was able in the merger to retain its charter, its organization, and its name.

As a consequence of the merger the Company entered the Oregon Country. It acquired there the interests and position of the North West Company. It obtained, also, by gift from the government, a monopoly of all British rights of trade west of the mountains. The monopoly was a reward for the merger and an instrument for defeating American traders who might, under the terms of the joint occupation of 1818, undertake a competition. The Company was thus, in 1821, the sole British occupant of the Oregon Country. It was almost the only occupant of any nationality, for Americans were not crossing the mountains at all in those years to trap or trade.

For three years the Company took little advantage of its privileged position in its new sphere. It was engrossed in the immense task of reorganizing and rehabilitating its demoralized trade east of the mountains. It had to entrust the country west of the mountains to the former employees of the North West Company. These men, suspicious of the new regime and leaderless, served without energy. They permitted, in the lower Columbia, a trade deterioration to continue that had already set in before the merger. They allowed the lower Columbia to register, on the books of the Company, a succession of annual net losses. They led the directorate of the Company to regard the lower valley as a forlorn hope. The Company considered abandoning the lower river as a western base of operations and withdrawing northward to the Fraser.[3]

[3] *Fur Trade and Empire: George Simpson's Journal*, Frederick Merk, ed. (Cambridge, 1931), xxi–xxxi.

In the autumn of 1824 George Simpson, the American field governor of the Company, appeared at Fort George. He had come over the mountains from Hudson Bay for the purpose of surveying the Columbia Department and determining its future. He was a young Scot of lowly origin but high ability, who had been sent to America after the merger. He had already established a reputation in the East for driving power and administrative genius. He came to the West, surmising that the deterioration of the lower Columbia was the result of inefficiency, listlessness, and waste. He found these suspicions verified and applied the correctives with accustomed energy. He completely overhauled the Columbia Department, replacing its old head by a new one whom he had brought with him. The new head was Dr. John McLoughlin, an administrator as gifted as the Governor himself, who was destined to become a power in the affairs of the West and to dominate the Oregon Country for the next twenty years.[4]

One of Simpson's labors in the winter of 1824–25 was the dismantling of historic Fort George on the site of Astoria. This was done at the recommendation of Canning. The fort stood on a bank of the Columbia which was sure to go, in a future partition of the Oregon Country, to the United States. In its stead Simpson erected a new fort north of the river, opposite the mouth of the Willamette. He named the new establishment "Fort Vancouver," in order to associate the Columbia River explorations of the Vancouver expedition with England's claim to the soil north of the river.[5]

These arrangements completed, Simpson was on his way back over the mountains in the spring of 1825. In the autumn he was in London ready to report on his activities and to make his recommendations. His recommendations were two. North of the Columbia, a vigorous program of expansion with a view to a permanent occupation of the country; south of the Columbia, a swift trapping out of the furs.[6]

An expansion north of the Columbia would involve a considerable outlay of capital and labor. The risks of such an outlay in an area of undetermined sovereignty, where national ambitions clashed, the Company well knew. It desired from the government, before

[4] *Ibid.*
[5] *Ibid.*, 124, 258. See also, Essay 1.
[6] *Fur Trade and Empire*, Merk, ed., *passim*, and Essay 4.

committing itself irrevocably to the new program, an assurance that it would have the future use of the central transportation system of the Oregon Country, the Columbia River. More specifically it wished assurance that in a future partition of the Oregon Country the government would see to it that the river remained adjacent to British territory. If a partition on that basis could be arranged, the Company preferred it to the uncertainties of the convention of joint occupation. That convention was a ten-year arrangement which would shortly expire.

As a result of Simpson's recommendations, on December 9, 1825, the London governor of the Company addressed a letter to Canning. He gave an account of what the Company had done and what it proposed to do in the Oregon Country. He wrote of the expansion the Company contemplated northward from the Columbia and behind the mouth of the Fraser. He declared that for this expansion the Columbia would be necessary. The river was the highway by which the country behind the mouth of the Fraser and that on the Columbia's own upper waters was provisioned. For the trade of the Oregon Country generally the river was required. The Governor suggested that the Oregon Country be partitioned. He called attention to the fact that on a recently published American map a boundary line had been drawn from the Rocky Mountains to the seacoast along the 49th parallel,[7] which, he thought, might be made improper use of in the future by the American government. He proposed a line that he thought would be fair to the United States and that would also answer the needs of the Company. The line began at the point where the continental divide is intersected by the 49th parallel. It fell southward along the continental divide to the place where Lewis and Clark crossed the mountains, said to be in latitude 46° 20′; thence it ran via Lewis' river (the Snake) to a junction with the Columbia, and thence, via the Columbia, to the sea. The Governor observed that this line would leave both the Columbia and Lewis' river free to be navigated by the subjects of the two nations.

[7] Cartographers in the United States in this period commonly depicted the northern boundary of the United States as established from the Rocky Mountains to the Pacific at the line of the 49th parallel. This was done either in ignorance or in excess of cartographic patriotism. The error was pointed out by Henry S. Tanner in his *A New American Atlas*, published in Philadelphia in 1823. Special commendation was bestowed on Tanner for this scholarly achievement by Jared Sparks, who reviewed the *Atlas* in the *North American Review*, XVIII (1824), 384–385.

Perhaps he did not know that the British government had offered the United States without result a much more favorable line than this in the negotiation of 1823–24. He sent with his letter a map on which he had marked his line and the location of the Company's posts in the Oregon Country. He made the suggestion, in conclusion, that Governor Simpson was in town and would be happy to attend any appointment the foreign secretary would be pleased to make should further information respecting the Oregon Country be desired.[8]

This was the letter that stimulated Canning to propose reopening the Oregon negotiation. The endorsement he wrote on it, upon reading it, was: "This is a very important Paper. The Map which accompanied it should be carefully preserved & the whole placed among the Papers belonging to the negotiation with the U. States. Did Mr. Addington see Gov. Simpson & take a memo. of his communication?"[9]

The meeting desired by Canning between Addington, the undersecretary of state in the Foreign Office, and Simpson was held. Its outcome was a questionnaire drawn up by Addington for Simpson to answer. The questionnaire and the answers Simpson made to it are equally revealing.

A first set of questions related to the agricultural possibilities of the Columbia valley, a matter in which Canning had an interest. It drew from Simpson an attractive picture of the lower Columbia as the seat of a future agricultural settlement. Both banks of the lower Columbia, Simpson reported, from the seaboard inland to the Cascade portage were covered with a great variety of fine, large timber. The soil of the lowlands he described as alluvial and rich and, where well located, as at Fort Vancouver, capable of producing large quantities of grain and pasturing numerous herds of cattle and hogs. The climate he described as delightfully temperate with little or no frost or snow.

A second series of questions related to the fur potentialities of the Columbia valley. Was the hunting ground immediately on the northern bank of the Columbia good? The answer Simpson gave was that immediately on the northern bank the hunting ground was nearly exhausted of furs, but that the back country was still

<hr />

[8] *Fur Trade and Empire*, Merk, ed., 257–260.
[9] *Ibid.*

productive and that in all the small rivers and lakes beaver was found. Simpson declared that the trade of the Columbia as a whole was still in its infancy and that the territories to the northward and southward of the river produced an equal quantity of furs.

A third series followed, concerning the country's outlets to the sea. The Columbia and the Fraser were particularly inquired about, and a comparison of the two as outlets was requested. This series went to the heart of the Oregon problem. If the Fraser was navigable it was a possible alternative to the Columbia as an outlet, and it lay wholly north of the 49th parallel. Simpson answered these questions by affirming that the Columbia was the only navigable river he knew between the interior and the coast. It was the only certain outlet for the trade west of the mountains, comprising thirteen of the Company's trading establishments. As for the Fraser, it was impassable. Its banks, in stretches of its course, formed precipices where the towing line could not be used, and its current was so impetuous as to render navigation in certain seasons out of the question. Simpson concluded his testimony with the round statement that in his opinion "if the Navigation of the Columbia is not free to the Hudsons Bay Company, and that the Territory to the Northward of it is not secured to them, they must abandon and curtail their Trade in some parts, and probably be constrained to relinquish it on the West side of the Rocky Mountains altogether."[10]

Canning had an even more compelling reason for wishing to reopen the Oregon negotiation. He was disturbed by the agitation that was going on in Washington for a military occupation by the United States of the mouth of the Columbia. This agitation, initially the work of a few zealots in Congress, had become of graver character. In December 1824 President Monroe had formally recommended to Congress that a military post be established at the mouth of the Columbia, "or at some other point in that quarter within our acknowledged limits."[11] Within sixteen days a Floyd committee bill, authorizing the establishment not merely of the post but of the territory of Oregon—a territory including all the country west of the Rocky Mountains and north of the 42nd parallel, with no restriction of northern boundary—had passed the House by an

[10] *Ibid.*, 260–266.

[11] James D. Richardson, *Messages and Papers of the Presidents* (Washington, 1896–1898), II, 262. "Within our acknowledged limits" was a cryptic phrase, which was intended, perhaps, to mean merely the south side of the Columbia.

overwhelming majority and had obtained a disquietingly large vote in the Senate.[12] In December 1825 Adams had repeated Monroe's recommendation and had added the suggestion that provision be made for a public vessel to explore the whole Northwest Coast of the continent.[13] His message had led to no actual legislation but had produced an aggressive committee report—the first of two reports of the Baylies Committee.[14]

These proceedings had been reported home regularly by the British ministers in Washington. In March 1826 they had been summarized, at the suggestion of Canning, by Addington, who had been an observer of some of them at close range while he was minister in Washington in 1824–25. A suggestion of Addington was before Canning that a series of British papers exhibiting the claims of England to the Oregon Country be published by Parliament as an antidote to the agitation in Congress and a warning to the American government against aggressive action.[15] The suggestion, apparently, did not commend itself to Canning. The proposal to reopen the Oregon negotiation was the alternative.

The proposal was accepted with eagerness by the American government. It opened the way for bringing not only the Oregon question but other stubborn Anglo-American issues to a settlement. The Oregon question and a sheaf of others were made ready for negotiation. The added issues were commercial relations with the British West Indies, which involved the colonial and navigation laws of England; the renewal of the commercial convention of 1815, which Gallatin and Rush had once renewed in 1818, but which was soon to expire; the northeastern boundary issue; the question of navigation of the St. Lawrence; and the still unsettled question of indemnification for slaves carried off from the United States in violation of the Treaty of Ghent. In quantity and complexity these issues formed a load more than an ordinary minister

---

[12] A description of the bill by Senator Dickerson of New Jersey is in *Congressional Debates*, 18 Cong., 2 sess. (1824–25), 690. The House vote on it is in 18 Cong., 2 sess. (1824–25), *House Journal*, 68–69, 78–79.

[13] *Messages and Papers of the Presidents*, II, 313.

[14] The first Baylies Report is printed in 19 Cong., 1 sess. (1825–26), *House Reports*, No. 35.

[15] H. U. Addington, "Abstract of Proceedings," March 9, 1826, F.O. 5: 221; Addington to Canning, May 2, 1826, F.O. 5: 221. See also same to same Dec. 28, 1824, British Museum, Additional Mss., 38746:69, and Vaughan to Canning, Jan. 30, 1826, F.O. 5: 210.

could carry. The resident minister of the United States in London, Rufus King, was old and unwell. The government decided to send a special plenipotentiary to join him. The obvious man for the place was Albert Gallatin.[16] He was prevailed upon to accept. When King was presently obliged by illness to resign, Gallatin was persuaded to become resident minister to England for the period necessary to bring a general negotiation to completion.

Instructions to Gallatin were prepared under the supervision of President Adams, who was more expert on Anglo-American affairs than his secretary of state, Henry Clay. On the Oregon question the instructions were that the line of the 49th parallel must be the limit of American territorial concession. It could be so announced. The only departure permitted from it was the concession to the British of the right to navigate the Columbia River and any of its branches which the line intersected from the point of intersection to the sea.[17]

These instructions displeased Gallatin. He had asked to be given some freedom, especially freedom to make again the Gulf offer he had made informally in 1818, which involved concession of a crucial area south of 49°.[18] He had wished to be permitted to enlarge that offer by the addition of the whole drainage basin of Juan de Fuca Strait. He believed that without these concessions he could reach no partition agreement with the British. He had been promised, while he was considering acceptance of the mission, that he would be permitted to write his own instructions. He reminded the President of this in letters of remonstrance against his instructions.[19] But the President was inflexible against any retreat from the line of the 49th parallel.

---

[16] Gallatin had already dealt with some of these issues as special envoy to England in the negotiation of 1818. He had an unrivalled knowledge of American finance and economy, a mind trained to cut through complex technical issues, and a European's insight into European modes of thought.

[17] Clay to Gallatin, June 19, 1826, *A.S.P.*, *F.R.*, VI, 644–646.

[18] See Essay 3.

[19] Gallatin to Clay, June 20, 29, 30, 1826, in *Writings of Albert Gallatin*, Henry Adams, ed. (Philadelphia, 1879), II, 307, 312–313, 319–320.

THE INFLEXIBILITY of the President on the issue of the 49th parallel was no mere intransigeance of an individual. It was the will of the Senate. It reflected the temper of the nation. The President made this clear to Gallatin in a later letter discussing the instructions: "One inch of ground [beyond the 49th parallel] yielded on the North-West coast . . . would be certain to meet the reprobation of the Senate."[1]

The line of the 49th parallel had been the consistent policy of American administrations ever since the Oregon Country had become an Anglo-American issue. It had been the policy of the Madison government. In the dark days of the War of 1812 Monroe had maintained it in his instructions to the peace commissioners at Ghent. In the Monroe administration Adams had defended it in two negotiations with the British—those of 1818 and 1823–24. If Adams had wished as President to retreat from that line he could not safely have done so. Retreat would have been politically disastrous.

Yet there was something paradoxical, in that day, about defending the line of the 49th parallel west of the Rockies. The whole trans-mountain region was believed, in the first quarter of the nineteenth century, to be beyond the reach of the government of the United States. The conviction of thoughtful Americans was that if this territory were acquired, it could not be permanently held. For the United States to attempt to hold and govern it would be to fly in the face of time, space, and the dearest conceptions of American democracy.

Between the western settlements of Missouri and the Pacific coast a vast barrens was believed to extend. The Great American Desert was there, a land of sterility, of dust storms and aridity. In the report of the Long expedition of 1819–20, the region between the parallels of latitude 39° and 49°, and between a line 500 miles east of the Rockies and the base of the Rockies, was declared unfit for cultivation, a region not habitable by a people dependent on agriculture, an area important chiefly as a check to too great an

---

[1] Adams to Gallatin, March 20, 1827, in Gallatin, *Writings*, II, 367–368.

extension of American population westward and as a protective barrier against the incursions of an enemy in that quarter. West of this waste rose the towering peaks of the continental divide, and beyond them stretched, as far as the Cascades, another desert of sand and alkali.[2]

For the crossing of this barrens only primitive means of travel were available—the horse, the ox, the canoe. No one of right mind dreamed of railroads ever ascending the heights of the Rockies or the Cascades. It was not until 1829, two years after the close of Gallatin's negotiation, that the first crude locomotive was put in motion in the United States. Steam had come to be applied to river transport but its use for ocean transport was a development of the future. The telegraph was a development yet further in the future.

The travel time of the Lewis and Clark expedition from St. Louis to the shores of the Pacific was eighteen months. That of Robert Stuart, the Astorian, on a return trip from Astoria to St. Louis in 1812–13, via the short cut of South Pass, was ten months. The sea voyage between the Pacific Northwest and the eastern seaboard by way of Cape Horn was a matter of six to eight months depending on the weather. Communication between the Northwest Coast and the eastern seaboard was often by way of a trip around the world.

The society that would be formed in the Oregon Country was expected to consist of a population drawn from the United States. It would be an offshoot of the United States. If it became a colony it could be governed, doubtless, from the United States. Colonies were governed from England that were even more remote. Yet, to Americans, a colonial government, permanently maintained over a people of their own kin, seemed repugnant. It would be contrary to the genius of American democratic institutions. If attempted, it would end, so it was believed, in subverting the liberties of the republic itself. The expectation and the wish of thoughtful Americans was that the society which would be formed west of the Rockies, would take the course that the American colonies had

[2] The report of the Long Expedition is in *Account of An Expedition from Pittsburg to the Rocky Mountains,* Edwin James, comp. (Philadelphia, 1823); see especially volume II, 361. See also Henry M. Brackenridge, *Journal of a Voyage up the River Missouri* (Baltimore, 1815); and Robert Greenhow, *History of Oregon and California* (Boston, 1844), 323. The persistence of the desert conception of the region beyond the 100th meridian is well traced in Ralph C. Morris, "Notion of a Great American Desert East of the Rockies," *MVHR,* XIII (1926–27), 190–200.

taken and that Spain's Latin American colonies had more recently taken. It would become independent.

Such a destiny was predicted and desired by Thomas Jefferson. He was, indeed, the progenitor of the idea. In one of the letters he wrote Astor regarding the future of Astoria, he declared that he looked forward with gratification to the time when people of United States origin would have spread themselves over the whole length of the Pacific West, "covering it with free and independent Americans, unconnected with us but by the ties of blood and interest, and employing like us the rights of self-government."[3] Jefferson gave that concept wide currency. He spread it by means of conversations with disciples and friends. Among the host of his disciples, who in the 1820's were persuaded that a Pacific republic, independent of the United States, would rise west of the mountains were Gallatin, Monroe, Crawford, Clay, Benton, and probably Madison.

The most vocal exponent of this concept in Congress or in the press was Thomas Hart Benton. In a speech delivered to the Senate on March 1, 1825, he admitted that the United States should have limits and that he was a limitationist. Where the northern and southern limits should be, he preferred, for the moment, not to say. They were fixed by the hand of Nature, and posterity would neither lack sense to see nor resolution to step up to them. He continued:

Westward, we can speak without reserve, and the ridge of the Rocky Mountains may be named without offence, as presenting a convenient, natural and everlasting boundary. Along the back of this ridge, the Western limit of the republic should be drawn, and the statue of the fabled god, Terminus, should be raised upon its highest peak, never to be thrown down. In planting the seed of a new power on the coast of the Pacific ocean, it should be well understood that when strong enough to take care of itself, the new Government should separate from the mother Empire as the child separates from the parent at the age of manhood.[4]

The conviction that a new republic would come to life in the Pacific West was, however, not a policy. It was merely the setting

[3] Jefferson to Astor, May 24, 1812, in *Works of Thomas Jefferson*, Paul L. Ford, ed. (New York, 1904–1905), XI, 244.

[4] *Congressional Debates*, 18 Cong., 2 sess. (1824–25), 712. The limitationists were apparently not unwilling that the United States should acquire territory provisionally beyond the Rocky Mountains in trusteeship for the future new republic.

for a policy. The policy that the government should adopt regarding the prospective infant—whether to generate it, or foster it, or remain aloof from it, or even to resist its coming—was the question. It was a question on which men widely differed. Romanticists, like Jefferson, who looked forward with gratification to the appearance of the infant, would have the United States give it fostering care and protection. Benton wished to go further. He would have the American government actually plant the germ; he would have the government occupy for that purpose the harbor at the mouth of the Columbia. Less generous or romantic persons urged that the government refrain from planting or fostering what would become a western rival. They warned that the new republic would drain the United States of capital and population; that in the fur trade of the Far West and in the commerce of the Orient it would become a national competitor.[5]

Monroe, as president, entertained the hope that a combination of seemingly divergent policies might be possible. In March 1824, some months prior to the message which called forth Floyd's bill, he proposed to recommend to Congress that a military post be built on the shores of the Pacific, either at the mouth of the Columbia or in Juan de Fuca Strait, as a protection to the national interests. He intended to combine with this recommendation a strong argument against the formation by the United States of any territorial settlements on that coast. He intended to give a decided expression of opinion, as part of the argument, that such settlements "would necessarily soon separate from this Union." The President read to his cabinet the draft of a message to Congress embodying these ideas.[6]

Opposition to the sending of such a message was at once expressed. It was expressed by all three cabinet members present, Adams, Calhoun, and Southard. The grounds of opposition were significant. They revealed that a new point of view regarding the destiny of the Pacific Northwest was taking its place beside the limitationist view. All the cabinet members approved the recommendation that a military post be built. But all doubted the

---

[5] For an example of this point of view see a speech by Wood of New York on Jan. 13, 1823, *Annals of Congress*, 17 Cong., 2 sess. (1822–23), 598–601.
[6] *Memoirs of John Quincy Adams*, Charles F. Adams, ed. (Philadelphia, 1874–1877), VI, 250–256.

expediency of a presidential declaration that a separation of settlements formed on the coast would necessarily soon occur. Calhoun and Adams maintained that no such separation would occur. Calhoun affirmed that "the passion for aggrandizement was the law paramount of man in society, and that there was no example in history of the disruption of a nation from itself by voluntary separation." Adams was the boldest and most extreme of those who rejected Jefferson's old theories. Accepting Calhoun's conclusions, though not his interpretation of history, he declared that "a government by federation would be found practicable upon a territory as extensive as this continent, and that the tendency of our popular sentiments was increasingly toward union."[7] The tendency of our popular sentiments, to which he referred, was another name for nationalism. Monroe, finding his advisers unanimous against him, concluded not to send the message in that form.

Parallel to the questions whether the territory west of the mountains could be held, or should be held, in the Union, was a third: Was it worth holding? Debate on this question was going on in the press and in Congress from the time of the restoration of Astoria to the conclusion of the Oregon Treaty in 1846. The opinions ventured ran the gamut, from the rhapsodies of Benton and Floyd, according to whom the country was a Garden of Eden, to the strident judgment expressed in a New York journal that the country was fit only for the seat of a penal colony.[8] The debate is hardly worth reporting. It was a display, for the most part, of ignorance and factionalism. The ignorance was at first almost unavoidable. The country was remote; its interior was not visited by American traders; it was occupied, after the collapse of Astor's enterprise, by no great American corporation comparable to the Hudson's Bay Company, having a stake in its resources and a centralized knowledge of them. The debate is an illustration of an important fact: that in the absence of reliable information the American public and government were at a disadvantage, as compared with the British government, in the formulation of Oregon policy.

Debate was also going on in Congress and in the press over individual stakes of Oregon diplomacy. It was going on especially

[7] *Ibid.*
[8] New York *Gazette*, March 16, 1822.

over the most important of all the stakes, the Columbia River. In this debate Benton, Floyd, and their followers gave free rein to imagination. They pictured the Columbia as forming, together with the Missouri, a channel of communication between the Pacific Ocean and the Mississippi River, and as connecting the Northwest Coast with St. Louis. Along this channel would flow the commerce to and from the Orient. Furs from the Oregon Country would flow to China. In return teas, silks, and spices would move to St. Louis. St. Louis would become the Venice of the New World. A modern Tyre would rise at the mouth of the Columbia.[9]

Realists sought to bring these flights of fancy to earth by adverting to the bar lying across the mouth of the river, the waterfalls and rapids that obstruct navigation higher up the river, and the mountains that separate the heads of navigation of the Columbia and the Missouri. They called attention to Vancouver's *Narrative*, containing Broughton's report on the bar, and the oral testimony regarding the bar of American traders having a knowledge of the Northwest Coast. They cited, also, accounts of the mountain barriers by explorers and traders who had crossed them.

In reply, the Benton-Floyd school cited John B. Prevost, the agent of the American government at the Astoria restoration, whose account of his experiences, written for the Department of State, was published in 1822. In his report he declared that the bar was less a danger than it was thought to be, that it had been crossed and recrossed without trouble by the vessel on which he had traveled, and that it could be made safe for vessels of almost any tonnage if the channel through it were marked.[10] By that report the issue of the bar was long befogged. Benton disposed of the problem of the mountain barrier between the Columbia and the Missouri by pointing to the ease with which the Lewis and Clark expedition had crossed from one river system to the other.

Another of the stakes of Oregon diplomacy, mentioned occasionally in early debates and becoming steadily more prominent later, was a deep-water harbor that would be suitable for a naval station

[9] The views of Benton are set forth in repeated editorials in the St. Louis *Enquirer* of the years 1819–1821; those of Floyd are in the Floyd reports of 1821 and 1822, 16 Cong., 2 sess. (1820–21) *H. Reports,* No. 45; 17 Cong., 1 sess. (1821–22), *H. Reports,* No. 18.

[10] The Prevost report is printed in 17 Cong., 1 sess., *H. Documents* (1821–22), No. 112.

of the United States. Such a harbor was at first identified with the mouth of the Columbia. But as the ineligibility of the mouth of the river became more apparent, search for a better one turned northward, toward Juan de Fuca Strait. In March 1824 a port within the strait was mentioned as an alternative to the harbor at the mouth of the Columbia in Monroe's undelivered message, and at about the same time congressional speeches began to reveal a desire for a naval station in the strait or the Gulf of Georgia.[11] Yet it was in just this period that Gallatin was proposing to concede these waters to the British.[12]

Associated, in congressional discussion, with the need for a naval station was the need for a base for whalers. Such a base, it was argued, was required for the New England whale fisheries in the Pacific, a large and growing interest, more important to the nation even than the maritime fur trade of the Pacific Northwest. The argument for a whaling base was an attempt to link the maritime Northeast with the fur-trapping West in support of an aggressive Oregon policy.

But the attempt was without result. New England whalers in this period operated almost altogether in the South Pacific. They used as their base increasingly, after the War of 1812, the Hawaiian Islands. A port on the Oregon coast would have been far out of their course. Spokesmen for the whaling interests in Congress repeatedly pointed out that they found among their constituents no interest whatever in an Oregon whaling base.[13]

This uncertainty in the executive, the press, and Congress concerning the worth and the destiny of the Oregon Country was probably absent from the mind of Adams. He seems to have

[11] J. Q. Adams, *Memoirs*, VI, 250–251. In 1822, at the time of the public discussion of the Russian ukase of 1821, William Sturgis, a Boston merchant prince and dean of fur traders on the Northwest Coast, wrote a series of letters to the *Boston Daily Advertiser*, which were brought to the notice of President Monroe. In these letters Sturgis graphically described the bar at the mouth of the Columbia and its perils. He recommended strongly that Port Discovery in the straits be selected for an American naval station (*ibid.*, VI, 429; *Boston Daily Advertiser*, Jan. 28, 31, Feb. 6, 20, 1822). See also a speech by Trimble of Kentucky, delivered in the House on Dec. 21, 1824, *Congressional Debates*, 18 Cong., 2 sess. (1824–25), 40. Harbors in the straits were preferable to the mouth of the Columbia for naval stations. But since they lacked connection by water with the interior they did not seem as desirable as the mouth of the Columbia for commercial purposes.

[12] See above, Essay 3.

[13] See *Annals of Congress*, 17 Cong., 2 sess. (1822–23), 424, 594–595, 598, 680. See also the testimony of William Sturgis in *Boston Daily Advertiser*, Feb. 6, 1822.

considered the area of high value and to have expected it to become part of the Union. Yet he did make declarations that flatly contradicted such a view and that must be taken into consideration by the historian. In 1818, in an interview with Charles Bagot, the British minister—the interview at which Bagot announced his government's decision to restore Astoria—Adams took pains to minimize the value of the Pacific West to the United States. In giving Bagot renewed assurances regarding the mission of the "Ontario," he declared, with ironic reference to Astor's enterprise, that the government "had no thoughts of making war at present for the empire of Astoria."[14] In a letter to Rush in the same period he directed the latter to remark to Lord Castlereagh "the minuteness of the present interests, either to Great Britain or to the United States, involved in this concern; and the unwillingness, for that reason of this Government to include it among the objects of serious discussion with them."[15] In instructions drawn shortly after for the negotiation of 1818, Adams, in declining a British proposal for the arbitration by the Tsar of the two western boundary problems, wrote: "But the delineation of an unsettled boundary across the western deserts of this continent, the title to establishments on the Pacific ocean, . . . where save pretensions, there is no object to any party worth contending for—to create burdensome commissions and make solemn references to a foreign sovereign for these, appears scarcely to be necessary, if altogether justifiable."[16]

On the other hand, Adams wrote exultingly in his diary on concluding in 1819 the treaty with the Spanish minister which fixed the 42nd parallel as the boundary separating Spanish and American claims in the Pacific Northwest: "The acknowledgment of a definite line of boundary to the South Sea forms a great epocha in our history. The first proposal of it in this negotiation was my own, and I trust it is now secured beyond the reach of revocation."[17] In 1845, at the height of the Oregon crisis, on learning that Polk had again offered the British the line of the 49th parallel, Adams commented in his diary that Polk should have demanded the whole of Oregon; that in the Monroe administration

---

[14] J. Q. Adams, *Memoirs*, IV, 94; Bagot to Castlereagh, June 2, 1818, F.O. 5: 132.
[15] Adams to Rush, May 20, 1818, *A.S.P., F.R.*, IV, 854.
[16] Adams to Gallatin and Rush, July 28, 1818, *A.S.P., F.R.*, IV, 378.
[17] J. Q. Adams, *Memoirs*, IV, 275.

and in his own he had made the offer of the line of 49° under the impression that it would be rejected; that its purpose had been to preserve peace and postpone the issue until such time as the United States could maintain its full claim, by an appeal to arms, if necessary.[18]

The likelihood is that Adams' disparagements of the Oregon Country were devices of policy, a tactic of chaffering such as is often practiced by seekers of real-estate bargains. His instructions to ministers at a foreign court were, to be sure, confidential and presumably candid. But such instructions are often written with a view to being communicated. Whatever the real views of Adams, he was in this case making use, for policy purposes, of a widely held American conviction that the Oregon Country was a region without value.

Yet it is evident from the unswerving determination with which the American government defended the line of the 49th parallel west of the mountains that a national interest of major importance was believed to be at stake there. If that interest was not material, if the American public was uncertain that the Oregon Country could or should be held, if expansionism was out of bounds there, what was the nature of this interest? It was political and ideological. In the Pacific West the American public and government were groping toward a wider conception of their democratic destiny in the New World. They were seeking to eliminate Britain, and Europe in general, from that part of the Pacific West which they considered to be in the orbit of the United States. Britain and Europe were to be contained outside the United States zone. Containment was the objective which gave shape and character to the Oregon problem as soon as it emerged from the mists of the Pacific.

The struggle to contain the British—to discourage their encroachments on the territory and sphere of the United States—was an old one in the history of the republic. It began immediately after the winning of American independence, with the effort to clear the British from the Northwest Posts. It continued in the resistance made to the British project of an Indian buffer state

[18] *Ibid.*, XII, 220–221. This recollection must be discounted as a reconstruction of old age. If postponement of the issue had been in Adams' mind solely, the compromise offer of the line of 49° would hardly have been made.

north of the Ohio, the resistance which finally halted that project in the Treaty of Ghent. It figured in the determination of the American government to keep the British from access to the upper waters of the Mississippi. It reappeared in the Astoria issue and in the protracted negotiation over the boundary in the region between the Lake of the Woods and the Rocky Mountains. The fight for the line of the 49th parallel in the Oregon Country was merely the projection to the Pacific of an old, embittered controversy.

Other European states whose influence Americans wished to push from their Pacific sphere were Spain and Russia. Spain had rights and possessions on that coast antedating all the others. Yet she was the first to be pushed to one side. By a treaty, signed in 1819 and ratified in 1821, she withdrew to the line of the 42nd parallel and ceded her rights north of it to the United States. She was ceding rights that, in view of the virtual independence of Mexico, were hardly any more hers to cede. Russia was pushed by a treaty, concluded in 1824, to latitude 54°40′. England, therefore, in 1826, remained the sole European rival to be kept out of the United States zone.

The policy of containing England was backed by intense national emotions. One of the emotions was pride in American republicanism and a wish to safeguard it against the encroachments of European monarchy. Another was zeal for American social democracy and contempt for the "bastard liberty"[19] of the British, with its aristocracy and its inequalities. A third was love of American liberty and the wish to keep at arm's length the monopolies, the established church, the spirit of reaction associated with Britain. A fourth emotion was traditional hatred for the British on the part of large segments of the American public. The followers of Jefferson who controlled the federal government hated the British. They could not forget British aggressions against the United States on sea and on land before and during the War of 1812. The adherents of Jackson, the opposition after 1825, equally hated the British, as they showed in the eagerness with which they came to the support of the "Old Hero" on the occasion of his execution

[19] The term was Jefferson's. Jefferson to Astor, Nov. 9, 1813, in *Writings of Thomas Jefferson*, Andrew A. Lipscomb and Albert E. Berghs, eds. (Washington, 1903–1904), XIII, 432–434.

of two British subjects in his famous raid into East Florida. Adams, more than almost any other figure in American public life, detested the British. He nursed against them a hate described by Stratford Canning as "ravenous."[20]

The concept of containment was broad enough to draw support from divergent sources of thought.[21] It drew support from Adams and other expansionists who had caught the vision of the extension of the United States to the Pacific and who saw in containment a means of keeping the Pacific Northwest open as a preserve for the

[20] Stratford Canning to Planta, Feb. 6, 1821, F.O. 5: 157. A softening in this anti-British feeling occurred in 1823 as a result of the recognition in the two countries that they might have a common interest in preventing interference by the Holy Alliance in Latin America. Dexter Perkins has emphasized this better feeling and has held that there was a *rapprochement* of the two governments in 1823. See his *The Monroe Doctrine, 1823–1826* (Cambridge, Mass., 1932), and *AHR*, XLII (1936–37), 155. Perkins has been challenged on this emphasis by Arthur P. Whitaker in *The United States and the Independence of Latin America, 1800–1830* (Baltimore, 1941), and by Edward H. Tatum in *The United States and Europe, 1815–1823* (Berkeley, 1936), each of whom has brought important new evidence to the problem. The improvement in feeling did not in any case extend beyond 1824.

[21] The popular appeal of this objective makes understandable the course which Congress took on the Oregon issue in the period of the 1820's. The congressional course, by any other test, seems contradictory and paradoxical.

In December 1824 a recommendation was sent to Congress by Monroe that the employment of a frigate be authorized for the exploration of the mouth of the Columbia "and the coast contiguous thereto." A like recommendation was made by Adams as president in the next year. The reason for these recommendations was that the waters of the coast from the Juan de Fuca Strait southward to the California boundary were less well known than those north of parallel 51. The coastal waters south of the strait had never been as much frequented by maritime fur traders as those between 51° and the Bering Sea. The southern waters contained few sea otter, the prime object of the trade, whose natural habitat was the colder water to the north. The survey of the southern shore line by Vancouver had been less thorough than that north of the straits. In 1822 William Sturgis suggested in public letters, which were brought to Monroe's notice, that a government survey of the southern shore line be made. The survey recommendations of Monroe, and later of Adams, were a result.

The attitude of Congress toward the recommendations was a test of the interest of Congress in an ultimate acquisition of the Oregon area south of 49°. The survey would have been a primary step toward acquisition, and one to which the British government could not have objected. The recommendations of the two presidents were ignored by Congress. No naval exploring expedition was despatched to the Pacific Northwest by the American government until the Charles Wilkes Expedition of the years 1838–1842.

Yet the belligerent Floyd bill, which challenged the British presence in the Oregon Country and flaunted the convention of 1818, was adopted by the House with alacrity in 1825. The bill attracted the votes of congressmen who wished their constituents to know that they supported a policy of containing the British in the Pacific Northwest. The bill won an overwhelming majority in the House and a large vote in the Senate.

American republic. It drew support equally from the limitationists of the Benton school. To them it meant keeping the Pacific Northwest open for the democracy of a new republic. The association of these ideas in Benton's mind appears in his Terminus speech of 1825. He urged in it that if the United States would plant the germ of a new republic at the mouth of the Columbia, she would "find herself indemnified for her cares and expense about the infant power . . . in the exclusion of monarchy from her [United States] border, the frustration of the hostile schemes of Great Britain, and, above all, in the erection of a new Republic, composed of her children, speaking her language, inheriting her principles, devoted to liberty and equality, and ready to stand by her side against the combined powers of the old world."[22]

In retrospect, the fight to contain Europe in the Pacific Northwest was an interim phase of American policy. It was a negative phase. It had appeal only while the American public was uncertain of the feasibility and value of holding the Oregon Country in the Union. It attracted to the support of the demand for the 49th parallel a national sentiment that was unanimous, however divergent in origin. It kept the Oregon issue and country open until the nation was ready to follow a more positive course. It was transmuted into expansionism as soon as the progress of invention and the growth of nationalism had given Young America an opportunity to convert the nation to a program of advance to the Pacific. In the meantime, when first openly avowed as American policy in 1823, it became a major irritant in Anglo-American relations.

[22] *Congressional Debates*, 18 Cong., 2 sess. (1824–25), 712. The reasons assigned by William Sturgis, in his influential 1822 letters to the *Boston Daily Advertiser*, for wishing the American government to take military possession of Port Discovery were much the same as those given by Benton. Sturgis wished an American military post within the straits as a means of keeping England and Russia out of that area. But he believed that no actual settlement should be made by the United States on the Pacific slope. He was persuaded that no such settlement could be permanently kept in the Union. See above, note 11.

PRIOR TO 1823 no avowal was ever made by the American government of a wish to contain Europe in the Pacific Northwest. Containment was sought behind the screen of a demand for a specific line of boundary. American administrations took the paradoxical position of insisting on a boundary at the line of the 49th parallel while persuaded that territory so won could never remain permanently within the Union. Containment sought in terms of a boundary aroused no European resentment and satisfied American feeling. If it had been sought in terms of preventing the spread of European systems of society and government in America it would have generated resentment in Europe and would, in negotiations with England, have been self-defeating.

In the instructions issued to American negotiators in the early Oregon negotiations the principle of containment of Europe remained concealed. It appeared only between the lines. In the instructions issued by Monroe in 1814 to the peace commissioners of the United States at Ghent the following language was used:

On no pretext can the British Government set up a claim to territory south of the northern boundary of the United States. It is not believed that they have any claim whatever to territory on the Pacific ocean. You will, however, be careful, should a definition of boundary be attempted, not to countenance, in any manner, or in any quarter, a pretension in the British Government to territory south of that line.[1]

In the negotiation of 1818 the language used by Adams in the instructions to Gallatin and Rush was:

The new pretension, however, of disputing our title to the settlement at the mouth of Columbia river, either indicates a design on their part to encroach, by new establishments of their own, upon the forty-ninth parallel of latitude, south of which they can have no valid claim upon this continent; or it manifests a jealousy of the United States—a desire to check the progress of our settlements, of which it might have been supposed that experience would, before this day, have relieved them.[2]

In actual negotiations containment was kept even more out of sight. It was screened behind a demand for needed rivers and

[1] Monroe to the American Plenipotentiaries, March 22, 1814, *A.S.P.*, *F.R.*, III, 731.
[2] Adams to Gallatin and Rush, July 28, 1818, *ibid.*, IV, 375-378.

harbors. In the negotiation of 1818 Gallatin gravely upheld the thesis of needed rivers and harbors in the Pacific Northwest though believing that all the territory there would in the end be the possession of an independent republic.

In 1823, a bolder course was taken. Containment was lifted to the surface of American policy. It was made the announced program of the United States in the Pacific Northwest. At the same time its range was vastly expanded. It was stretched to cover the whole American hemisphere. A correlative was added to territorial containment. European states were warned against any extensions of colonial systems of trade exclusion to areas they claimed on the Pacific coast. The United States government asserted that the two Americas had come to be occupied by independent nations as a result of successful revolutions, and that they were consequently no longer open to new European colonization or extensions of colonial systems of exclusive trade.

Adams stated this thesis in an instruction sent to London for Richard Rush, in connection with the Oregon problem, on July 22, 1823. He phrased it as follows:

A necessary consequence of this state of things will be, that the American continents, henceforth, will no longer be subject to *colonization*. Occupied by civilized, independent nations, they will be accessible to Europeans, and to each other, on that footing alone; and the Pacific Ocean, in every part of it, will remain open to the navigation of all nations in like manner with the Atlantic.

Incidental to the condition of national independence and sovereignty, the rights of interior navigation of their rivers will belong to each of the American nations within its own territories.

The application of colonial principles of exclusion, therefore, cannot be admitted by the United States as lawful, upon any part of the Northwest Coast of America, or as belonging to any European nation. Their own settlements there, when organized as territorial Governments, will be adapted to the freedom of their own institutions, and as constituent parts of the Union, be subject to the principles and provisions of their Constitution.[3]

Five months after this instruction was written its thesis was incorporated, in language phrased by Adams, into the December message of President Monroe to Congress.[4] It became one of the

[3] Adams to Rush, July 22, 1823, *ibid.*, V, 792–793.
[4] *Messages and Papers of the Presidents*, II, 217–218.

three theses in the amalgam of ideas that is known as the Monroe Doctrine, the other two being: no European intervention in the affairs of the revolted states of Latin America and no American intervention in the affairs of Europe. It is itself known as the doctrine of noncolonization. It was the brain child of Adams. It is the one element in the Monroe Doctrine which is credited by historians without dissent to the Secretary of State.

It was developed in part to defend American trade interests and rights on the coast of the Pacific Northwest. It was directed, in its trade aspects, at Russia. The Russian Tsar, in 1821, had issued an extraordinary ukase closing the waters of the Northwest Coast north of the 51st parallel to non-Russian vessels. He had forbidden non-Russian vessels to come within a distance of one hundred Italian miles of the coast.[5] The decree was an encroachment on the established rights of the United States and of England. By implication it was an assertion, also, of Russian sovereignty over the whole coast north of 51°. It collided with the territorial claims of both the United States and England. It more especially collided, in that latitude, with the maritime rights of the United States and the territorial claims of England. The American and British governments contemplated a united front against Russia on this issue. Adams drew up the instruction to Rush of July 22, 1823, with this possibility in mind. On the same day that he sent off the Rush instruction he sent another of the same purport to Henry Middleton, the American minister at St. Petersburg.[6]

In March 1826, several years after the noncolonization doctrine appeared, Adams described it altogether as a principle of trade. He attributed it exclusively to the trade presumptions of the ukase of 1821. He was then President of the United States and presented this interpretation in a message to Congress in which he defended the doctrine against attacks that had been made on it by the opposition. He asserted that the doctrine rested on reasoning "equally simple and conclusive": namely, that the Americas, by virtue of having become occupied by independent states, were no longer open to extensions of colonial systems of exclusive trade.[7] This trade attribution was later taken over at its face value by his-

[5] The ukase is printed in *A.S.P., F.R.*, IV, 857–861.
[6] Adams to Middleton, July 22, 1823, *ibid.*, V, 436–437, 445.
[7] *Messages and Papers of the Presidents*, II, 334–335.

torians of the doctrine and became the standard emphasis. The doctrine was explained as a policy of the "open door" for the Pacific Northwest, a program of keeping unobstructed the avenues of trade in the New World.[8]

This explanation was too simple. It did not comport well with the language of the doctrine or the facts regarding it. One important fact which it left unexplained was that the doctrine was addressed to England as well as to Russia, and was given, in the Rush instruction, its most emphatic and detailed form. With England the United States had no issue of trade exclusion in the Pacific Northwest. On the contrary the United States and Britain had a trade agreement there, the convention of joint occupation of 1818, and Adams believed that the British government might join the American in a combined front against Russia on the ukase issue.

The ascription of the doctrine so exclusively to the Russian ukase is difficult to reconcile even with the facts regarding the ukase. The ukase was issued in the late summer of 1821. It was brought to the attention of Adams in January or February of 1822. It was followed by an extended correspondence with the Russian foreign office via the American minister in St. Petersburg and the Russian minister in Washington. Adams made no use of the doctrine of noncolonization against the ukase while it was a genuine trade issue. In August 1822 Middleton notified Adams that the Russian foreign office had assured him the ukase would not be carried out. In July 1823, when the non-colonization doctrine was formulated, the ukase had long been, as a trade problem, a dead issue.[9]

Noncolonization as a principle was not single in purpose. It was double, territorial and commercial. It was mainly territorial, and incidentally commercial. It was a ban on new colonization by Europe. Its name defines its major purpose. It was a principle of territorial containment.

It was containment in extreme form. It was containment directed no longer to a modest United States sphere of influence—to territory on the Pacific coast contiguous to that of the republic—but widened to apply to a hemisphere. The American sphere of influence was conceived to be the western world. This was a stretch-

[8] See Perkins, *The Monroe Doctrine, 1823–26*, chap. i.
[9] The documents relating to the ukase are in *A.S.P., F.R.*, V, 432–471; also in *Alaska Boundary Tribunal Proceedings*, 58 Cong., 2 sess. (1903–1904), *Sen. Documents*, No. 162, II, 31–93.

ing of concept congenial to Adams. He believed that North America, in all its length and breadth, would be absorbed some day into the United States.[10] The noncolonization doctrine seems, in his mind, to have been a measure that would keep North America open as a preserve for the republic of the United States to expand over at leisure.

Even in the case of Russia the noncolonization doctrine was largely territorial. The document in which it was explained to Middleton was entitled, "Observations on the Claim of Russia to Territorial Possessions on the Continent of North America, communicated with Mr. Adams's letter...."[11] The ascription of the doctrine so exclusively to trade and to the ukase in 1826 was a tactic of policy. In 1826 Adams had learned to his cost that the territorial emphasis of the doctrine was blocking his objectives with Canning. He was facing at that time a new Oregon negotiation with England, and was preparing to mute the territorial theme. His plenipotentiary in that negotiation was to go to the length of privately disavowing the doctrine.

The doctrine was directed, in its territorial aspects, principally at England. British containment was what was uppermost in the mind of Adams. The doctrine was given its fullest and frankest formulation in the Rush instruction. It was asserted less aggressively against Russia. In the Middleton instruction it was not even incorporated into the body of the instruction but was relegated to an accompanying document, the last of a series of ten such documents.

The challenge to England in the doctrine was given point by a proposal that accompanied it in the Rush instruction. The proposal was innocent enough on its surface but carried a sting. Rush was directed to suggest to Canning a joint occupation by three states—England, Russia, and the United States—of the Oregon Country for a period of ten years. Rush was to propose, with a view to a definitive future demarcation of boundaries, that no more British settlements be established south of the 51st parallel or north of the 55th parallel, that no more Russian settlements be made

[10] J. Q. Adams, *Memoirs*, VI, 250–251.
[11] See references cited in note 9. Adams asserted the noncolonization principle to the Russian minister in Washington orally five days before he incorporated it in the Rush and Middleton instructions. This assertion was the first appearance of the doctrine.

south of the 55th parallel, and no American north of the 51st. Should Britain earnestly insist on the 49th parallel, however, the United States would consent to carry that line to the sea, this being the boundary east of the Rocky Mountains. The sting in the instruction was the proposed restriction upon England north of the line of 55°. Adams was there intervening in an area that had hitherto been assumed to be a zone of only Anglo-Russian rivalry. What Adams had in mind in this area and in this instruction has remained an historical enigma. He was reconciled to permitting the country north of 55° to go to Russia and had proposed this to Russia in July 1823. To England, however, he showed in the instruction, he was unwilling it should go.[12]

The forces which shaped and timed the noncolonization pronouncement in the Monroe message were not crisis factors such as shaped the companion pronouncement of nonintervention. On the Northwest Coast there was no crisis in 1823 to call forth such a doctrine. The Russian situation was taken merely as an occasion for giving forth the doctrine. Adams himself suggests this in the message of 1826. How little there was of emergency in the doctrine is indicated by the proposals that accompanied it in the July 1823 instructions. They amounted to an offer to leave the region north of 49° to England and to Russia, an offer followed by a treaty in 1824 which left to Russia all the area north of 54° 40′ and also the exclusive trade of its territorial waters, subject only to the reservation to the United States of a ten year trading privilege. A trading post of the Russian American Company at Bodega Bay in California cannot have been the occasion of the pronouncement. It had been built as early as 1812, and Adams was not sufficiently alarmed by it to make it an issue in the Russian negotiation of 1824. With Britain there was similarly little in the way of crisis in 1823 on the Northwest Coast.

The enunciation of the noncolonization doctrine seemed to Albert Gallatin premature. It seemed so to him as late as 1846.[13]

---

[12] Adams may have had in mind establishing bargaining leverage in this latitude for the United States which could be used to obtain commercial concessions for American vessels from Russia in the portion of the Northwest Coast that would be assigned to Russia. This is hinted at in Richard Rush, *Memoranda of a Residence at the Court of London* (Philadelphia, 1845), 470, and in *Alaska Boundary Tribunal Proceedings*, I, pt. 1, 28.

[13] A. Gallatin, *Letters on the Oregon Question*, 17.

In 1848 Calhoun declared that the doctrine had appeared in the message of Monroe without any previous cabinet deliberation on it. He condemned it as having been impolitic, unclear in formulation, "broader than the fact"—which was a manner of saying that it was extreme—and that it exhibited "precipitancy and want of due reflection."[14]

The conception upon which the doctrine seems to have been predicated, that the United States would expand as a federal republic over all North America, was unrealistic and wild. Even today, in an age when travel has come to approach the speed of sound, the concept of a federal republic of the United States embracing the whole continent is as remote and extravagant as ever. In 1823 it was not merely extravagant, but inconsistent with other concepts of Adams. A United States authority, extending over an entire continent, inevitably meant, whatever it might be called, colonialism or autocracy. Both were abhorrent to Adams. In 1821, in a Fourth of July oration directed at Great Britain, which won Adams wide notice, he bitterly assailed colonialism as a system based on immorality.[15] Yet a United States, stretched to the dimensions of a continent, would inevitably have generated a new colonialism.

In 1823 Adams was a leading candidate for the succession to the presidency. He had proved himself an exceptionally energetic and able secretary of state. He was in a strategic office for the succession. He was the outstanding northern candidate, supported as such by states that had become sensitive on the slavery issue as a result of the clash over the admission of Missouri into the Union. In an era of virulent factional rivalries, he was the target of attack by the adherents of every other contender for the presidency. His rivals sought to fasten on him the charge that, as a New Englander, he had consistently betrayed western interests. His great diplomatic

---

[14] John C. Calhoun, *Works*, Richard K. Crallé, ed. (New York, 1853-1855), IV, 462. The instruction to Rush probably did not receive the careful scrutiny of Monroe. The President was of the opinion that any society formed in the Pacific Northwest would be beyond the reach of the American government and would necessarily, if formed, soon separate from the Union. He was of that opinion as late as March 1824. In the Rush instruction, however, the Adams thesis was asserted, that settlements formed on the Pacific coast, would, when organized as territorial governments, be "constituent parts of the Union" and "subject to the principles and provisions of their [United States] Constitution." See above, p. 128.

[15] John Quincy Adams, *An Address Delivered at the Request of a Committee of the Citizens of Washington: on the Occasion of Reading the Declaration of Independence, on the Fourth of July, 1821* (Washington, 1821).

triumph, the Adams-Onís treaty was denounced as an unnecessary sacrifice of Texas to Spain.[16] The most damaging charge hurled at him was that he had been unduly soft in dealing with England. The adherents of Clay, Floyd among them, charged, in the famous Jonathan Russell affair of 1822, that he had exhibited an undue willingness at Ghent to concede the navigation of the Mississippi River to the British—"to let the British into the heart of our country"—in exchange for the continuation to New Englanders of the fisheries liberty.[17] He was accused by Benton of having betrayed the West on the Oregon issue. Benton, on February 17, 1823, made a survey of the issue in a Senate speech which was loaded with political dynamite.[18] He read the instruction which Adams had written Gallatin and Rush in 1818, in which the New Englander had referred to the "minuteness of the present interests, either to Great Britain or to the United States, involved in this concern [Oregon]; and the unwillingness, for that reason of this Government to include it among the objects of a serious discussion with them."[19] Benton noted the fact that Prevost, the agent of the State Department who had been sent to the mouth of the Columbia in 1818 to receive the restitution of Astoria, had traveled going and coming, as a guest on a British ship of war.[20] The ominous circumstance was recalled that the convention of 1818, of which the Oregon agreement of joint occupation was part, opened with an article securing to New England fishermen the liberty of curing fish on the unsettled coasts of Newfoundland and Labrador. The joint occupation agreement itself, Benton charged, left England in virtual possession of the Oregon Country. These were charges that an aspirant to the presidency could not leave unanswered.

Adams was eager for the presidency. He had been quietly nursing the ambition throughout his secretaryship. He did not confess this freely even to himself, but his private correspondence

[16] Carl Schurz, *Henry Clay* (Boston, 1887) I, 162–165; *St. Louis Enquirer*, March 31, 1819.

[17] J. Q. Adams, *Memoirs*, index; *Writings of John Quincy Adams*, Worthington C. Ford, ed. (New York, 1913–1917), VII, 250–367; and *The Duplicate Letters, the Fisheries and the Mississippi: Documents Relating to Transactions at the Negotiation of Ghent, Collected and Published by John Quincy Adams* (Washington, 1822).

[18] *Annals of Congress*, 17 Cong., 2 sess. (1822–23), 246–251. See also *St. Louis Enquirer*, March 17, 1819.

[19] See above, pp. 35–36.

[20] See Essay I.

and his diary reveal it clearly and his family was well aware of it. He watched the maneuvers and twistings of his rivals with jealousy and bitterness of soul. His comments on them in his diary were written in acid. His Puritan conscience forbade his descent into the ring with his rivals. He believed that the office seeks the man, and not the man the office. When the opportunity offered to strike successfully at his detractors, as it did in the Jonathan Russell affair, he struck with crushing and unmerciful force. He kept this issue of personal politics alive in the press until even the appetite of that politics-hungry generation was satiated. Then he followed it up with a lengthy pamphlet.[21] His private correspondence from May 1822 to April 1823 is dominated for more than a hundred pages of printed matter by this issue.[22]

Adams realized that the most damaging of the charges against him, if permitted to stick, was that he had been weak in the face of British encroachments in the West. This was a charge to which an answer could be given without a descent into the hurly-burly of politics. Instructions issued by the Department of State on important foreign issues passed with surprising promptness into public knowledge by the road of congressional calls upon the executive for documents. The challenge to England and to Russia in the July instructions and in the December message of the President would serve as a resounding answer to detractors.

The trumpet blast of noncolonization is not to be explained primarily in these political terms. It was the expression of a universal desire of the American public to contain Europe in the Pacific West. It reflected the deepest convictions of Adams, who, like Canning, his British counterpart, identified his own intense nationalism, his inordinate expansionism, and a high tone in addressing foreign governments, with the national good. The doctrine was a typical illustration of the uncertainty of Adams' judgment, an inability to sense that tactics of aggressiveness which had been used with success against Spain in 1819 would not be profitable against England, especially in an Oregon negotiation in which real British concessions would have to precede a settlement. These elements all contributed to the doctrine. But the blast and its timing cannot be fully understood, in the absence of any real crisis and in the light of the

[21] See the references cited in note 17.
[22] J. Q. Adams, *Writings*, VII, 250–367.

risks it created in the coming British negotiation, without a recognition of the fact that July and December 1823 were the eve of a presidential election.

The doctrine was made known to Canning gingerly and piecemeal by Rush. The injection of so explosive an issue into a negotiation sufficiently difficult in itself Rush postponed as long as possible. As a first step he prepared merely a memorandum of the tri-partite partition proposal of Adams, which he carried to a conference with Canning. He found Canning confined to bed by an attack of the gout and apparently less aggressive than usual. When the foreign secretary learned that the American boundary demand had been lifted to the 51st parallel he merely ventured the remark that it was beyond anything England had anticipated. But on Rush's departure he examined the memorandum left with him and for the first time became aware of the proposed restriction on Britain at the 55th parallel. He wrote Rush immediately:

> What is here? Do I read Mr. Rush aright? The United States will agree to make no settlement north of fifty-one, on Great Britain agreeing to make none south of that line. So far all is clear. The point of contact is touched, and consequently the point of possible dispute between the United States and Great Britain; but the memorandum goes on, "or north of fifty-five"!
>
> What can this intend? Our *northern* question is with Russia as our *southern* with the United States. But do the United States mean to travel *north* to get *between* us and Russia, and do they mean to stipulate against Great Britain, in favor of Russia, or reserve to themselves whatever Russia may not want?[23]

The answer Rush was obliged to give was "that it was even so."[24]

The noncolonization doctrine was fully disclosed to Canning only after it had been made public in the Monroe message. It seemed to him the colossal impertinence of an upstart state. It seemed an attempt to interdict a process of European colonization that was as old as the voyage of Christopher Columbus. It seemed as bizarre as the doctrines that underlay the ukase of 1821. It appeared to be a challenge to British colonization of every part of the Oregon Country and of all other unappropriated portions of North America. His rage over the doctrine was intensified by the

[23] Richard Rush, *Residence at the Court of London* (Philadelphia, 1845), 468–469.
[24] *Ibid.*

section of the Monroe message in which the American government took upon itself singly to warn Europe against intervention in Latin America. That section of the message stole his own thunder. It asserted for the United States the role of protector of Latin America, which he was ambitious to play in the eyes of the world and in the eyes of his British constituents. His rage over these elements in the message burned in him throughout his final years as Foreign Secretary and as Prime Minister.

As a result Anglo-American issues became exacerbated. Those relating to the Pacific Northwest became impossible to settle. The project of a joint Anglo-American negotiation with Russia over the ukase issue ended in failure, and this was the prelude to the failure of the separate Anglo-American negotiation over Oregon, begun early in 1823. In the separate negotiation, the noncolonization doctrine, finally resorted to by Rush as a support to the American position in the Oregon Country, was met by a flat denial of its validity on the part of the British: "The British plenipotentiaries asserted, in utter denial of the above principle, that they considered the unoccupied parts of America just as much open as heretofore to colonization by Great Britain."[25] According to Rush, the anger of Canning over the noncolonization doctrine was chiefly responsible for the stalemate in which this negotiation, like the preceding one, ended.[26]

In 1826 Canning was still at white heat. His anger had become intensified by the growing agitation in Congress for the military occupation of the mouth of the Columbia. To Canning, noncolonization and the agitation were components of a single American policy of aggression. They aroused all his combative instincts.

In 1826 Adams, now president, was ready to subordinate the preaching of noncolonization to the practical necessities of negotiation. He had learned prudence from the reception accorded by Canning to his doctrine. In the instructions which he drew for the Gallatin negotiation, he permitted the doctrine quietly to recede into the shadows cast by concrete demands. He swerved "not an inch of ground" from the demand for the 49th parallel, and he

---

[25] *A.S.P., F.R.,* V, 563.
[26] Rush, *Residence at the Court of London,* 470–475. Canning to British Commissioners, May 31, 1824, *Some Official Correspondence of George Canning,* Edward J. Stapleton, ed. (London, 1887), II, 76–85; Hughes to Gallatin, Dec. 10, 1826, Gallatin Papers, New-York Historical Society. See also Gallatin to Clay, Dec. 20, 1826, *A.S.P., F.R.,* VI, 658–659.

made clear privately to Gallatin that he had not changed his views as to his principle.[27] But he permitted the didactics of the doctrine to be withheld. Of this withholding Gallatin made full use for purposes of conciliation. He did so to a degree that might have startled Adams had he known it. At the third meeting with the British plenipotentiaries, according to a report made to Canning, Gallatin

repeated with some emphasis an observation which he had already made with respect to the denial of the right of future colonization by Europeans in any portion of the New World, of a principle which had been maintained by his predecessor (Mr. Rush) in conformity with the language of the then President of the United States, Mr. Monroe. That doctrine, Mr. Gallatin said, he had no instructions to put forward, or even touch upon. The Committee of the House of Representatives, he added, had in their report on the subject of the Columbia River, made during the last session of Congress, disclaimed the principle advanced by Mr. Monroe; that the American Government, also, had no intention of acting upon it was evident from the circumstance of their having proposed to Great Britain a certain line of boundary beyond which it was clear that the latter would have the right and power to establish whatever colonies they pleased. It could not be expected, Mr. Gallatin added, that a Government should go further than this in renouncing a doctrine once avowed by them, but we might judge of their intentions by their acts.[28]

This private disavowal by a minister of the United States of a declared policy of his government is a measure of the feeling which that policy had aroused in British foreign office circles. It registered temperatures that had to be reduced. It was a measure of the difficulty of the task which Gallatin faced in 1826.

[27] On March 20, 1827, the President privately wrote Gallatin: "For the causes of this present soreness of feeling we must doubtless look deeper than to the report of a committee of our House of Representatives, or to the assertion by the late President that the American continents were no more subject to future colonization from Europe. As the assertion of this principle is an attitude which the American hemisphere must assume, it is one which no European power has the right to question; and if the inference drawn from it of danger to *existing* colonies has any foundation, it can only be on the contingency of a war, which we shall by all possible means avoid. . . ." A. Gallatin, *Writings*, II, 366–367.

[28] Huskisson and Addington to Canning, Dec. 7, 1826, F.O. 5:219. The Baylies report to which Gallatin referred, contained the comment on the noncolonization project: "We do not propose to enter into the discussion of the principle asserted by Mr. Monroe, that no part of the continent of North America is now to be considered as open to European colonization. For ourselves we can only say that we are not disposed to quarrel with any nation for colonizing any portion of the American wilderness, without the limits of the United States." 19 Cong., 1 sess., *H. Reports* (1825–26), No. 213, p. 14.

IN ENGLAND there was no public opinion comparable to the American on the Oregon question. None had been raised by persistent agitation. Public discussion of the question was conspicuously absent. There was no Oregon debate in Parliament at any time prior to 1840; indeed, hardly any thereafter. No parliamentary committee report on the issue ever appeared. The question was similarly unnoticed before the forties in the British press. The forces shaping Oregon policy in England were under the surface; they operated more quietly than in the United States.

Most active of the forces shaping Oregon policy was the Hudson's Bay Company after 1821. The Company was almost the only direct force. Its influence was exerted privately; it preferred to remain out of public sight. It published no reports. It discouraged publication by its employees even of narratives of their adventures in the fur trade. Its method was to persuade cabinet members in strategic positions. It exerted influence especially on Canning, who, in the years from 1822 to the time of his death in 1827, very nearly determined the Oregon policy of the British government.

The influence exerted by the Company was not due to any major trade interest that it guarded in the Columbia valley. The Columbia trade of the Company, in terms of empire values, was surprisingly slight. The extent of it was indicated by Governor Simpson in response to a query presented to him in the Addington questionnaire. The query concerned the annual profits of the Company in the Columbia district and whether the profits arose principally from the northern or the southern part of the district. Simpson evaded the issue of the profits. He gave instead the somewhat more impressive figure of the gross value of the furs taken. The gross value he gave was between £30,000 and £40,000, which was divided about equally between the northern and the southern parts of the Columbia valley. This was a total less than the gross of many a Lancashire textile establishment. Simpson was careful to preface his testimony by the observation that the trade of the Columbia was yet in its infancy, which was, however, an opinion of doubtful accuracy.[1]

[1] *Fur Trade and Empire*, Merk, ed., 263.

The explanation of the Company's influence with Canning was probably the identity of its aims and his. Its representations of facts and its formulations of policy lent support to positions he wished to take in the Cabinet regarding the building of the empire and the stimulation of British trade. In Gallatin's opinion the Company exerted a smaller influence on Oregon policy than the North West Company had once done. Gallatin expressed this view at the close of his negotiation. He did not explain the decline, but it was probably the result of the growing objection in England to all government-intrenched monopolies. Gallatin reported, however, that the Company had been and would continue to be the principal bar to a definitive settlement of the boundary. "Of the monopolizing, rapacious, and unfriendly disposition of that company," he reported to Clay, "you are well apprised."[2] One indication of its influence was the ready response Canning made to the letter of the London governor suggesting the reopening of the Oregon negotiation.

Emotional forces were important elements shaping British Oregon policy. One of them was the pride Britons felt in the Empire, in the magnitude of the Empire, in the thought that upon the Empire the sun never set. Englishmen were stirred by the very remoteness of the Northwest Coast, by the thought that in this far corner of the world there would some day rise a flourishing British colony and commerce. These were emotions that found reflection in the columns of the London *Times*. They were the spirit of Canning.

Of the same substance were British recollections of the triumph of Pitt over the Spanish in the Nootka Sound affair. To many Britons the Northwest Coast and Nootka Sound were synonymous terms. Gallatin was struck by the importance of the Nootka Sound tradition in British thinking on the Oregon issue. It was especially a factor in the thinking of Canning, who was a disciple and a political heir of Pitt.[3]

But by no means all Britons viewed the Empire with pride. Some—the philosophically minded "little Englanders"—viewed it as a liability. They believed that England had attained greatness

[2] Gallatin to Clay, August 10, 1827, *A.S.P., F.R.*, VI, 694.
[3] *Ibid.*; also Canning to British Commissioners, May 31, 1824, in *Some Official Correspondence of George Canning*, II, 78.

and prosperity not by any possession of colonies, but by capacity to manufacture cheaper and better and to carry on commerce more profitably than other nations. They regarded colonies, British North America particularly, which cost more to administer than the revenue they produced, as a drain on the mother country. In 1825 John Ramsay McCulloch, the eminent Scottish statistician and economist who was a leading exponent of such views, declared in an article in the *Edinburgh Review:* "We defy any one to point out a single benefit, of any sort whatever, derived by us from the possession of Canada, and our other colonies in North America. They are productive of heavy expense to Great Britain, but of nothing else." "Every man of sense," McCulloch affirmed "knows, that Canada must, at no distant period, be merged in the American republic."[4] Such a fate for Canada many Englishmen, including Alexander Baring, contemplated with equanimity.

"Little Englanders" believed that the Pacific Northwest would become an independent state. It would, they were sure, follow the course which the Latin American provinces of Spain and, earlier, the United States had taken. The spectacle of the dissolution, continent wide, of the Spanish empire in America profoundly affected the thinking of these men. The independence of the Latin American states had had for its immediate effect a great enlargement of British markets, profits, and influence in diplomacy. The prospect that the Pacific Northwest would become independent was welcome to them for similar reasons.[5] But if the philosophy of the "little Englanders" touched some members of the British government it had no place in the thinking of Canning.

Other emotional forces than the love of empire stamped themselves upon British Oregon policy. Among them was jealousy and apprehension of the growth of the United States. Jealousy was keen regarding the territorial expansion of the republic. The United States in 1783 had extended westward only to the Mississippi. In 1803 it had advanced at one stride to the Rocky Mountains. In 1812 it had declared war in order, so the English believed, to conquer Canada. During the war it had edged into

---

[4] XLII (1825), 291–292. For an indignant reply to this article see *Quarterly Review*, XXXIII (1825–26), 410–429.

[5] Alexander Baring was an illustration of the "Little Englander" who believed that an independent state would rise in the Pacific Northwest. He was a merchant prince of London.

West Florida. In 1819–1821, it had acquired East Florida and, in addition, Spanish rights to a large part of the Northwest Coast. Its citizens and its ambitions were flowing into Texas. The United States was becoming the colossus of the New World. Its population was increasing by geometric progression. Of this increase a considerable part was drawn by immigration from Britain.

Even greater jealousy and anxiety was felt in England regarding the sea growth of the United States, the expansion of the American merchant marine. That development seemed to the British a challenge to them in their traditional sphere of supremacy. The American merchant marine had grown phenomenally during the quarter century of the wars of the French Revolution, when it was the only important neutral carrier on the ocean. It had become, next to the British, the greatest in existence. The alarm that its growth had caused in England had been a major factor in producing the War of 1812. In the period following the war, a period of intense shipping depression and severe competition for freights, Americans were outdistancing the British. They seemed to be gaining on the British in all the commerce lanes of the world. They seemed especially to be gaining in the Pacific.

The commerce gains of the Americans in the Pacific were attributed in England to the privileges in the China trade held by the East India Company. Under an ancient charter, that company had once possessed sole rights of British trade between Britain and all the coasts and islands in the Pacific and Indian oceans. In 1813 Parliament had passed a statute which paved the way for the termination of the China monopoly. Under the statute the India trade was opened at once to independents. However, the sole and exclusive rights of British trade to and from China and the sole British rights in the tea trade to and from all places between the Strait of Magellan and the Cape of Good Hope were continued to 1834. Parliament had also provided, in the interests of the East India Company, that any British vessel clearing for a port within the Company's limits must be of a burden of at least 350 tons.[6]

The Pacific coasts of North and South America lay within the

---

[6] *British Statutes*, 53 George III, c. 155. The act provided that after 1831, on three years notice by Parliament, the China monopoly of the Company should expire.

Company's limits. Britons could ship furs from those coasts to China only in vessels of the Company. In 1793, following the Nootka Sound affair, Parliament had somewhat eased this restriction. It had permitted independent traders to ship furs from the Northwest Coast to China in vessels which the East India Company licensed.[7] The Company felt obliged, in view of Parliament's action, to grant such licenses whenever applied for. But it required the furs so shipped to be sold in China for bills of exchange or cash. Furs could not be bartered for tea or other China produce, which meant a reduction in their sales value by 20 per cent or more. The vessels bringing the furs had to sail away empty from China or be sold. Finally, the 350-ton requirement on vessels clearing for points within the Company's limits meant the virtual exclusion of British vessels from the trade between the Northwest Coast and China since on the Northwest Coast smaller vessels were better suited to enter the bays for furs. The net effect of the Company's restrictions was to make of the Pacific what Richard Rush in 1819 described as a "void" in British independent enterprise.[8]

Into this void American enterprise sailed. At Canton, Americans developed a trade in the years between the close of the American Revolution and the early 1820's which was of greater value than that of the East India Company. In 1818 no less than 214 American vessels, according to a list offered in evidence before a committee of the British House of Lords, were absent from the United States on trading voyages to China and India.[9] American vessels not only supplied the markets of the United States, formerly the possession of the British, with all the tea, silk, and other oriental goods consumed, but those of continental Europe with nearly all their tea requirements. Americans even did the carrying from British ports to China of British manufactures, a trade from which British independents were excluded.

An outcry was raised in England against these burdens on British commerce in the Pacific. It was an outcry led by the shipping and commercial interests. Its climax came in 1820–21, when, in both houses of Parliament, committees were investigating and holding

[7] *Ibid.*, 33 George III, c. 52.
[8] Rush to Adams, April 14, 1819, State Department, England, Despatches, 23. Rush gives a graphic account, in this despatch, of the British alarm over the growth of American commerce in the Pacific.
[9] *British Parliamentary Papers*, 1821, VII, Document 476, pp. 88–91.

hearings on the problem.[10] In the testimony submitted to these committees the opponents of the East India Company all came to similar conclusions. British shipping was being rapidly replaced, in the commerce of the Pacific, by American. Even without the fettering restrictions of the Company, British vessels could barely meet American competition. Vessels in which the trade to the Orient was best carried, vessels of small tonnage, were more cheaply built in the United States, where timber costs and taxes were lower, than in England. Vessels of every tonnage were more cheaply victualed in the United States than in England. American seamen were, in general, superior in character and in enterprise to the British. They were normally permitted to operate, in the trade of the Northwest Coast, on shares with the owners. The trade to the Orient was highly profitable to Americans. Its profits equaled the cost of the entire consumption of oriental produce in the United States, as affirmed in a report made to Congress by the Lowndes committee on currency.[11] This rich trade, and indeed the Pacific, was being bestowed, critics maintained, upon Americans by the shackles which the East India Company imposed on British commerce.

In 1820 Edward Ellice, a prominent member of Parliament and partner in the North West Company, testified before the Lord's Committee on the baneful effects exerted by the East India Company privileges on the trade between the Northwest Coast and China. He did so in terms of the experiences of his own company. He testified that his company had experimented for several years with fur shipments in its own vessels, under license from the East India Company to China. The experiment had failed because the furs could not be exchanged for tea and the vessels had been obliged to sail from China empty. The North West Company had been forced to turn to Americans to market its furs in China. The mode of operation that had been adopted was to ship British manufactures in a British vessel to the American port of Boston. At Boston the goods were delivered to the American house of Perkins and Company. They were shipped in a vessel of that company to the mouth of the Columbia. The goods were there left with the

[10] See *Brit. Parl. Papers*, 1821, VI, Doc. 746; VII, Doc. 476.
[11] *Ibid.*, VII, Doc. 476, p. 6. The Lowndes report is in *Annals of Congress*, 15 Cong., 2 sess. (1818–19), 791.

agents of the North West Company. In the same vessel, under the American flag, the North West Company's furs were taken to China. So taken, they could be bartered freely for teas or other China produce. The return cargo was sent to the United States for sale. For these services Perkins and Company were paid a percentage of the proceeds. The savings effected by the North West Company, under this mode of marketing, as against the license system of the East India Company, were declared by Ellice to amount to 50 per cent.[12]

In reply to such critics the spokesmen of the East India Company denied that the privileges of the Company were an adverse influence on the total of British commerce in the Orient. They denied especially that any connection existed between the Company's privileges and such growth as had occurred in American oriental shipping. They attributed the initial American growth to the fact that for almost a quarter of a century Americans had been able to take advantage of the absorption of Europe in fighting. The postwar growth they minimized. Such postwar growth as had occurred they explained in terms of the cheapness of American shipbuilding, the low rate of American taxes, and the willingness of American traders to deal in teas of inferior quality.[13]

The trade from the Northwest Coast to China in American vessels the East India Company spokesman declared to be of slight extent. From statistical tables, based in part on an American authority, Adam Seybert, they showed that in 1818–19 the value of the furs taken to China by Americans was $372,000 as compared with $7,414,000 in silver dollars and a total of all American imports into China of $10,017,000. From other Seybert tables they showed that the Northwest Coast trade of Americans had been at its height in 1799–1800, and that it had since steadily declined, with the single exception of the year 1816–17.[14]

The attitude of the British government on this issue was that the privileges of the East India Company were an unfortunate inheri-

[12] *Brit. Parl. Papers*, 1821, VII, Doc. 476, pp. 92–100.
[13] *Ibid.*, VII. See especially the testimony of Charles Grant, a director of the East India Company, pp. 155–195, and accompanying tables. See also VI, Doc. 746, pp. 302–325.
[14] *Ibid.*; also Adam Seybert, *Statistical Annals* (Philadelphia), 1818. The increase occurring in 1816–17 is probably a reflection of the arrangement made between the North West Company and Perkins and Company described by Ellice.

tance from the past, that they should be restricted within the narrowest limits legally possible, but that they bound the state and must be endured until they expired in 1834. This was the attitude of Canning. In 1820, when he was President of the India Board, he strongly urged the Company to relinquish some of its less used privileges in the interests of the nation, but when the Company refused to yield he accepted its decision.[15]

The Orient was to Canning, as it was to all imaginative statesmen of his day, a vast unexploited opportunity. Its fabled wealth, its teeming millions, its stores of teas, silks, and spices—all the elements that had once fired the mind of Marco Polo—were an invitation still held out to the West. The East was a golden market to which Britain would send, once the fetters of the East India Company had been broken, her surplus for exchange.

It was against such a background that the Oregon issue was projected in Canning's thinking. The issue had for Canning a setting strikingly like that which Benton and Floyd gave it in Congress, though its ending was hardly the same. The trade of the Columbia valley, still slight, would expand. The Columbia would become the seat of a flourishing British colony. Between it and the Orient and Britain would flow a world-circling commerce that would be the glory and the power of Britain. This was the vision by which the policy of Canning was shaped when he became secretary for foreign affairs in Liverpool's cabinet.[16]

British apprehensions regarding the growth of the American merchant marine were evident elsewhere than in the Orient. During the period of Gallatin's London negotiation they were evident particularly in the British West Indies. The trade of the British West Indies had once been of mutual advantage to Americans and to the islanders. Food and lumber, which could not be produced in sufficient quantity in the islands, nor obtained at low enough prices from British North America, had been brought from New England. In exchange molasses had been given, for which New England afforded the best market. This exchange was desired by the island planters on as free a basis as possible. It was opposed by

---

[15] Canning to Chairman of the East India Company, May 17, 1820, *Brit. Parl. Papers*, 1821, VII, Doc. 476, pp. 393–394; and Robinson to Canning, June 7, 1820, *ibid.*, 394–399.

[16] See below, pp. 158–159.

other empire interests, especially by the British shipping interests, which expected to have a monopoly of the carrying trade within the empire, and by the maritime provinces of British North America, which expected to have their stake in the markets of the islands protected. After the American Revolution pressure was exerted in England to have restrictions placed on the trade of the revolted colonies with the islands. The result was that the trade was kept on a precarious basis, opened by orders in council when food shortages developed in the islands and kept closed at other times.[17]

In 1822, under an act of Parliament, sponsored by Castlereagh and Robinson, the trade was opened to vessels of the United States on a basis approaching reciprocity. The result was that the trade and the carrying had been virtually engrossed by the Americans. In 1825 Parliament, under the leadership of William Huskisson, adopted a far-reaching series of laws covering trade and navigation in the whole empire. The series was part of Huskisson's great program of reform of the trade and navigation system. By one of the laws new rates of duty were established on foreign imports into the islands. By another the trade between the islands and Great Britain was restricted to British ships. By a third law an offer was made to throw open the foreign trade of all British colonies, including the islands, to any foreign countries which, having colonies, would extend similar privileges to British ships in their colonies or which, having no colonies, would extend most-favored-nation privileges to British ships. The laws were intricate. It was impossible, without authoritative explanation of them, to determine their bearing on American commerce with the islands. The American Department of State and committees of Congress, after careful consideration of the offer contained in them, decided to attempt nothing in the form of legislation but to leave the problem to negotiation.

Gallatin was given instructions to deal with the problem. On arriving in England, he was confronted by a British order in council closing the islands to American vessels on the ground that the offer

[17] An admirable exposition of British policy is found in Gerald S. Graham, *Sea Power and British North America, 1783–1820*, Harvard Historical Studies, XLVI (Cambridge, Mass., 1941). A good study by an American is Vernon G. Setser, *The Commercial Reciprocity Policy of the United States* (Philadelphia, 1937).

contained in the statutes of 1825 had not been acted on by the American government in time. The order in council was the work primarily of Canning and Huskisson, whose interests in the reform of the British navigation system were outweighed, where the United States was concerned, by apprehensions over the growth of the American merchant marine. Gallatin sought vainly throughout his mission in London to obtain a revocation of the order. His negotiation regarding Oregon was dogged, as it had been in 1818, by a clash over a different issue on which the British were peculiarly sensitive.

British apprehension over the growth of the American merchant marine extended to the allied problem of naval supremacy. A merchant marine is the nursery of a navy. If the American merchant marine were to equal the British, the American navy would not long remain inferior to the British. In the War of 1812 the American navy had given a good account of itself, hopelessly outnumbered though it was. In individual encounters at sea and in fleet actions on the Great Lakes it had outfought the British. Its successes had been a rude shock to the British. In any future general war the United States would be aligned, it was assumed, with France. She had been thus aligned in the two preceding wars. The prospect of such a combination, when the navy of the United States would equal England's was not attractive to the British.

In the writings and speeches of British publicists and statesmen these apprehensions were a recurring theme. They began to appear as early as the Napoleonic wars. In 1805 they appeared in the widely read and widely influential pamphlet of James Stephen, *War in Disguise; or, The Frauds of the Neutral Flags*. This pamphlet, written to the thesis that the ostensibly neutral commerce carried between the West Indies and continental Europe was actually a contraband trade and a vital service to Napoleon, gave warning to the British public that the expanded marine of the United States, which was a "vast excrescence" on the natural body of the American marine, was one that "in various quarters, is peculiarly likely to displace, by its extended dimensions, the maritime interests of England."[18]

[18] James Stephen, *War in Disguise; or, The Frauds of the Neutral Flags* (London, 1805), 135.

In the period of the 1820's such views were privately or publicly expressed by the two members of the British government who were the most intimately concerned with the Oregon negotiation, Canning and Huskisson. They were expressed in 1824 by Canning with great clarity in a memorandum prepared for the members of the British government on the question of the revolted new states of Latin America:

Lastly: We have spoken of the United States of North America as our rivals in commerce and influence with the New States; but there is another and more formidable light in which they should be viewed.

The great and favourite object of the policy of this country for more than four centuries has been to foster and encourage our navigation, as the sure basis of our maritime power. In this branch of national industry the people of the United States are become more formidable rivals to us than any nation which has ever yet existed; more so even than the Dutch, whose rivalry in this respect occasioned several successive wars between the two countries.

The views and policy of the North Americans seem mainly directed towards supplanting us in navigation in every quarter of the globe, but more particularly in the seas contiguous to America.

Let us recollect that as their commercial marine is augmented their military marine must proportionately increase. And it cannot be doubted that if we provoke the New States of America to give a decided preference in their ports to the people of the United States over ourselves, the navigation of these extensive dominions will be lost to us and will in a great measure be transferred to our rivals.

Let us remember, then, that peace, however desirable, and however cherished by us, cannot last for ever. Sooner or later we shall probably have to contend with the combined maritime power of France and of the United States. The disposition of the New States is at present highly favourable to England. If we take advantage of that disposition, we may establish through our influence with them a fair counterpoise to that combined maritime power.[19]

Similar views were given public expression by Huskisson in a widely noticed speech in Parliament in May 1826—the speech which proved to be the forecast of the order in council closing the British West Indies to American vessels. The United States, Huskisson declared, is England's most formidable rival "in commerce, in

---

[19] Canning Memorandum, Nov. 30, 1824, in *Despatches, Correspondence and Memoranda of Arthur Duke of Wellington*, Arthur R. Wellesley, ed. (London, 1867–1880), II, 358.

navigation, in naval power, and maritime pretensions." It had obtained an unfair and unwise preference in the West Indian Trade Act of 1822.

Upon what principle of fairness, upon what principle of sound policy, were we to continue this preference exclusively to a power, towards which, God knows, I entertain no feeling of hostility—far from it; but, when I am speaking of that nation in a British House of Commons, it is not improper to say, that in matters of navigation and naval power, there exists, towards us, a spirit of rivalry in the United States; a spirit of which I do not complain, but which incline every Englishman to doubt the wisdom of any measure, tending to encourage the growth of the commercial marine of America, by giving to it privileges greater than are permitted to the shipping of other states—states less jealous of our maritime ascendancy in time of war, and, at all times, confining their views upon the ocean to the industrious employment of their sea-faring people, without looking to the ulterior object of one day disputing with us the dominion of that ocean.[20]

Not merely jealousy but a general ill will was nursed by the governing classes of England against the United States. The ill will was in part a residue of the bitterness evoked by the War of 1812. But it was more deep-seated. The United States was regarded by the British governing classes as a rebellious and ungrateful child that had twice, in unnatural alliance with a traditional foe, made war on its parent. Its republican form of government was an affront. Its democratic cast of society was a menace. Its very successes, broadcast by the Radicals in the opposition, seemed to threaten the established order in England.

The press of upper class society gave unmistakable evidence of this ill will. The London *Times*, the Tory press, and the conservative Whig press, were all hostile to the United States. *The Times*, the most powerful of British journals, was outstandingly hostile. It exhibited this feeling in a consistent high-lighting of the clashes that occurred between the two countries, and in a steady, carping criticism of things American. In 1818 it sought to stir up an exhausted people to a new war pitch over Jackson's raid into East Florida and his execution of Arbuthnot and Ambrister. It kept that issue alive throughout the Anglo-American negotiation of 1818 and well into 1819. It denounced as stupidities and as weakness any

---

[20] *Hansard's*, 2nd ser. XV (1826), 1182. Another statement by Huskisson of the same tenor is found in *ibid.*, XVII (1827), 646–647.

concessions Castlereagh made to the United States. In discussing things and persons American its habit was to refer to them sneeringly as "republican," which, in its columns, was a term of reproach. It demanded that the navigation policy of England be based on the assumption that the United States was a rival to England in peace and a likely enemy again in war.[21] It regarded British subjects who emigrated to the United States, if of the better class, as guilty of the crime of ingratitude to their country; if of the class described by Morris Birkbeck as having settled in Illinois, it dismissed them as a "bad set," whom it was a happiness to have got quit of, though it was the government's duty to prevent others from following their example. It represented American society as a mixture of boorishness and vulgarity. The tone it maintained toward the United States was a lofty superiority and the criticisms it offered were poisoned by sarcasm and the barbed remark.[22]

Yet society in England was far from unanimous in such hostility to the United States. The commercial interests in England, especially those favoring freer British navigation and trade laws, were, in general, well disposed toward the American republic. Liverpool, the chief center of British-American trade, was a traditional center of pro-Americanism. In the manufacturing cities that relied on the United States for markets and raw materials there was friendly understanding. Individuals in every British party and class were tolerant toward the United States. Alexander Baring, a Tory of the liberal wing, was an old advocate of Anglo-American reconciliation. In a pamphlet entitled *An Inquiry into the Causes and Consequences of the Orders in Council*, published in 1808 as a reply to Stephen's *War in Disguise*, he urged that the success and prosperity of the United States ought to be welcomed in England, that three-fourths of the proceeds of the sale of American produce on the continent of Europe was paid ultimately to England in the purchase of British manufactures.[23] Brougham, a champion of the United States in the fight over the orders in council prior to the War of 1812, continued to be after the war a consistent advocate of Anglo-American reconciliation. Castlereagh, a high Tory, sought quietly to improve Anglo-American relations.

[21] *The Times*, May 14, 1818.
[22] This characterization rests on an examination of the London *Times* for the years 1818–1828.
[23] See especially p. 162 of the pamphlet.

Even the *Times* occasionally relented in its anti-Americanism. In 1818 it printed a protest from one of its readers against its editorial thesis that America was the rival of England in peace and might be again an enemy in war. This was the protest:

It is somewhat difficult to perceive how that nation should be our enemy in peace which, in its habits, its laws, its institutions, and its language, most resembles our own, and which, owing to the influence of all these reasons, is our best and most extensive customer. . . . Consider but for a moment the relative positions of the two countries, and observe the raw material she affords for us to work up, and recollect how the industry of our people is supported by her demand for manufactured articles of every description. Ask Staffordshire, and the county palatine of Lancaster; ask Birmingham; nay, ask London herself, what they experienced when that valuable market was interrupted; and is there not every reason for union, and none for quarrel?[24]

An especially vigorous friendliness toward the United States was maintained in the 1820's by a small group in British politics, the Radical Whigs. This group not merely defended, it lauded the United States. It held up democratic America as an example for Parliament to follow. In democratic America, it pointed out, stability and order were maintained without repressive "Six Acts"; the franchise was reformed; government was economical; taxes were low; the masses were spared the burdens of sinecures, extravagance, and inefficiency; religious equality was assured to Catholics and every other religious group; commerce was unhampered by trade or navigation monopolies; a general prosperity prevailed in contrast to the dislocation and misery prevalent in England during much of the postwar period.[25]

Such views the Radicals carried to the public in the columns of the crusading London daily, the *Morning Chronicle*. They spread them, also, in such weekly or provincial journals as the *Examiner*, the *Manchester Guardian*, and the *Scotsman* of Edinburgh. The *Edinburgh Review*, the leading Whig quarterly, exhibited such leanings on occasion. The political figure from whom the Radicals took their inspiration was Charles James Fox, the Whig, who

[24] *The Times*, May 22, 1818.
[25] This characterization is based on an examination of the *Morning Chronicle* from 1818 to 1828. I have also examined the *Edinburgh Review* and a broken set of the *Scotsman* for this period.

throughout his life had been a champion of Anglo-American reconciliation.

But the Radicals were a minority and a discredited one. In 1826 the prevailing disposition of the British public and government was unfriendliness toward the United States. Gallatin believed the unfriendliness greater than it had been at the close of the War of 1812. He wrote Clay shortly after his arrival in London:

There is certainly an alteration in the disposition of this Government towards the United States since the year 1818, when I was last here. Lord Castlereagh and Mr. Robinson had it more at heart to cherish friendly relations than Mr. Canning and Mr. Huskisson. The difference may however be in the times rather than in the men. Treated in general with considerable arrogance till the last war, with great attention, if not respect during the years that followed it, the United States are now an object of jealousy and a policy founded on that feeling, has been avowed.[26]

In October 1826, shortly before the opening of his negotiation, Gallatin wrote this private warning to the President:

Although all my faculties are exerted . . . in trying to accommodate differences and to remove causes of rupture, it is impossible for me not to see and feel the temper that prevails here towards us. It is perceptible in every quarter and on every occasion, quite changed from what it was in 1815–21; nearly as bad as before the last war, only they hate more and despise less, though they still affect to conceal hatred under the appearance of contempt. I would not say this to any but to you and your confidential advisers, and I say it not in order to excite corresponding feelings, but because I think that we must look forward and make those gradual preparations which will make us ready for any emergency, and which may be sufficient to preserve us from the apprehended danger.[27]

In April 1827, near the end of his mission, Gallatin again wrote:

I do not believe that there is a single question between us in which the Ministers will not be supported by the public opinion of the country in taking rank ground against us. Our dependence for friendly arrangements rests solely on the superior sense of the Ministers.[28]

[26] Gallatin to Clay, Sept. 22, 1826, Gallatin Papers, N.-Y.H.S., Mission to England, May 3–Dec. 19, 1826.
[27] Henry Adams, *Life of Albert Gallatin* (Philadelphia, 1879), 621.
[28] Gallatin to Clay, April 28, 1827, Gallatin, *Writings*, II, 371–372.

CHAPTER V · THE BRITISH CABINET
AND THE OREGON ISSUE

THE MINISTERS in the British Cabinet upon whose "superior sense" Gallatin was obliged to depend in the negotiation of 1826–27 were Canning and Huskisson. They were the members of the Cabinet with whom he had direct contact. They were hardly a safe dependence for any American seeking friendly arrangements from Britain. Canning had been an obstacle to such arrangements for years. In the critical period, 1807–1809, when the United States was being subjected to the injuries and indignities from which it finally took refuge in war, he occupied the Foreign Office. His was the spirit which appeared in the famous November orders of 1807, the orders that, together with impressment, were the grievances which eventually drove the United States to war; his was the reluctance to make amends for the outrage of the Leopard-Chesapeake affair; and his was the disavowal of the Erskine agreement, which might have preserved the peace, a disavowal which he accompanied with the insulting charge that the American government had deliberately overreached Erskine.

In his second term as foreign minister, from 1822 to 1827, Canning was as implacable against the United States as in the first. He was hot with resentment over the Monroe message of December 1823; he was annoyed by the agitation in Congress over the Oregon issue; he was distrustful of American purposes in Cuba. He detested the republicanism of the United States; he was utterly and openly contemptuous of its democracy; he thought its government tricky. His mood in dealing with the American government is indicated in a note he sent Liverpool in 1825, after an interview with the aged Rufus King regarding the future of Cuba:

I set him right upon these points; on which, if his Government blunder as sincerely as he appears to do, there is perhaps no harm done beyond the loss of time, but if—as the suspicion sometimes comes across me—this bonhomie is affected by the U.S.G. for the express purpose of being enabled to cry out and take a new line on the disappointment of their groundless expectations, why then the Yankees may be just the rogues that we have always hitherto taken them to be, but which I was willing to hope they might have resolved to be no longer.[1]

In any territorial issue in which Britain was concerned Canning was a true disciple of Pitt, an intense nationalist and imperialist. At his death the London *Times*, which was his devoted admirer in his later years, eulogized him "as an eloquent expounder and advocate of that policy which fixed a lever on every foreign soil whereby to raise the British empire to honour and prosperity."[2] The Oregon Country was soil that he believed would raise the British empire to honor and prosperity, and the Hudson's Bay Company was the lever by which he hoped to do it.

Huskisson was a personal and political follower of Canning. He owed his admission into the Cabinet to Canning's influence. He shared Canning's jealousy of the maritime growth of the United States. He was not otherwise, however, in the opinion of Gallatin, hostile to the United States.[3] On the Oregon issue he seemed to Gallatin to hold temperate views.

The Cabinet, in the spring of 1826, when renewed discussions of the Oregon question began, was the same Tory body that had been in office in the two earlier Oregon negotiations. It had been in power since the beginning of the War of 1812 and, with growing age, had become increasingly inharmonious. Until the spring of 1827 it was held together by the tact and character of its leader, a moderate, Lord Liverpool. It consisted of three groups, a nucleus of ultra Tories and high churchmen, a moderate group, and a Canning element comprising, chiefly, Canning and Huskisson. The ultra Tories distrusted and disliked Canning. They did so largely on personal grounds, though also on account of his advocacy of Catholic emancipation. They remembered, and did not forgive, the intrigue he had earlier carried on in the Cabinet against Castlereagh, ending in a duel. They considered him underhanded, an adventurer in politics, an insincere rhetorician, a man possessed of "talents without character."[4] So deep was their distrust of him that when,

---

[1] Canning to Liverpool, August 6, 1825, *Some Official Correspondence of George Canning*, I, 283.
[2] *The Times*, Oct. 16, 1827.
[3] Gallatin to Clay, August 14, 1827, Gallatin, *Writings*, II, 382–383.
[4] *Hansard's*, new series, V (1821), 426.

in the spring of 1827, Liverpool was obliged by the collapse of his health to resign and the King invited Canning to head a new cabinet, they refused to serve under him, and Canning was driven into forming a government in alliance with the Whigs.[5]

As soon as the Cabinet began its discussion of the Oregon issue a division appeared in its ranks. The division was occasioned by a suggestion made by Liverpool that the old American proposal of the 49th parallel be given reconsideration.[6] How the members divided and how close the division was cannot be ascertained. All that is known is that Liverpool, who usually stood with Canning, was ranged on one side and that Canning was on the other. The division was evidently close, for it remained long unresolved and eventually had to be compromised. In the meantime Canning carried on a persistent campaign of propaganda within the Cabinet to turn Liverpool and his abettors away from any thought of new concessions to the United States.

Canning's initial step was to order Addington to prepare a memorandum evaluating the claims of England and the United States to the Oregon Country. The order was given shortly after Canning made his proposal of a new negotiation to the American minister in London. The Addington memorandum, when presented on May 10, proved less an evaluation of claims than a partisan defense of that of England. It was reckless in assertion and calculated to mislead rather than instruct uninformed readers. It flatly asserted that Francis Drake, the first British mariner on the Northwest Coast, had explored the entire coast from latitude 37° to 48°, though the fact that Drake had sailed no farther northward than latitude 42° or 43° was already well known to the scholarly world. The memorandum boldly questioned Robert Gray's discovery of the Columbia. It dismissed the Lewis and Clark expedition with a mention of its name. It refurbished Canning's shallow thesis, developed in 1824, that the United States had weakened, not strengthened, its title to the Oregon Country by acquiring the title of Spain and that the two titles necessarily invalidated each other. It resurrected the theory that Astoria had been purchased, not captured, by the

---

[5] *The Greville Memoirs*, 1814–1860, Lytton Strachey and Roger Fulford, eds. (London, 1938), I, 170–177.

[6] Canning to Liverpool, May 17, June 11, 1826, *Some Official Correspondence of George Canning*, II, 55, 58.

British during the War of 1812 and that the claim of the United States to its restitution should have been resisted.[7] Addington was a protégé of Canning. His work was a complete vindication of the position his chief had hitherto taken on the Oregon question, and wished to take again.

The memorandum was promptly submitted by Canning to Liverpool. Copies of it were distributed to the members of the Cabinet together with the printed papers of the preceding negotiations. In a covering letter Canning outdid Addington. He flatly denied what Addington merely questioned: that Gray had discovered the mouth of the Columbia. He declared in a concluding sentence that he did not know how to contemplate surrendering England's claims.[8]

Liverpool was unconvinced. He asked for further information. The two questions on which he wished more data were:

1st. What is the *value* of the trade carried on upon the North West Coast of America, and from thence through the interior?

2nd. Would the amended Projet of the United States (viz. the 49 Degree of Lat.) afford us any facilities as to outlet for our Communications by Nootka and other ports, and how far would such communications be less advantageous than those through the Columbia?
I should think Huskisson might be able to furnish *full* information on the *first*, and to *procure* some on the *last*. We must naturally expect that questions will be put during the discussion on both these points.[9]

The first of these inquiries was a pointed one. Liverpool knew, evidently, that the value of the trade of the disputed Oregon area would be shown by statistical data to be slight. Canning's response, in his reply to Liverpool, was to anticipate the data. He wrote:

But it is not from what our trade is now, that the question is to be estimated. It is when China shall be open to English as well as American commerce that the real value of settlements on the northwest coast of America will become apparent.[10]

A fortnight later Canning had the information that Liverpool desired ready to distribute to the Cabinet. It consisted of the letter

[7] Memorandum of H. U. Addington, May 10, 1826, *ibid.*, II, 110–115.
[8] Canning to Liverpool, May 17, 1826, *ibid.*, II, 55.
[9] Liverpool to Canning, June 23, 1826, in William Huskisson Mss., British Museum.
[10] Canning to Liverpool, June 24, 1826, *Some Official Correspondence of George Canning*, II, 62.

that the Governor of the Hudson's Bay Company had sent Canning the preceding December; also Addington's questionnaire to Simpson, and Simpson's replies to it.[11] These Hudson's Bay Company materials were depositions for Canning in that they stressed the indispensability of the Columbia River as a channel of communication to the sea.

A long covering letter was sent with these documents by Canning which is highly significant. It not only pointed out the importance of the Hudson's Bay Company material but added powerful emotional arguments against the cession of the north side of the Columbia to the United States. Canning referred to the "blunder" the Cabinet had made while Castlereagh was in office in returning Astoria to the United States. This was an appeal to the fears of Liverpool, who had been Prime Minister at the time. Canning asked Liverpool to observe that the restoration had been determined on by the Cabinet

not only with the full knowledge that the Yankees have sent a ship of war to take possession of the settlement, without a shadow of right thereto, but that this fact, (the preparation of the Yankees to invade and wrest from our N.W. Cy. a settlement theirs by purchase) is put forward as a motive for surrendering it under a forced construction of the Treaty of Ghent: and then think what a task it will be to justify this transaction to Parlt., if upon this transaction we rest our justification for abandoning the whole N.W. Coast of America to the Yankees. I feel the shame of such a statement burning upon my face by anticipation.

Yet, Canning went on to say, withdrawal from Astoria had not been, after all, ill policy:

It [Astoria] lies on the south side of the Columbia, to which we are not unwilling to abjure all claim, keeping the north to ourselves, staking the midstream as our boundary. The cession of Astoria was therefore in furtherance of our present proposition. It now makes our present ground stronger by showing how willingly we departed from that part of it which we thought untenable.

But this is only true, if we maintain our present ground immovably. If we retreat from that, the cession of Astoria will have been but the first symptom of weakness, the first of a series of compliances with encroachments which, if not resisted, will grow upon success. There are

[11] The list of papers distributed is given in the Peel Mss., British Museum.

two points—one of a political, the other of a commercial character—which I anxiously desire you to bear in mind in the discussion of this question.

1st. That the ambitious and overbearing views of the States are becoming daily more developed, and better understood in this country.

2nd. That the trade between the Eastern and Western Hemispheres, direct across the Pacific, is the trade of the world most susceptible of rapid augmentation and improvement. Between China and Mexico, it is now going on largely. Morier has brought me some specimens of China manufactures imported into Mexico, which vie with what we get through India in England.

We cannot yet enter into this trade, on account of the monopoly of the E.I. Cy. But ten years hence that monopoly will cease; and though at that period neither you nor I shall be where we are to answer for our deeds, I should not like to leave my name affixed to an instrument by which England would have foregone the advantages of an immense direct intercourse between China and what may be, if we resolve not to yield them up, her boundless establishments on the N.W. Coast of America.[12]

The concluding portion of Canning's letter unmasked a strange and unexpected element of strength in his position. It presented evidence straight from the enemy's camp of the soundness of his strategy. A confidential communication had been received by Canning divulging the important information that Gallatin was dissatisfied with his Oregon instructions. The message had come while Gallatin was still in America. It must have moved across the Atlantic with the speed of a diplomatist's mail pouch. The sender's name Canning withheld in transmitting the document to his chief. He may even have removed the signature at the wish of the sender. He referred to the document in forwarding it merely as "paper No. 1."

Who the sender was and how the information he gave was obtained are problems which cannot with certainty be solved. Neither "paper No. 1" nor an accompanying "paper No. 2," referred to below, have survived in the collected correspondence of Canning or Liverpool. The only clue Canning's letter gives is that the person who was the source of the information was known to Gallatin and was expected to be able to send warning back to Gallatin to get his instructions liberalized.

[12] Canning to Liverpool, July 7, 1826, *Some Official Correspondence of George Canning*, II, 72–74.

Though a definitive answer to the mystery cannot be given, it is possible, by piecing together scraps of scattered information to construct at least a conjecture. In the early summer of 1826 a letter was written to Sir Charles Bagot by an American, Christopher Hughes, which is known to have contained the news of Gallatin's appointment to the London mission, and in all probability carried also the information regarding his dissatisfaction with his instructions. Sir Charles Bagot was then British ambassador at The Hague. He had been elevated to the knighthood for his earlier services as minister plenipotentiary to Washington. He was a member of the ruling aristocracy of England, closely connected by marriage with the Duke of Wellington. He was a protégé of Canning, with whom he was in frequent familiar correspondence.

His informant, Christopher Hughes, was American chargé d'affaires in Brussels. He was well known to Gallatin, having served while a youth as one of the secretaries to the American commissioners at the Ghent peace conference. He had once been a neighbor of the Gallatins in Baltimore. He was the son-in-law of Senator Samuel Smith of Maryland. He was thus related to Robert Smith, brother to Samuel, once secretary of state of the United States. Hughes was a young man of social rather than intellectual distinction, widely known in European diplomatic circles for his family connections, his social graces, and his prowess as a punster. Such of his letters as have survived, private and public, reveal a person gossipy and rambling of mind rather than penetrating. He was vain and eager to exhibit the access he had to high sources of information in Washington. He was in frequent private correspondence with Sir Charles Bagot, to whom he signed himself under his nickname, "Uncle Sam." Like his Baltimore connections he was an exponent of Anglo-American reconciliation. He saw in Sir Charles Bagot the shining exemplar of that policy. He was partial also to Canning, the great man, who in 1823, while momentarily pressing the project of a joint Anglo-American front against the Holy Alliance, had dazzled him, as he was passing through England, with special attentions.

The transmission to Hughes from Washington of the information regarding Gallatin's instructions was probably via Senator Smith. In the late spring of 1826 Gallatin was in Washington conferring with Clay and Adams regarding his instructions. A meeting occurred at that time between him and Senator Smith. The meeting was probably at the request of the Senator who had a special interest in one of the items on Gallatin's agenda, the problem of the American trade to the British West Indies. Smith had once been a wealthy merchant in the West Indies trade. He was a power in Senate politics, a forceful debater, president *pro tempore* repeatedly of the Senate, a general who had served with some distinction in the War of 1812. He was, however, an intriguer, given to cabal and to methods of indirection. He was unfriendly to the Adams administration and was eager to embarrass it politically. Gallatin had much reason to be wary of the Smith family, but because of the Senator's position and his special concern with some parts of the approaching mission, seems to have talked to him rather freely regarding the probable length of term of his mission and his disappointment over his instructions. A part of this confidence Smith at once betrayed by causing an unsigned communication to be sent to a newspaper hostile to the administration—the Richmond *Enquirer*—regarding the term of the mission with a view to embarrassing the administration. It was probably Smith, or some member of his family who wrote Christopher Hughes the news of the mission and the fact of Gallatin's disappointment over his instructions.[13]

Hughes may have hoped, in passing this information on to Bagot, that by exhibiting the conciliatory temper in which Gallatin was embarking on the mission, he would advance the cause of Anglo-American reconciliation. The use Canning made of the information to shape the thinking of Liverpool is best described in his own words:

At the same time that I press upon you the danger of concession, and the benefits of holding out on this question, it is a satisfaction to be able to present to you some prospect of more facility in the negotiation than probably you venture to expect, or than I expected before yesterday, when the enclosed paper No. 1 fell into my hands.

[13] This account is based on the following sources: Hughes to Mrs. Gallatin, Nov. 14, 1826, Clay to Gallatin, June 21, 1846, and Feb. 24, 1827, in Gallatin Papers, N.-Y.H.S.; Canning to Liverpool, July 7, 1826, in *Some Official Correspondence of George Canning*, II, 74–75; Hughes Papers, Library of Congress; *George Canning and His Friends*, Captain Josceline Bagot, ed., II, 199, 284–287, 296–301, 314; *Congressional Debates*, 19 Cong., 2 sess. (1826–27), 402–418; Richmond *Enquirer*, June 9, 1826. The editor of the Richmond *Enquirer* was Thomas Ritchie, bitter political foe of Clay and Adams.

That paper was not wanted to make me feel assured either that our case is good, or that we have an interest of the deepest importance and heaviest responsibility in maintaining it. But I derive from it a hope which I had not before—that the goodness of our case is felt in the quarter in which it is most useful that it should be felt; and I have thought it advisable in that hope to let it be understood, that we are impressed with the duty of maintaining it. Hence the other enclosure, No. 2, which commits nobody but me, but which may prepare the person for whose warning it is written, either to obtain a modification of the instruction, which he may already have received from his Gov't., before he sails, or to prepare them for expecting to be called upon to modify it hereafter.[14]

Shortly after posting these materials Canning received a printed document on the Oregon question through the regular diplomatic channels from Washington. The document was the Second Report of the Baylies Committee of the House of Representatives. It was a thoroughgoing examination of the British claim to the Oregon area, especially of the claim derived from the voyage of Sir Francis Drake. From British sources it demonstrated that Drake could not have sailed higher than latitude 42° or 43° on the coast. It defended the claims of the United States and Spain and, in its concluding pages, charged Britain with inordinate imperialist ambition and uttered a half defiance of England on the issue of the Northwest Coast. Its tone was such as a committee of Congress, with its eye fixed on constituents, was likely at that time to indulge in.[15] The report infuriated Canning. He declared it was "almost tantamount to a declaration of War" against England. He refused to be persuaded that committee reports of Congress do not, any more than speeches delivered on the floor of Congress, reflect the views of the executive. He made the document the occasion for pressing to adoption the order in council closing the British West Indies to American vessels, as Gallatin was afterwards informed.[16] A more immediate use he made of it was to send it to Liverpool with the note:

I cannot forbear selecting the enclosed despatch of Mr. Vaughan's from a mass which I received last night, and requesting your attention

[14] Canning to Liverpool, July 7, 1826, *Some Official Correspondence of George Canning*, II, 74–75. No copy of "paper No. 2" could be found in the Bagot Mss. in the possession of the Bagot family.

[15] This report is printed in 19 Cong., 1 sess., *H. Reports* (1825–26), No. 213.

[16] Gallatin to Clay, Nov. 27, 1826, State Department, England, Despatches, XXXIII, National Archives.

to it and its enclosure. After such language as that of the committee of the H. of Representatives it is impossible to suppose that we can tide over the Columbia, or can make to ourselves the illusion that there is any other alternative than either to maintain our claims or to yield them with our eyes wide open.[17]

Liverpool was silenced at last. Canning was able in November 1826, in drawing up the instructions for the negotiation with Gallatin, to write that the government had not changed its position on the Oregon issue since 1824,[18] when it had stood immovable at the Columbia River. Liverpool had been won over, perhaps, by the testimony of the Hudson's Bay Company that the river was indispensable to it; or he might have been angered by the Baylies report, or he might merely have preferred to avoid a clash with his headstrong colleague.

The lines of the negotiation were now drawn. The Americans were intrenched at the 49th parallel. The British had staked their claim at the midstream of the Columbia. Both were prepared to stand fast. This was not a favorable prospect for the success of the negotiation.

[17] Canning to Liverpool, July 14, 1826, *Some Official Correspondence of George Canning*, II, 115.
[18] Canning to Huskisson and Addington, Nov. 10, 1826, F.O. 5: 219.

THE PLENIPOTENTIARIES chosen to deal with Gallatin were Huskisson and Addington. Huskisson was chosen for his expertness in the commercial phases of the negotiation. He had, in 1823–24, dealt with Rush on these issues. Addington was a specialist on the boundary problems. He was the voice of Canning in the negotiation. On all topics, as Gallatin later observed, he was "extremely difficult."[1]

The conference opened on November 15, 1826. It promptly placed the Oregon issue at the head of its agenda. The British plenipotentiaries asked Gallatin to report upon a proposal which their government had made to Rush in 1824 and which Rush had taken for submission to the American government—the proposal that the boundary be the 49th parallel from the Rockies to the Columbia, and thence be the channel of the Columbia to the sea. Gallatin reported that this proposal had been declined by the American government. He then submitted his counterproposal. It was the old American offer—the undeviating line of the 49th parallel. As tactfully as possible Gallatin gave notice that on this line his government would insist. At the same time he offered the important new concession permitted by his instructions. The United States would make the navigation of the Columbia and any of its tributaries intersected by the 49th parallel perpetually free to British subjects from the point of intersection to the ocean, provided the waters below the point of intersection should prove on examination to be "navigable by boats." This proposal was taken by the British, without comment, for reference to their government.[2]

A discussion of claims took place at the second session and continued through later sessions. Gallatin shone in the debate. He presented the case of the United States with a clarity and a cogency that had never been given it before and that continued to illumine it in all the later Oregon negotiations. He showed that the United States had claims to the whole valley of the Columbia, the adjacent seaboard, and much more. But he concentrated his argument on the country between the 42nd and 49th parallels. His case was based

[1] Gallatin to Clay, July 29, 1827, *A.S.P., F.R.,* VI, 684.
[2] *Ibid.,* 652, 655.

on a variety of grounds, of which discovery was one. Discovery of the mouth of a river was recognized in the civilized world as giving the nation of the discoverer claims of sovereignty to the entire valley of the river and to the adjacent seaboard. Gallatin demonstrated that Britain had relied in the past on this principle. He showed, from the testimony of Vancouver, that Gray had discovered the mouth of the Columbia. He also proved that the interior waters of the river had been first explored by Americans— by the Lewis and Clark expedition. With regard to the waters washing the southern end of Vancouver Island he showed that their discovery had been a gradual process in which traders and explorers of various nations, Spanish, British, and American, had shared. Vancouver had encountered Spanish explorers in the Gulf of Georgia at the time of his great survey, and they had accompanied him around the island. The United States had acquired all the rights created by Spanish exploration.

To the rights derived from discovery the United States had added, as Gallatin showed, those of colonization. Americans had established Astoria at the mouth of the Columbia and other posts in the interior. Though Astoria had been taken by British arms in the War of 1812, it had been later restored to the United States in accordance with the Treaty of Ghent. The United States also had rights, Gallatin maintained, that derived from the contiguity of its territory to that which was in dispute. Between parallels of latitude 42° and 49° the United States adjoined the Pacific Northwest. It was the land mass of which the Pacific Northwest was the extension. From the United States would come, in the not distant future, the population which would occupy that wilderness. Gallatin showed that the civilized world, and England especially, gave adherence to the principle that contiguity creates territorial rights. He demonstrated that the British sea-to-sea charters of the colonial period in America had been based on this principle. His argument throughout was a masterly combination of cogency of reasoning and moderation of statement.[3]

The British case was addressed to the thesis that no nation had a sound claim to sovereignty in the Oregon Country, that the region was still a no-man's land, open to all comers, and that it would go,

[3] *Ibid.*, 652–655, 666–671; also Huskisson and Addington to Canning, Nov. 23, 1826, F.O. 5: 219.

and should go, to the power that occupied it. The British made a point of not even claiming rights of exclusive sovereignty there. They claimed merely limited rights, which they defended on grounds of prior discovery and occupation. They had taken this position as against Spain in the Nootka Sound controversy of 1790. They had departed from it momentarily in their negotiation with Gallatin in 1818 when they had claimed rights of exclusive sovereignty.[4] Now they were returning to their earlier position, a position easier to defend. They had no very good claim south of the straits, certainly not as strong a claim as that which the United States held after acquiring the rights of Spain. Their emphasis on rights of occupation accorded well with the fur-trade position they had been developing in Oregon after the War of 1812.

The arguments used in support of the British claims were partly those of prior discovery. The achievements of British explorers south of 49° on the coast were emphasized, especially those of Drake, Cook, Meares, and Broughton. Meares was shown to have been at the mouth of the Columbia before Gray, though it had to be conceded he had failed to recognize the nature of the opening he had seen. Broughton was shown to have sailed farther up the Columbia than Gray. The explorers whose discoveries in the waters about Vancouver Island were stressed were Barkley, Dixon, and Vancouver. The explorations and settlements which had been made in the interior by the North West Company were also cited. The discovery Gray had made of the mouth of the Columbia was challenged on the ground not only that he had been preceded by Meares, but that he had been a mere private adventurer. The Spanish claims held by the United States were challenged on three grounds: that exploration had not been followed in the case of Spain by permanent settlements; that Spain, by the Nootka Sound convention, had abandoned her claim to exclusive sovereignty on the Northwest Coast;[5] and that her claims must in any event be regarded as conflicting with and weakening the United States claims, rather than as supplementing them. The British case was set forth in a formal statement, incorporated later in the protocols. It was probably drawn with a view to publication at an early date in the documentary series of Congress.

[4] Gallatin to Clay, August 7, 1827, A.S.P., F.R., VI, 693.
[5] A.S.P., F.R., VI, 662–666.

The British effected a quiet retreat in the course of this argument. They all but formally acknowledged the sovereignty of the United States in the region south of the Columbia. They not only presented no defense of their claim on that side; they called the attention of Gallatin to the fact that the Astoria site had been abandoned by the Hudson's Bay Company and that a new fort had been erected by the Company on the north side.[6] They were acting in this on the principle Canning had enunciated to Liverpool in his letter of the preceding July, that England would strengthen her claim north of the Columbia by exhibiting a willingness to yield ground on the southern side.

In the argument of both sides the principle of convenience was invoked. It was invoked chiefly against the proposals the opposite side made. The British brought it to bear against the American proposal of the 49th parallel to the sea. They showed that that line would sever the tip of Vancouver Island and place the entire straits south of the truncated island within the United States. Gallatin invoked the same principle against the British proposal of the Columbia River line. He showed that the channel of the lower Columbia for a considerable distance runs close to the north shore, so close, that if the river were made the boundary the British would have complete control of its navigation. He pointed out also that on the whole Northwest Coast, from the northern boundary of California to Juan de Fuca Strait, not a single port deep enough for an American naval station was to be found; that the port at the mouth of the Columbia was unusable, because of the bar, except for light vessels of commerce; that north of the 49th parallel the coast abounded in harbors suitable for naval stations; that if all the deep-water harbors inside the straits were to pass to England, the exclusive naval command of the Northwest Coast would pass to England with them.[7] This argument was a strange one to come from the lips of a man who a few months earlier had been urging Adams and Clay to yield to the British all the waters in the Gulf of Georgia and the strait of Juan de Fuca. The argument was Gallatin's discharge of an obligation imposed by his instructions. Privately, in all probability, he deemed it academic. He was one of those who believed that an independent republic would rise in the Pacific

[6] *Ibid.*, 651.
[7] Gallatin to Clay, Nov. 25, 1826, *ibid.*, 654–655.

Northwest, which would take over the harbors there, south, as well as north, of the 49th parallel.[8]

While this debate was going on, the British Cabinet was considering behind the scenes Gallatin's combined offer of the 49th parallel and the Columbia River navigation. It decided to reject the offer. The decision represented Canning's unwillingness to yield the lower river to the United States. It reflected also British objection to the conditional nature of the river navigation proposal.[9]

In announcing the rejection the British plenipotentiaries indicated that they intended to make a counteroffer. They inquired of Gallatin first, however, whether he was authorized to deviate from the 49th parallel as a boundary. This was an improper probing into his instructions, but Gallatin, sensing that it was intended to open the way for a new offer, chose not to rebuke it. He replied that he must adhere to the 49th parallel as a basis. But he would entertain a proposal for deviation from this basis, designed for mutual convenience, provided it was consistent with the basis. Any deviation made to the south must be compensated for by an equivalent at the north. Gallatin did not indicate the nature of the deviation he had in mind, but he later wrote Clay that he intended an exchange of the southern extremity of Vancouver Island for part or all of the valley of the Columbia north of 49°.[10]

The British followed this lead with their new proposal, which contained a concession beyond the traditional offer of the line of the Columbia. They proposed to concede to the United States, in the region adjoining Juan de Fuca Strait, a quadrilateral of territory, a detached tract, comprising roughly the Olympic Peninsula. The tract was to be bounded on the north by the strait of Juan de Fuca; on the west by the ocean; on the south by a line drawn from a point south of Gray's Harbor to Hood's Canal; on the east by Hood's Canal and Admiralty Inlet to the straits. The offer was intended to give the United States a portion of the deep-water harbors inside the straits, especially Port Discovery, which Vancouver had described as particularly excellent.[11]

[8] Grant and Addington to Dudley, August 6, 1827, F.O. 5: 230. Two reports were made to Dudley on this day; the one here cited was private.

[9] Gallatin to Clay, Nov. 25, 1826, A.S.P., F.R., VI, 652–655.

[10] Gallatin to Clay, Dec. 2, 1826, ibid., 655–656.

[11] Canning had instructed the British plenipotentiaries to offer Gallatin at the outset merely the harbor of Port Discovery, with a semicircle of territory around

The offer was doubtless a compromise in the Cabinet—a compromise between the views of Liverpool and those of Canning. It was an attempt to satisfy the American demand for a deep-water harbor inside the straits without loosening the British grip on the lower Columbia. As an added attraction, the British proposed that neither state should ever in the future erect works at the entrance to or on the banks of the Columbia which would impede the free navigation of the river.

As a bid for agreement the offer was woefully inadequate. It was the offer of an enclave. It was the presentation, for an American naval station, of an isolated tract of land hemmed in on every side by British territory or by water that would be dominated by the British navy. Gallatin at once rejected the offer. He declared that even to take it for reference to his government would be inconsistent with his instructions.[12]

As a rejected offer it now became a recording problem. It was made so by the British. They wished to exclude all record of it from the minutes of the conference. They wished the offer to be regarded as having been informally made. Gallatin would have agreed to this, but he was further asked to agree to a positive statement in the protocol that no new offer had been made. He resisted such a statement as contrary to the truth. The British finally relented and agreed that the offer should be recorded as made, though with a reservation that it was not to be regarded as prejudicing their position in the future.[13]

The offer did prejudice their position in the future. Its very presence on the protocol, notwithstanding the reservation to the contrary, formed a precedent of concession north of the Columbia. What was more significant, it revealed British irresolution in defending their position north of the river. Canning, having won his

---

it five miles in radius. This instruction they carried out. Only after the offer had been rejected by Gallatin "with some vivacity" did they make the final quadrilateral offer authorized by Canning. Of the initial offer and its rejection no record was made in the protocol (Canning to Huskisson and Addington, Nov. 30, 1826, F.O. 5: 219; Huskisson and Addington to Canning, Dec. 7, 1826, F.O. 5: 219; *A.S.P.*, *F.R.*, VI, 656, 660).

[12] See the references cited in the footnote above.

[13] Gallatin to Clay, Dec. 5, 1826, *A.S.P.*, *F.R.*, VI, 657; Gallatin to Addington, Dec. 4, 1826, Gallatin Papers, Bundle 9. The British plenipotentiaries wrote Canning that they permitted the offer to be recorded because they wished to display in the protocol the government's "earnest desire to accommodate matters" (Huskisson and Addington to Canning, Dec. 7, 1826, F.O. 5: 219).

triumph over Liverpool three weeks before, had now abandoned it. He had warned the premier that the Cabinet must maintain its position immovably at the Columbia. "If we retreat from that," he had predicted, "the cession of Astoria will have been but the first symptom of weakness, the first of a series of compliances with encroachments, which, if not resisted, will grow upon success." In agreeing to the enclave offer, Canning had himself retreated; he had himself betrayed a symptom of weakness; he had contributed to a "series of compliances with encroachments" which prepared the way for the later advance of the United States to the line of the 49th parallel.

In the meantime, after Gallatin's refusal even to refer the enclave offer to his government, the conference recognized that it could reach no agreement to partition the Oregon Country. It decided to stop trying. It turned, instead, to the more modest undertaking of continuing the convention of joint occupation of 1818. That convention, a ten-year covenant, was due to expire in two more years. To the task of renewing it the conference turned at its third session.

AS SOON as the conference turned to the task of renewing the convention of joint occupation a complication appeared. The complication was a British proposal to insert into the convention an interpretative stipulation in the form of a second article and to make the acceptance of it by the American government a condition of the renewal. The stipulation was that neither contracting party, during the lifetime of the convention, would "assume or exercise any right of exclusive sovereignty or dominion over any part of the said [Oregon] country, nor form therein any establishment in support or furtherance of any such claim."[1]

The meaning of the stipulation was spelled out for Gallatin by the British. The key word in it was the word "exclusive." If the stipulation were accepted, the right to assume or exercise any exclusive sovereignty or dominion over any part of the Oregon Country would be renounced by the two governments. The right to establish any military post in that country would be given up. Initially Gallatin understood that only a military post exclusively commanding the mouth of the Columbia River would be regarded by the British as an infraction of the stipulation, but later it became clear that any American military post which was government-established would be regarded as a violation of the agreement. The establishment of a distinct territorial government by either power over the Oregon Country would also be ruled out. Each government, however, would retain the right to extend its territorial laws over its own nationals in this wilderness, though not over the nationals of the other, and each would retain the right to try, and to punish, its own nationals for offenses committed there. Any impediment to the free navigation of harbors and rivers, any levying of duties or establishment of customs houses, any removing or disturbing of the settlements of either party by the other, would be infractions of the stipulation; though, as Gallatin, in a letter home observed, they would have been infractions under the existing convention without the stipulation. The net effect of the stipulation would have been,

[1] *A.S.P., F.R.,* VI, 657.

if approved, the renunciation by either party of the right to erect any military post or establish any distinct territorial government in the Oregon Country during the lifetime of the convention.[2]

The stipulation was Canning's project. It was probably what he had in mind when first he proposed to the American government that an Oregon negotiation be held. He could not confidently have expected any boundary settlement, opposed as he was to the concessions that a settlement with the United States would have entailed. The stipulation could be hoped for; it could be made a condition of the renewal of the convention. The stipulation would satisfy immediate British purposes. It would give the Hudson's Bay Company time to fasten its grip on the region north of the Columbia. It would be the answer given to the agitation in Congress to erect an American military post at the mouth of the Columbia and an American territorial government over the whole of the Oregon Country. It would tie the hands of American Floyds for the term of the renewed convention.

A plausible argument was offered by the British plenipotentiaries for this plan. The argument was that the stipulation merely clarified the intent of the convention. The intent of the convention, the British said, was to suspend the right of exercising sovereignty in the Oregon Country. This was evident from the fact that the convention was an agreement of joint occupation, an agreement that the Oregon Country should be free and open to the nationals of both parties. No nation, in any case, the British said, ever had rights of exclusive sovereignty in the Oregon Country. Such rights would some day come to the nation that settled the country.[3]

With the question of the stipulation the British connected the question of the term for which the convention should be renewed. The term that Canning would have favored if the stipulation could have been agreed upon was fifteen or twenty or even twenty-five years instead of ten. The lengthened term would fit well into the purposes of the Hudson's Bay Company.

Gallatin met the stipulation proposal as his instruction required. He referred it to his government. He had been directed to refer to Washington any British proposal that involved a substantial change

---

[2] Gallatin to Clay, Dec. 20, 1826, *ibid.*, 658–659.
[3] Gallatin to Clay, Dec. 5, 1826, August 7, 10, 1827, *ibid.*, 657, 691, 694.

in the convention; he was authorized to agree only to a simple renewal for a ten year period.[4] He sent the proposal home in December 1826. He received the reply of the President, through Clay, in March of the following year. The reply was a rejection in unequivocal terms of the proposal. The delivery of the reply was delayed until the end of May, owing to the cabinet crisis in England caused by Liverpool's illness and retirement.[5]

Despite the rejection Canning still had hopes that the stipulation might be vendible. He offered it in a new dress. On June 19 Gallatin was informed by the British plenipotentiaries that a simple renewal of the convention for a period of ten years would be acceptable— but only on the condition that a declaration embodying the British understanding of the convention be permitted to appear in the protocol: namely, that both parties were restricted "from exercising, or assuming to themselves the right to exercise, any exclusive sovereignty or jurisdiction over the territory mentioned in that article.[6]

Gallatin rejected this proposal. He pointed out that to admit this declaration into the protocol would be tantamount to inserting in the convention the stipulation which the American government had already given notice it could not accept. If the British were to insert this declaration into the protocol, it would become necessary for him to reply with a counterdeclaration, setting forth the American view of the convention. Of what avail would an agreement then be, accompanied by two declarations of such opposite char-

---

[4] Gallatin did suggest, however, omitting from the convention the clause referring to "claims of any other Power or State," which had been written into the instrument originally as a protection to Spain and Russia. He believed that this clause had become obsolete as a result of the treaties the two powers had made. His suggestion was not approved by the British, who preferred to adhere to the thesis that the Oregon Country was a vacant region, open to all comers.

Gallatin also made the suggestion informally that only the "debateable ground" of the Oregon Country be put under the convention if it was revised, and that all the rest of that country be assigned at once in exclusive possession to one or the other of the two claimants. What he regarded as the "debateable ground" he did not say, but he wrote home that he had in mind the area north of 49°. The suggestion did not appeal to the British (Gallatin to Clay, Dec. 5, 12, 1826, *A.S.P., R.F.*, VI, 657, 658; Clay to Gallatin, Feb. 24, 1827, *ibid.*, 646–647; *ibid.*, 660; Huskisson and Addington to Canning, Dec. 7, 1826, F.O. 5: 219).

[5] *A.S.P., F.R.*, VI, 676; J. Q. Adams, *Memoirs*, VII, 226.

[6] *A.S.P., F.R.*, VI, 677, 678; Dudley to Huskisson and Addington, June 18, 1827, F.O. 5: 230.

acter? He declared he would be unable to renew the convention if accompanied by any British declaration purporting to explain its meaning or intent.[7]

At this stage Gallatin was in a position to expound the American view of the meaning of the convention. He had been unable to do so while uncertain of the verdict of the President on the projected stipulation and had contented himself merely with expressing his preference for a simple renewal. He had the knowledge necessary for an authoritative exposition of the convention. He had been one of the authors of the instrument. He proceeded to analyze it with a clarity and force that on both sides of the Atlantic illumined the subject as long as the compact remained in effect.

The convention, he held, was what it appeared on its face to be, and nothing more. It was a commerce agreement, a free trade agreement, a compact of joint exploitation. Its intent was to keep the Oregon Country open to the commerce and settlement of the nationals of both parties, free from any obstruction by the government or subjects of either. On the issue of sovereignty the convention was silent. It left that issue where it had found it. By the convention neither party was precluded from exercising exclusive sovereignty in the Oregon Country so long as no interference occurred with the freedom of commerce and settlement of the other.[8] Gallatin was stating facts of history. He had been asked in the negotiation of 1818 by the British to agree to a declaration in the convention that neither party would exercise under it any sovereign or territorial authority in the Oregon Country against the other, and he had refused. He had taken the position that the convention was a commercial agreement. The convention had been kept deliberately silent on the issue of sovereignty.[9]

As for the erection of a military post in the Oregon Country, Gallatin held that it was forbidden to neither party by the convention. A military occupation would be an infraction only if it interfered with the freedom of commerce and settlement which the

[7] Gallatin to Clay, August 7, 1827. *A.S.P.*, *F.R.*, VI, 691; Grant and Addington to Dudley, August 6, 1827, F.O. 5: 230.

[8] Gallatin to Clay, August 7, 1827, *A.S.P.*, *F.R.*, VI, 691–693.

[9] See Essay 3. In 1821, when the first of the Floyd bills came before Congress, the British Cabinet decided that it did not conflict with the convention of joint occupation (Castlereagh to Stratford Canning, April 10, 1821, F.O. 116: 8; Canning to Stratford Canning, April 14, 1821, F.O. 116: 6). The Floyd bill is printed in *Annals of Congress*, 16 Cong., 2 sess. (1820–21), 958–959.

convention protected. The erection of a military post by the United States might become necessary for the safeguarding of American traders and settlers against Indians and lawless whites, or for the protection of the Indians themselves against aggression. Military posts, which Congress and the President had merely contemplated, the British already had in the stockaded forts and the powerful organization of the Hudson's Bay Company.[10]

A territorial government established by either party in the Oregon Country would, like a military post, be no infraction in itself of the convention. It would be an infraction only if it obstructed the freedom of trade and settlement which the convention assured. The United States might deem it necessary to form a territorial government in the Oregon Country as a means of maintaining order in a remote wilderness inhabited by savages and licentious traders. It would in that case be doing only what the British government had already done.

The British government had established the Hudson's Bay Company in the Oregon Country. To that company it had given a monopoly of British rights of trade. A powerful incorporated company, operating to the exclusion of private British traders, was in itself a territorial government. Through such agency Britain had long governed extensive and populous regions in the Orient. Experience in North America had shown that, where private British traders competed with each other for the peltry of savages, disorder and bloodshed occurred. When, however, there was an exclusive company, its agents governed; all other British subjects were its servants. All were kept in order and restrained from committing outrages on each other and on the Indians.[11]

Nothing was wanting then to a complete system of government but courts of law for the trial of criminal and civil cases. Such courts the British Parliament, in 1821, had established. A criminal and civil jurisdiction had been erected for certain parts of British North America and for the Oregon Country in the same act which authorized the monopoly given the Hudson's Bay Company. Courts for inferior criminal and civil cases, presided over by justices of the peace, had been established. Capital and other high offenses, and all civil suits above a certain amount, had been placed under the juris-

[10] Gallatin to Clay, August 7, 1827, *A.S.P.*, *F.R.*, VI, 691–693.
[11] *Ibid.*

diction of the courts of upper Canada. No provision had been made in the act for exempting citizens of the United States in the Oregon Country from this jurisdiction.[12]

The United States might have reason to complain of the act, Gallatin said, not as a breach of the convention of 1818, but as an infraction of the right of sovereignty claimed by the United States over the Oregon Country. If such complaint had not been made it was probably because the act had not been literally enforced.[13] But Great Britain, which had assumed as much jurisdiction as was necessary for protecting her subjects and maintaining order, could not complain if the United States adopted measures for the same object, even if the measures were not precisely the same as those Great Britain had found sufficient.

The American government could not create an incorporated monopoly in the Oregon Country. Incorporated monopolies were incompatible with the genius of American democratic institutions. The American mode of trade was competing companies and competing individuals. The American mode of control in a wilderness area was the territorial form of government. The United States might consider it necessary to establish a territorial form of government in the Oregon Country as a means of preserving peace and order among its citizens and giving them protection. Whatever the United States might contemplate in this respect, it had never yet actually exercised sovereignty or jurisdiction in that country. By this exposition Gallatin justified his government's rejection of the British proposal of a stipulation and his own rejection of the British project of a declaration in the protocol.[14]

The British were enough impressed with this exposition and the rejections to withhold further efforts to obtain a declaration on the issue of a territorial government. But they continued, as required

---

[12] *British Statutes*, 1 and 2 George IV, c. 66.

[13] The act was apparently not known to the American government prior to 1827. Its adoption by Parliament seems to have escaped the notice of Rush. Its existence was discovered by Gallatin only in April, 1827. The British plenipotentiaries denied that the act was designed to apply to any except their own nationals in the Oregon Country. See Gallatin to Clay, April 21, 1827, State Department, England Despatches, xxxiii; same to same, August 7, 1827, *A.S.P., F.R.*, VI, 691–693; Huskisson and Addington to Dudley, June 8, 1827, F.O. 5: 230; Addington to Gallatin, June 20, 1827, Gallatin Papers, N.-Y.H.S.

[14] Gallatin to Clay, June 22, 23, 1827, *A.S.P., F.R., VI*, 677–678; 681–683.

by their instructions,[15] to press for a declaration on the issue of military posts. On June 26, at the eleventh conference, they announced that they would agree to a simple renewal of the convention, provided they could insert in the protocol one or the other of two declarations—(1) that the contracting parties had no right to take military possession of the Oregon Country, or (2) that if the United States did establish military posts in that country, Great Britain would do the same. They expressed a preference for the first of these declarations. The second might be construed in the United States as a threat. They declared that their government did not wish to erect military posts; it would do so only in self-defense.[16]

Gallatin at once rejected this proposal. He informed the British that he could not agree to a renewal of the convention if accompanied by any declaration in the protocol attaching any construction or interpretation whatever to the agreement. The proper place for such a declaration was not the protocol, but a communication addressed by the British government to the American government through the ordinary diplomatic channels.[17]

It was clear by now that the campaign of the British to write their own interpretation into the convention would not succeed. In the course of the debate one position after another had been taken by them only to be abandoned. The end had now clearly come. Renewal of the convention, *totidem verbis*, or no convention at all, had become the choice. The British protested to Gallatin that a convention of joint occupation, renewed without definition and known to mean opposite things to the signatories, would be hardly better than no convention at all. Inwardly they felt it would be somewhat better. A convention, amicably made and signed, even if without definition, would place a moral restraint on American aggression. The undefined convention had served British purposes well enough in the past. It had been a factor in preserving peace in the Oregon Country. It had permitted British fur companies to maintain their domination of that country. It would be likely to be of even greater utility in the future. A reorganized and reinvigo-

[15] Dudley to Huskisson and Addington, June 18, 1827, F.O. 5: 230.
[16] Gallatin to Clay, June 27, 1827, *A.S.P., F.R.,* VI, 680; Grant and Addington to Dudley, August 6, 1827, F.O. 5: 230.
[17] *Ibid.*

rated Hudson's Bay Company was at the beginning of a new program of expansion.

On July 21, after every hope of agreement on a declaration in the protocol had vanished, the British plenipotentiaries made their final move. They informed Gallatin that they would accept a simple renewal of the convention, though in view of the American rejection of the stipulation, they would agree to it only on a short-term basis. The short-term basis had become preferable since it would permit the convention to be quickly terminated on evidence that the United States had embarked on a plan of military occupation of the Oregon Country. The British also suggested that they would give consideration to any form of a temporary renewal Gallatin might wish to propose.[18]

Gallatin readily approved the principle of a short term renewal. He also suggested the form. The British had shortly before proposed that the commercial convention of 1815 be renewed for an indefinite period, subject to the condition that it could be terminated on a twelve-months' notice by either party. That form, Gallatin suggested, should be applied to the convention of joint occupation. This was acceptable to the British. On August 6 the convention, so framed, was engrossed and signed. Its renewal had been a labor of eight months.[19]

[18] *A.S.P., F.R.*, VI, 687; Grant and Addington to Dudley, August 6, 1827, F.O. 5: 230.

[19] Gallatin to Clay, August 7, 9, 1827, *A.S.P., F.R.*, VI, 691–694. The August 7 dispatch is an admirable brief résumé of the negotiation.

IN THE COURSE of the months of negotiation Gallatin had come increasingly to feel that something more than the renewal of the naked convention was needed to safeguard the peace in the Oregon Country. He considered the Canning stipulation no sufficient safeguard—it would merely restrict the rival exercise of exclusive sovereignty. What was needed was an agreement regulating in specific terms the relations between the two occupying powers in the Oregon Country—a field contract for the period of the joint occupation. In referring home the Canning stipulation Gallatin had suggested that he be given authority to conclude such an agreement. He had been disappointed when the President had authorized merely the renewal of the convention. He believed that an opportunity had been lost. He had loyally carried out the President's wishes, but he continued to feel that a supplementary agreement was necessary.

To pave the way for such an agreement Gallatin had carried on informal conversations with the British plenipotentiaries and with Canning while the formal negotiations were still in progress. These conversations are a significant phase of the conference. They throw light on the nature of the joint occupation and the problems which it raised. They exhibit Gallatin in his characteristic role of peacemaker and they make more understandable his proceedings in the conference. The recordings of the conversations are British and must be used with caution, since they are *ex parte*, colored perhaps by British prepossessions, and catch ideas in the process of evolution.[1]

The recordings show that Gallatin, on June 9, some months after the arrival of the letter from home ordering a mere renewal of the convention, confided to the British that he believed citizens of the one nation, apprehended in the commission of crime within the limits or possessions of the other in the Oregon Country, should be transferred by their captors to the other to be dealt with under

[1] Two letters reporting these conversations were sent to the Foreign Office by the British plenipotentiaries, both of the same date. One is official, the other unofficial. The official report is Grant and Addington to Dudley, August 6, 1827, No. 6, F.O. 5: 230. The unofficial report (*ibid.*), the more valuable of the two, carries no dispatch number.

the laws and tribunals of their own government. On the same occasion he evidently also expressed the opinion that it might be inexpedient for the United States to erect military posts in the Oregon Country. He added, to quote the British report,

that it would surely be the greatest folly imaginable for two powers like Great Britain and the United States to be quarrelling about a matter of such very minute present interest to either. In the United States it would be still greater absurdity than in Great Britain, since in the natural course of things, if Great Britain were not forced into colonizing the country, it must necessarily, from its proximity to the United States, fall eventually into the hands of that Power, or rather, Mr. Gallatin said, it would fall into the hands of neither. It would be peopled by both, but mainly by the United States, and would eventually, as its population and internal organization advanced, render itself independent of both.[2]

At a later conference he returned to the subject of the military posts. He was reported to have said that he did not see how the United States could dispense entirely with such a post in the Oregon Country. One would be needed to give support and protection to American citizens who would settle in that country. He thought an agreement might be reached permitting each nation to establish one such post, the size of its garrison to be limited.

Gallatin was reported to have felt that an interval of time was necessary before a new agreement should be attempted. Issues had been raised by the proposed British stipulation that required further study. On both sides of the Atlantic the national temper was unfavorable at the moment to a calm and dispassionate consideration of the problem. In the United States, Congress and the people, with scarcely an exception, regarded the American claim to the Oregon region as indefeasible, as admitting neither doubt nor dispute, and the British claim as a deliberate and unjust aggression on it. But when the clouds which at present enveloped the issue had had time to clear away, he did not despair of some more substantial and definite arrangement being concluded.[3]

[2] The conviction that an independent republic would arise in the Pacific Northwest remained with Gallatin throughout the life of the joint occupation agreement. It was asserted by him in 1846, at the height of the Oregon crisis, in the concluding letter of a series originally published in the *National Intelligencer,* and subsequently republished as a pamphlet. See Albert Gallatin, *Letters on the Oregon Question* (Washington, 1846), No. 5. Alexander Baring also adhered to the same view to the end.

[3] See the references in Chapter VI, note 8.

Gallatin sought to prepare his own government in the same way for a new negotiation. He sent Clay, shortly after signing the convention, a long letter devoted to this problem, which was designed for the eyes of the President. The letter is one of the most revealing documents of the negotiation.[4] It opens with a statement, made "with confidence," that the British government had no wish at present to colonize the Oregon Country; that they viewed that country with indifference; that they believed when it was settled it would not long remain a colony either of Britain or of the United States; and that they were willing to let the settlement of it take its natural course.

However, they would not be prepared to agree now, nor for some time in the future, to such a partition of it as the United States desired and had a right to claim. They would not be supported in doing so by British public opinion. The Hudson's Bay Company, though perhaps less favored now than it had once been, would continue to be the principal bar to a partition settlement. Such a partition as would be satisfactory to the United States would not be possible until the citizens of the United States had acquired a respectable footing in that country.

In the meantime the British government would feel itself bound to protect existing establishments created by British capital and enterprise. Recollections of the high ground assumed by Britain toward Spain in the Nootka affair would have their influence, and national pride would prevent any abrupt relinquishment of British claims. But Great Britain "did not seem indisposed to let the country gradually and silently slide into the hands of the United States"; and she was anxious that it should not, in any event, become the cause of a rupture with the United States.

As evidence that the British government was willing to permit the disputed region silently to "slide" into American possession Gallatin cited the fact that the British plenipotentiaries had sedulously avoided in the negotiation setting up a claim to exclusive sovereignty over any part of the Oregon Country; that they had reverted, instead, to the doctrine advanced in the Nootka affair of a wilderness unoccupied and open to all. Such an exposition of the nature of the British claim, Gallatin thought, was far more signifi-

---

[4] Gallatin to Clay, August 10, 1827, *A.S.P., F.R.*, VI, 694–696.

cant than any of the arguments advanced by the British in support of it.[5]

Since Great Britain would permit the region to pass to the United States, provided peace were preserved, it was important for the American government to consider the measures necessary to prevent conflicts. A number of these were suggested in Gallatin's letter for the President's consideration. The desires expressed in Congress for an American territorial jurisdiction in the Oregon Country, Gallatin felt, could be satisfied without any formal agreement. On this issue, he observed, the British had at first been particularly sensitive. He had relieved their apprehensions in great part by the explanations he had given and the comparisons he had made of the British and American modes of extending jurisdiction. He thought the issue could be arranged by extending the jurisdiction of an established territory of the United States over the trans-mountain country and defining the country over which the jurisdiction was extended in general terms similar to those used in the act of Parliament of 1821.

On three issues, Gallatin felt, a definite agreement should be made. From his informal talks with the British he could report what the British desires on these issues were. The first was an agreement that no customs house should be erected nor any duties raised by either party on tonnage, merchandise, or commerce in the region west of the Rockies.[6] This restriction, he thought, was already implied in the convention—in the requirement that the country be free and open to the vessels, citizens, and subjects of the two powers. He observed that the extension of the revenue laws of the United States to that quarter would be undesirable, that if duties were exacted on merchandise intended for the Indian trade, the citizens of the United States would not be able to compete with the Hudson's Bay Company.

The second measure proposed was that the citizens and subjects of the two powers in the Oregon Country should be amenable only to the jurisdiction of the courts of their own nation. Gallatin

[5] *Ibid.* Also same to same, Dec. 20, 1826, *ibid.*, 658.

[6] The Floyd bills of 1821 and 1824 each included an authorization to the President to open a port of entry within the Oregon Country and to extend the revenue laws of the United States to it. The bill of 1824 extended the revenue laws to the whole area west of the Rocky Mountains and north of 42° without specifying a northern boundary. See Chapter I, note 12, and Chapter VII, note 9, of this essay.

believed that an agreement on this subject was indispensable. Without one, it would hardly be possible to avoid collisions.

The third measure desired by the British was an agreement that no military post be established by either power in the Oregon Country. Gallatin thought that this was the most difficult part of the whole problem. He wrote that he had repeatedly explained to the British, with some effect he had at first believed, why Great Britain could dispense with a military force in the Oregon Country while the United States could not. In the later discussions, however, it was the point on which they had been most tenacious. The establishment of a military post, they felt, would be a formal national occupation, and one of such notoriety that Great Britain could not permit it to be done without following suit. If the United States built forts, Great Britain indubitably would do the same. The real objection, from the American point of view, to embarking on a race of armaments would then appear. Great Britain, with a far greater military establishment than the United States, could, without much inconvenience, send out larger detachments for service to Oregon. And if Great Britain did once take military possession, the result, quite apart from the danger of collisions, would be that she would find it much more difficult to withdraw voluntarily at a later time from the area she had occupied.[7]

The thesis in Gallatin's letter that the British viewed the Oregon region with indifference and were willing to permit it to slide into American possession in the future was doubtless based on conversations with members of the British government. It is entitled to the respect due the judgment of a highly competent observer, and it did represent views in some circles in British politics. But it could not have represented the views of Canning, and if Canning persuaded Gallatin to the contrary, he was another of the diplomats of that generation who practiced the arts of the real-estate agent.

The action taken by the British and American governments on Gallatin's plan was to shelve it. The plan had been designed for the future; it was relegated to the indefinite future. In England, Canning died two days after the signing of the convention; the government that succeeded him was an interim one without energy. In the United States, Adams was in no mood to make concessions on the Oregon issue to the British. Even if he had been, his administra-

[7] The above account is a paraphrasing of the report of Gallatin.

tion was moving toward a close. He was beset in Congress by a factional opposition of extraordinary virulence, which would have flayed him if he had agreed to Gallatin's suggestions.

Throughout the negotiation Gallatin had been trying to lead the two governments on the road to a real peace. He had been the reconciler, the seeker of compromise. He had been manifesting his conviction that the diplomatist is more than the advocate of national gain, that he is also the minister of peace. He had been almost internationalist in outlook, Swiss rather than Yankee. He had sought initially to narrow the gap between national demands and to bridge it. When this proved impossible, he had sought to build a basis for a secure truce. His labors were the expression of an innate cosmopolitanism and a spirit of moderation. They were the result of his eagerness for Anglo-American reconciliation. They were perhaps also a response to his conviction, shared with his lifelong friend Alexander Baring, that the region west of the Rockies would become an independent republic. But even Gallatin could not reconcile the conflicting desires of a Canning and an Adams, each representing an extreme and irascible nationalism.

THE CONFERENCE closed in September 1827. It closed with an output hardly commensurate with the year and a half of planning and discussion that had gone into its sessions. The sum of its achievement was the renewal of two conventions—joint occupation and the commercial convention of 1815—and an agreement to refer the issue of the northeast boundary to the decision of some friendly sovereign. The prime object of the negotiation, at least ostensibly—the partition of the Oregon Country—had failed.

Yet the negotiation, even in its Oregon phase, was not a complete failure. It was a success in that it lowered tensions which had developed to the danger point on the opposite sides of the ocean. In the United States the feeling had become virtually unanimous that the British case in the Oregon Country was meritless, that their presence south of 49° was a sheer encroachment, that containment of them was a vital need. In Congress the limitationists, who wished to reserve the Oregon area for a new republic, and the expansionists, who desired to acquire it for the United States, had joined forces and were moving irresponsibly toward a showdown with the British. Misinterpreting the quietness of the British press and Parliament,[1] and encouraged by the 1824 message of President Monroe, they had put through the House by an overwhelming majority the Floyd bill which was designed to push the British from the Oregon Country. In England, Canning was storing up wrath. He regarded the noncolonization doctrine of the American executive and the militant proceedings of Congress as all of one piece—to expel Britain from a country where he had ambitions for the British Empire.[2] In 1826 he was, if not yet in a mood for a rupture with the United States, at least in what Adams described as a "waspish" mood.[3] That mood was reflected at the conference in the excessive "susceptibility" which Gallatin described the British plenipotentiaries as exhibiting in the Oregon discussions, and in the repeated warnings that they issued to Gallatin of the seriousness with which

[1] Addington to Canning, May 2, 1826, F.O. 5: 221.
[2] Gallatin to Clay, Dec. 20, 1826, A.S.P., F.R., VI, 658–659.
[3] Adams to Gallatin, Dec. 12, 1827, Gallatin, *Writings*, II, 398.

any aggressive action taken by Congress would be regarded by the British government.[4]

This explosiveness was reduced by the negotiation. It was reduced partly by the conciliatory temper and moderation brought by Gallatin to the discussions. It was reduced further by the forceful yet tactful presentation he made of the American claim to the Oregon Country and the American conception of the intent of the joint agreement. Canning and Huskisson and the Cabinet were undoubtedly given an education on this issue in the course of the negotiation.

A similar education was effected in the United States. The Adams administration and its successors were taught by the reports of Gallatin the unwisdom, from an American point of view, of any congressional measure that would drive England into a military occupation of the Oregon Country. The public in the United States was similarly educated. The education was hastened by a tradition of American democracy that the documents of important negotiations with foreign states should be promptly published. In 1828 the documents of the Oregon negotiation were submitted by Adams to Congress and were published.[5] In the protocols appeared the elaborate defense by the British of their claim, prepared in all probability with a view to its publication in the United States. The protocols made clear the sobering fact that Britain would fight if aggressive action were taken by Congress on the Oregon issue.

It was probably no accident that congressional agitation on the issue tapered off after the negotiation.[6] It was certainly no accident that the agitation was no longer fed by messages from American presidents. By 1830 a quiescent stage in the controversy had been reached, which continued to the end of the decade. It was not until the 1840's, until the movement of American pioneers into the

---

[4] Gallatin to Clay, Nov. 25, 1826, *A.S.P., F.R.,* VI, 652–654; same to same, Nov. 27, 1826, State Department, England, Despatches, xxxiii.

[5] 20 Cong., 1 sess. (1827–28), *H. Documents,* No. 199.

[6] In the session of 1828–29, when the last of the Floyd bills was brought before the House, the attack on it was led by persons who relied for their ammunition on the published documents of the 1826–27 negotiation. The ablest speech by far against the bill was made by James K. Polk, the future president. It was an exposition almost entirely of the conflicts between the bill and the renewed convention in terms of information taken from the published documents of the negotiation. The bill was decisively defeated by the House. See *Congressional Debates,* 20 Cong., 2 sess. (1828–29), 129–132.

Oregon Country had attained considerable proportions, with resulting political agitations, that the Oregon issue again became explosive.

In the meantime the convention of joint occupation justified the faith which Canning had placed in it. It permitted the Hudson's Bay Company to dominate the whole Oregon Country, south as well as north of the Columbia River. The Oregon Country became a British sphere of influence and remained so, uncontested to the end of the fur-trade era.

Such a result Adams undoubtedly foresaw when he agreed to the renewal of the convention. The Senate similarly foresaw it in ratifying the agreement. American fur traders operating on a small scale in the Oregon Country could not hope by their individual competition to displace a great British corporation. They had not done so in the case of the North West Company which had held the Oregon region to 1821. Still less could they hope to do so against a mammoth corporation such as the Hudson's Bay Company.

The American government, nevertheless, was acting with hard-headed and far-sighted realism in renewing the convention. Adams and the Senate recognized that whether or not the convention was renewed the Hudson's Bay Company would remain a fixture in the Oregon Country. Military action alone could loosen such a grip with any promptness, and military action the United States was not prepared to resort to. If the convention were permitted by the American government to lapse, the Hudson's Bay Company would remain in the Oregon Country despite the claims and rights of the United States. If the convention were renewed, the Company would be there by American sufferance.

From the point of view of the American government the renewal of the convention was a wise adjournment of a controversy. It was an adjournment to the day when the Oregon Country would be occupied by American settlers. To Gallatin this was what the renewal meant. It was what he had in mind in reporting to his government that no satisfactory boundary line would be obtainable "until the citizens of the United States shall have acquired a respectable footing in the country."[7] It was what Adams had in

[7] Gallatin to Clay, August 10, 1827, *A.S.P., F.R.*, VI, 694. Gallatin made the following prediction regarding the advance of American settlement into the Oregon

mind, also. On March 20, 1827, in a letter to Gallatin in which the failure of the partition negotiation was discussed, he referred at some length to the intransigeance of the British and the uncompromising spirit of Congress and concluded: "In this temper of the parties, all we can hope to accomplish will be to adjourn controversies which we cannot adjust, and say to Britain, as the Abbé Bernis said to Cardinal Fleuri, 'Monseigneur, j'attendrai.' "[8]

Country in his statement of the claims of the United States, delivered to the British, December 19, 1826: "Under whatever nominal sovereignty that country may be placed, and whatever its ultimate destinies may be, it is nearly reduced to a certainty that it will be almost exclusively peopled by the surplus population of the United States. The distance from Great Britain, and the expense incident to emigration, forbid the expectation of any being practicable from that quarter but on a comparatively small scale. Allowing the rate of increase to be the same in the United States and in the North American British possessions, the difference in the actual population of both is such that the progressive rate which would within forty years, add three millions to these, would, within the same time, give a positive increase of more than twenty millions to the United States. And if circumstances, arising from localities and habits, have given superior facilities to British subjects of extending their commerce with the natives, and to that expansion which has the appearance, and the appearance only, of occupancy; the slower but sure progress and extension of an agricultural population will be regulated by distance, by natural obstacles, and by its own amount" (A.S.P., F.R., VI, 670).

[8] Gallatin, *Writings*, II, 368.

ESSAY 6 · THE OREGON QUESTION IN THE WEBSTER-ASHBURTON NEGOTIATIONS*

IN 1763 Great Britain and her thirteen American colonies finished a collaboration and began a quarrel. They finished in triumph together the expulsion of France from the continent of North America, a work that had occupied them three quarters of a century. They began a quarrel destined to occupy them another three quarters of a century and to create bitterness between them comparable only to that they had once directed against France.

From 1765 to 1775 they quarreled over the issue of parliamentary taxation. They went to war over it. They emerged from the fighting with harsh memories of bloodshed, of Indian atrocities, of the harrying of Tories, of the alliance of one of them with the ancient enemy, France, and of the final separation. Next they clashed over the separation treaty. Before they could resolve that set of differences, they drifted into yet others arising out of the wars of the French Revolution—conflicts over the rights of neutrals at sea, the impressment of American seamen, and the responsibility for Indian uprisings on the Ohio. They fought over these a second war. They emerged from it with old issues undecided, memories again rubbed raw, and new issues added. They had now, less than ever, the will to compromise their differences. They had formed the habit of allowing differences, old and new, to pile up unresolved. By 1840 the accumulation had become so large and so heated that a spark could have set it off into a third war.

This prolonged hostility varied in intensity from period to period. Under special circumstances it cooled into something not far removed from reconciliation. In the Federalist period, when control of government in both countries was held by political parties motivated by a common dislike for, or fear of, revolutionary France, the

* Reprinted from the *Mississippi Valley Historical Review*, XLIII (December 1956).

relations of the two governments considerably improved. In the Washington administration the Jay mission was successful in averting an Anglo-American war. In the Adams administration, when the Federalists clashed with France over issues leading to the undeclared naval war of 1798, an actual co-operation with England was briefly achieved. In 1823 the two governments momentarily gave thought to issuing a joint declaration of opposition to any armed intervention by the Holy Alliance in the affairs of Latin America.

But any softening of the old antagonisms was the exception. Discord was the rule. Efforts to eliminate causes of friction were always handicapped by the bitterness of feeling nursed in the two countries against each other. Especially was this the case where controversies were prominent enough to be in the public eye. In such, if either side made concessions to the other it did so in fear of the reprobation of its own public. Agreements reached were likely to be narrow in scope. If wider, they were exposed to vehement press attacks. The agreements of the Federalist period and the near accord of 1823 were succeeded by explosions of popular emotion more violent than usual.

In the early forties, however, a new climate seemed to be developing in Anglo-American relations. A desire to clear away accumulated conflicts and to seek a reconciliation was beginning to be felt. Time had removed some of the barriers to a reconciliation. The generation which had fought the War of the American Revolution had passed, and a new generation, which had fought in neither Anglo-American conflict, had reached maturity. The world had long been at peace. The imperious necessities of belligerence no longer drove the British to impose arbitrary sea rules on the merchant marine of neutrals. Impressment of American seamen had ended. The British navigation system, an old source of friction, had been given up. The United States had emerged as an important power and was now treated by England more as an equal. A major economic affliction—a world-wide business depression, which was the aftermath of the Panic of 1837—had fallen upon both peoples. The distresses which it produced were reminders to the two that they were dependent for prosperity on each other. In each nation the commercial, banking, industrial, and even some of the farming interests, were eager for tranquillity in the relations of their governments in order that the health-giving exchange of their national surpluses might be restored as rapidly as possible to normal.

In 1841 the governments of the two countries were well disposed toward each other. For the first time since the presidency of John Adams they were simultaneously and equally desirous of ending their disputes and effecting a reconciliation. In England the government of Sir Robert Peel came into office, succeeding a cabinet in which for ten years the truculent Lord Palmerston had directed foreign policy. The new secretary for foreign affairs, Lord Aberdeen, was a lover of peace, and of Anglo-American peace in particular. In the United States the Whig administration of William Henry Harrison had been established as a result of the presidential election of 1840. In this administration Daniel Webster, an Anglophile, and a potentate of the party, was secretary of state. Edward Everett was the American minister at the Court of St. James.

The most pressing issue between the two governments was the boundary dividing their possessions in America. This boundary, now a symbol of good will in international relations, was then, and especially in the years 1837–1841, a line of discord. From the Atlantic to the Pacific it was a succession of embers, each ready to be fanned by some gust of national feeling into a conflagration. At the northeast the Maine-New Brunswick section had been in dispute for more than half a century. It had become in the years 1838–1839 the scene of private and public disturbances known as the "Aroostook War." On the border between New Hampshire and Quebec, in the upper basin of the Connecticut, another conflict smoldered, an ominous manifestation of which was the formation in the 1830's of a squatters' "Republic of Indian Stream."[1] In neighboring New York, inflammatory incidents were occurring one after another along the Niagara boundary, notably the destruction by a Canadian force of a river steamboat, the *Caroline*, moored on the American side of the river, and the later explosive affair of Alexander McLeod arising out of it. Just west of the Great Lakes another dispute smoldered concerning the Grande Portage, a carrying place around the falls of the Pigeon River, strategic for the fur

[1] A scholarly work on this subject is Roger H. Brown, *The Struggle for the Indian Stream Territory* (Cleveland, 1955).

trade and for the connection it gave with the transportation systems of the Far West.

In the Far West the unresolved Oregon issue was again becoming a menace to peace. In an earlier period it had generated such episodes as the British seizure of Astoria, the "Ontario" affair, and the diplomatic crisis of 1825–1826. It had become less explosive after the agreement, reached in 1827, to renew the convention of joint occupation. But in 1841 it was flaring up again as a result of the migration of American pioneers to the valley of the Willamette. A resolution introduced into Congress in January, 1841, directing the President to serve notice on England of the termination of the convention of joint occupation, was an omen of new dangers.[2] At stake in this dispute was a vast wilderness, an area forty times the square mileage involved in the Maine controversy.

Issues other than boundary disputes confronted the two governments. One of these was over the maritime slave trade, a trade forbidden by most Christian nations to their subjects but carried on clandestinely by adventurers using false flags. The British government in the effort to suppress it sought to obtain from other governments treaties conferring on their navies mutual rights of visit to suspected slavers. The authorities of the United States, with memories still fresh of earlier British visitation and search of vessels in quest of sailors to impress, were unwilling to participate in such a program. Related to this issue was another, arising out of the American domestic slave trade and marked by the incident of the brig *Creole*, which had created excitement in the southern states of the Union.

A clearance of this accumulation of critical issues was more than ordinary diplomacy could effect. It required, in the judgment of the British government, a special negotiation. For such a negotiation the city of Washington was considered the best seat. Late in December, 1841, the British ministry determined to send a special mission to the United States. It prevailed on Lord Ashburton to be its head and gave him sole charge of the negotiation. The resident British minister in Washington, Henry S. Fox, was allowed no part in it. Fox had long shown ill will toward the United States and its

---

[2] This resolution, referred to in the instructions to Ashburton, had been brought before the Senate by Lewis F. Linn of Missouri. It was not passed. *Senate Journal*, 27 Cong., 2 Sess. (1841–1842), 81.

institutions that had disturbed Peel and was to lead shortly to his recall.[3]

Ashburton was a happy choice. As former head of the great London banking house of Baring Brothers, he had an outlook that was international rather than narrowly national. He was widely respected for ability, integrity, and public spirit. He ranked high in the counsels of the Conservative party. He might have been, if he had wished, a cabinet member in the Peel government. He was especially well qualified for a mission of reconciliation to America. He had been a lifelong defender of American causes in England and was recognized as such in the United States. His house had arranged the loan by which the Louisiana Purchase had been financed. He had stoutly supported the position of the United States in the controversy preceding the War of 1812. He had facilitated the peace negotiations at Ghent which brought that war to an end. His house had been a distributor of American state and corporation securities to British investors. He was a personal friend of Webster. His wife was the daughter of a prominent American financier. The appointment of a British lord of this eminence to a special mission at Washington was flattering to the pride of Americans and was hailed with pleasure by the American press.

The negotiation which followed marked a turning point in Anglo-American relations. It marked the end of an era of the piling up of controversies and the opening of an era of their systematic removal. Indicative of the change was an altered temper in the conduct of the negotiation. The stiff formalities, the maneuvering for advantage, the clashes over the form of minutes, the distrusts and tensions of earlier negotiations were absent. The negotiators dealt with each other informally, without minutes, in a spirit of give-and-take and mutual trust. Indeed, they entered, while in the preliminary stages of the Maine discussions, into a virtual conspiracy with each other to disarm the intransigents on that issue in each other's public and to make possible a compromise settlement. The treaty concluded by them was a major achievement. It was epoch-making in the number and magnitude of the controversies it put to rest.

[3] Sir Robert Peel to Lord Aberdeen, November 17, 1841, Peel Papers (British Museum); Lord Ashburton to Aberdeen, May 12, 1842, Aberdeen Papers (British Museum).

But it was incomplete. It contained no settlement of the Oregon dispute. For this dispute Webster and Ashburton had been able to find no solution. They had resolved to postpone the search for one. That was the acceptance of failure. It meant the frustration of the desire of the two governments for a sweep of all their controversies. It meant the projection of the controversy into the era of the organized migrations of pioneers to the Oregon Country and the resultant burgeoning of the issue into a war crisis in 1845–1846.

An isolated failure in a negotiation otherwise successful is a subject that challenges study. It raises the question of the nature of the impediments by which the failure was caused. In the Oregon negotiation the impediments were not, it is clear, of a kind intrinsic in the problem. They were not, as they had been in earlier Oregon negotiations, irreconcilable clashes of interest. These had passed with the passing of the lower Columbia fur trade. Any differences of interest remaining in 1842 were reconciled in 1846, under the adverse conditions of a war crisis, by a partition agreement which was mutually advantageous and well received. In that agreement new means of settlement played no part. The means employed were old. The central idea—a partition line via the Strait of Juan de Fuca—had been intimated as a solution as early as the negotiation of 1826 by Albert Gallatin.

The impediments to an agreement in 1842 were essentially procedural. They were such as are common in diplomacy—hasty and uninformed preparation for the Oregon portion of the negotiation by the persons charged with it in England, including excessive dependence on subordinates; misinterpretations in Washington by each negotiator of what was said or done by the other, with resulting inaction and delays; finally, fatigue, illness, and the eagerness of the negotiators to escape the exhausting summer heat of Washington, which led to a premature cessation of their labors. The negotiators got bogged down in a morass of procedures that were defective, and frailties that were personal, and the opportunity for a complete clearance of Anglo-American controversies passed.

The first step into the morass was a set of instructions drafted on the Oregon issue for Lord Ashburton. The instructions were a historical anachronism. They amounted to a retraction of a quarter of a century of British offers. They authorized two proposals of partition of the Oregon Country, one designed to open the bargaining, the other to be presented if the first failed. The first was an offer of a line starting where the crest of the Rocky Mountains is intersected by the forty-ninth parallel, dropping southwardly along the crest to a meeting with the Snake River, and thence following the channels of the Snake and the Columbia to the sea. This was a line less favorable to the United States by far than any ever proposed by the British in preceding negotiations. It reserved to England not only all the Oregon Country north of the forty-ninth parallel, but, of the portion south, nearly all of the present states of Washington and Idaho. It left the United States not much more of the Oregon Country than the present state of Oregon. Not even in 1818, at the outset of the Oregon negotiations, had the British government ventured to propose such a division.[4]

The second authorization was a line along the forty-ninth parallel from the crest of the Rocky Mountains to an intersection with the Columbia River, and thence along the channel of the river to the sea. This line had been offered repeatedly by the British in earlier negotiations and had been as often rejected. It was nevertheless made the final British offer. Ashburton was given no authority to make any concessions north of the Columbia River.

In an earlier negotiation, in 1826, George Canning had offered a tract of land to the United States north of the Columbia—a tract adjoining Juan de Fuca Strait. He had made the offer to meet the insistent American demand for a share in the harbors inside the Strait, particularly for a harbor that could be used as a naval base. The area offered was an enclave; it was surrounded on every side by British territory or waters which the British navy would be able to dominate. Albert Gallatin, the American representative, had rejected the offer for this and for other reasons. Even that unattractive proposal Ashburton was not given the power to renew.

The instructions represented a general retreat from earlier British proposals. They constituted a policy of retrogression. So little did they reflect the conciliatory temper and purpose of the mission that a series of questions arises concerning them. Who was their author? Under what circumstances were they prepared? Why were they

---

[4] The Ashburton instructions are in Aberdeen to Ashburton, February 8, 1842, Foreign Office, 5: 378. They are printed in *Papers Relating to the Treaty of Washington* (6 vols., Washington, 1872–1874), V (Berlin Arbitration), 218–19.

so restrictive? These are questions more easily asked than answered. The Foreign Office, which prepares instructions, screens its inner workings from the prying eyes of the historian by a shield of anonymity.

Instructions of importance were ordinarily a joint product of the secretary for foreign affairs, who represented the ministry, and the career staff. The secretary took primary responsibility for decisions of policy. The career staff concerned itself more largely with implementation. In some cases participation in the drafting of instructions was permitted to the person for whom they were intended, as it was to Ashburton in the case of the Northeastern boundary instructions.

In the drafting of the Oregon instructions, however, neither Aberdeen nor Ashburton participated directly. Aberdeen merely gave formal approval. He was engrossed at the time in the multitudinous duties of adjustment to his new office. He had world-wide issues of Britain's foreign relations to direct. Among the issues of the Ashburton mission, with which he had hastily to acquaint himself, were those of the Northeastern boundary, the affair of the *Caroline*, the McLeod affair, and the right of visit at sea in peacetime, all more urgent than the Oregon problem. To the Oregon problem he was a newcomer. He had never been obliged to deal with it while previously secretary for foreign affairs.[5]

Even less a participant in the drafting of these instructions was Ashburton. He had never had more than a secondhand or general knowledge of the problem. He seems to have considered it an overdrawn issue. He believed that the Pacific Northwest would ultimately become part neither of the British Empire nor of the United States, but would organize itself as an independent republic.[6] He considered the Northeastern problem his chief concern. Of this he had long had a personal knowledge, arising partly from the fact that in Maine lay the Bingham estate of his wife's family.[7] The career staff of the Foreign Office thus was left with virtually no policy direction in the drafting of the Oregon instructions.

---

[5] The instructions were submitted for comment to selected members of the cabinet. They elicited no very useful responses.

[6] Ashburton to William Sturgis, April 2, 1845, *House Exec. Docs.*, 42 Cong., 3 Sess. (1872–1873), No. 1, pt. 6, p. 37.

[7] Frederick S. Allis (ed.), *William Bingham's Maine Lands, 1790–1820*, Colonial Society of Massachusetts, *Publications* (Boston), XXXVI-XXXVII (1954).

The career staff labored under other handicaps. It was given little time for the preparation of any part of the instructions. Peel and Aberdeen wished the negotiation in Washington to open at the earliest possible moment in order that its result could be acted on by the Senate of the United States before the adjournment of Congress in the summer of 1842. The Senate's Whig majority, elected in the political overturn of 1840, was favorable to an Anglo-American understanding. But whether its control of the Senate would continue long was uncertain. The Whig party had become deeply divided as a result of the death of Harrison and the clash of the party chiefs with John Tyler. If a treaty were to be held over to the opening of Congress in 1843 it might come before a body that had been changed in its political complexion by the autumn elections. Ashburton was, therefore, early in February, 1842, hustled off to America, though even the Northeastern portion of his instructions was not yet in final form.

More serious than the precipitance with which the Oregon instructions were drawn was the disorganization of the staff drafting them. The staff was at that time virtually leaderless. It had lost its veteran head, the permanent under-secretary for many years, John Backhouse. He had become incapacitated by illness and had resigned shortly before the Ashburton mission was undertaken.[8] Lord Aberdeen had been obliged, before the drafting of the Ashburton instructions could go forward, to set out on an emergency hunt for a new permanent under-secretary. The person he found was Henry Unwin Addington.

Addington was a retired diplomat, well versed at one time in the issues of Anglo-American relations. He had been particularly well informed on the Oregon and the Maine issues. He had been British minister in Washington in 1824–1825, when the agitations of John Floyd and Thomas H. Benton in Congress had brought the Oregon question, in an irritating form, to the notice of himself and of the British foreign secretary, Canning. He had served Canning shortly afterward in London, preparing for the Gallatin mission which was to take up the Oregon and the Maine problems. He and William Huskisson had been the British plenipotentiaries in the 1826 negotiations on these issues with Gallatin.[9] He was in 1842 the sole British

---

[8] *Annual Register, 1845* (London, 1846), App. 313.
[9] See Essay, 5, pp. 111–112, 156–157, 164.

survivor of those negotiations. He had good family connections. He was the nephew of a former British prime minister of the same family name. On January 14, 1842, he was invited by Aberdeen to become permanent under-secretary in the Foreign Office. He accepted on a temporary basis at first, but a few months later took an appointment without limit of time.[10] He continued in this office until 1854, and thus was permanent under-secretary throughout the critical last years of the Oregon controversy.

He had been in his earlier years a protégé of Canning. He had absorbed the unfriendly attitude of his master toward the United States. In the 1826 negotiation he had been, as Gallatin reported home, "extremely difficult."[11] He was still, in 1842, a disciple of Canning rather than of his new chief in his approach to American problems. In the Northeastern portion of the Ashburton instructions his preconceptions had to be subordinated to the wishes and the knowledge of Aberdeen and Ashburton. In the Oregon portion he was his own master.

His preconceptions concerning the division of the Oregon Country dated back to the Oregon negotiation of 1826. More directly they stemmed from a proposal the Hudson's Bay Company had sent the Foreign Office in 1825. That proposal was to draw a line starting where the crest of the Rocky Mountains is intersected by the forty-ninth parallel, dropping southwardly along the crest to the Snake, and thence following the channel of the Snake and the Columbia to the sea. This line had been the concept of George Simpson, the Company's American administrator, and it reflected the Company's grasping policy. It had intrigued Canning. He had directed Addington to take testimony concerning it from Simpson, with the result that Addington had become infected with the virus of British fur trade imperialism.[12]

But Canning had been too realistic in the end to offer such a line to the United States. He had already in 1824 offered the United States a much more favorable one—the forty-ninth parallel to the Columbia and the Columbia to the sea. He had contented himself

---

[10] Henry U. Addington to Aberdeen, January 16, 1842, Aberdeen Papers.
[11] Albert Gallatin to Henry Clay, July 29, 1827, *American State Papers, Foreign Relations* (6 vols., Washington, 1832–1859), VI, 684.
[12] See Essay 5, pp. 111–112, 156–157.

in 1826 with renewing the 1824 offer. When it had been declined, he had made his enclave offer, which Gallatin had also declined.[13] If Addington, in 1842, had used the realism practiced by his old master, he would, in drafting the Oregon instructions, have offered first a line not widely differing from the initial offer of 1826. Instead, he exhumed the Hudson's Bay Company proposal of Simpson, already in 1826 an anachronism, and dressed it up as a first offer.

As a second offer Addington authorized the Columbia River line, thrice before offered in negotiations to the United States and thrice refused. He made this the final authorization—the final resort of Ashburton for reaching an agreement. He withheld altogether from the instruction the enclave offer of 1826. He did not even inform Aberdeen of the fact that in a preceding negotiation such an offer had been made.

If Aberdeen had known that such an offer had once been made he would probably have wished to renew it. He might even have wished to enlarge it. The fact that Canning had been ready to give ground north of the Columbia to that extent would have seemed to Aberdeen important. It was evidence that so redoubtable an imperialist as Canning recognized the reasonableness of the American demand for a share in the harbors of Puget Sound and the straits, and was willing to make some concession to meet it. Aberdeen might conceivably have used the Canning offer as a means of reconciling the cabinet to the terms of settlement agreed to soon after in the treaty of 1846.

But Aberdeen was completely without knowledge that the enclave offer had ever been made. He did not have knowledge of it until November, 1843, more than a year after the conclusion of the Webster-Ashburton negotiation. He then learned of it, not from his own Foreign Office staff, but from Edward Everett, the American minister in London.[14]

It seems all but incredible that in 1842 the enclave offer could have been wholly unknown to Aberdeen. The offer was a matter of

[13] *Ibid.*
[14] Edward Everett to Aberdeen, November 30, 1843, Aberdeen Papers; Everett to Abel P. Upshur, December 2, 1843, Everett Papers (Massachusetts Historical Society, Boston).

public record. It had been so for years. It was printed among the documents of the negotiation of 1826, which Congress had ordered published in 1828.[15] Yet in 1843 Aberdeen gave Everett his personal assurance that he had been completely unaware of it. He had to be shown proof of it before he even gave credence to it.[16] His word was accepted by Everett at full value. Aberdeen was a man of such integrity of character that a personal falsehood from him, which in this case would have served no purpose, is more difficult to credit than his statement that he did not know of the offer.

Even more remarkable than Aberdeen's confession of ignorance was an assurance he gave Everett a few days later that Addington himself had no recollection of such an offer having been made. That assurance "staggered" Everett, who knew that Addington had been one of the plenipotentiaries who had made it. Everett thought for a moment he might himself have been in error; that the offer might have been made in a preceding negotiation. He returned to the documents of the negotiation of 1826 to reassure himself, after which he sent Aberdeen the page reference to it in the minutes of the negotiation.[17]

The inability of Addington to recollect the enclave offer may well have been a case of diplomatic forgetfulness. It is difficult to account for otherwise. Addington not only was the maker of the offer, but, after it had been rejected, had sought to keep it from being entered on the minutes. He and his colleague, Huskisson, had asked of Gallatin that it be omitted, on the ground, not altogether truthful, that it had been unofficially made. Gallatin had given his consent to omitting any reference to it. But when he had been asked, in addition, to enter the positive statement on the minutes that no offer beyond the Columbia River line had been made, he had refused on the ground that such a statement would be a falsification of the record. Addington and Huskisson had finally permitted the offer to be entered on the record with the reservation that it was not to be regarded as prejudicing the British position in the future.[18] Such a history ought to have left some imprint on

[15] *House Docs.*, 20 Cong., 1 Sess. (1827–1828), No. 199.
[16] Everett to Aberdeen, November 30, 1843, Aberdeen Papers.
[17] Everett to Upshur, December 2, 1843, Everett Papers; Everett to Aberdeen, November 30, 1843, Aberdeen Papers.
[18] See Essay 5, pp. 168–169.

any mind of ordinary retentiveness even at a distance of sixteen years, and Addington had a reputation in London for accuracy of memory.

Nor did he have to be wholly dependent on memory. He had the records of the 1826 negotiation. It is hardly conceivable that he did not read them to refresh his memory prior to drafting the Oregon instructions. Evidence that he did so, and with some care, is afforded by his exhumation of the Hudson's Bay Company proposal of 1825 in exact form. The enclave offer was conspicuously in evidence in the 1826 records. It was in evidence in Canning's instructions to his two negotiators, in their progress reports, and in the minutes of the negotiation.[19]

A remark which Addington dropped to Edward Everett in the summer or autumn of 1843 heightens the suspicion that his lapse of memory in 1842 was diplomatic. Addington was discussing informally with Everett a new Oregon negotiation for which the British and American governments were preparing. He casually declared that in the new negotiation "he was disposed to take higher ground" than had been taken by his government in 1826.[20] By this remark he produced alarm in the mind of Everett, who some months later, with relief, reported to Washington an assurance given him by Aberdeen that in the new negotiation the British government would at least abide by the proposals it had made in 1826.[21] The higher ground Addington was disposed to take in 1843 he had probably thought it desirable to take in 1842, and the forgetting of the enclave offer would have made the ascent easier.

Addington conceived of himself, perhaps, as regaining ground lost to the United States in earlier negotiations. He knew that Canning had been reluctant in the 1826 negotiation to make the enclave offer, that he had made it only in response to pressure from Lord Liverpool, the prime minister. He had given Canning loyal support as a subordinate in that negotiation in resisting concessions to the United States. He knew of Aberdeen's reputation for concession in dealing with foreign states. In drafting the Oregon in-

---

[19] *Ibid.*, pp. 110–111, 168–169. The minutes of the negotiation are printed in *A.S.P., F.R.*, VI, 639–706.
[20] Everett to Upshur, November 14, 1843, Everett Papers.
[21] *Ibid.*

structions he may have conceived of himself as defending empire interests too easily yielded by his new chief. If this is the explanation of his loss of memory, it would not be the only occasion in the history of international relations when the policy of a new administration has been resisted and thwarted by a bureaucracy representing the point of view of an earlier government.

Documents other than the instructions had to be readied for the Oregon negotiation, especially transcripts of confidential records for Ashburton's reference purposes in Washington. The staff of the Foreign Office had the duty of providing these. The ones actually provided were relatively few, four for the Oregon negotiation as compared with fifteen for the Northeastern. Those for the Oregon negotiation, according to a list preserved in the Foreign Office, were a set of the minutes of the negotiation of 1823–24, a copy of the letter containing the Hudson's Bay Company partition proposal of 1825, a memorandum consisting of a defense of the British claim to the Oregon Country which had been prepared by Addington for the 1826 negotiation, and a historical survey, not of much value, of the Oregon controversy.[22] Omitted was a copy of the minutes of the 1826 negotiation. This was a strange omission. It deprived Ashburton of the record of the most recent of the series of the Oregon negotiations, which if he had had an opportunity to read, would have given him knowledge of the enclave offer.[23] Ashburton was, like Aberdeen, apparently unaware of the enclave offer throughout his negotiations with Webster.

The Foreign Office staff revealed its disorganization also by its failure to obtain current information bearing on the Oregon issue. It gathered current information regarding neither the trade nor the needs of the Hudson's Bay Company in the lower Columbia Valley. The trade and needs of the Company had changed materially since the preceding Oregon negotiation. Trapping in the area had almost ceased; the fur bearing animals had been trapped out. Agriculture was establishing itself: farming by Americans south of the river; grazing, by a subsidiary of the Hudson's Bay Company, north of the river. The river itself was steadily becoming

[22] Foreign Office, 5: 378.
[23] Copies of the documents of the 1826 negotiation were in the archives of the British mission in Washington by the close of 1843. The date of their arrival cannot be ascertained. They may have been sent in connection with the marking of the Northeastern boundary by the British and American surveyors.

less important to the traders. The perils of its bar, the difficulties of its channel above the bar, the formidable interruptions to navigation upon the middle reaches of the river, all long troublesome to the Company, had already led to serious consideration of a shift of base to a new site at the southern tip of Vancouver Island, a shift actually made in 1844–45.[24]

If such information had been assembled by the Foreign Office, it might well have induced a reconsideration of the old British insistence on a boundary staked at the midstream of the river. It might have made acceptable to Aberdeen and the cabinet some new basis of a settlement, for instance a settlement which merely reserved to the Hudson's Bay Company the right to a free use of the river, as was done a few years later in the treaty. Recognition might then have been given to the need of the United States for a foothold on the Juan de Fuca Strait which would have met the American requirement of a usable harbor on the Pacific.

Information for any such reconsideration of Oregon policy was convenient to hand. At the Hudson's Bay House in London, the headquarters of the Company's far-flung territories, there was a unique collection of Oregon materials. The annual field reports of the Company's Oregon operations were in constant use there. They were filled with detailed descriptions of the trade and transportation needs of the valley of the lower river. To these reports the government had rights of access, for the Company was a semipublic corporation, enjoying special government privileges in the Oregon Country. Canning had used their information in preparing for the Oregon negotiation of 1826. He had directed Addington to obtain a synthesis of it from Simpson. For a negotiation later than that of Ashburton the Foreign Office obtained information concerning the affairs of the Columbia from the Company.[25] But in preparing for the Ashburton instructions it appears not to have been in touch with the Company at all.

Instead, the Foreign Office acted on information gathered in 1826. On this basis it staked the British claims immovably at the midstream of the Columbia. It omitted the enclave offer; it undertook to cut the United States off entirely from harbors at the straits.

---

[24] See Essay 8, pp. 245–254; also Joseph Schafer (ed.), "Letters of Sir George Simpson, 1841–1843," *American Historical Review*, XIV (October 1908), 70–94.
[25] See references in n. 24.

And in the briefings of Ashburton the same program was stressed. The retention by England of the north bank of the Columbia was pressed upon Ashburton as the "great desideratum." Rigidity became intrenched as policy in the absence of new information and fresh appraisal, with results that were to be recorded upon the outcome of the negotiation.

With instructions not yet completed for part of his agenda, Ashburton left London for America early in February, 1842. He went in state on a frigate of the navy, partly for the purpose of honoring the United States. Arriving in Washington early in April, he found Webster planning to bring the governments of Maine and Massachusetts into the Northeastern boundary negotiation. This required approval by Ashburton, and caused a delay of several months in the opening of this part of the negotiation.

While he and Webster waited for the commissioners of Maine and Massachusetts, they held conferences on items on the agenda which, in the interval, could be disposed of. On the Oregon issue they held a conference soon after Ashburton's arrival. It was exploratory in nature, intended to locate bases for an agreement. It located, instead, the shoals of the Addington instructions. The conference opened with a *pro forma* offer by Ashburton of the first partition proposal of his instructions. This was declined. Then the second offer was made—the line of the forty-ninth parallel to the Columbia and the Columbia to the sea. This, Ashburton made clear, was his final offer—it was the full extent of his powers. By Webster it was neither accepted nor rejected. He complained merely that the line would leave the United States without a single safe harbor on the Pacific.

Thus at the very outset, the negotiators were on shoals—the shoals on which every Oregon negotiation from the first had gone to wreck. In all the earlier negotiations the British had anchored themselves at the river, which was the central transportation system of the Oregon Country. Their determination had been to possess at least the north bank of the river, which would insure them free use of its channel. The Americans had taken their position at the straits, seeking harbors that could be obtained only if the boundary line were located north of the river.

Webster appears to have come to the conclusion, when he learned of the limits of Ashburton's instructions, that a peaceful end to the

Oregon dispute could be reached only if a new approach to it were taken. He intimated to Ashburton that the new approach might lead to the Mexican province of California, just south of the Oregon Country. There lay the magnificent harbor of San Francisco. If this could become the possession of the United States by an agreement satisfying England and Mexico, the need of the United States for harbors at the straits would be relieved. An Oregon treaty permitting the partition line to be at the Columbia River might then become acceptable. The idea intrigued Ashburton, who took it for reference to his government.

Only one connected account of this important conference, written by a participant, is extant—a letter sent by Ashburton to Aberdeen on April 25, 1842. This is so revealing a document that it deserves to be quoted at length. Ashburton wrote:

The Oregon or Columbia river boundary, I hope to settle satisfactorily, and by this I mean to carry our line down to the river, which seems from a careful examination of all the information furnished me to be the great desideratum. I shall make no settlement in this case on any other terms.

The Americans evidently attach great importance to their territory on the Pacific, although at present they have few if any settlers there, and as they have located the great body of Indian tribes which they have forced back from the countries east of the Mississippi, on the head waters of the Missouri towards the Rocky Mountains and the Pacific, it will not be easy for their Western settlements to spread in the usual manner in that direction for many years to come. What they are principally looking to is to have a harbour of their own on the Pacific. The mouth of the Columbia is a barred and indifferent harbour, but they say that the estuary to the North of it, entered, I believe, by the Strait of Juan de Fuca is the only good harbour on this part of the coast, and hence the obstinacy with which they have hitherto persisted in carrying the boundary line further north. In a preliminary conversation with Mr. Webster I told him plainly that I could make no arrangement in this matter which did not give us the joint use with them of the northern branch [the main channel] of the Columbia River. After complaining that this would leave them no harbour he intimated that this might be managed if they could make a settlement of boundaries with Mexico, so as to give them the harbour of San Francisco (a very good one I believe) in latitude 37½. I said that we could take no part in any arrangement of this description, but that although I had no power to enter upon the subject at all, I believed that we should make no objection to any arrangement of the kind, provided the cession by

Mexico were voluntary. Here this matter now stands. We shall probably get our boundary with the understanding I mention, but without waiting for our Treaty the conclusion of their arrangements with Mexico with which we are to have no concern.

This acquisition of the harbour of San Francisco seems to have been a project of some standing; for Mr. Everett spoke to me of it before I left England. I doubt whether in any case we could interfere with effect to prevent this arrangement, unless it were attempted to be forced upon Mexico. We shall therefore probably do well to avail ourselves of the circumstance of this expectation to settle satisfactorily our own boundaries. I much doubt whether the Americans will for many years to come make any considerable lodgment on the Pacific. The Indians are in great force there and naturally jealous of and hostile to them.[26]

A striking feature of this letter is the prediction Ashburton made in it that he would reach a settlement of the Oregon question and that the line of settlement would be the Columbia River. That prediction is made twice and with confidence. It was based on what Ashburton described as an "intimation" from Webster. The intimation was of a plan under which Mexico would be induced to cede territory in California, sufficient to include the port of San Francisco, to the United States; England would acquiesce in the cession; the United States would accept a partition line in Oregon at the Columbia River. That plan, as amplified later by Webster,[27] is now known among historians as the "tripartite" plan.

As a mere intimation it was open to differences of interpretation. And it was differently interpreted. By Ashburton it was taken to mean that its parts were separable, that a partition line at the Columbia could be independently, and at once, agreed to and that a subsequent negotiation would take place between the United States and Mexico concerning a cession in California. To Webster it seems to have meant that the parts would be interlocked, that they would move forward together, that an Oregon partition and a California acquisition would be simultaneous. To Webster, also, the plan appears to have been for the long run, something for a future negotiation. At least he took no early steps to acquire territory in California. On May 30, 1842, he received from Waddy Thompson, the American minister in Mexico, who was an enthusiast for American expansion over California, an unsolicited but

[26] Ashburton to Aberdeen, No. 2, April 25, 1842, Foreign Office, 5: 379.
[27] Webster to Everett, January 29, 1843, *The Writings and Speeches of Daniel Webster*, J. W. McIntyre (ed.), 18 vols. (Boston, 1903), XVI, 393–94.

urgent recommendation that a negotiation with Mexico for the acquisition of California be opened.[28] Webster made no reply to it until June 27, 1842, after the Oregon negotiation either had already been or was about to be abandoned as a failure.[29] The likelihood is that the version of Webster's intimation reported by Ashburton was colored by wishful thinking.

Viewed retrospectively, the Webster-Ashburton talk on Oregon was less promising than Ashburton in his cheerful report of it indicated. It was in truth a failure as soon as Webster learned of the rigorous limits imposed on the negotiation by the instructions. The intimation he offered was probably intended to suggest merely how a future escape might be found from the consequences of a present failure. Further discussions of the subject were adjourned, with no clear understanding that they would be resumed. In Ashburton's mind the expectation was that they would be resumed, if the response of the British government to the intimation proved favorable. Actually, they were never resumed. The problem was simply shelved.

The chief agency in this failure was the instructions Ashburton had received. They rendered an agreement virtually impossible. Contributory to the failure were the gaps in Ashburton's knowledge left by the briefings given him. The impact of these gaps on the negotiation appears at a number of points. It appears in the lack of understanding Ashburton seems to have had of the importance to Americans of a harbor on the Pacific. He wrote, as of knowledge he had newly discovered, that what the Americans "are principally looking to is to have a harbour of their own on the Pacific," that the mouth of the Columbia was a barred and indifferent harbor, that the estuary entered by the Strait of Juan de Fuca was the only good harbor on this part of the coast, and hence "the obstinacy with which they [the Americans] have hitherto persisted" in their efforts to carry the line of partition farther north. It appears in the unawareness shown by Ashburton of the enclave offer. He could hardly have been as cheerful as he was regarding the prospect of a boundary at the Columbia River

---

[28] Waddy Thompson to Webster, April 29, 1842, State Department Despatches, Mexico, Vol. XI (National Archives). The letter took a month to reach Washington.

[29] Webster to Thompson, June 27, 1842, Claude H. Van Tyne (ed.), *The Letters of Daniel Webster* (New York, 1902), 269-70.

if he had known that his government in a preceding negotiation had offered the United States harbors at the straits. It appears in the assurance with which he wrote: "I mean to carry our line down to the river, which seems from a careful examination of all the information furnished me to be the great desideratum. I shall make no settlement in this case on any other terms."[30]

The impact made by the instructions on Webster and on the turn he gave the negotiations can only be conjectured. It is not recorded. Webster was, of course, unaware of the manner in which the instructions had been drafted. He could not suppose otherwise than that they represented a matured decision of the British cabinet. He doubtless believed that the unyielding temper they exhibited, and especially their retreat from even the enclave offer, represented a hardening of the British attitude, a warning that the United States must not expect, in its search for harbors, ever to cross the Columbia. He apparently turned to California as the only hope of averting a future clash with England over the harbor issue. It is significant that the earliest official suggestion of an Anglo-American apportioning of the Oregon and California harbors occurred in his intimation at the meeting at which the restrictiveness of the Addington instructions was laid bare.

California had been for years a goal of American expansionists. It had attracted them in all sections of the United States. Even in the Northeast, traditionally cold to expansionism, the superb harbor of San Francisco, offering a port of trade to the Orient, had been considered worth an effort to acquire. Its general attractiveness had been played on by Andrew Jackson in his administration.[31] It had been reflected in the Waddy Thompson exchange of letters with Webster and in Edward Everett's conversation with Ashburton in England to which Ashburton referred. It was felt by Tyler, and even by Webster, who overcame in this case the misgivings he normally felt regarding American expansion to the Pacific.[32]

[30] Ashburton to Aberdeen, No. 2, April 25, 1842, Foreign Office, 5: 379.

[31] See, for example, William H. Wharton to Thomas J. Rusk, [February 16, 1837], George P. Garrison (ed.), *The Diplomatic Correspondence of the Republic of Texas* (Part I), American Historical Association, *Annual Report*, 1907 (2 vols., Washington, 1908), II, 193–94. For a general discussion, see Robert G. Cleland, "The Early Sentiment for the Annexation of California," *Southwestern Historical Quarterly* (Austin), XVIII (July, 1914), 1–40.

[32] In the letter to Thompson, Webster wrote, after an admonition concerning expansionism: "Nevertheless, the benefits of the possession of a good Harbour on

Under the tripartite plan, as subsequently spelled out to Everett, enough of the California province to include San Francisco would be acquired by the United States. It would be acquired peaceably, in exchange for the assumption by the United States of debts owed to American citizens by Mexico. A payment of modest proportions might also be made to Mexico if that should prove necessary.[33] According to the plan, England would bestow her blessing on the transaction. Without taking any active part in it she would agree to view it with benevolent neutrality. She had interests of her own in California, as in other parts of Mexico, by virtue of her trade, her investments, and her position in Central America. She was believed in some American circles to have territorial designs herself on California. She would subordinate these designs and interests if she agreed to a cession of part of the province to the United States. She would in effect sanction the diminution of the assets of one of her debtors. She would receive as compensation the area that lay between the Columbia River and the Strait of Juan de Fuca.[34]

This plan, in its Anglo-American aspects, seemed to suggest an exchange of equivalents. On the surface it appeared an exchange of American territorial claims in the straits region for British concessions in California. Actually, the plan could have had no such appearance to Webster. England had in California no concessions of real substance to offer. She had, as Webster believed, no territorial designs of her own to surrender there.[35] Neither her creditor status in Mexico nor her strategic position in Central America would suffer real impairment from a Mexican sale to the United States

---

the pacific is so obvious, that to that extent, at least, the President strongly inclines to favor the idea of treaty with Mexico." Webster to Thompson, June 27, 1842, Van Tyne (ed.), *Letters of Webster*, 269–70. In 1845, Webster wrote to his son: "You know my opinion to have been, and it now is, that the port of San Francisco would be twenty times as valuable to us as all Texas." Webster to Fletcher Webster, March 11, 1845, *Writings and Speeches of Webster*, XVIII, 204.

[33] For this amplification of Webster's intimation see Webster to Everett, January 29, 1843, *Writings and Speeches of Webster*, XVI, 393–94.

[34] In his letter of January 29, 1843, to Everett, Webster departed from his intimation of 1842 in one important respect. He suggested that the United States retain a small area north of the Columbia, an area corresponding to the enclave Canning had once offered, but enlarged a little so that it would rest on the Columbia River. In 1846, in a private letter, Webster reverted to his willingness to take the unmodified Columbia River line to the forty-ninth parallel. Webster to Franklin Haven, February 2, 1846, *ibid.*, XVIII, 216.

[35] Webster to Thompson, June 27, 1842, Van Tyne (ed.), *Letters of Webster*, 270.

of part of northern California. In a tripartite deal her contribution would be her neutrality, and nothing more. This might have value if the transfer needed to be forced from Mexico. But if it were to be voluntary, as the plan postulated, it would have little value. To a voluntary transfer, as Ashburton observed in his letter to Aberdeen, England would be unable to offer effective opposition in any case. What England would get under the plan would be without cost. She would get gratis from the United States a region which for a quarter of a century American governments had resisted relinquishing: the harbor area between the Columbia and the straits, the commercial prize of the Oregon Country.

If this was the tripartite plan, what explanation is to be made of Webster's even conceiving it? What explanation is to be made of his intimating it to Ashburton? These are questions never directly answered by Webster. But the preceding history of the Oregon problem answers them indirectly. For more than a quarter of a century, in repeated negotiations, the Oregon problem had shown itself resistant to the ordinary diplomatic solvents of give-and-take. It had proved to have embedded in it that despair of diplomats—an intersecting of rival national ambitions. British ambition had been to hold the north bank of the Columbia River as an assurance of continued British use of the central transportation system of the Oregon Country. American ambition had been to gain that bank as an assurance of reaching the harbor waters inside the straits. In 1842 these ambitions seemed to be cutting across each other with greater implacability than ever. British determination to remain at the Columbia had apparently grown stronger. The omission of even the enclave offer from Ashburton's instructions had the appearance of defiance, almost, of American wishes. In the American Congress the agitation of Senator Lewis F. Linn for a radical solution of the Oregon issue was gathering momentum. How then was a collision to be avoided?

San Francisco lay outside this crossing of rival ambitions. It was a port universally desired in the United States. Its acquisition would detour American ambitions out of the danger zone at the north. A cession by Mexico of enough of the remote fringe of her territory to transfer the port would probably be made without too much protest or too high a price. By such an arrangement all possibility of a future Anglo-American clash over the Oregon issue would be averted. The tripartite plan was Webster's escape from the shadow Addington had cast over the negotiation.

Whatever its origin, the tripartite plan was a flight from reality, even in the matured form later communicated to Everett. It would have been agreed to by no American Senate of that era. It would have been denounced by expansionists as a betrayal of the nation. What the expansionists were intent on having was not a choice between harbors at the straits or in California, but harbors in both latitudes and, in addition, the entire provinces in which they lay. If Webster's plan had been of the sort understood by Ashburton, if it had envisaged the signing away of American claims to the Oregon harbors before the United States had acquired the one in California, its author incredibly misconceived the appetite and determination of American expansionists. A plan after that pattern, incorporated into the Webster-Ashburton agreement, would have sunk the entire agreement in the storm it would have let loose in the Senate.

A few weeks after Ashburton's letter reporting the intimation had been sent home, its prediction that the area north of the Columbia would be yielded by the United States was put to test. The United States exploring expedition commanded by Lieutenant Charles Wilkes, which had been absent from the United States nearly four years, examining the shores of the Pacific Northwest among others, returned home. It brought back a wealth of information regarding the mouth of the Columbia and the coasts adjoining it.[36] It gave a very unfavorable report of the harbor at the entrance to the Columbia, and a highly favorable one of the harbors inside the straits. The information it gave on these subjects was not new; but it came with new emphasis to a community that had expanded its horizons and enlarged its desires on the Pacific. The glamour and interest associated with the cruise attached themselves to the

---

[36] The first reports of the expedition appeared unofficially in the press. An official report, exclusively on the Oregon Territory, was written under the date of June, 1842, for Secretary of the Navy Abel P. Upshur, who withheld it from publication. The reason it was withheld was probably its advocacy of such policies as 54° 40' and military occupation by the United States of the Oregon Country. Wilkes gave a synopsis of his cruise as a lecture before the National Institute on June 20, 1842, and this was subsequently published. He made a special report on the hazards of crossing the bar at the mouth of the Columbia, which is printed in *Senate Docs.*, 29 Cong., 1 Sess. (1845–1846), No. 475. The first full printing of the *Narrative of the United States Exploring Expedition* appeared in five volumes in 1844. The work appeared, also, in repeated later editions.

information released by its spokesmen to the press. The new publicity spurred interest in the pioneering potentialities of the Oregon Country. Any possibility that the tripartite solution of the Oregon problem might be acceptable was shattered. It was shattered even in the mind of Ashburton. A fortnight after the expedition returned, on June 29, 1842, he wrote home:

With reference to the subject of Boundaries, I am sorry to have to express my apprehension that I shall not be able to do anything with that on the Pacific. The exploring expedition just returned from a cruize of nearly four years brings a large stock of information about the Columbia River. The public is at present busy with this subject and little in a temper for any reasonable settlement. It must, therefore, I fear, sleep for the present.[37]

The recognition that the issue must sleep for the present was belated. The issue had already, for more than two months, been asleep—ever since the initial Oregon conference. Ashburton had failed sooner to recognize this fact partly because his vision had been blurred by the glitter of the tripartite intimation, partly because he had not yet fathomed a trait in Webster that was to become more evident during the closing meetings of the Maine negotiations, a willingness to give assurances and make promises larger than he could fulfill.[38] Ashburton had finally seen reality in the form of the public response in the United States to the press reports of the exploring expedition. Then he recognized that the tripartite project, as a present reliance, was a delusion.[39] When that became evident he was ready to shelve the whole problem.

His readiness to shelve the problem was an unpleasant surprise to Aberdeen and Peel. It seemed to them a flight from duty.[40]

[37] Ashburton to Aberdeen, No. 10, June 29, 1842, Foreign Office, 5: 379.
[38] Ashburton to Aberdeen, July 13, 1842, Aberdeen Papers. Ashburton wrote: "My real difficulty is with Webster who yields & promises everything, but when it comes to execution is so weak & timid and irresolute that he is frightened by everybody and at last does nothing. I have attached too much importance to his concessions which I thought worth something, but which he is wholly unable to realize."
[39] A similar disillusionment occurred later in the case of Aberdeen. The initial response of Aberdeen to the tripartite intimation was favorable. It continued to be favorable as late as the autumn of 1842. But by February, 1843, it was otherwise. At that time Aberdeen informed Everett that England preferred not to be a party to an American acquisition of California, though she would make no objection to an American purchase of it if Mexico were willing to sell, which he greatly doubted. See Everett to Webster, October 17, 1842, and February 27, 1843, Everett Papers.
[40] Everett to Webster, October 17, 1842, *ibid.*

They were unaware as yet of the difficulties they themselves had created for Ashburton in approving the Addington instructions. They had been misled by the optimism of Ashburton's earlier report. They still desired as much as ever that the Oregon problem be settled. This was part of their hope for a sweep of all outstanding issues with the United States and for the resounding triumph it would give over the preceding administration. If the negotiation could have been continued, it is possible a liberalization of instructions could have been obtained in London under the promptings of Edward Everett. If a settlement on some new basis could have been reached, subsequent, perhaps, to the completion of the Maine agreement, it could have been submitted separately to the Senate.

But to Ashburton any prolongation of his stay in Washington would have been out of the question. He could hardly be induced to remain long enough to conclude the Maine agreement.[41] He had come to America in the expectation that his mission would be completed within four months. He was impatient to have done with it. He was sixty-seven years old, and he labored under the infirmities of age.[42] He was tortured by the heat and humidity of the summer in Washington. In that "oven," as he described it, he was unable to work by day or to sleep by night.[43]

He did not consider the Oregon question urgent. He did not foresee that it would soon become a threat to Anglo-American peace. He underestimated the Oregon fever which was spreading in the West and transforming the issue while he and Webster temporized. His knowledge of the conditions affecting migrations to the Oregon Country was defective. He believed that a great body of Indian tribes, forced out of the area east of the Mississippi, had been relocated on the headwaters of the Missouri, where it would interpose a barrier to the migration of Americans over the Rockies. He nursed misconceptions as to the deterring effect of the Indians resident in the Pacific Northwest upon the migrations. He

[41] Webster to Everett, June 28, 1842, *Writings and Speeches of Webster*, XVI, 375–76.
[42] Ashburton to Aberdeen, December 22, 1841, and April 26, 1842, Aberdeen Papers.
[43] Ashburton to Aberdeen, June 29 and July 28, 1842, *ibid.*; Ashburton to Webster, July 1, 1842, in George T. Curtis, *Life of Daniel Webster* (5th ed., 2 vols., New York, 1889), II, 113 n.

doubted that for many years to come Americans would make "any considerable lodgment on the Pacific." He entertained, besides, the reassuring conviction that an independent republic would rise on the shores of the Pacific, which would ultimately remove the Oregon issue as a disturber of Anglo-American relations. He felt free, because of such ideas, to yield to the temptation to shelve the problem.[44]

Webster also felt free for similar reasons to put the problem aside. His health was bad. He labored under a chronic ailment that was always acute in the heat of the Washington summer. According to Ashburton, at the end of July, he looked as if he would not "much outlive our treaty and I would not answer for myself if the work were to last long."[45] In Webster's mind was rooted the same conviction as in Ashburton's that an independent republic would rise before long in the Pacific Northwest which would possess itself of the Columbia and of the harbors at the straits.[46] The territory itself he valued little. He considered the Pacific Northwest a poor country.[47] He was fearful of the results of national expansionism. In common with other Whigs of his day he accepted a doctrine earlier formulated by Jefferson, and treasured for a time by Democrats, that any democracy which annexed territories lying at a great distance did so at its peril. In his reply to Waddy Thompson concerning California, he admonished this expansionist: "In seeking acquisitions, to be governed as Territories, & lying at a great distance from the United States, we ought to be governed by our prudence & caution; & a still higher degree of these qualities should be exercised when large Territorial acquisitions are looked for, with a view to annexation."[48]

Besides, Webster believed that if necessary the Oregon issue could be settled by way of the tripartite plan. He had hopes of being appointed to the court of London, in replacement of Everett, upon completion of the Ashburton negotiation. In London he would be able to implement the tripartite plan by direct dealings with the

---

[44] *Hansard's*, Third series, LXVI (1843), 59.

[45] Ashburton to Aberdeen, July 28, 1842, Aberdeen Papers.

[46] Speech at Faneuil Hall, November 7, 1845, *Writings and Speeches of Webster*, XIII, 314.

[47] Webster to Everett, January 29, 1844, *ibid.*, XVIII, 179.

[48] Webster to Thompson, June 27, 1842, Van Tyne (ed.), *Letters of Webster*, 269. See also Webster to "Mr. Bigelow *et al.*," January 23, 1844, *ibid.*, 289-94.

British government.[49] He found it seductively easy, therefore, to agree with Ashburton that the settlement of the issue should be postponed.

The decision to postpone was, in fact, inescapable. It was ordained by Ashburton's instructions. The instructions—retrogressive in character, prepared without direction or information by subordinates imbued with the spirit of imperialism of an earlier day —sent a chain reaction of confusion flowing through the negotiation. At the outset they misled Webster, who did not fathom their lowly origin, as to what was Britain's ultimate goal. Anglophile himself, compromising in temper, possessed of an elastic conscience about putting the property of others to his use, he responded to their surprising rigidities with a misty and unrealistic intimation. This, in turn, misled Ashburton into hoping for an easy agreement, with the result that neither he nor Webster, nor their governments, came to grips with the realities of the problem. Frailties of health and the lack of recognition of new forces stirring in the United States merely brought a final avowal of a failure that had been foreordained.

In itself, postponement of the settlement of an international issue is not a failure. It may, in some cases, be actually constructive. It may provide an opportunity for passions to cool, for information to be gathered, for the healing forces of time to operate. But in this case postponement had no such compensations. What it did was to allow the solution of the Oregon problem to drift away from an existing period of good will, away from the momentum of the achievements won in the negotiation, and into the era of the covered wagon migrations, the politics of expansionism, and the war crisis of the Polk administration.

[49] Webster to Everett, January 29, 1843, *Writings and Speeches of Webster,* XVI, 393–96.

ESSAY 7 · ARBITRATION ONLY AT THE CANNON'S MOUTH!

THE STRANGE vicissitudes and partial successes of the Webster-Ashburton negotiation were followed by a deterioration of Anglo-American relations. The "Battle of the Maps" was fought, consisting of charges and countercharges of cartographic dishonesty that had been resorted to in arriving at the Northeastern boundary settlement. The "Battle" was opened by Lord Palmerston to prove the Peel government's ineptitude in the negotiation. It was taken up in the United States to prove Palmerston's trickiness in hiding important cartographic evidence during his incumbency of the Foreign Office. The warfare transferred its bitterness to the Oregon dispute. It alerted nationalists on each side to the likelihood of similar chicanery in Oregon negotiations yet to come. It led to increased agitation in Congress to force a settlement of that issue by serving "notice" on the British of American intention to terminate the old convention of joint occupation.[1]

By the autumn of 1843 Lord Aberdeen was aware of the need for a new negotiation. London would have been preferred by him as the seat for the negotiation and Edward Everett, the American minister there, as the negotiator for the United States. Everett was trusted by Aberdeen and was popular even with the opposition in London. But politically Washington was the better seat for the negotiation. This was partly because Everett was less trusted by his own government than he was by the British. He was a hangover from the Whig days of the Tyler administration, which had already moved far into its Democratic days. Furthermore, a new British minister was needed in Washington to replace Henry S. Fox, who was out of favor there. Richard Pakenham, the British minister to Mexico, on a visit to London at the time, was promoted to the Washington legation. His instructions were drawn by Aberdeen in consultation with Everett.

[1] The agitation to serve notice became a major subject of debate in Congress in 1843.

The instructions went as far toward satisfying the Oregon demands of the United States as was possible without special cabinet authorization. They repeated every concession ever proposed to the American government. In addition they directed Pakenham to offer the United States any harbors it might want between the line of the 49th parallel and the Columbia, including those on Vancouver Island, as free ports. If these concessions should prove insufficient Pakenham was instructed to propose arbitration.

Unofficially Aberdeen widened the authorized concessions prior to Pakenham's departure in December 1843 for Washington. Orally he added concessions of a major order. He took this step because he was not sanguine of results from the written instructions, as he confessed to Pakenham. He directed Pakenham to draw out from the American Secretary of State, if possible, a modified version of the old American offer of 49°. The modification was to consist of stopping the line at the water's edge so that it would not apply to Vancouver Island. The line should go out to sea via the Strait of Juan de Fuca. All ports south of this line, inclusive of the mouth of the Columbia River, should be free ports to Great Britain; also, the navigation of the Columbia should be common to both sides. Aberdeen warned Pakenham that he did not have cabinet consent for these concessions, but hope could be given the American negotiator that a proposal along these lines would be favorably considered by the British government. A letter confirming these conversations was sent by Aberdeen to Pakenham on March 4, 1844.[2]

In the United States the climate was less favorable in 1844 than it had been in 1842 for a fruitful Oregon negotiation. The flow of pioneers to the Oregon Country was on the increase. On the increase, also, was "All Oregon" agitation in Congress, and its tone was violent. In American politics an ominous union of the issues of "All Oregon" and "immediate annexation" of Texas was forming. The air was filled with the feverishness of an oncoming presidential canvass.

In the State Department, the successors to Daniel Webster (Abel P. Upshur and John C. Calhoun) were Texas-minded rather than

---

[2] The official instructions are in Aberdeen to Pakenham, Dec. 28, 1843, Foreign Office 5: 39. The unofficial ones are in Aberdeen to Pakenham, March 4, 1844, Aberdeen Papers, British Museum. The evidence of conversations prior to Pakenham's departure is in Pakenham to Aberdeen, March 28, 1844, *ibid.*

Oregon-minded. They were Southerners, and exceedingly pro-slavery in their thinking. Upshur, it is true, desired a new Oregon negotiation on a compromise basis, but his career was cut short by an explosion on the warship "Princeton" soon after Pakenham's arrival. As for Calhoun, he had a preference for "masterly inactivity" in Oregon matters, and he carried on negotiations with Pakenham unenergetically. In the summer of 1844 he gave Pakenham warning that any British proposal, short of the old American proposal of 49°, would meet certain defeat in the Senate, and that the same fate would meet any British proposals of arbitration. A conviction became established in Pakenham's mind that an attempt to extract a proposal from Calhoun of the kind contemplated in his unofficial instructions would end in failure.[3]

With the advent of Polk to the White House in 1845, the climate in Washington for an Oregon settlement became even less favorable. Polk was committed, by a campaign letter prior to the Democratic nominating convention of 1844, to a program: "not to permit Great Britain or any other foreign power to plant a colony or hold dominion over any portion of the people or territory of either [Oregon or Texas]." He was further committed to that program in running for the presidency on the Democratic platform in 1844 and by his Inaugural Address to Congress. Yet a few months after the Inaugural, in continuing the languishing negotiation inherited from Tyler, he directed the new Secretary of State, James Buchanan, to offer what his predecessors had so long been offering—the line of the 49th parallel. His proposal did not include what his predecessors had included—a British right to share in the navigation of the Columbia south of the line of 49°. The proposal seemed to Pakenham so far short of what even his unofficial instructions had contemplated that he rejected it. He did not even take it for reference to his government. Indeed he went so far as to ask, in the conventional language of diplomats, for an offer "more consistent with fairness and equity." Polk's reply was to order the withdrawal of his proposal. Though the minister was disavowed by his government and was privately directed to obtain a resubmission of the proposal, the President would not move. The negotiation—the fifth in the series—came to a close.

[3] St. George L. Sioussat, "John Caldwell Calhoun" in Samuel F. Bemis, *American Secretaries of State* (New York, 1928–29) V, 193–197; Claude H. Hall, *Abel Parker Upshur* (Madison, 1963).

The President next took the issue to Congress. In his first annual message he recommended termination of the 1827 convention of joint occupation. He asked for a congressional notice of termination to become operative a year after the notice was served. He added that then "we shall have reached a period when the national rights in Oregon must either be abandoned or firmly maintained. That they can not be abandoned without a sacrifice of both national honor and interest is too clear to admit of doubt."[4] Expansionists in Congress promptly brought into the two houses joint resolutions of "notice." These moved slowly, through a flood of oratory in the succeeding months, toward a vote.

In the Oregon Country, in the meantime, the settlements of the rival nationalities on the opposite sides of the Columbia showed signs of rising tensions. The settlements of the Hudson's Bay Company lay on the north side of the river, clustered about the fortified posts of the Company. The settlements of Americans lay south of the river in the valley of the Willamette. Turbulent American elements were threatening to cross the river and to seize the Company's lands. Some threatened to set fire to the houses and to pillage the stores of the Company. The Company strengthened its fortifications and called for naval protection. Here were all the ingredients of a borderers' clash. Were one to occur, it was likely to echo through the excitable Middle West. It could spark off an explosion into war in the charged atmosphere of Anglo-American relations.[5]

To ward off such a disaster the Peel government pressed arbitration again. It did so as soon as Pakenham's negotiations with Buchanan had ended. Obeying instructions, Pakenham urged arbitration with an earnestness that increased as the controversy came nearer and nearer to a showdown. His first proposal was that an equitable division of the region in dispute be made the arbitrator's assignment. This was at once declined by Buchanan on the ground that to agree to it would be to admit that there was substance to the British claims to Oregon, which the President had just denied.

Pakenham next proposed that the arbitrator's duty be to determine whether either claimant had a complete title to the region,

---

[4] J. D. Richardson, ed., *Messages and Papers of the Presidents, 1789–1897* (Washington, 1907), IV, 397.
[5] See Essay 8.

with the understanding that if neither was found to have one, the arbitrator should make a division of the country "according to a just appreciation of the respective claims of each." This, Buchanan also declined, after cabinet consideration.[6] In informing the crestfallen British minister of the decision, Buchanan sought to enliven the conversation with humor. Referring to a Pakenham proposal to nominate the Republic of Switzerland or the government of Hamburg or Bremen as arbitrator (a proposal made in concession to the American feeling that no crowned head of Europe could be impartial as arbitrator where a republic was a party) Buchanan replied he was personally opposed to any arbitration, but that, if he were compelled to choose one, he would select the Pope, "that both nations were heretics and the Pope would be impartial."[7] The literal-minded Englishman, beset by forebodings of the consequences of his errors, did not at once recognize the humor, and his final humiliation was to have it labeled for him as such.

Rejection of arbitration with such remorseless finality was part of Polk's program of pressure. It was intended to convey to the British his determination to settle the issue without further delay, even by force, if necessary. The President consented cheerfully, therefore, to a request which came from the Senate on Webster's motion for copies of recent Oregon exchanges between the State Department and the British representative in Washington in which the arbitration issue had been prominent.[8] This material was promptly published. It heightened in England the sense of crisis impending in the Oregon controversy, which was what Polk intended.

As a consequence a request was made in Parliament for copies of British Oregon correspondence with Pakenham. The request came in the form of a motion by the Earl of Clarendon in the Lords, and its purpose was clearly to spread the British case before the British public and the world. The Earl was a leading spokesman of the Whig opposition in the Lords. But the opposition had be-

---

[6] The several British proposals are printed in *Parliamentary Papers* (1846), LII, 109–184. The American replies appear in John B. Moore, ed., *Works of James Buchanan* (Philadelphia, 1908–11), VI, 349, 350, 355, 357, 370. See also *Sen. Docs.*, 29 Cong., 1 Sess. (Serial 473), No. 117, 4–10, and in (Serial 478), No. 489, 34–39.

[7] Moore, ed., *Works of Buchanan*, VI, 351.

[8] *Cong. Globe*, 29 Cong., 1 Sess., 274–275 (Jan. 29, 1846); Richardson, ed., *Messages and Papers*, IV, 422. The documents appear in *Sen. Docs.*, 29 Cong., 1 Sess. (Serial 473), No. 117.

come by this time[9] a virtual ally of Peel in a common program to repeal the Corn Laws. Clarendon opened his request with a warm commendation of the conciliatory spirit of Aberdeen's foreign policy, and especially of his arbitration proposals to Polk. He continued with views which strikingly illustrated British desires for a peaceful outcome of the dispute.

Concerning arbitration he declared that his noble friend had given evidence, by the very sweep of his proposals, by his willingness to refer to arbitration both the issue of title and of partition, and by his willingness to accept as arbitrator any sovereign or government or group of individuals, "that however confident we ourselves may be of the validity of our own claims, yet so little desirous are we of obstinately adhering to them, that we are anxious that our whole case should be submitted to any impartial tribunal, and are ready to abide by its decision." Such a course would show the world Britain's eagerness for peace. War over the Oregon Country would, he said, be disgraceful.

The whole fee simple [there] is well known to be of such insignificant value as not to compensate the losses and miseries that one single month of war must produce. It is true there does exist in the United States a party so reckless as to be ready to engage in war—true it is that by this party we have been rudely assailed—that our claims have been repudiated, and our whole policy misrepresented; but I must say I think that for this party, great allowance must be made, and we must not be too prone to take offence at what may be attributed to the peculiar institutions of the United States—to the immediate influence of the popular will, and the electioneering habits of public men in America—motives of action with which we ourselves are always more or less familiar at home.

Clarendon declared it a moral impossibility that this reckless party represented the majority of the American people. He could not believe a people and government would rush into an unjust war, especially at a "moment when America, of all countries in the world, will be the foremost and largest partaker in the enlightened system of commerce which we, for our own welfare . . . were about to adopt—and the intelligence of which, I understand, has been read in America with all the satisfaction it was calculated to excite."

[9] The date is March 17, 1846.

In concluding the speech Clarendon made a suggestion, which, though not at all germane to his request for documents, must have been pleasing to Aberdeen. The suggestion was that the resolution of notice which the American Senate was then debating should be viewed by the British government, if adopted, not as a hostile declaration, but "simply as a determination on the part of the American people, that the whole question shall be settled within a twelvemonth, but in a manner satisfactory to the honour and interest of both countries, and therefore calculated to render more enduring those friendly relations which have hitherto subsisted between them, and which in their mutual influence . . . will never be dissolved."[10]

In England a call for documents relating to an uncompleted negotiation with a foreign state was seldom welcomed by the government. It smacked too much of the modes of a democracy. But in this case it was answered favorably at once by Aberdeen, and, in the Commons a few days later, by Peel. The documents as published covered the period 1842 to March 1846. They heavily accented the offers of arbitration made by Pakenham and the rejection of them all by Polk. They let the world see the difference between the British and American attitudes toward arbitration.[11]

Several conjectures as to Clarendon's speech are worth offering at this point. One is that the speech had been pre-arranged with Aberdeen in the hope of achieving ends both parties desired. A like cooperation had been employed earlier by the government and the opposition in response to Polk's Inaugural Address. A second conjecture relates to the extraneous remarks of Clarendon on the notice resolution then before the American Senate. The remarks were that Aberdeen should consider a resolution of notice as not necessarily belligerent, but as evidence of a determination of the American people to get the Oregon issue peacefully settled within a twelvemonth. That excellent suggestion could easily have been made privately to Aberdeen. The fact that it was made publicly may well mean that it was intended to be heard across the Atlantic. Certain it is, that it was heard by the friends of peace in the American Senate and that it encouraged a willingness on their part to serve

---

[10] *Hansard's Parliamentary Debates,* LXXXIV, 1114 (March 17, 1846). See also pp. 1277–1280.
[11] See references cited above in n. 6.

a notice that was couched in conciliatory terms, so that it could be interpreted in England as an invitation to a new negotiation.[12]

In the meantime Polk's grim-visaged rejection of arbitration was viewed differently in America by the two parties and within the parties. Whigs deplored it. This was not because they considered arbitration an ideal mode of resolving the Oregon dispute but as a better mode of resolving it than war. They preferred direct nego-tiation but were willing as a last resort to have arbitration. That mood was well expressed in a letter of Edward Everett to Dr. Henry Holland, court physician and friend of Aberdeen, which was written on March 27, 1846, at the height of the crisis. The letter may have been intended for the eyes of Aberdeen.

But though I would have agreed to arbitration as an honorable mode of settling the present difficulty & though I consider the reasons for which Mr. Buchanan declined it quite unsatisfactory, there *is* a reason why I think it would have worked inequitably against us. Arbitration between two powerful parties is but another name for splitting the difference. In order therefore that it may be applied fairly each party before the arbitration must have insisted so steadily on its extreme claims that the attention of the arbiter will be distinctly drawn to their extent. This you have done. From the negotiation in 1824 down you have maintained that the Nootka convention gave you a right to the whole region west of the mountains. We, however, from the first agitation of the controversy, although alluding to an extension far up our coast & specifically to 61° or 62°, urged our right to the valley of the Columbia with so much greater emphasis & offered the 49th degree so promptly at the outset of the negotiation, that this line [49°] came to be regarded as that of our extreme claim. I happen to know that when, in 1843 our members of Congress began to talk of 54° 40′ it was regarded on your side as a novelty. This impression has no doubt since been weakened, but I well recollect being unable to convince one of the most intelligent of my colleagues in London that the question was *not* how the territory between 49° & 42° should be divided, but how the territory between 54° 40′ & 42° should be divided. In other words, having first, in the way in which we conducted the negotiation in effect submitted our claim to arbitration, that is, having split the difference ourselves, we should, by avowedly submitting it to arbitration, be very apt to have it split again. I have, however, kept this view to myself, not wishing to do anything which would discourage arbitration.[13]

[12] See Essay 13, pp. 387–388.
[13] Everett to Dr. Henry Holland, March 27, 1846, Edward Everett Papers, Massachusetts Historical Society.

Views like Everett's were held by peace Democrats also, especially by those from the Cotton South. These are illustrated in the position of Calhoun. As Secretary of State he had steadily refused Pakenham's arbitration proposals. He had considered arbitration a last resort, to be used only after every other had been exhausted. But by 1846 he had come to favor arbitration "if nothing better can be done."[14] The peace elements among Whigs and Southern Democrats in the crisis of 1845–46 were exhibiting unity, thus, even in the stand they took on arbitration.

Among expansionists, on the other hand, the arbitration offers of the British were denounced as a trick, which unless rejected by the administration would destroy the future of the United States on the Pacific. The postulate of this element was the same as Everett's. It was that arbitration in a territorial dispute is another name for splitting the difference. The difference in the Oregon Country was the core of territory between the offers which each nation had made to the other—in other words, the territory between the Columbia River and the 49th parallel. If that core were to be halved, the half falling to the United States would lie south of the vital harbors at the Straits. This view was set forth with special cogency in an editorial published in March 1846, by the influential Democratic journal, the New York *Evening Post*, of which William Cullen Bryant was editor. The editorial was one of a series directed to the problem, which for clarity of view and trenchance of presentation was unsurpassed elsewhere in the American press:

We have never heard any body admit that we ought to be deprived of the advantage of a port on the Pacific. If there are any who are for giving up to Great Britain, Puget Sound and its passages to the Ocean, and yielding to her the entire command of the Northwest Coast, they are careful not to make their opinions public. They have at least the grace to be ashamed of them.

Yet there are certain indirect methods, understood by politicians, of getting at a desired result, without appearing to seek it openly. Those who rail at the administration, as the whig journals continue to do, for not accepting the offer of Great Britain to submit the dispute to arbitration, do in effect renounce the right of the United States to harbors on the Pacific. To our minds, the result of such an arbitration is almost certain. Great Britain had offered our government the mouth of the

14 American Historical Association, *Annual Report* (1899), II, 677.

Columbia in latitude 46 as a boundary; we on our part, had offered the parallel of 49. The intermediate space is covered by various titles or pretenses of titles advanced on both sides. The arbitrators must be an exception to their class if they would not propose to terminate the controversy by dividing this space between the two governments, and fixing the boundary between them, somewhere about 47 degrees and 30 minutes, which would completely exclude us from all access to the Pacific. They would say, as thousands in this country are now saying: 'This is a dispute which can only be settled by compromise; each party in a case like this, must yield something of its claims.' If they set out with this position, the only question would then be, what sort of a compromise should be awarded? What concessions should be exacted of each party? The most obvious, the most easy, and, at first sight, the most plausible method of settling this question, would be to take a middle point between the last offer made by the United States and the last offer made by Great Britain. We have as little doubt that after having decided the controversy in this manner, and left us high and dry on the rock-bound shore of the Pacific, without a shelter for a skiff, the arbitrator would plume himself on his strict impartiality. To censure the rejection of the offer of arbitration, therefore, is the same thing as to contend for renouncing all maritime advantages on the northwest coast . . . .[15]

This was in part the thesis of the Polk administration. It appeared in a dispatch of Buchanan to Louis McLane, the American minister to London, explaining the rejection of the arbitration proposals:

Independently of the reason prominently presented in my reply, that the President does not believe the territorial rights of this nation to be a proper subject of arbitration, there are other powerful reasons against such a course, which might have been stated had it been deemed proper in a communication to the British minister. These you can use as occasion may require.

In the first place, without pretending to know the opinions of individual Senators, I hazard but little in asserting that no treaty for arbitration could obtain the constitutional majority of the Senate necessary to its ratification. Several of the Senators who might assent to a compromise upon the parallel of forty-nine degrees, would not be willing to jeopard by arbitration the possession of the harbors on Admiralty inlet and Puget's sound south of that parallel. Indeed, for commercial purposes, the United States might almost as well abandon the whole territory as consent to deprive themselves of these harbors; because south of them, within its limits, no good harbor exists.[16]

[15] New York *Evening Post*, March 25, 1846.
[16] Buchanan to McLane, Feb. 26, 1846, in *Sen. Docs.*, 29 Cong., 1 Sess. (Serial 478), No. 489, pp. 40–41.

Polk and his expansionist associates objected to arbitration, however, on other grounds. Any European arbitrator, they felt, was likely to be biased against the United States, either because of dislike of republican institutions, or because of ties to the British. Moreover, Polk and Buchanan considered British offers of arbitration to be mere maneuvers of politics, made in full knowledge that they would be rejected. Aberdeen had been warned by McLane that any British arbitration offers made on the Oregon issue would be rejected in all probability. The pressing of them seemed, therefore, confirmation of the view that the real purpose of the British in making them was either to avoid a concession which might be politically embarrassing to make, or to postpone a settlement, or to establish a propaganda case, in the event of a war, before the neutrals of the world. All these objections and suspicions entered into Polk's rejection of arbitration. But the determining objection was the danger that the national interest would suffer a major disaster if an arbitration should end in the loss of every usable harbor on the Pacific shore to which the United States then had any claim.

Yet Peel had been driven to pressing arbitration by dangers which he considered no less menacing to British national interest. If the Americans were to be satisfied, the whole area between the Columbia and the Straits would have to be given up. Everything the British government had refused for a quarter century to yield would have to be conceded, including numerous loyal subjects of the crown. And this would be done under Polk's menaces. An enterprising opposition would certainly describe the yielding as an abject surrender, indeed a disgraceful one, deserting the national honor and rendering the crown contemptible in the eyes of the world. Arbitration would free the government from these dangers. Even if the arbitration were to result in the loss of the entire substance of the dispute, nothing more than substance would be lost. Honor would be secure.

In British eyes, moreover, the Oregon issue was just the sort that could be referred safely to an arbitrator. The country was a remote and unattractive wilderness.[17] It seemed of little potentiality to the British public. British trade opportunities there were being exploited

---

[17] For a temperate British discussion of the Oregon issue stressing the agricultural unattractiveness of the country in terms like those of Clarendon and also urging arbitration, see *British and Foreign Review*, XVI (1844), 560–586.

by a British monopoly established by Parliament in 1821, a monopoly unpopular on general principles, and more particularly as affecting fur prices to British consumers. Domestic issues of far-reaching consequence could be attended to if this embarrassing issue could be referred to an arbitrator. If worse came to worst, if arbitration were offered and declined, and war should follow, the United States would stand convicted in the court of world opinion of having initiated it.

Peel, especially, was attracted to such ideas and it was he who imposed on the hesitant Aberdeen his own insistence on recourse to arbitration.[18] And yet Peel, in the last analysis, was himself being driven by the course of history. For it was the prolonged series of abortive Oregon negotiations and the steady British rejections of American offers made in them that was driving him on.

While the two governments wrestled with the past in this way, John Quincy Adams, who had helped to produce the past, went forward with new ideas in Congress. At the age of seventy-eight he represented his state energetically in the lower house of Congress. His expansionism was as aggressive as ever, though no longer where territory that might fall to slavery was at issue. For years he had been the leader of the nation's anti-slavery forces in the House, in a vain effort to prevent the annexation of Texas. Embittered by defeat on that issue he had heightened his demands for northern territory. He insisted, now, on All Oregon, without admitting, as did the Ohio abolitionist, Joshua Giddings, that he hoped to redress thus the balance of gain which the South had upset by annexing Texas.[19]

On learning in December 1845 of Polk's emphatic public declaration that he would never again offer the British the 49° line so rudely rejected, Adams cynically wrote in his diary that Polk would nevertheless accept it from the British, if they offered it. He wrote, further, that he and Monroe, in earlier days, had acted under the conviction that the offer of 49° would be rejected, that this offer had been intended to gain a postponement of the issue until the United States had grown sufficiently strong to maintain its full claim by an appeal to arms if necessary.[20]

[18] See Essay 8, n. 53, and Essay 9.
[19] The Giddings speech appears in *Cong. Globe*, 29 Cong., 1 Sess., App. 72ff (Jan. 5, 1846).
[20] Charles F. Adams, ed., *Memoirs of John Quincy Adams* (Philadelphia, 1874–77), XII, 220, 221.

The memory of Adams in so writing had grown constructive with age, for what he wrote was at variance with the facts of history, and, still more, with good sense. If those early offers had been made to be rejected, they assuredly would not have been set at 49°. They would have been set north of 49°, far enough north to have saved the nation bargaining margin for the future.

Early in 1846, while the House was debating its resolution to serve "notice," Adams aligned himself with the war hawks of the West. He did so in three major speeches, in which he charmed 54° 40′ men by his extremism, but startled his own constituents and the Anglo-American world. In each speech he urged that the notice be served. He urged that a real occupation by Americans of the whole Oregon Country be made as promptly after notice as the terms of the convention permitted. He cited with approval Frederick the Great's "military way of doing business." He carefully spelled this out. In the case of Silesia, Frederick the Great had occupied first and negotiated afterwards; he had possessed himself of the province on the day he sent a minister to the court of Austria to negotiate for it.[21]

In a second speech Adams carried the thesis of prompt occupation one step further. Occupation, he asserted, is the foundation of all title. Without it there is nothing complete in title. By the British no occupation is intended. They intend to keep the Oregon Country in a barbarous state for hunters, savages, and wild beasts. The American people will occupy, will make the wilderness blossom as a rose, they will increase, multiply, and subdue the earth. For dramatic effect Adams called on the clerk of the House to read from Genesis the verses in which the command is given: "Be fruitful and multiply, and replenish the earth, and subdue it." The 8th verse of the 2nd Psalm was also called for, wherein it is declared that to him who will occupy, the heathen is given for his inheritance, and the uttermost parts of the earth for his possession.[22] In a final speech he developed the thesis, dear to Polk, that the British had no valid claim to any part of the Oregon Country on any ground whatsoever.[23]

[21] *Cong. Globe*, 29 Cong., 1 Sess., 127 (Jan. 2, 1846).

[22] *Ibid.*, 340ff (Feb. 9, 1846). Adams made a prophesy which became popular with the war hawks, that if England were to make war with the United States over the Oregon Country she would soon find herself fully occupied in maintaining herself in rebellious Ireland.

[23] *Ibid.*, 662–664 (April 13, 1846).

This ultraism dismayed peace proponents in the United States and in England. They shook their heads at the spectacle of such intransigeance. The religious-minded took exception to the use of Holy Writ in such a cause. They thought the speeches little short of blasphemous. Edward Everett wrote Louis McLane: "He will not allow England an inch of land on the Pacific:—thinks they have no case nor claim. N.B. Three times offered to compromise the question on the basis of the 49th degree, twice as Secretary of State and once as President!"[24] In Congress a Southern Whig interrupted Adams on the floor of the House to make the same point, which Adams considered a personal affront.[25]

From England the anti-slavery idealist and pacifist, Joseph Sturge, wrote Adams a gentle admonition on the warlike tone of his speeches, to which Adams replied in a long letter, overflowing with bitter memories of two wars forced by Great Britain on the American people at the cost of great national suffering, and suffering of himself and family.[26] Adams alienated even his Massachusetts constituents in this strange crusade. They withheld from him, as he had to admit on the floor of Congress, their customary support. Their sympathies lay in this case with Calhoun, of all persons.

If Adams gave support in these speeches to the cause of the war hawks he could not make that cause succeed. For the war hawks were the minority of reckless men, mentioned by Clarendon, and they were already powerless in the grip of the peace Whigs and the Southern Democrats. The peace coalition was moving in Congress and in the nation toward Clarendon's suggestion of a notice resolution clothed in friendly terms which would be accepted in England as an invitation to reopen direct negotiations.

In the Senate this coalition made its final move as soon as the Senate rules of debate permitted. On April 16, 1846, it set aside a harsh form of notice desired by the 54° 40′ chairman of the Foreign Relations Committee and approved a substitute that was everything Clarendon could have wished. The Senate induced the House soon after to approve a conciliatory conference-form of resolution.

[24] Everett to McLane, Jan. 1, 1846. Edward Everett Papers, M.H.S.

[25] *Cong. Globe*, 29 Cong., 1 Sess., 339 (Feb. 9, 1846). The New York *Journal of Commerce* commented on Jan. 9, 1846: "But Mr. Adams has too long been under the government of his antipathies to hope for anything better of him during the little remnant of his life."

[26] Adams to Joseph Sturge, April 1846, John Quincy Adams Letter Books, Private, Adams Papers, M.H.S.

It did all this by majorities that were overwhelming. It gave Polk discretion as to sending the resolution forward, which was just what Polk did not want.[27] He had been wanting Congress on its own responsibility to send a harsh and determined form of notice. He bowed, however, to the wishes of Congress and sent the mild form as it was, which was a shock to his followers, but only the beginning of ruder shocks to follow.

In London the notice was at once accepted as an invitation to reopen negotiations. It led to the framing of an offer by the cabinet with Louis McLane offering guidance from outside. The offer bore a striking resemblance to the one which Aberdeen had orally directed Pakenham, two and a half years before, to try to draw from the American Secretary of State. It specified a partition line along the 49th parallel to Admiralty Inlet and from that point to the sea via the Strait of Juan de Fuca. With regard to the Columbia it departed a little from what Aberdeen had specified in his informal instruction. It reserved rights of navigation on the river to the Hudson's Bay Company, though not to British subjects generally. It yielded this much to the wishes of Polk. It also gave protection to possessory rights of the Company to lands it occupied south of 49°, to which Polk had made no objection. The offer was the work of a few days of placid cabinet consideration.

This proposal reached Polk on June 6. Its terms were short of his All Oregon demands. Indeed, they were short of demands which he had been secretly prescribing as minimal to McLane. He had already betrayed softness in deciding to send the mild notice to London. Further softness would be shown if he sent the proposal to the Senate for advice. The Senate was notoriously controlled by its peace coalition. Still, the Mexican War was on, and a dispute with England ought not to be left dangling, impeding prospects of that war. After all, the offer from the British was not far short of offers his predecessors had made repeatedly and even he had made. Asking advice from a Senate committed against the 54° 40′ program was sure to infuriate the 54° 40′ men whom he had inspired. It would be prudent, therefore, to have cabinet support for the move. Unanimity of that support was essential. Unanimity was asked from

[27] *Cong. Globe*, 29 Cong., 1 Sess., 680–683 (April 16, 1846). The mover of the resolution in the Senate was Reverdy Johnson, a Maryland Whig, but the form was Crittenden's. See *below* p. 387. For the background of Crittenden see Albert D. Kirwan, *John J. Crittenden* (Lexington, 1962).

the cabinet. All but Buchanan, who had presidential aspirations, responded favorably at once. Buchanan was harried into line and then actually wrote the necessary letter asking Senate advice. In the letter the President stoutly maintained he still adhered to the position taken by him in his message to Congress on the Oregon issue, and he would, if the Senate declined to give advice, reject the British proposal. However, he would sink his personal views and conform his actions to the advice of the Senate if it were given. The Senate did give advice, and quite promptly. It advised, by an overwhelming vote, that he accept the British proposal as it stood. To this advice he conformed his actions. He ordered the proposal formalized into a treaty, which the Senate then ratified by more than the two-thirds majority needed. The treaty was hurried off to London, where it was proclaimed by Peel as his last act in office amid a chorus of commendations from all sides.[28]

An over-all assessment of the course of Polk on the Oregon issue is necessary to an understanding of the arbitration element in it. It is the more necessary because of the deviousness of the course Polk took. He had committed himself, as many another Democrat had, in the 1844 campaign, to an All Oregon program, without taking the program too seriously. Once in the White House he felt obliged to convert the commitment of himself and of others into tactics of boldness to be used against the British, though the objective he had in mind was not more extensive than the line of 49°. The tactics became adamant rejection of arbitration, a tough message to Congress in December 1845, a recommendation regarding the serving of notice, encouragement to pioneer occupation of Oregon, and stimulation of the war element in Congress and in the nation. Tactics of this sort tend to be demagogic. But Polk's were something more. They were designed to recreate margin lost when Adams, Albert Gallatin, and Richard Rush in 1818, at the opening of a negotiation, had offered a line at 49°, and had persisted in it later.

The tactics of Polk were all too apparent. Also the threats, which were part of them, had too little home support, and too little naval support; they seemed to the public too risky, too clumsy, too offensive. They were offensive especially to the coalition of peace elements which had firm control of Congress. Calhoun put his

[28] See Essay 13.

finger on the weakness of the tactics near the close of the Senate debate on notice, when he observed that intimidation is a hazardous tactic even as used against a feeble nation. Used against a nation as great and powerful as the British, it would be self-defeating. The hollowness of the tactics became more apparent when, at the end of the notice debate in the Senate, the two houses adopted a pacific resolution and the President elected to send it to London.

One element in Polk's tactics was well based. It was rejection of arbitration. The reasons assigned for rejection in official documents did not seem good to a moderate Whig such as Everett. But other reasons, past and present, had seemed good to him, as noted in his discerning letter to Dr. Holland. A past reason was the repeated offers of 49° which had brought the issue to a state where it was hardly arbitrable. The present reason was the state of public opinion in the United States. Public opinion regarding an arbitration varied only in the degree of unwillingness to accept it. In expansionist circles the feeling against it was vehement. It was based on fear of the prejudices which any Old World arbitrator would bring to bear on a republic, on fear of a damaging award in a vital sector of the national life, and on fear of the effect of an award on the future of Manifest Destiny.

Vehemence against it was attributed to Andrew Jackson, and his spirit was brought back to life to testify against it. In an editorial on the Oregon issue written by John L. O'Sullivan (a leading exponent of Manifest Destiny) the dead hero was made to express himself strongly on the subject. O'Sullivan was engaged, on July 4, 1845, in a patriotic battle with the editor of the *New York Tribune*, who had come out for 49° and for an arbitration, if necessary. O'Sullivan considered the combination of the two ideas ominous. It meant willingness on the part of the *Tribune* to take less than 49° from an arbitrator. He wrote:

> When disputes like the present arise, they [Americans] must carefully ascertain that which is right, and then maintain it at all hazards. Or, in the immortal words of the dying hero, on whose mighty mind the history of the past formed a part of the picture filled out with prophetic visions of the future [Manifest Destiny]: "There must be no arbitration but at the cannon's mouth!"[29]

[29] *New York Morning News*, July 4, 1845.

Whether or not this testimony was apochryphal, it was enough for the Democratic masses in the United States. It rendered arbitration intolerable. In other circles, where arbitration might have been tolerable, it seemed so only as a last resort. Since this was the state of public opinion in the United States it was well that direct negotiation of the issue was resumed in the spring of 1846. A direct negotiation had become by then feasible and promising as a result of the formation of peace coalitions controlling governmental decisions on both sides of the Atlantic. A successful direct negotiation then proved surprisingly easy, considering how stubborn the dispute had been and how heated it had become.

ESSAY 8 · THE OREGON PIONEERS AND THE BOUNDARY *¹

IT IS a truism in American history that the success of the United States in the Oregon boundary negotiations was due in considerable measure to the Oregon pioneers. They brought pressure to bear on the British government during the final stages of the Oregon negotiations, and this was a factor in winning for their country the empire of the Pacific Northwest. But what the nature of this pressure was, how direct it was, or how great its effectiveness, are questions that have never been carefully investigated. They deserve attention, for they go to the heart of Oregon diplomacy and determine the place of the Oregon pioneers in American diplomatic history. They are the province of this study.

Proper analysis of this subject necessitates at the outset a survey of the stakes of Oregon diplomacy. They were not as extensive as at first sight they seem. Nominally the whole of the Oregon country was at issue, the vast domain extending from the Rocky Mountains to the sea and from California to Alaska. But the region about which dispute really centered was the comparatively limited area lying between the Columbia River and the forty-ninth parallel, the triangle now constituting the central and western thirds of the state of Washington. As early as 1818 the British government had intimated a willingness to divide the Oregon country at the line of the Columbia River and the forty-ninth parallel, and this it definitely offered to do in 1824, 1826, and 1844. It further offered in 1826 and 1844 to yield to the United States a large segment of territory north of the Columbia, intended to satisfy the determined

---

* Reprinted from the *American Historical Review*, XXIX (July 1924).

¹ This paper, read at the meeting of the American Historical Association at Columbus, Dec. 28, 1923, is part of a larger study of the Oregon question begun some years ago in the Seminar of Professor Turner at Harvard University. I need not say how much I owe to him in the way of stimulating suggestions made then and since.

American demand for a share in the harbors of Puget Sound.[2] These proposals the American government had declined. That embracing the Puget Sound harbors had been unacceptable because the proffered area in which they lay would have been isolated from the body of the United States, an enclave in British territory. But the offer had served a useful purpose from the American point of view. It had committed the British government to a line of partition even more favorable to the United States than the Columbia River.[3] And this was years before any pioneers had begun to settle in Oregon.

Similarly, though with somewhat less certainty, the American government stood committed to the line of the forty-ninth parallel. This it had offered as a compromise from the very beginning, and, when in 1844 Calhoun attempted to extend again the field of dispute, Pakenham, the British minister, cut him short, informing him that he "was not authorized to treat about any territory lying to the north of the 49th parallel of latitude, which was considered by Her Majesty's Government to form the basis for the Negotiation, on the side of the United States, as the line of the Columbia formed that on the side of Great Britain."[4] So clear had this mutual delimitation of the field of dispute become by the time of the later Oregon negotiations that in 1844 Pakenham recommended to his government that it offer full cession to the United States of the territory south of the Columbia in return for the yielding by the United States of the territory north of the forty-ninth parallel, a proposal which interested Lord Aberdeen but which he did not press because he foresaw that it would be rejected by the American government.[5]

With these facts as a guide we may now turn to assessing the influence of the Oregon pioneers on the boundary negotiations. It has been supposed that they determined the character of the final

[2] The region bounded by Fuca's Strait, Hood's Canal, and a line drawn from the southern extremity of Hood's Canal to the southern point of Gray's Harbor.

[3] "It is true that in submitting this last proposition [1826] we distinctly stated that, in case it was rejected, we should consider it as in no way committing us to the adoption of any course for the future. But it is obvious that a proposition of this kind once made, must always involve the practical difficulty of subsequently assuming any less extensive basis of negotiation." Aberdeen to Pakenham, Dec. 28, 1843, Public Record Office, F.O. 115: 83.

[4] Pakenham to Aberdeen, Sept. 28, 1844, F.O. 5: 408.

[5] Aberdeen to Peel, Oct. 17, 1844; Peel to Aberdeen, Oct. 19, 1844. Peel MSS., British Museum. A similar suggestion was under discussion in the negotiations of 1826–1827.

settlement by simply taking possession as farmers of the territory in dispute.[6] Five thousand American settlers wielded the pen, it is thought, that wrote the Oregon Treaty, demonstrating that in diplomacy possession is nine points of the law. It is a plausible theory. But it collapses at the prick of the fact that in 1846 all or practically all the American pioneers in Oregon were located in the Willamette Valley, on the south side of the Columbia River—just that part of the Oregon country which ever since 1818 the British government had been willing to concede to the United States. American occupation in other words was of an area that did not need to be won.

North of the Columbia River, on the other hand, in the region really at issue, the total number of American settlers was eight. Seven of these with their families under the leadership of M. T. Simmons, famous in the history of the state of Washington as its first permanent white settler, had established themselves in October, 1845, at the head of Puget Sound. At Jackson Prairie near the Cowlitz Landing was an Americanized Englishman. That was the extent of American occupation north of the Columbia; and of American commercial activity here, there was in 1846 none.

British interests, on the other hand, agricultural as well as commercial, were strong. Fort Vancouver was in this region, on the north bank of the Columbia River, so located in 1824 in place of old Fort George south of the river at the special request of George Canning, the British minister of foreign affairs, and so named by Governor Simpson in order to link the claims to the soil which

---

[6] This is the view which the Oregon pioneers themselves advanced through their delegate in Congress when seeking their 640-acre donations. See Memorial of J. Q. Thornton, *Sen. Misc. Doc.* no. 143, 30 Cong., 1 sess. It is the theory which underlies a fundamental part of the Marcus Whitman legend. See also Joseph Schafer, "Notes on the Colonization of Oregon," in *Oregon Historical Quarterly*, VI (1905), 390; Katherine Coman, *Economic Beginnings of the Far West* (New York, 1925), II, 163; Lady Frances Balfour, *Life of Aberdeen* (London, 1922), II, 134. This view was given perhaps its baldest expression by President Harding in his Meacham, Ore., address: "But stern determination triumphed, and the result was conclusive. Americans had settled the country. The country belonged to them because they had taken it; and in the end the boundary settlement was made on the line of the forty-ninth parallel, your great Northwest was saved, and a veritable empire was merged in the young Republic." *New York Times*, July 4, 1923. For a modified view see Joseph Schafer, *A History of the Pacific Northwest* (New York, 1918), 181–184, and "Oregon Pioneers" in G. S. Ford (ed.), *Essays Dedicated to Frederick Jackson Turner* (New York, 1910), 35.

Great Britain advanced to the discoveries and survey of Vancouver.[7] That this post under the chief factorship of Doctor McLoughlin controlled the commerce, particularly the fur trade, of the region north of the Columbia no one can doubt; indeed, it dominated the commercial life of the whole Oregon country, including even the American settlements in the Willamette. But this establishment represented also a powerful agricultural interest. At the fort ten or more entire sections of land were held for the Hudson's Bay Company. Twelve hundred acres of this were under cultivation, the remainder pastured 700 brood mares, 1,600 hogs, and cattle and sheep to the number of 3,400. There were employed here more or less regularly in the fields, dairies, mills, shops, and stores of the great establishment from 150 to 200 men, who, with their Indian wives and half-breed children, comprised a settlement that already in 1837 was estimated by Lieutenant Slacum to contain from 750 to 800 souls.

Four other establishments of the Hudson's Bay Company, or of its subsidiary, the Puget Sound Agricultural Company, lay between the Columbia River and the forty-ninth parallel. Fort Okanagan, near the river of the same name, was of minor importance. Fort Victoria at the tip of Vancouver Island was new but rapidly developing. Fort Nisqually was the center of the herding and farming activities of the Puget Sound Agricultural Company, where on a tract of 167,000 acres there were pastured 5,800 sheep, 200 horses, and 1,850 cattle. Cowlitz Farm was another extensive property, embracing 3,500 acres, of which 1,400 acres under cultivation produced yearly more than 10,000 bushels of grain and the remainder pastured 100 horses and sheep and cattle to the number of 1,500. Eighty-five men were attached to these four establishments, who with their families added their quota to the weight of British occupation.[8] Nineteen Canadian families, retired servants of the Hudson's Bay Company, and a Roman Catholic mission were established

[7] Pelly to Canning, Dec. 9, 1825, printed in *Oregon Historical Quarterly*, XX (1919), 27.

[8] The data used in this paragraph are gathered from Warre and Vavasour's Report, Oct. 27, 1845, conveniently printed in *Oregon Hist. Quar.*, X (1909), 60; Report of the Puget Sound Agricultural Company, Jan. 14, 1846, F.O. 5: 460; Slacum's Report, Mar. 26, 1837, in *House Committee Reports*, no. 101, 25 Cong., 3 sess. Lord Aberdeen had at his disposal the Report of the Puget Sound Agricultural Company when he framed the Oregon Treaty.

near the Cowlitz River.[9] Clearly British influence outweighed American in this contested area; and if occupation had determined its fate in 1846, it must inevitably have become British territory.

Nor may we assume that these facts were unknown to the British Foreign Office. Lord Aberdeen was well aware of them and understood their meaning. Indeed he overestimated the British advantage, for he did not know when he framed the Oregon Treaty of the little American settlement forming at the head of Puget Sound. His latest advices from the Northwest Coast were those brought by Lieutenant Peel, who sailed from the Straits of Fuca on September 26, 1845,[10] whereas the Simmons party did not reach Puget Sound until near the end of October.[11] What was in his mind when he formulated the Oregon Treaty and despatched it to Washington may be seen from one of the private letters of instruction which he sent with it to Pakenham. He emphasizes in this the extent of the sacrifice Great Britain was making in conceding to the United States the line of the forty-ninth parallel, which will "interfere with the possessions of British colonists resident in a district in which it is believed that scarcely an American citizen as a settler, has ever set his foot."[12]

American negotiators were likewise aware of these facts, though naturally they were disposed to keep them dark. It is significant that Calhoun, famous advocate of "masterly inactivity," who in his negotiations with Pakenham in 1844 first stressed as an important diplomatic fact the moving of the pioneers into Oregon, remained vague as to their location and spoke not of the present but of the future when he said "that the whole region drained by it [the Columbia River] is destined to be peopled by us."[13] Congressmen

[9] Vavasour's "Report," Mar. 1, 1846, in *Oregon Hist. Quar.*, X (1909), 91. Warre and Vavasour under date of Oct. 26, 1845, report 90 families, but this is an error. *Ibid.*, p. 56. Lieutenant Peel, Sept. 27, 1845, reports eight families, F.O. 5:459.

[10] Gordon to Secretary of Admiralty, Oct. 19, 1845, F.O. 5: 459.

[11] Captain Gordon's report casually noticed that the head of Puget Sound had been "lately taken possession of by an American Party." This referred to the claims-making expedition of Simmons and some others in July, 1845. Simmons was the speculator type of pioneer who early penetrated this northern region in search of a mill site. *Ibid.*

[12] Aberdeen to Pakenham, May 18, 1846. Privately printed (unpublished) *Correspondence of the Earl of Aberdeen*. I am indebted to Lord Stanmore for access to this printed correspondence; also for courteous permission to use the Aberdeen MSS.

[13] Calhoun to Pakenham, Sept. 3, 1844, printed in *Sen. Doc.* no. 1, 29 Cong., 1 sess., pp. 146–153.

blurted out more openly what was well known to the State Department. Owen, of Indiana, for example, on January 3, 1846, asks a question and answers it:

Is there an American settler now living north of the Columbia? So far as I know or believe, not one. I have recently conversed with an intelligent gentleman who has spent some years in that country; and he informs me that the moment a citizen of the United States attempts to settle north of the river—on the *British* side as they persist in calling it —the Hudson Bay Company—the East India Company of that region— sees to it that they are removed, and caused to emigrate south of the stream.[14]

McClernand of Illinois asserted five days later in the same debate:

An idea was purposely inculcated in Oregon, by the British authorities, that the settlements of the Americans south of the Columbia would be acquiesced in by that Government; but that all such north of that stream would be contested, if needs be, at the point of the bayonet. This idea was attended with the effect of restricting the settlements of the two countries to different sides of the river. While the Americans were settling the south, Great Britain, as a counterpoise, would fill up the north—convert her temporary settlements, for the purposes of trading and fishing, under the convention, into permanent agricultural and commercial communities . . . .[15]

Four other references to the same facts were made on the floor of the House by Rhett, Douglas, Giles, and Caleb Smith in a single week of debate.[16] We must then abandon this theory that American pioneers brought pressure to bear on the government of either country by occupation of the area in dispute.

It would be more correct to say that they sought out the Willamette Valley, partly because of a previous certainty that it would eventually be allotted to the United States. They regarded this as important, for, apart from patriotism, it meant American land policy and the probable donation to them of their 640-acre preemptions. That they knew the Willamette was in no real sense contested territory when they located there it is easy to demonstrate. The Canadian servants of the Hudson's Bay Company who first settled in it realized that it was to become American territory and some of them hesitated to go there on that account, as Dr.

[14] *Cong. Globe,* 29 Cong., 1 sess., 1845–1846, p. 135.
[15] *Ibid.,* p. 167.
[16] *Cong. Globe,* 29 Cong., 1 sess., pp. 135, 142, 160, 173.

McLoughlin testifies, fearing discrimination.[17] Jason Lee located his mission there in 1834, partly because he wished to work in what would normally become American soil.[18] Slacum, special agent of President Jackson, told the Canadians here in 1837, much to their joy, that "although they were located within the territorial limits of the United States, their pre-emption rights would doubtless be secured them when our Government should take possession of the country."[19] Alexander Simpson, who spent several days in the Willamette in 1840, found the settlers "aware that under American law" their pre-emption rights were not unlimited and choosing their locations accordingly.[20] Dr. McLoughlin reported in 1844: "As to the immigrants come this year [1843] they have placed themselves all on the South side of the Columbia River in the Wallamette, Falaty Plains, about Fort George and Clatsop, and give out that they believe the Columbia River will be the boundary."[21]

But what really determined the flow of American pioneers into the Willamette Valley was its unusual agricultural attractiveness. Its beautiful prairies and oak openings, constituting an island in a sea of forest that swept otherwise practically unbroken from the Cascades to the Pacific,[22] made it the ideal land of the pioneer. Here was the perfect combination of fertile soil, timber in quantity sufficient for all needs, yet not so heavy as to require years of clearing, and close at hand a river that led to a market. American pioneers could not resist such allurements. Many of them undoubtedly believed in a vague way, when they set out for Oregon, that they had a mission to save it for their country from the clutches of the Hudson's Bay Company, and this may even have been a minor motive in putting some of them in motion. But once arrived on the Columbia, it was not patriotism but the call of the soil and the certainty of American land title that took them south of the river.

Such facts will explain also why Americans were so late in beginning settlement of the disputed country north of the Colum-

[17] Oregon Pioneer Association, *Transactions*, 1880, p. 49.
[18] H. K. Hines, *Missionary History of the Pacific Northwest* (Portland, 1899), 87.
[19] Slacum Report, in *House Committee Rept.* no. 101, 25 Cong., 3 sess., p. 40.
[20] A. Simpson, *Oregon Territory*, (London, 1846), 38.
[21] McLoughlin to Simpson, Mar. 20, 1844, Hudson's Bay Company Archives Journal, no. 1652 A.
[22] Isaiah Bowman, *Forest Physiography* (New York, 1911), 146.

bia. This was a heavily wooded area, as Dr. McLoughlin more than once pointed out to his superiors when they complained of the slow growth of the Puget Sound Agricultural Company. There were few districts in it that were attractive from the point of view of the time, and of these the most eligible were already held by the two allied British corporations. It is not surprising then that as long as good land was to be had in the Willamette, which was at least until 1846, Americans were for the most part ready to leave the northern region in British possession.

More sensational explanations of this situation were heard in Congress. Again and again during the debates of the middle 'forties, the two houses were told that it was the Hudson's Bay Company which prevented settlement here by force, intimidation, or bribes. Such charges, made in exaggerated terms and always without proof, were of course baseless. But, on the other hand, it is reasonably clear that adventurous spirits among the Americans, or speculators who might have wished early to penetrate the northern district in search of mill or town sites, were restrained from going by the well-known opposition of the great fur-trading corporation. Mere words of discouragement, or insistence by so powerful a person as McLoughlin that the district was certain eventually to go to Great Britain, would ordinarily alone have been enough to do this. "The English residents," writes Lieutenant Howison, who visited the Columbia in the summer of 1846, "calculated with great certainty upon the river being adopted as the future dividing line, and looked with jealousy upon the American advance into the northern portion of the territory, which had some influence in restraining emigration."[23] McLoughlin, it is fair to say, emphatically denied opposition of any kind. Reporting to the British consul general in the Sandwich Islands in March, 1845, the facts of the well-known Williamson episode,[24] he said,

As it has been asserted by Gentlemen of high character in the Senate of the United States that the Hudson's Bay Company had opposed the settlement of American citizens on the north bank of the Columbia

[23] *House Misc. Doc.* no. 29, 30 Cong., 1 sess., p. 4.

[24] Williamson was a Willamette settler who attempted in February, 1845, to stake out a claim on land held by the Hudson's Bay Company near Fort Vancouver and was evicted at the order of McLoughlin. H. H. Bancroft, *History of the Pacific States* (San Francisco, 1886), XXIV [*Oregon*, I], 459.

River, I beg to inform you that there is not even a shadow of truth in the report. The Hudson's Bay Company has opposed the entrance of no settler into any part of the country, except within the limits of their improvements.[25]

It ought also to be said that shortly after this letter was written, having first tried to discourage M. T. Simmons from making the first permanent American settlement in Washington and having failed, McLoughlin turned about and gave him and his party generous assistance.[26] But undoubtedly in the Willamette community the Hudson's Bay Company was known to desire Americans to remain south of the Columbia River, which helped to keep them there, as is interestingly shown in the ebullition that followed the arrival of Lieutenant Howison and the U.S. *Shark* in the summer of 1846:

> Before the arrival of the "Shark," [the Fort Vancouver officials report to London] the Americans with very few exceptions were settled in the Willamette and other districts to the Southward of the Columbia River, and from an impression that it would ultimately become the boundary of the United States possessions on the West side of the mountains, they never showed much inclination to take lands on the north side where moreover the country from being densely wooded, is by no means so attractive or favorable for settlement as the beautiful plains of the Willamette. The case was reversed when Captain Howison in the very unreserved communications he made to his Countrymen told them that the United States would never accept of any boundary short of 49° and that this settlement at Fort Vancouver and all the Country South of that line would certainly become United States property. This opinion resting on the authority of a person in whom they had confidence and falling in with their own prepossessions on the subject produced an ellectric effect in the settlements, which put the whole host of Yankee speculators and deputations in motion all rushing towards "Vancouver" to be in time for a snatch at the loaves and fishes, not a morsel of which was to be left for us, the rightful owners, as they made no secret of their intentions to take possession of every acre of land in this neighborhood in defiance of any rights thereto, on the part of the Hudson's Bay Company.[27]

[25] McLoughlin to Miller, Mar. 24, 1845, F.O. 5: 459. McLoughlin unquestionably opposed, as a matter of business, settlement in sites on either side of the Columbia where trade of a petty sort might be carried on with Indians.

[26] C. A. Snowden, *History of Washington* (New York, 1909), II, 429.

[27] Board of Management at Fort Vancouver to Governor and Committee of the Hudson's Bay Company, Nov. 2, 1846, F.O. 5: 481. For Lieutenant Howison's version see *House Misc. Doc.* no. 29, 30 Cong., 1 sess., pp. 18, 19.

Politically, as well as economically, the Hudson's Bay Company successfully held off American snatchers after loaves and fishes north of the Columbia. Dr. McLoughlin was able to defeat every effort they made to extend their political control across the river. The facts of that contest need merely a brief summary. Prior to 1844 the pioneers' provisional government made no attempt to exercise authority north of the Columbia River, nor did it even fix a definite northern limit for the area over which it claimed jurisdiction. But in June, 1844, at the instance of the Clatsop Methodist mission it organized Clatsop County with boundaries extending northward across the Columbia River. McLoughlin, who happened at the time to be in Willamette Falls, promptly made protest, pointing out that not a single American settler was to be found north of the Columbia at this point, that to enact such a measure was simply to furnish "an argument to demagogues in both countries, to enable them to embarrass both Governments, and prevent the Boundary being settled,"[28] and that since they could not, after all, determine matters of diplomacy "it was not good policy for them to start subjects which might lead to difficulties, but limit their legislation to what the circumstances of their case actually required, so as to keep peace and order among them." His argument prevailed, and an amendatory act was passed which struck off from "any counties heretofore organized" the parts lying north of the Columbia River.[29] But this concession proved unpopular in the community, for it was held to constitute a recognition of British claims to the Columbia River boundary, and at its December session the legislature passed a new measure declaring Oregon Territory to extend all the way to 54° 40′. Since the provisional government made no attempt to exert authority north of the Columbia, however, this resolution was hardly more than an expression of sentiment. But by the summer of 1845 it had become apparent that a common control was necessary for the preservation of order and mutual good relations, and to this end a compact was entered into between the Hudson's Bay Company, representing the British side of the river, and the provisional government, representing the American. By the terms of this compact the fur-trading corporation agreed to take a hand in the provisional government and to pay

28 McLoughlin to Simpson, Mar. 20, 1845, F.O. 5: 443.
29 F.O. 5: 440.

taxes. In return it was left in actual control of administration in the region north of the Columbia, and this area, which the provisional legislature in a hostile spirit had just voted to divide into two districts bearing the names of Lewis and Clark, was at McLoughlin's demand, after a heated debate and close division, organized as a single district bearing the name of Vancouver. By this compact, as a careful student of it has keenly observed,[30] McLoughlin was able to maintain the character of the territory north of the Columbia River as the special preserve of the Hudson's Bay Company, and such was its status as long as the boundary question remained unsettled. Lord Aberdeen was well aware of these facts, and, in conceding to the United States the line of the forty-ninth parallel, he understood that he was surrendering a district which politically as well as economically was dominated by British colonists.[31]

But it would be a mistake now to conclude that the Oregon pioneers did not influence the boundary treaty at all. They did influence it both indirectly and directly. How much they did it by way of modifying British public opinion is a difficult matter to determine. No doubt their presence on the Willamette in growing numbers was a factor enabling the British Cabinet in 1846 to make concessions toward a settlement which would not have been possible before. But on the other hand the London *Times* was well aware that Americans were settled only on the south side of the Columbia, that the disputed region north of the river was in Hudson's Bay Company control, and that to concede the forty-ninth parallel was to surrender important British vested interests.[32] As a potential military force[33] in case of war the Oregon pioneers aroused British apprehension,[34] and perhaps that helped to produce concessions which made a peaceful settlement possible. But such an hypothesis is somewhat weakened by the private correspondence

[30] R. C. Clark, "Last Step in Provisional Government", in *Oregon Hist. Quar.*, XVI (1915), 313.

[31] The Hudson's Bay Company made a practice of submitting to the British Foreign Office copies of correspondence from Oregon on matters of political or diplomatic interest. See McLoughlin to Simpson, Mar. 20, 1845, F.O. 5: 443; Pelly to the Foreign Office, Mar. 28, 1845, F.O. 5: 440; McLoughlin to Pelly, Nov. 15, 1844, F.O. 5: 444.

[32] London *Times*, May 9, Nov. 20, 1845; Mar. 16, 1846. But see Joseph Schafer, "Oregon Pioneers", in *Turner Essays in American History*, 35.

[33] For this suggestion and the phrasing of it I am indebted to Professor F. J. Turner.

[34] Peel to Aberdeen, Feb. 23, 1845, Peel MSS., British Museum.

exchanged between the leaders of the British Cabinet, the Duke of Wellington, and Lord Metcalfe in Canada,[35] from which it appears that they realized that if war came it would be decided, and the fate of Oregon would be decided, not in the Far West, but in Canada, on the Great Lakes, and on the sea. Even in Oregon the Hudson's Bay Company in case of war would not have been helpless, as it effectively controlled ammunition, and could count on the support of the British navy, and at least a part of the eighty thousand Indians under its domination in the Pacific Northwest. More effective as a factor in the negotiations was the danger, recognized by both governments, that local conflicts between the pioneers and the Hudson's Bay Company might develop into a general conflagration. No doubt this had considerable influence in hastening a settlement on the basis of mutual concessions.

But there is a positive contribution of real significance which the Oregon pioneers made to the boundary settlement. It is that they led the Hudson's Bay Company to shift its main depot from the old and famous site on the Columbia River to a new location at the tip of Vancouver Island. This they did by arousing in the mind of George Simpson, field governor of the Company's territories, fears for the safety of the valuable stores concentrated at Fort Vancouver. Simpson profoundly distrusted the Willamette settlers. In his private correspondence he persistently classed all of them together as "desperate characters." He seems to have considered the provisional government of the same stripe, for when in 1845 he reported that the Clatsop Point settlers had hesitantly given in their adhesion to it he observed: "Well was it for them that they did so, as this infant Government appears to be very energetic, the Bowie knife, Revolving Pistol and Rifle taking the place of the Constable's baton in bringing refractory delinquents to justice."[36] Emigrants en route to Oregon being of the same stamp as those already there, he was concerned for the safety of Fort Hall and warned its chief officer in the spring of 1846 to be on guard against pillaging.[37] Fort Vancouver's vast stores he proposed to put as far as possible out of reach of harm.

[35] See particularly the Peel MSS. for 1845–1846.
[36] Simpson to the Governor, etc., of the Hudson's Bay Company, June 20, 1845, War Office, 1: 552.
[37] Simpson to Richard Grant, June 27, 1846, H. B. Co. Archives, Journal, No. 1721.

Even before the major migrations to Oregon had begun, while Jason Lee was still preaching the way for them in the East, Simpson scented danger and began stirring the London office to action.

Missions [he reported in 1839] are now established at three different points on the Columbia, and every Trapper who straggles away from his party, seats himself down on the Wilhamet, now with our retired servants and Indians forming a Settlement of about 100 families; and from the measures that have been taken by Missionary and Emigration Societies in the States, it is confidently expected a large body of settlers will find their way there by sea and land this season. While their means were small, and without external support, they were quiet and orderly, confining themselves to their Agricultural pursuits; but as their numerical force encreases, tranquillity it is to be feared will give way, and composed as their society at present is, and is likely to be, for some time to come, of men of desperate character and fortune, we count on the law of the strongest becoming the law of the land. In that case, our tenure of the trade, and of the Establishments on the Columbia river, will be both dangerous and uncertain, unless the boundary be immediately determined; as every citizen of the United States, who knows the country even by name, contends we are intruders, without a shadow of right to be there, and among the Wilhamet settlers few will be scrupulous as to the mode or means of asserting their imaginary rights.[38]

"We think," replied the London office, instructing McLoughlin regarding a new main base, "the object becomes more necessary as the influx of strangers to the Columbia increases."[39]

But McLoughlin was slow to act, for he had become old at Fort Vancouver, and was tied there by private interests. Fort Victoria was, therefore, not under construction until the spring of 1843, and it required Simpson's intervention again to bring about the actual shift of base in 1845. When the latter learned on New Year's Day, 1845, that President Tyler had urged Congress to facilitate emigration to Oregon, foreseeing that this meant a large increase in migration the next summer, he immediately sent directions to McLoughlin.

From what we know of the character of the people proceeding to settle west of the mountains, I think we cannot be too much on our guard against lawless aggression. I have, therefore, strongly to recommend that no more goods be kept in depôt at Vancouver than may be absolutely necessary to meet immediate demands, and that the

[38] Simpson to London Office, July 8, 1839, H. B. Co. Archives, Journal, no. 1406.
[39] London Office to McLoughlin, Dec. 31, 1839, H. B. Co. Archives, General Letter Book, no. 625.

reserved Outfit[40] for the Columbia River be kept at Fort Victoria and all goods intended for the coast at Fort Simpson, so as to be as much as possible out of reach of the troublesome people by whom you are surrounded at present. I would, moreover, recommend that the furs be collected at Fort Victoria instead of the Columbia, and that in future, the ships for England take their departure from thence, while the ships from hence will proceed thither direct (before entering the Columbia River) depositing there all reserve Outfits, merely taking to Vancouver the articles required for immediate distribution or sale.[41]

Simpson's judgment on the Willamette settlers and on their government was of course warped by prejudice, but his fears for the safety of the stores at Vancouver were warranted. Emigrants to Oregon in this period were no longer God-fearing New England missionaries. Predominantly they were from Missouri and states neighbor to her—communities notorious for turbulence and readiness to self-help. Missouri contributed more than a majority[42]—the state that had just expelled from their homes fifteen thousand Mormon settlers in the dead of winter with a loss of property estimated by Joseph Smith at a million dollars—the state that was soon to win notice again by the exploits of its border ruffians. Southern uplanders, contentious, ignorant, and suspicious, they went to Oregon inflamed against the Hudson's Bay Company by the charges of such men as Kelley, Slacum, and Spaulding, printed in government documents, that it oppressed American settlers in the Willamette, or the atrocious accusation of Benton that it incited Indians to murder American trappers, five hundred of whom had already been slain.[43] Powerful emigrant trains arriving in Oregon destitute and starving, and believing such tales, were capable of attempting any mischief, and it was partly to avert disaster that McLoughlin gave such generous aid to the companies of 1843 and 1844.[44] Residence for a year

[40] The Hudson's Bay Company kept always at Fort Vancouver a year's supply of goods ahead of current requirements in order to be insured against the chance of wreck of the annual supply ship from England. This was the reserved outfit.

[41] Simpson to McLoughlin, Jan. 1, 1845, H. B. Co. Archives, Simpson Letter Books.

[42] McLoughlin to London Office, Nov. 20, 1844, H. B. Co. Archives, Journal, no. 1711. Lieut. Wm. Peel wrote to Gordon (Sept. 27, 1845, F.O. 5: 459): "They (American settlers) are almost all from the Western Provinces and chiefly from the Missouri." Dr. White wrote to the Secretary of War in Washington at the time of the Williamson episode that too great a portion of Oregon's population came from the Western states "for one moment's safety in our present condition." See Bancroft, *Oregon*, I, 460.

[43] McLoughlin to Simpson, Mar. 20, 1845, F.O. 5: 443.

[44] McLoughlin to J. H. Pelly, July 12, 1846, H. B. Co. Archives, Journal, no. 1721.

or two in the Willamette dispelled much hostility, but there were always abundant opportunities for friction in the economic relations of monopoly-hating pioneers with a foreign corporation that dominated, even if benevolently, the life of the community. Particular soreness was felt that a corporation whose charter was believed to grant the right to hold land only for trading purposes had engrossed many of the choicest farming, mill, and town site locations in the country, and this jealousy extended even to the Company's retired servants in the Willamette. A curious echo of Missouri Mormon troubles sounds out of a report brought to McLoughlin early in 1845 of an alleged attempt by some thirty or forty Americans to organize a party whose object was to drive out of the Willamette all the Canadians and others having Indian or half-breed families who held lands there.[45] Similar feeling animated the attempts of bold spirits like Williamson, Alderman, McNamee,[46] and others to stake out claims on lands occupied by the Hudson's Bay Company near Fort Vancouver, and it eventually found successful expression after the Oregon Treaty in the gradual seizure by American settlers, treaty terms notwithstanding, of much the greater part of all the lands and much of the cattle held by the Company and its subsidiary in the region between the Columbia River and the forty-ninth parallel.[47] Beside the danger of spoliation was that of incendiarism, ruffians like Alderman and Chapman, who nursed grievances, having openly threatened to set fire at opportunity to the premises at Fort Vancouver.[48] McLoughlin, as well as Simpson, saw these dangers and took such measures as he could to forestall them, strengthening the defenses of Fort Vancouver in 1844, appealing for naval protection to British authorities in 1845,[49] and, when that brought slow

[45] McLoughlin to Simpson, Mar. 3, 1845, F.O. 5: 443; McLoughlin to Governor and Committee, Mar. 28, 1845, H. B. Co. Archives, Journal, no. 1742; Douglas to Governor and Committee, Dec. 7, 1846, F.O. 5: 481.

[46] Above, p. 241. For the Alderman incident, see McLoughlin to Gordon, Sept. 15, 1845, F.O. 5: 459. For the McNamee incident, see Board of Management to H. B. Co., Nov. 2, 1846, F.O. 5: 481.

[47] These spoliations are described in the testimony taken by a commission under the treaty of 1863 "for the final settlement of the claims of the Hudson's Bay and Puget Sound Agricultural Companies," and they are in part the basis of the award of $650,000 made to the Hudson's Bay Company in 1869. See Report of British and American Joint Commission, 14 vols., in Library of Congress.

[48] McLoughlin to H. B. Co., Nov. 20, 1845, in *Am. Hist. Rev.*, XXI (1915–1916), 112.

[49] *Ibid.* See also Lieutenant Howison's Report, in *House Misc. Doc.* no. 29, 30 Cong., 1 sess., pp. 18, 19.

response, yielding to the wish of the orderly element among the Americans that he give in his adhesion to the provisional government. Simpson's measure was more thorough, and it is easy to agree with him in his formal report of it to London headquarters that it was required.

The proceedings in Congress [he observes] and other reports in the public prints, which find their way to the Wallamette by every opportunity, seem to influence the minds of the great body of the most ignorant settlers against us, who look upon us as intruders, and if they were not overawed in some degree by the semblance of law that exists, and a feeling that we are in a situation to resent any aggression that might be openly attempted, there would be no salvation, either for the lives or property of British Subjects. Notwithstanding a certain degree of popularity, which the Company's officers enjoy, arising from the hospitalities and assistance that have been rendered to almost every American who has come to the Country, the Honble. Company as a body is looked upon with much jealous rancour and hostility, leading to serious apprehensions on the minds of the Council that the Depot at Fort Vancouver, and the other posts within reach of these people, are not safe from plunder. These apprehensions have determined us on giving directions that the business in the neighborhood of the Wallamette Falls be contracted as much as possible, and that the great bulk of the property in depot at [Fort] Vancouver be removed to Fort Victoria, which is intended to be made the principal depot of the Country, as you will observe by the instructions contained in the accompanying copy of my despatch . . . .[50]

There were, to be sure, other considerations, ordinary requirements of business, that demanded the creation of a new main depot away from the Columbia River. The decline of the fur trade in the valley of the Columbia,[51] the perils of the bar at the entrance of the river, and uncertainties as to the boundary settlement were powerful factors dictating the change. Eventually they would have brought it about even without the intervention of the Americans in the Willamette. Indeed, the Hudson's Bay Company had been contemplating the transfer for at least ten years. But it required the menace of the Willamette settlers to crystallize these factors into action, and action just when the boundary negotiations were at a stage to be influenced by it.

[50] Simpson to Hudson's Bay Company, June 20, 1845, Public Record Office, War Office I: 552.
[51] *Am. Hist. Rev.*, XXI (1915–1916), 127.

So quietly was this shift of base made that hardly any American understood at the time what was happening; but it did not escape the notice of Lord Aberdeen. He knew of it in 1845 and welcomed it for the promise it offered of a peaceful solution of the Oregon controversy. Sincerely desirous of composing this critical issue he had reconciled himself by December, 1843, to substantially the terms of settlement later laid down in the treaty of 1846.[52] But he had found it impossible to win over Peel, the prime minister, or the remainder of the Cabinet.[53] They no doubt feared the clamor which an active opposition would raise over what was virtually a surrender to the demands of the United States. The Cabinet was still unpersuaded when the news came in 1845 of the shift of base of the Hudson's Bay Company. That event put a new political face on the situation. The Hudson's Bay Company had unwittingly revealed by its move that it no longer regarded the Columbia River as a vital trade route or an indispensable outlet for its western provinces to the sea; that a watercourse which looked imposing on the maps was of so little real promise for anything but a fur-trade commerce that it was being relegated by the British interest which best knew its

[52] Aberdeen to Pakenham, Mar. 4, 1844, Aberdeen MSS. This letter was found by Dr. Schafer, the scholar of the Oregon question, in the Aberdeen MSS., and was in part printed in his article, "British Attitude toward the Oregon Question," in this *Review*, XVI (1910–1911), 296. Dr. Schafer seems to believe that this letter represented the views of the British Cabinet in 1844, as well as those of Lord Aberdeen. That would make it, if true, a document of first importance. But it does not represent the views of the Cabinet, as the correspondence presented in the following note shows.

[53] Peel to Aberdeen, Sept. 28, 1844, Peel MSS. "I incline to arbitration rather than any important concession beyond former proposals. If I recollect right there are on record in the F.O. very strong opinions, both with reference to considerations of policy and justice, as to the impropriety of carrying concession beyond certain defined limits. I should not be afraid of a good deal of preliminary bluster on the part of the Americans. The best answer to it would be to direct the *Collingwood* to make a friendly visit when she has leisure, to the mouth of the Columbia." As late as Apr. 18, 1845, Lord Aberdeen instructed Pakenham (F.O. 5: 423) to add to previous offers to the American government merely that of allowing "all ports within the disputed territory south of 49° N. L. whether on the main land or on Vancouver's Island to be made perpetually free Ports," and adds: "Beyond this degree of compromise Her Majesty's Gov't could not consent to go. Should you therefore have an opportunity of making such a proposal, and should it be rejected, you will have no alternative but to recur to the demand for arbitration." Privately he wrote on the same day (Aberdeen MSS.) that if Buchanan should propose the 49th degree to the sea, "I should not like to regard his proposal as perfectly inadmissable. It is possible that by some modifications it might be accepted, though I do not think it at all likely, and of course you will give no encouragement to the notion, but recur to arbitration in the event of our terms being rejected."

potentialities to secondary uses. To yield this river to the United States could not involve serious national loss, nor under the circumstances lay the government open to partisan attack or national outcry. And surrender of the Columbia was the key to the peaceful settlement of the Oregon boundary.

Previous Oregon negotiations had all gone to shipwreck on the issue of the Columbia River. American negotiators had steadily sought as their prime objective in Oregon a share of the harbors in and about Puget Sound, the only safe harbors on the Pacific to which at this time the United States had any claim. To obtain these however, in satisfactory status, American territory must embrace both banks of the Columbia River and extend beyond it to the forty-ninth parallel. Great Britain, on the other hand, was determined to hold one bank of the river which was considered the St. Lawrence of the West, the only outlet for the western provinces of British North America to the sea.[54] The mere territory between the Columbia and the forty-ninth parallel was not a real obstacle to a settlement, for it was held by British negotiators and public in no high esteem.[55] Nor did Great Britain consider it essential to shut the United States off from all good harbors on the Pacific—its proposals of 1826 and 1844 are evidence of that. Britain's determination in all the earlier negotiations not to retreat from the line of the Columbia was due to the exalted conception which its Foreign Office had of the river's value as a highway of commerce.

This exaggerated notion the Hudson's Bay Company had naturally taken no pains to dispel so long as the fur trade on the Columbia was prosperous and growing. On the contrary, its officers had wrought diligently to confirm it. That appears clearly in the following excerpts from a letter written by Governor Simpson to the British Foreign Office in January, 1826, in response to a list of queries submitted to him by H. U. Addington. Whatever may be the significance of the queries,[56] no one could fail to be impressed with the reply. Indeed it is not impossible that in the emphatic presentation of the value of the Columbia highway here made we have an expla-

[54] London *Times*, Jan. 3, 17, 1846.

[55] Aberdeen to Gurney, Feb. 20, 1842, printed in Lady Frances Balfour, *Life of Aberdeen*, II, 137. Lord Aberdeen refers to the region as "a few miles of pine swamp." London *Times*, Oct. 1, 1845, and Mar. 5, 1846.

[56] More evidence is needed before venturing an opinion on the general drift of these queries. The negotiation of 1826 is the one in which the British government first advanced to the offer of the enclave north of the Columbia River.

nation of the failure of the negotiations of 1826—the last negotiations prior to the critical ones of the 'forties.

6. Query:—Is the Country northward of the Columbia favourable for Land and water communication?

Answer:—The Country to the Northward of the Columbia is not favorable for Water communication with the Coast on account of the impetuosity of the current at particular Seasons in the different Rivers, and frequent chains of Rapids and dangerous falls, and the communication with the Coast by Land is quite impracticable, on account of the mountainous character of the Country, which is covered with almost impenetrable Forests.

7. Query:—For what extent of Country does the Columbia River furnish an outlet for Trade? Specify this exactly and according to the latest and most accurate accounts.

Answer:—The Columbia is the only navigable River to the interior from the Coast, we are acquainted with, it is therefore the only certain outlet for the Company's trade west of the Mountains, comprehending that of thirteen Establishments now occupied.

10. Query:—What comparison does Frasers River bear in magnitude and capacity for the purposes of Trade with the Columbia? Is the native population on its banks dense or not—well disposed or not—warlike or pacific?

Answer:—Frazers river is not so large as the Columbia and not to be compared with it for the purposes of Trade, the depth of water found at its entrance was about 3 fathom: the banks are generally high and steep, covered with Timber, and such places as are sufficiently low and clear for the site of an Establishment bearing marks of having been overflown in the Seasons of high water. About 70 miles from its entrance the navigation is interrupted by Rapids and Falls, so as to render it nearly impassible, and according to the best information I have been able to collect, the banks of the River about 150 Miles up, form precipices where the towing line cannot be used, and the Current so impetuous at certain Seasons, as to render it impossible to use either the Setting Pole or Paddle, Canoes being the only craft that can attempt to stem the Current at any Season. . . .

11. Query:—Could the Fur produce to the North of Frazers river and West of the Rocky Mountains be conveniently transported by means of this River for Shipment to other Countries?

Answer:—From all the information I have been able to collect respecting Frazers river, it is not my opinion that it affords a communication by which the interior Country can be supplied from the Coast, or that it can be depended on as an outlet for the returns of the interior. I will further altho' unasked take the liberty of giving it as my opinion that if the Navigation of the Columbia is not free to the Hudson's Bay Company, and that the Territory to the Northward of it is not secured to them, they must abandon and curtail their Trade in some parts, and probably be constrained to relinquish it on the West side of the Rocky Mountains altogether.[57]

Nineteen years after this letter was written its author was executing the retreat which we have noticed from the Columbia to Vancouver Island. Lord Aberdeen at the same time was seeking escape from an impasse in the Oregon negotiations which Pakenham had brought about at Washington by cavalierly rejecting instead of taking *ad referendum* Polk's proposal to draw the Oregon boundary at the forty-ninth parallel. Under these circumstances Lord Aberdeen wrote to Peel:

If it should ever be possible to effect a settlement between ourselves upon terms, I think the following might perhaps be accepted; and I should be very unwilling to concede more. I would carry the 49th parallel of latitude as the boundary *to the sea*, and give to the United States the line of Coast to the South of this degree. This would leave us in possession of the whole of Vancouver's Island, and the northern shore of the entrance into the Straits of John de Fuca. The navigation of the Columbia to its most remote accessible point, should be common to both parties at all times; and all the ports between the Columbia and the 49th parallel, whether on the main land, or in the island, should be Free Ports. I believe that this would give us everything really worth contending for, and it would seem to coincide with the notions of the Hudson's Bay Company, who have lately established their principal settlement on Vancouver's Island.[58]

[57] Simpson to Addington, Jan. 5, 1826, H. B. Co. Archives, Corr. with Govt., no. 721.

[58] Aberdeen to Peel, Sept. 25, 1844 and Oct. 17, 1845, Peel MSS. See also Everett to Aberdeen, Jan. 28, 1846, Aberdeen MSS. Everett, who had lately returned to America from his ministry at the Court of St. James, wrote to Aberdeen freely on the Oregon question, which their cordial friendship permitted him to do:
"Again the 'Times' [London *Times*, Jan. 3, 1846] greatly errs in representing the Columbia River and its mouth as the line of communication between Hudson's Bay and China. To a party having settlements on the lower waters of the Columbia this river and its mouth are of course the outlet and a very poor outlet. But of the territory north of 49 it is not the outlet on account of the falls. I am well advised by practical men, that if the 49th degree is adopted as the Boundary, not the smallest part of your trade would descend the Columbia, although the navigation should be free. The pass through the mountains used by the Hudson's Bay people is north of 49; and all their trade both of export and import, would of preference pass the Straits of Fuca. I learned from Your Lordship a year ago, that, although you have at present the free range of the Country, the Hudson's Bay Company have been removing their principal station from the banks of the Columbia river to the south end of Vancouver's Island. I consider it even probable that *we* shall desert the mouth of the Columbia for some port within the Straits of Fuca."

These were the terms, slightly modified, which in the spring of 1846 Lord Aberdeen wrote into the final Oregon settlement. He had translated the Hudson's Bay Company's retreat from the Columbia into a treaty of peace.

American westward expansion was in large measure the work of rough frontiersmen, men who at the cutting edge of civilization had developed habits of direct action and self-help. Such men were hard to control anywhere, and in the Spanish border-lands, weakly held and badly governed, they quickly brought on revolution and annexation to the United States. But West Florida, Texas, and California are not Oregon. In the Pacific Northwest American pioneers were confronted by sterner stuff than Spaniards or Mexicans— the British government and the Hudson's Bay Company. Direct action and turbulence were there held remarkably in leash by the power and wisdom, in considerable part, of a single great corporation. But the Hudson's Bay Company, much feared, was itself afraid. It is a phenomenon by no means new, two hostile elements facing and fearing each other. In Oregon this led, for once, not to war but to peace.

ESSAY 9 · BRITISH PARTY POLITICS AND THE OREGON TREATY*

THE OREGON boundary question was a diplomatic problem involving a kernel of reality and an enormous husk. The husk took on more and more the character of chaff as the controversy ripened, though politicians and public never altogether realized it and diplomats refused for tactical reasons to acknowledge it. To a proper analysis of the Oregon negotiation of 1846 the separation of the kernel from the chaff is essential.

Separation of the two discloses the fact that the Treaty of 1846 from a British point of view was not a compromise but a surrender. A mere fragment of the immense territory stretching from California to Alaska and from the Rocky Mountains to the sea which diplomats and politicians argued about was in 1846 actually in dispute. The area in question was a tract lying between the offers the two governments had repeatedly made to each other, a triangle bounded on the north by the 49th parallel and on the south and east by the Columbia River—the area now the western two-thirds of the state of Washington.[1] Not even the entirety of this triangle was in dispute, for in 1826 the British government had offered the American a considerable detached headland or *enclave* north of the Columbia, fronting on the Strait of Juan de Fuca.[2]

---

* Reprinted from the *American Historical Review*, XXXVII (July 1932).

[1] In the Oregon negotiations of 1826 Albert Gallatin gave an intimation of willingness to accept a partition line along the 49th parallel which stopped short at the Strait of De Fuca so as to leave to Great Britain the whole of Vancouver Island. See Gallatin to Clay, Dec. 2, 1826, *American State Papers, Foreign Relations* (6 vols., Washington, 1832–59), VI, 655–656.

[2] President Polk in his inaugural of March, 1845, and in his message to Congress of December, 1845, publicly asserted the claim of the United States to the whole of the Oregon Country. But in the interval between these addresses he formally offered to the British minister in Washington a settlement on the basis of the 49th parallel. And when that offer had been summarily rejected and had been withdrawn, he still permitted it to be known in London that he would submit to the American Senate a settlement on the basis of the 49th parallel. President Polk in his public declarations was acting on the theory "that the only way to treat John Bull was to look him straight in the eye."

This triangle was of importance to the two governments not so much for its intrinsic worth as for its water appendages. The Columbia River which washes the base of it was regarded by uninformed English opinion as the future outlet of western Canada to the sea. At the apex of the triangle, clustered about the Straits, lies that group of magnificent roadsteads and harbors (the western counterpart of the waters of New York) which the American government felt it must at least share, and share by tenure more secure than that of an *enclave*. No American government could even consider surrendering the entirety of those harbors. They were the only safe ones on the western coast to which the United States at that time had any claim. This held American negotiators immovable at the line of the 49th parallel.

If the government of the United States could not and would not move from the line of the 49th parallel, if to obtain harbors it had to engross the whole area to the Straits, any British government that undertook to bring the menacing controversy to a close had to agree to a surrender. Surrender was necessary of the whole dis-puted triangle, of the majestic stream of the Columbia, and of the great crescent of harbor waters sweeping through De Fuca Strait to Puget Sound. More difficult even than such a sacrifice of substance was the sacrifice required of British pride. For more than a quarter of a century and through five negotiations, British governments had resisted American pretensions to the triangle on the ground of the superiority of British title to it. That was an elevation from which it was difficult to descend. Since the earlier negotiations the triangle had been occupied by British subjects in considerable numbers, servants of the Hudson's Bay Company and employees on the farms and pastures of the Puget Sound Agricultural Company. Practically no Americans were there as settlers, indeed none, so far as Lord Aberdeen knew.[3] If in diplomacy possession is nine points of the law the triangle was already British. To give it up, to retreat from the Columbia River boundary, was to abandon British vested interests and to expatriate British subjects. It was to retreat from the boundary of British prestige.

Lord Aberdeen, the secretary for foreign affairs in the Conserva-tive government of Peel, was eager for a pacific adjustment of all outstanding differences with the United States. Conciliatory and

[3] See Essay 8, pp. 238–239.

peace-loving, he saw nothing within the triangle that was worth the risk of war. Of the territory itself he had a low opinion; he was well aware that the Columbia could never be an outlet for western Canada to the sea; and he recognized the essential reasonableness of the American demand for a share in the harbors about the 49th parallel. Personally he was willing as early as December 1843 to settle the dispute on the basis of the American line to the Straits.[4]

What gave him pause was the political difficulty of so complete a surrender. Peel's strength in Parliament was mortgaged to an extensive program of domestic reform. That might be jeopardized if the government became exposed to the reproach of having abandoned in America the interests and honor of the nation. The British public to be sure was uninformed as to Oregon and even less interested. Unless the nation was roused it might not feel that its rights and honor were being betrayed. But the Whig Opposition was watchful and among the Whigs was Palmerston!

Lord Palmerston had already demonstrated what he could do under such circumstances in 1842 when he fell foul of the treaty closing the Northeastern boundary controversy. That treaty, though a compromise, was by no means unfavorable to England. Indeed it was probably more favorable than the abortive arbitral award made when Palmerston was secretary for foreign affairs in 1831 by the king of the Netherlands, a judgment which Palmerston would have been willing to accept. Lord Ashburton had obtained over and above that award 893 square miles of the terrain in dispute, and had secured in addition what the military experts of the government had most at heart, a frontier line considerably farther removed than the Dutch line from the river St. Lawrence, one that appeared more easily defensible and better suited to the require-ments of a road between Quebec and Fredericton. Lord Ashbur-ton's treaty had been received by the British public with relief if not with enthusiasm. Many notable Whig leaders had approved it and likewise an influential portion of the Whig press. Yet Lord Palmerston in the columns of the *Morning Chronicle* and in Parlia-ment had made it the subject of a sensational partisan attack. He had denounced it as "one of the worst and most disgraceful treaties

<hr/>

[4] Aberdeen to Pakenham, Mar. 4, 1844, and Pakenham to Aberdeen, March 28, 1844, Aberdeen MSS.

that England ever concluded";[5] he proposed to brand across it for all time in red letters of shame the word "capitulation"; and he scourged the government which was responsible for it as inept and pusillanimous. He returned to the fire on the occasion of the "Battle of the Maps," and thereafter discharged into the government camp intermittently for several years shells loaded with the charge of "capitulation." His cannonading proved ineffective. The treaty was too clearly a wise settlement to be made a partisan issue; there was too great division regarding it within the ranks of the Whigs themselves, and the Whig chieftain, Lord John Russell, took his stand too reluctantly and too half-heartedly at the side of his fighting colleague. But the assault gave warning to the Conservative ministry of the danger of agreeing to any future settlement that would lay the government open to the charge of a real capitulation. That was what Lord Aberdeen had in mind when in response to urgent appeals of the American minister at the Court of St. James for a settlement of the Oregon controversy he gave always the same mournful answer—that his government could not concede what previous British governments had again and again refused.[6] The shadow of Lord Palmerston hung during the last two critical years over the only solution of the Oregon controversy that held the prospect of peace.

It was to dispel that shadow that Edward Everett at the end of December, 1845, when the two nations seemed to be drifting helplessly into war over the Oregon question, sent an appeal to Palmerston's political associate, Lord John Russell. In it he eloquently prayed the Whig chieftain to grant immunity to the Conservative government—immunity without which the concessions could not be made to the United States that were necessary to bring the controversy to a pacific close. His letter is well worth reproducing at length. It is an analysis of the Oregon question by an

[5] Palmerston to Russell, Sept. 24, 1842, Public Record Office, Russell MSS.
[6] See Everett to Webster, Dec. 28, 1843, Everett MSS. In this private letter Edward Everett reported to the American Secretary of State: "I have strenuously urged upon Lord Aberdeen the *reasonableness* of running the 49th parallel of latitude to the sea, as a principle of compromise. His only difficulty (I really think) is that this proposal has been three times rejected; and the ministry does not dare to agree to terms, which have in all former negotiations been refused." See also Everett to Upshur, Feb. 2, 1844, and Everett to Calhoun, Feb. 28, 1845, Everett MSS. See also McLane to Buchanan, March 3, 1846, Department of State, England Despatches, vol. 56, National Archives.

able observer, one who had just returned to America from a four years' service as American minister at the Court of St. James, where he had enjoyed to an unusual degree the confidence of leaders of the government and the Opposition alike.

Boston, U. S. A.
28 Dec. 1845.

My dear Lord John:
  In pursuance of an intimation which I made to you before I left London and which seemed acceptable to you, I will now undertake to give you very briefly my view of the existing controversy between the two countries. It is proper in the outset to state, that I am not in the confidence of our own government, and know nothing of their views, beyond what may be gathered from the ordinary sources of public and private information. The present state of the controversy seems to be the following. Our government has offered to yours the 49th degree of latitude to the Pacific Ocean, with a free port, or ports as you wish, on the south end of Vancouver's island. You have offered to us the 49th degree till it strikes the Columbia River thence down that river to the Pacific, with a detached territory north of the Columbia, including a port within the Straits of Fuca, and such other free ports as we wish. These offers with the exception of the Free ports on the two sides are the same which were made and rejected in the former negotiations.
  Our offer of the 49th, as originally made in 1818, and renewed in 1824 and 1826, was—I have always understood rejected by the British Administration of those days, under the suggestion of the North West and the Hudson's Bay Companies, that the navigation of the Columbia river was absolutely necessary to an advantageous possession of any part of the back country partially drained by it. I believe that this representation, as a matter of geographical fact, is entirely unfounded. The bar at the mouth of the Columbia and the terrific surf that breaks upon it make it nearly inaccessible, and all navigation is stopped by the falls at the distance of 80 or 100 miles from the sea. . . . I admit the difficulty, on the part of your Government,—substantially in the same hands now as in 1818-1826, of agreeing to what they then rejected. The point of honor and consistency must be saved; but in proportion as the rejected proposal was really equitable, such modification as may be insisted upon, to save the point of ministerial consistency, ought to be moderate. Such a modification has been offered by our government in the form of free ports on the southern extremity of Vancouver's island. I think that the cession of that extremity would be by us agreed to; in other words that our Government would agree to the 49th parallel till it strikes the sea, leaving to you the whole of Vancouver's Island. This to you is a very important and substantial modification of

the proposal formerly rejected.[7] Whether your ministers will accept it is a question for themselves; but their course will no doubt in a great degree depend upon yours. If you choose to rally the public opinion of England against this basis of compromise, it will not be easy for Sir R. Peel and Lord Aberdeen to agree to it. If you are clearly of opinion, as a point of public interest or honour that this compromise ought not to be agreed to, you will of course encourage the ministers in rejecting it. But if the only point to be saved is one,—*not of national but merely of ministerial consistency*, it will I think deserve your most serious consideration—yours and that of your friends—whether you will encourage and stimulate the government to plunge into a war, *for the sake of adhering to the worst traditions of Lord Liverpool and Lord Castlereagh.* . . . I pray you to pardon the freedom of this letter. It is dictated by the feeling, that Peace between the two countries is the great interest of the world, and that its preservation is wrapped up in the folds of your mantle. May God guide you to a wise decision.[8]

An appeal such as this might well have produced in England a response other than its author intended. For it was a delicate thing that an American, and particularly one so recently minister to England, should implore a leader of the Whig party to give immunity to a Tory government for the purpose of facilitating a surrender to the United States of the whole substance of a dispute. When the appeal was sent for comment to Lord Palmerston he reacted to it adversely.

C. T.　2 Feb. 1846.

My dear John Russell:
Many thanks for Everett's very skilfull letter which does credit to American diplomacy; and no less to the writer's penetration. . . . The Americans appear to have but one formula for boundary negotiations which runs thus; we say that we have a clear right to the whole of the thing which is in dispute, but we will prove our moderation by ceding to you for ample equivalent a small and comparatively little valuable portion of it; we are all of us determined to seize and keep the remainder whether you will or no; and if you do not agree to these terms you will be the cause of the war which we shall make agst. you. Their notion of the way of saving the honor of the party with whom they are dealing is as if the gentleman on the road after taking the traveller's purse should keep the sovereigns to satisfy his own claims and give back a shilling or two to save the wounded honor of the person with whom he was thus making *an equitable distribution*[9] of the matter in dispute.

---

[7] But Albert Gallatin had already intimated a willingness to make this modification in the negotiations of 1826. See *ante*, note 1.

[8] Everett to Russell, Dec. 28, 1845. Courtesy of the Huntington Library.

[9] The underscoring is Palmerston's.

I have not much studied this Oregon Question, but a look at the map, and Everett's admissions seem to shew that his proposed distribution is somewhat of this character. . . ."[10]

Lord John Russell's reaction, however, was more favorable, and was likewise more significant. In response to the appeal, early in February, 1846, he took the momentous step necessary to preserve Anglo-American peace. On his own responsibility he gave the Conservative minister of foreign affairs assurance of party truce on the Oregon question. "My opinion", he afterwards informed Lord Palmerston, "upon the whole is that we may well and with due regard to our own interests give up the Columbia river, and I have let Aberdeen know privately that he will have no opposition from me on that ground."[11] That meant commitment on the Oregon question not merely of Lord John Russell but of his party associates, since they could not without a party rift publicly denounce what he had approved; it meant that in the ministry, Lord Aberdeen was relieved of the restraints of colleagues arising from political timidity, that at last, as secretary, he had a free hand in the Oregon negotiation—the freedom to make such a treaty of concession as personally he had been willing since December, 1843, to conclude. There remained only for the American government to signify its willingness to reopen the suspended negotiations by a courteous notice of the termination of the convention of joint occupation, and a treaty could be drawn that would bring to a close a dispute which for over a year had been a menace to the peace of the world.

Lord John Russell was induced to give this momentous promise not solely, of course, nor even primarily, by the power of an eloquent letter. As a parliamentary leader he based his decisions on weightier considerations. He acted on Edward Everett's appeal because it coincided with what he conceived to be prudent Whig policy. Party interest, as identified in his mind with the good of the state, was what influenced him to grant the Oregon truce, and the student who would know the history of the settlement of 1846 will search for it in British party politics, and particularly in the inner politics of Her Majesty's Whig Opposition.

Whig Opposition politics were directed in these years by no lofty political principles distinguishable from Conservative, either

[10] Palmerston to Russell, Feb. 2, 1846, Broadlands, Palmerston MSS. Courtesy of Sir Wilfred Ashley.
[11] Russell to Palmerston, Feb. 3, 1846, *ibid.*

in the field of domestic or foreign administration. Party exigency was almost their sole guide. In the field of domestic politics the two parties differed almost as much within their own ranks as from each other and Lord John Russell and Sir Robert Peel might have exchanged party leadership with no substantial alteration of views. Whigs and Peelites, indeed, after the announcement by the Conservative ministry of its purpose of repealing the Corn Laws, were in practical coalition for a half year as against the rebellious Protectionists of the Conservative party. In the domain of foreign administration there was an equally slight difference of principle between the two parties. Theoretically the Whig party was sympathetic toward revolutionary liberalism on the continent of Europe, and to give it support favored an *entente cordiale* with revolutionary France; whereas the Conservative party was favorable to the governments and views of the old Holy Alliance. Yet Lord Palmerston, who had favored an *entente cordiale* during the Grey ministry, himself wrecked it in the Turco-Egyptian crisis of 1840, in which he aligned England with the three chief autocracies of Europe to defeat and humiliate France; and Lord Aberdeen, on the other hand, made the revival of Anglo-French cordiality the main work and the chief glory of his five years of office.

What distinguished Whig from Conservative administration of foreign affairs was less a principle than a man. It was Lord Palmerston, whose personality and temperament constituted the fighting ground of British foreign politics throughout the years of the Oregon crisis. Lord Palmerston had been foreign secretary in Whig administrations twice between the years 1830 and 1841, first in that of Lord Grey, the elder, and again in that of Lord Melbourne. He had acquitted himself to the satisfaction of all in the first. He had given proof of sagacity and of energy; as a negotiator he had shown moderation; and as a cabinet colleague he had been loyal and coöperative. But under the laxer control of Lord Melbourne he had developed the qualities that characterized the Palmerston of later tradition. He had become high-handed and self-willed, fond of giving the lead to Europe and of leading audaciously where there was danger, rejoicing in movement rather than in quiet, in argumentative and tactical triumphs rather than in the maintenance of good will, giving offense to foreign governments and statesmen by the jauntiness and flippancy of his tone, and exhibiting in general the characteristics which later called forth the embittered description of him as "half hornet, half butterfly."

He had revealed these qualities particularly toward the end of the Melbourne administration, and the resulting reverberations still ran through British politics in the closing years of the Oregon negotiation. In the Turco-Egyptian crisis of 1840 his mode of checking an Egyptian pasha who, with the support of France was warring upon his master, the sultan of Turkey, had wrecked the Anglo-French understanding, and brought Europe to the verge of a general war. "He steered the ship [in that crisis] with astonishing self possession and admirable dexterity, and he brought her safely through the storm; but the storm was mainly of his own brewing. A daring pilot in extremity he certainly was, but he was also a pilot who loved to steer straight for the breakers."[12] He displayed these qualities in America and in the Far East, and when he left office in 1841 upon the defeat of the Melbourne government, though his personal prestige was at its highest, he left France embittered and humiliated, the rest of Europe breathless and uneasy, America, as a result of the *impasse* over the Maine boundary, in a dangerous state of irritation, and the Orient closed to British trade by the Opium War.

As a member of the Opposition he was still the stormy petrel of British foreign politics. His purpose there was to concentrate his party's fire upon his successor, Lord Aberdeen, whose management of the foreign office was a direct challenge to his own. Lord Aberdeen was the apostle of peace. In his temperament there was none of the zest of the tournament nor the love of contention that characterized the Whig viscount. He had a dread of war, which he regarded as the bitterest of human calamities, and he conceived of his ministership as an opportunity to clear away controversies old and new that threatened to lead to armed collision. France and America seemed to him particularly to guard the gates of Janus so far as England was concerned, and these two powers he made it his special object, after the irritations of Palmerston's last years, to placate and restore to a spirit of good will. He was in this eminently successful. He was able, in spite of a series of provocative episodes, to reëstablish cordial relations with France; and with America, to come to a settlement of controversies that had defied

---

[12] *Eng. Hist. Rev.* (1886), I, 117–118. I have made free use of the admirable characterizations in this anonymous article.

adjustment for generations. But Lord Palmerston regarded his policy as one of utter feebleness and low spirit, prostrating the prestige and honor of England and entailing the ultimate defeat even of its own purposes by encouraging in foreign governments a spirit of encroachment. *"We give up everything,"* he complained to Greville in the autumn of 1842, "universal concession the rule of action, and . . . there can be no difficulty in settling questions if we yield all that is in dispute."[13] "Resistance at home and . . . concession abroad," he protested again in 1844, were the key to Conservative policy,[14] and the Ashburton capitulation, the negotiations over the right of search, the diplomacy of Texas, the direction given to Spanish affairs, the management of the Tahiti and Morocco episodes, all seemed to him to illustrate this feebleness of grasp abroad set off by reaction at home.

This view he undertook to impress upon the public by constant vehement speeches in the House of Commons and by inspired articles in the daily press. He had formed a connection near the close of his term of office with the proprietor of the leading London Whig newspaper, the *Morning Chronicle*, and this became under his tutelage a lash upon the back of Lord Aberdeen. In the *Morning Chronicle* it was not necessary to maintain the same restraints on utterance as in the House of Commons, and there the foreign policy of the government was denounced as cowardly truckling to France and America, and these two countries by way of foil, were pursued with a recklessness of vituperation that gave concern even to the leaders among the Whigs. During the war on the Ashburton Treaty Lord John Russell seems to have thought it necessary to convey to his colleague some anxiety over the course of the *"Viscount Chronicle,"* as it was called, but the answer which Palmerston made was: "With regard to the *Chronicle*, I am inclined to doubt the expediency of endeavouring to exercise too minute a control over a paper whose general tendencies are right. A horse sometimes goes the safer for having his head given to him."[15]

---

[13] C. C. F. Greville, *A Journal of the Reign of Queen Victoria* (3 vols. London, 1885), II, 104.

[14] *Hansard's Parliamentary Debates*, LXXVI, 1870–1875.

[15] Palmerston to Russell, Nov. 14, 1842, Russell MSS. Palmerston went on in this letter to say that he could not recollect having seen any articles in the *Chronicle* about France to which fair objection could be taken, but that "while all the French papers are teeming every day with abuse of England, it cannot be surprising if now and then a newspaper writer's blood should boil over, and his

To engage thus in a course of international irritation was politically hazardous. The times called not for excitement but for quiet. The Western world in the late 'thirties and early 'forties was in a state of profound business depression following upon the panic of 1837, and merchants and manufacturers in a country which found its prosperity in overseas trade were eager to avoid unnecessary agitations tending to retard the return of business confidence. Spokesmen of the Conservative party in Parliament and in the press played upon this feeling and in replying to Lord Palmerston denounced him and the *Morning Chronicle* and the party which tolerated them as a war faction. The London *Times*, which constituted itself the special defender of Lord Aberdeen though it was independent in politics, never lost an opportunity to contrast the fevered state of British foreign relations at the close of Palmerston's régime with the good will and the quiet under Lord Aberdeen[16]

---

indignation should vent itself in some few remarks; nor, I confess, does it appear to me that such little occasional raps on the knuckles, even if they were given, would have an injurious effect upon our international relations."

16 See especially London *Times*, Jan. 3, Dec. 29, 1843, Nov. 18, 1844, Mar. 31, Dec. 12, 26, 1845. The article of Dec. 21, 1843, is an illustration: "It forms no part of the conditions of the trust by which the foreign affairs of a great nation are confided to the Ministers of the Crown, that they should strive to assert an irritating and impertinent right of interference on all imaginable occasions; that they should use their power not so much to promote their own laudable designs as to thwart the policy of their neighbours; or that they should make the dignity of the country consist in an arrogant defiance of the world. These indeed were the distinguishing characteristics of the foreign policy which was in full operation under the late Administration, and which still affrights the world with its angry but impotent thunders in the columns of the Opposition press. It is more brilliant to squander money than to adjust the balance of the public accounts; and it is more exciting to dash along in the heady current of strife and of adventure, than to compose the stable framework of those alliances upon which the peace of the world depends. But, happily for the world, the time is, in this country at least, gone by when a nation could be imposed upon by the din and the display of its own follies and crimes, and future Ministers who may attempt to speculate on the pugnacious temper or the irritable vanity of the people will probably perish from political life like the late Foreign Secretary—distrusted by his own party, despised by the sober sense of the nation, and dreaded by the rest of the world.

"The time is however arrived at which this slow and difficult task of reconciliation may be said to be accomplished. To a very great extent the poisonous seeds which were so profusely scattered by Lord Palmerston in every corner of the habitable globe have been eradicated. Our present object is not to revive old grievances. . . . The names of Affghanistan, China, the United States, Syria, Spain, and France suffice to awaken these associations in every mind; and they mark out, like so many monumental pillars, the huge and irregular circle of the aberrations of the British Cabinet. On each of these points some urgent and alarming difficulty was to be encountered; on none was there any fixed principle of action or permanent pledge of peace. . . . Lord Palmerston in his administration of our foreign

and to stress the injury done to British trade, particularly in America and in the East, by the course which Lord Palmerston had pursued there. According to the *Times*, the Whig ex-secretary was a "great anti-commercial diplomat,"[17] and *Punch* pictured him as the "God of War."[18]

For Whig politicians it was particularly embarrassing to be reproached with harboring a war faction. The Whigs were the party of the commercial and manufacturing classes as the Conservatives were of the landed aristocracy, and to incur at a time of business depression the charge of nursing a war element was damaging to the organization. What resulted therefore from Palmerston's activities in the years from 1840 to 1845 was that he produced in the Whig directorate anxiety and resistance, particularly in the group that stood at the right hand of Lord John Russell. From being the stormy petrel of British foreign politics he became that of his own party.

This dissatisfaction evinced itself in episode after episode in the years from 1840 to 1845. In the Turco-Egyptian crisis it took the form of a succession of party crises within the cabinet. Lord John Russell, representing the group that was alarmed at the prospect of a general European war, more than once threatened to resign, which would have brought the government tumbling to the ground.[19]

In the assault on the Ashburton Treaty a large majority of the party directors including its most powerful personages, Lord Clarendon, Lord Lansdowne, the Duke of Bedford, Lord Spencer, Lord Brougham, Lord Morpeth, Edward Ellice, Charles Buller, Benjamin Hawes, the Barings, and others took exception to their colleague's violence, and in some cases did so openly. Charles Greville on December 20, 1842, records in his diary:

---

affairs either recognized no such principles, or, which amounts to the same thing, he did not scruple to betray them, as when he sacrificed the alliance of France and England to such an object as the re-integration of the Porte into two pashalics of Syria. At home we viewed such conduct with distrust; but abroad the manifestation of such a policy . . . occasioned nothing short of universal terror; for it indicated the transfer of the vast influence of England from the cause of peace to the schemes of discord. . . ."

[17] London *Times*, Aug. 4, 1842.

[18] *Punch*, X, (1846), 23.

[19] See G. P. Gooch, ed., *Later Correspondence of Lord John Russell, 1840–1878* (London, 1925), vol. I, ch. 1; also H. L. Bulwer, *Life of Viscount Palmerston* (3 vols., London, 1870–74), II, Bks. XII–XIII.

Clarendon told me that when he was at Bowood there was a sort of consultation between him, Lord Lansdowne, and John Russell, about the 'Morning Chronicle' and Palmerston, . . . Lord John having been already stimulated by the report (which his brother, the Duke, had made him) of the opinions of himself, Lord Spencer, and other Whigs, who had met or communicated together on the same subject. The consequence was that John Russell wrote a remonstrance to Palmerston, in which he told him what these various persons thought with regard to the tone that had been taken on foreign questions, especially the American, and pointed out to him the great embarrassment that must ensue as well as prejudice to the party, if their dissatisfaction was manifested in some public manner when Parliament met. To this Palmerston replied in a very angry letter, in which he said that it was useless to talk to him about the Duke of Bedford, Lord Spencer, and others, as he knew very well that Edward Ellice was the real author of this movement against him. He then contrasted his own services in the cause with that of Ellice, and ended, as I understood, with a tirade against him, and a bluster about what he would do.[20]

The Palmerston letter referred to here has been preserved, and it fits Greville's description:

Now, as I have no respect whatever for Ellice's opinions when coming straight from himself, I am not prepared to defer to them a bit the more because they come echoed back from others. But if those others choose to follow him in these matters, let them do it. I pretend to guide nobody, except as far as reasons which I may give in Parliament, and arguments which I may there employ, may influence the minds of fair and impartial men. All that I claim for myself is freedom of action according to the best judgment I can form of the interests of my country; and that freedom I shall always exercise as long as it may please Heaven to continue to me my faculties, whether Radicals or old Whigs are pleased or displeased with the line I may think it my duty to take. If I am right, I am quite sure that my arguments and reasoning will have weight in the country, even if not in the House of Commons. If I am wrong, I shall be proved to be so, and perhaps then I may alter my own opinions.

I quite agree with you that we ought not, as an Opposition, to provoke or irritate either America or France, or indeed any other foreign power; but, on the other hand, I do not see why we should truckle to them.[21]

According to Greville, Lord John "wrote again, temperately, remonstrating against the tone he [Palmerston] had adopted, and

[20] Greville, II, 130–131.
[21] This letter is printed, though with elision of names, in H. L. Bulwer, *Life of Viscount Palmerston*, III, 113–118. It is worth reading in its entirety.

telling him that the persons whose sentiments he had expressed were very competent to form opinions for themselves, without the influence or aid of Ellice. This letter elicited one much more temperate from Palmerston, in which he expressed his readiness to cooperate with the party, and to consult for the common advantage, but that he must in the course of the session take an opportunity of expressing his own opinions upon the questions of foreign policy which would arise."[22]

Not merely anxiety but party suspicion was produced by the violence with which Palmerston assailed the Ashburton Treaty. Some of his colleagues could explain his eagerness in attack only on the theory that he was making a play for party leadership—that he was undertaking to outbid Lord John. This was the feeling entertained, according to Lord Brougham, by many Whigs,[23] and something of the sort seems to have been in the mind of the Duke of Bedford when he wrote to Lord John, his brother, on November 6, 1842:

Rely on it that if Palm. attempts or rather continues to attempt to give a direction to the party and to public opinion thru' the newspapers without concert he will dissatisfy the Whig party very much. He has now got possession of the M. Chronicle and some influence with the Globe, and is so industrious in his writings and so off hand in all he says that he will disgust the best of the old Whig party.[24] I see that it is not

[22] Greville, II, 130–131. The *Journal* is particularly illuminating on the politics of the "Ashburton War." On Sept. 24, 1842, after a visit to Palmerston, Greville wrote: "It was amusing to me to read in the columns of the 'Chronicle' all that I had been hearing Palmerston say, *totidem verbis;* his articles were merely a repetition of his talk, and that as exactly as if the latter had been taken down in shorthand. As far as I can judge, he will, however, fail to carry public opinion with him; he will not be entirely supported by the writers on his own side, nor by his political adherents . . . the fact is that Palmerston's determination to find fault with everything that is done in the Foreign Office, and the indiscriminate abuse which he heaps upon every part of our foreign policy, deprives his opinion of the weight which it would be entitled to, if he was only tolerably impartial. I never saw so much political bitterness as that which rankles in the hearts of himself and his wife. He abuses the acts of the Government, but he always does so with an air of gaiety and good humour . . . but under this gay and gallant exterior there burns a fierce hostility, and a resolution to attack them upon every point, and a more unscrupulous assailant never took the field. She talks a great deal more than he does, and it is easy to see, through her graceful, easy manner and habitual urbanity, how impatient they are of exclusion from office, and how intolerant of any dissent from or opposition to his policy and opinions." *Ibid.*, II, 105–106.

[23] Brougham to Napier, Nov. 4, 1842, British Museum, Napier MSS.

[24] The old Whigs—the Russells, the Greys, the Spencers, and others—never altogether admitted Palmerston to the bosom of the party. They considered him always something of an interloper, and he was, in truth, a Canningite rather than a Whig.

only on the American question but also on the public affairs of France that a system of irritation is kept up, after the fashion of Thiers which we condemn here. If the M. Chronicle wd. leave the French papers alone it wd. be much better, but Palm. is not to be ruled. . . .[25]

Palm. was indeed not to be ruled. Regardless of the feelings or suspicions of his colleagues he went his way. He carried his war on the Ashburton Treaty well into 1843, though with so little party support that in the midst of the final debate on it for lack of a quorum the House was counted out.[26] In January, 1845, Charles Greville visited him at Broadlands and found him "full of vigor and hilarity, and overflowing with diplomatic swagger. He said we might hold any language we pleased to France and America, and insist on what we thought necessary, without any apprehension that either of them would go to war, as both knew how vulnerable they were, France with her colonies, and America with her slaves, a doctrine to which Lord Ashburton by no means subscribes."[27]

In January, 1845, Thomas Macaulay sought to warn his colleague against views of this sort in a communication that lost none of its force by its tact:

Many thanks for your most interesting letter. I agree with almost every word of it. That your foreign policy was energetic and brilliant is allowed even by your detractors. I am firmly convinced that it was also wise and truly pacific. I concur too in your opinion that we have not, since we were in opposition, done anything to merit the imputation that we are a war party. Nevertheless that imputation, as you are aware, has been thrown on us by the men now in power here, by the French tribune, by the press both of France and of Germany, and perhaps as you suspect, by intriguers in our own ranks. It has as you observe found credit with many foolish and ignorant members of our party. I should go farther, and should say that it has found credit with many members of our party who however unjust and ill informed on this point, cannot be called generally foolish or ignorant. Nobody, I am sure, knows better than yourself that of all imputations which can be thrown on a body of politicians, that of being a war party is, in the present temper of the public mind, the most damaging. If this be so, we ought, I think seriously to consider by what means, compatible with the faithful discharge of our duty to our country, we can get rid of this imputation. And, indeed, to clear ourselves from unjust aspersions, and to keep our friends united, is a part, and not an unimportant part of our duty to our country.

[25] Bedford to Russell, Nov. 6, 1842, Russell MSS.
[26] *Hansard's*, LXVII, 1313.
[27] Greville, II, 264.

You will think that I am too much inclined to look at foreign politics with reference to their bearing on domestic politics. The truth is that with respect to foreign politics properly so called, I shall not venture to offer you any advice. For I know that you understand them infinitely better than I. But I have some opportunity of observing the temper of our party both in parliament and out of it. Now the temper of our party is one of the circumstances, though only one of the circumstances, which we ought to consider when we debate questions touching foreign policy. An English statesman cannot take his own way like Richelieu or Alberoni. It is to no purpose that he concerts the best plans for the security and glory of the Empire, that he sees to the very bottom of the designs of all the courts of Europe, that he knows exactly how far he may safely dare and where it will be prudent to stop, unless he carries with him the parliament and the country. It may be an evil that a man of your eminent capacity for the conduct of great affairs, should be under the necessity of consulting the prejudices of people who do not know the difference between the Texas question and the Oregon question, and who confound Doost Mahommed with Mehemet Ali. But this is the price which we pay for the advantages of representative government. It is vain to complain of the stupidity and ignorance of our friends. If they were all as stupid and ignorant as Joseph Hume or Williams of Coventry, it would still be necessary for us to win their confidence, because without that confidence we can effect little or nothing for the public.

I am therefore very deeply mortified when I see indiscretions committed which tend to alienate our friends and to accredit the calumnious assertions of our enemies. . . .

But I must stop; and indeed I ought to ask pardon for my prolixity. I am not aware that your views and mine are at all incompatible. You have certain opinions as to the course which England ought to take in her dealings with foreign powers; and in those opinions I generally concur. But in order that those opinions may find favour with Parliament and with the country, I hold it to be indispensable that we should appear before the public as what we really are, sincere friends of peace.[28]

No argument, however, except one, could bring Lord Palmerston in these years to alter his course. That one was the bitterness of disappointment of office. In December, 1845, Sir Robert Peel, on account of divisions within the cabinet over a proposal to repeal the Corn Laws, resigned. The Queen called upon Lord John Russell to form a government, which the latter, after careful consultation with the leaders of his party over questions of policy, agreed to do.

[28] Macaulay to Palmerston, Jan. 9, 1845, Broadlands, Palmerston MSS. Courtesy of Sir Wilfred Ashley.

Now Lord John undertook to apportion the different offices. He saw Lord Palmerston and told him that the Queen had some apprehension that his return to the Foreign Office might cause great alarm in other Countries, and particularly in France, and that this feeling was still more strongly manifested in the City. Whether under these circumstances he would prefer some other office for instance the Colonies? Lord Palmerston declared that he was not at all anxious for office and should much regret that his accession should in any way embarrass Lord John, that he was quite prepared to support him out of office, but that his taking another Department than his former one would be a public recognition of the most unjust accusations that had been brought against him, that he had evinced throughout a long official life his disposition for peace and only in one instance broke with France, that that matter was gone by and that nobody had a stronger conviction of the necessity to keep in amity with that power than himself. Upon this Lord John said that he could not form a Government without him and shewed himself quite satisfied with Lord Palmerston's declaration.[29]

If Lord John was satisfied with this declaration, not so other Whigs. A declaration could not erase from their minds a record of five years. Lord Grey (the son of the former prime minister) was in particular unsatisfied. He anticipated, if Palmerston should return to his old post, controversy and even war with France or America. At the last moment he expressed his determination not to enter Lord John's cabinet unless Palmerston were assigned some other department than that of foreign affairs. His own wish, he afterward explained to Lord John, would not have governed him except that he had found it "universally concurred in. I believe there is not one of those who were to have been our colleagues who does not think that his taking a different office would have been a great advantage."[30] To Lord John, however, such dissension within the party was a final discouragement to taking office. His would have been at best a minority government and to go forward in it without the united support of his colleagues, and without Grey as party spokesman in the Lords, seemed impossible. He abandoned his attempt, therefore, and the Queen found it necessary to call Sir Robert Peel again to her aid.

[29] Queen Victoria, "Memo of Parting Interview with Lord John Russell, Windsor Castle, Dec. 20, 1845," British Museum, Peel MSS.
[30] Grey to Russell, Dec. 19, 1845. Published in *Eng. Hist. Rev.*, I, 129–131. Thomas Macaulay was among those who privately concurred with Lord Grey in his objections to Palmerston's return to the foreign office.

For Lord John thus to fail after he had agreed to form a government was a blow to himself and to his party. The reasons for his failure were promptly uncovered in the press, and in the Conservative and independent journals the "Whig abortion," as it was gleefully termed,[31] was represented as new proof of Whig impotence, a reflection on the party leadership, and an affront to the Queen. Even the Whig journals were reduced to debating which of their two leaders, Palmerston or Grey, was most at fault. Le Marchant, one of the party chiefs, thought to extract sweet from bitter by the reflection that at least the party had demonstrated that it was not so greedy for office as its critics had charged at the end of the Melbourne administration when it had stayed in office two years too long. Macaulay, however, replied that the discredit was only increased. "We stayed in when we ought to have gone out, and now we stay out when we ought to have gone in."[32]

Especially damaging to the party was the alarm with which the business and governmental circles of Europe had received the news of Palmerston's prospective return to power. "The City," as the Queen had observed, had been deeply apprehensive.[33] Public securities in London and on the Continent had fallen,[34] and in Paris the head of the house of Rothschild was reported to have commented on the unhappy faculty which Palmerston had of bringing down the "fonds" of all Europe without warning.[35] Similar reports of uneasiness and objection had come from the various European chancelleries. If Louis Philippe did not actually express "insurmountable repugnance" to Lord Palmerston, as Henry Reeve re-

---

[31] London *Spectator*, Dec. 27, 1845. The thesis advanced in some accounts that Lord John Russell used the Grey-Palmerston episode as a pretext to escape forming a minority government is not borne out by the facts. Russell and his party associates voted to accept the Queen's invitation to form a government at a party conclave on Dec. 18 after a full discussion of the difficulties of governing in a minority and in spite of failure to obtain from Peel more than a general promise of support in abolishing the Corn Laws. The Grey-Palmerston episode occurred on the following day in connection with the distribution of offices. If Russell had wished to avoid office he had his opportunity to do so with credit to himself and to his party on Dec. 18. It is unlikely that he would have waited for the pretext of party dissension, which was discreditable to his leadership and to his party in the eyes of the public. But see A. L. Cross, *History of England and Greater Britain* (New York, 1914), p. 945.

[32] Greville, II, 339.

[33] *Ante*, p. 271.

[34] London *Times*, Dec. 22, 1845; see also N.Y. *Journal of Commerce*, Jan. 24, 1846.

[35] Greville, II, 345–346.

ported, or refer to him as "l'ennemi de ma maison," the Paris and London papers at least believed that such were his sentiments, and the accession of Palmerston, it was thought in Paris, would shortly be followed by the fall of Guizot, who was a defender of the *entente cordiale*, and by Thiers's return to power.[36] And when the news came of the failure of Lord John's attempt at government, the sigh of relief which went up from all Europe was illuminating. Guizot wrote to the French ambassador in London, "Ma joie est grande."[37] Palmerston, he said, had recently been making advances to him. "On est venu en 24 heures me communiquer deux lettres de lui, très explicites, très amicales, fort convenables, du reste, pour lui-même, maintenant son passé avec dignité, tout en promettant le meilleur avenir. Je ne doute pas qu'il eût eu bonne intention. Mais le caractère et l'habitude sont plus forts que l'intention."[38]

Prince Metternich, according to the British ambassador in Vienna, received the news of Palmerston's prospective accession with deep anxiety. "When, however, it was known that Lord John Russell had failed in his attempt, and that Sir Robert Peel had, with most of his former colleagues resumed the Government of the country, his satisfaction was very great. He sent for me, and read to me the account which he had received, and having concluded, he added: 'Maintenant, mon cher, nous pouvons dormir tranquillement en nos lits.' "[39]

Such a demonstration, abroad and at home, of the effect of Palmerston's activities was a lesson to Whig leaders. It taught them that even for an Opposition intransigence in foreign affairs may be a two-edged sword. It taught Lord John Russell in particular the need of taking a hand in formulating the foreign policy of the Opposition, of counteracting by his own efforts, since Palmerston was not to be controlled, the damaging impression abroad that the Whig party was in the hands of a war faction.

On the Oregon question Lord John himself had peace amends to make. He had delivered an aggressive speech in Parliament the preceding April replying to President Polk's inaugural. He had created in it an impression of belligerence on the Oregon question and of unfriendliness in general toward the United States. He had criti-

---

[36] *Ibid.*
[37] Guizot to Jarnac, Dec. 22, 1845, Aberdeen MSS.
[38] *Ibid.*
[39] Magenis to Aberdeen, Jan. 12, 1846, Aberdeen MSS.

cized the spread of American slave territory and the lust for territorial aggrandizement exemplified in the annexation of Texas. He had predicted that the indefiniteness of the southern boundary of Texas would invite still further American aggression upon Mexico. He pronounced the President's statement on Oregon a "blustering announcement," a thing that perhaps hardly needed to be said, and made an aggressive defense in turn of British title to Oregon and in particular to the Columbia River boundary. The Columbia he declared to be a valuable highway and harbor, which added to the confusion already existing on that point in British minds. He believed the Columbia to be "the only port . . . on that coast, . . . whilst, in order to show the extent of the river, it is enough to state that it is 1,600 yards wide, at a distance of 90 miles from the mouth. It is obvious that the increase of trade which must take place between this [Oregon] country and China will render it more important, as that is the only port on that part of the coast. There may be one established near Nootka Sound; but it is not, I believe, approachable, and is surrounded by high mountains; and probably will not for hundreds of years, if even then, be made available." He took his stand squarely on the line of the Columbia as the partition line of Oregon, taking no account even of Canning's headland offer of 1826 until informed of it by Sir Robert Peel.[40] In America, where he had been considered a friend of democratic governments, his speech produced a distinct shock.

It was in a very different mood that Lord John returned, after the "Whig abortion," to the Oregon question. The question was then in its most critical stage; it was the only explosive issue at that time in British foreign relations. He took his stand on it now unreservedly for concession and conciliation, and he took it with a forcefulness and an explicitness that betrayed his purpose to fix it as his party's stand, and to fix it thus in the full sight of the world. On January 12, 1846, on being presented the freedom of Glasgow, he proposed to his audience the toast, "Peace with all nations." He said as reported by the *Manchester Guardian:*

He need hardly say they desired peace with all nations, and there was only one nation at present with whom any serious question of difference might occur, and that was the United States of America. He wished to repeat what he said that morning, that the point of honour upon

[40] *Hansard's*, LXXIX, 178–201.

which nations might be in such a state of difference as to be impossible to be conciliated, did not now exist as a point of difference between them and the United States.—(Cheers.) When the president of the United States made his inaugural message, it did strike him that there were in that message declarations to which Great Britain, as an independent power, could not submit. Since that time, it appeared by the late message of the president, that a proposition for a compromise was made to her majesty's minister at Washington. Now, after that, without entering on the question whether the terms offered were sufficient or not, and the sufficiency of those terms would, he trusted, be deliberately considered by her majesty's government, the proposition showed that the government of the United States were ready to settle this question by negotiation. The question of more or less territory,—whether they were to obtain one-half, and the United States one-half,—whether they were to obtain a harbour in a particular position, or the United States to have that harbour, these were questions on which it would be disgraceful for two such nations to go to war.—(Immense cheering.) He begged to state thus briefly those views, because he thought declarations had been made on the subject of a very pernicious tendency. He believed the question was now in this position—that the majority of the people of the United States, and the majority of the people in this kingdom, wishing heartily all peace, the respective governments would be able to arrange this matter without going to war.—(Cheers.) With these few words he begged to give, 'Peace with all nations.'—(Great cheering).[41]

Commenting editorially on these remarks a few days later, the independent London *Spectator* observed:

One point on which he bestowed some pains is remarkable. He proposed the toast or sentiment of 'Peace with all nations,' and made a little lecture at Ministers on the necessity of bringing the [Oregon] negotiations with the United States to a peaceful issue. Can the man, you ask, who speaks in this way, seriously have meant to intrust the Foreign Office to Lord Palmerston? Why do you not see that that appointment is the very cause of the lecture? Lord John is doing his best to keep the warlike tendencies of his friend's method of diplomacy out of sight.[42]

Lord John gave even more striking evidence of Whig penitence in Parliament at the opening of the new session. On January 23, 1846, in the debate following the speech from the throne, he took occasion publicly to rebuke Pakenham, the British minister at Washington, for having rejected, without reference to his govern-

[41] *Manchester Guardian,* Jan. 17, 1846.
[42] London *Spectator,* Jan. 17, 1846.

ment, President Polk's offer to partition the Oregon Country by the line of the 49th parallel. "I confess," he said, "I think that was a hasty proceeding upon the part of the Representative of her Majesty."[43]

Nor was Lord John's Oregon intervention limited to mere general approval in public of the policy of concession. Early in February, 1846, on receipt of Edward Everett's letter, he privately gave Lord Aberdeen the momentous truce assurance regarding the specific issue of the surrender of the Columbia. And this he did without previous notification to Lord Palmerston!

Lord Palmerston was obliged, also, to yield to the logic of the events of December, though his conversion was neither permanent nor prompt. By his later career he bore out the truth of Guizot's observation that the force of habit and character would ultimately prevail in him over good intentions. He postponed his public penance until he was brought again in spring, after the winter of Whig misfortune, under the warming influence of the hope of office. By spring the Conservative party was completely shattered. Peel's former Protectionist supporters, who considered themselves betrayed by his conversion to the abolition of the Corn Laws, pursued him in Parliament and out with relentless fury. His life was in the hands of Lord John throughout the session of 1846, and the political world knew it was being spared only until the great reform which Whigs alone could not encompass was placed upon the statute books. Prospective return to office rendered it incumbent upon Palmerston to quiet the apprehensions and party dissensions of December. He proceeded, therefore, in the spring of 1846 to make his peace with the world. He did it partly by maintaining silence himself on foreign affairs in Parliament, and partly by inducing the *Morning Chronicle* to lower its tone. It was a change of heart that did not escape the keen observation of the London *Times*. Upon the fall of the Peel government in the summer of 1846 its editor wrote:

Seven months have elapsed since we were induced, by what then appeared to be the abrupt termination of Sir Robert Peel's Administration, to take a parting survey of the events which had marked, and the principles which had guided, the foreign policy of the Government for the last five years. The interval of time which has elapsed since last

[43] *Hansard's*, LXXXIII, 152.

December has largely added to the tribute of respect and gratitude which we then paid to the Minister especially intrusted with the foreign relations of the country; and the incidents which caused or accompanied Lord John Russell's failure in the attempt to form an Administration at that time, demonstrated that the force of the contrast between the Foreign Secretary and his proposed successor was felt, not only by this country and the world, but even in the impervious precincts of the Whig party. There is, happily, no ground or occasion to repeat that contrast at the present time. No sooner had hopes of office removed the despondency of indefinite opposition than a spirit of tacit acquiescence, tending to imitation, succeeded the reckless and absurd system of attack which had been directed for several years against the foreign policy of the Government. A total silence on these important topics was observed in Parliament; and even the principal organ of the Whig party in the press participated in the same mild influence. The lesson of last December was not lost upon so acute a statesman as Lord Palmerston. He perceived, as quickly as his opponents, that a Minister whose accession to power is viewed with consternation, distrust, and hostility by every Cabinet in the world, was *ipso facto* disqualified from maintaining those amicable relations with other States which he must desire to cultivate, and from exercising that influence which he ought to possess. An excursion to Paris at Easter sufficed to convince our neighbours, that whatever may be the defects of the Whig Foreign Secretary, they do not consist in a sombre or deliberate hostility to the French nation, and a decent understanding has been re-established between the parties, which we hope no fresh ebullitions of impetuosity will interrupt.[44]

Special homage to the peace opinion of the world was rendered by Palmerston in the Easter excursion, here mentioned, to Paris. The visit was his first in sixteen years, and by French statesmen and the French press it was recognized as a quest for the reconcilation that was necessary to his return to office. This end it quite achieved. The spectacle of so redoubtable a warrior come on a pilgrimage to Canossa flattered and disarmed Paris. Guizot reported to Lord Aberdeen:

Il est en droit de dire, qu'il a été bien reçu. On a vu, dans son voyage, une réparation du passé, un temoignage éclatant du besoin, et du désir, qu'il ressentait de se montrer bien avec la France. Déjà, au mois de décembre dernier, les incidents de votre crise ministérielle, et l'obstacle qu' avaient opposé au retour de Lord Palmerston les souvenirs de 1840, avaient flatté l'amour propre de notre public. Sa venue à Paris dans le but évident d'effacer ces souvenirs a été une nouvelle satisfaction. L'animosité s'est calmée. La curiosité et la courtoisie sont venues à sa place.

44 London *Times,* June 29, 1846.

Lord Palmerston n'a rien negligé pour cultiver cette disposition. Il est allé avec empressement, au devant du bon accueil. Il a vu tout le monde. Il a répété à tout le monde qu'il etait, autant que personne, ami de la paix, de la France, partisan de l'entente cordiale, et bien décidé a la continuer, s'il lut arrivait de revenir au pouvoir.[45]

Lord Aberdeen in reply to this letter wrote:

I understand that Lord Palmerston is quite delighted with his reception at Paris; and I should have been very sorry if he had returned with any other feelings. As my great object, whether in or out of office, is to strengthen the good understanding between the two countries, I rejoice that any possible cause of estrangement should be removed. Lord Palmerston may very possibly again fill the office which I now hold; and, in that case, I think you will have done well by enabling him to come here pleased and satisfied, and confident of a cordial reception by the Government which he had most reason to dread.

It would have been a very poor compliment to me had you sent back Lord Palmerston discontented and affronted; and, in truth, no one would have regretted it more than I should have done, from the manner in which it might have affected our future relations. I have never desired to injure Lord Palmerston; on the contrary, at the time of our Ministerial crisis in December, I endeavoured by every means in my power to smooth his advent to office. Party men, or mere politicians, will not understand this conduct, and I doubt if Lord Palmerston comprehends it himself, but you will have no such difficulty.

Whatever may have been the effect in Paris of Lord Palmerston's visit, it has been of the greatest service to him in this country. It has proved to the great merchants and capitalists of the city, who were very apprehensive of the effect likely to be produced by his accession to power, that he is not only tolerated but cherished by the Government and people who were supposed to be most hostile to him.[46]

The visit to Paris was observed and approved in the British press. The *Spectator* reported that Lord Palmerston had been widely

[45] Guizot to Aberdeen, Apr. 28, 1846. See also Guizot to Aulaire, Apr. 28, 1846, Aberdeen MSS.

[46] Aberdeen to Guizot, May 5, 1846, Aberdeen MSS. Lord Aberdeen was genuine in the sentiments expressed in this letter; still, he and Peel felt a little annoyed at the French government for having removed by their reception of Palmerston an obstacle to the return of the Whig party to power. Peel wrote to Aberdeen after reading Guizot's letter: "I care very little about these things, but the reception given in this country by the Queen and the Government to a political opponent of M. Guizot (Thiers) was different from that which has been given in Paris to Lord Palmerston. The difference was greater than any difference in the positions of the two parties could justify." Peel to Aberdeen, Apr. 30, 1846, Aberdeen MSS. Guizot took warm exception to the word "cherished," in his reply to Lord Aberdeen. See Guizot to Aberdeen, May 10, 1846, and Madame de Lieven to Aberdeen, May 9, 1846, Aberdcen MSS.

"introduced into good and great society where he has been diligently 'doing the amiable.' " It continued:

If his motives for this opportune trip after an absence of sixteen
years are only to be guessed, the probable effects of it are obvious
enough. Some said that when the Whigs last came into office, King
Louis Philippe expressly objected to Lord Palmerston as Foreign Secretary. That the astute old King should commit such an impertinence, is
unlikely. According to another guess, a reluctance was felt in a mansion
whose hospitality Louis Philippe had shared,[47] to select as the special
channel of communication with France, the King's 'favourite aversion.'
No doubt, it would have been very awkward; and it would therefore
be much more convenient to the agreeable Viscount if he could remove
all those little dislikes. So he has been making a round of calls in Paris,
just as a candidate for the English Parliament calls on the voters. If
such a thing were done by a French statesman in London, what would
not the Paris papers exclaim against the truckling to 'la perfide Albion'?
We British have no such inflammable suspicions. We have no very
lively feelings at all about Lord Palmerston's present plans; and, in the
possible event of his return to office, should he possess the good will of
the Parisians, and should he feel some necessity for retaining that good
will, we in England should be all the better pleased—should think him
all the cleverer for it, and all the safer as a Minister.

But the most interesting part of the matter is the effect of personal
intercourse in softening even national animosities. . . . Lord Palmerston
was accounted in Paris as the evil genius of Europe. The evil genius
visits Paris. The eye seeks his foot, and lo! it is not cloven. He walks, he
bows, he smiles! He is invited to dinner, and he comes! He eats, and can
of course digest; he listens, and therefore can ruminate. He utters liberal
sentiments. In short, he is human and not inhumane. If you tickle him,
he will laugh though, of course, the Parisians did not ascertain that fact
experimentally. . . . The Devil is not so black as he is painted. King
Louis Philippe is quite charmed with Lord Palmerston; the events of
1840, it is now believed in Paris, were but an official necessity, like the
big talking in the Chambers two or three years ago.

What a pity this same plan is not universally applied. Let Queen
Victoria begin by inviting President Polk to dinner, and asking General
Cass or Mr. Allen to look in to tea; there is no saying what remarkable
enlightenment of views on the Oregon question might follow, and not
illegitimately follow, such an interchange of amenities.[48]

No further interchange of amenities was necessary. Lord Aberdeen was able to dispatch to America in May, 1846, terms of an

---

[47] The reference is to Queen Victoria.
[48] London *Spectator*, Apr. 18, 1846.

Oregon Treaty that without a single alteration proved acceptable to the American Senate. He found the security to do so in the chastened mood of the Whig Opposition, and in particular that of its "enfant terrible." He found the haze of political smoke that still remained from the crisis of 1840, the assault on the Ashburton Treaty, and the "Battle of the Maps" a screen under which to win the peace of the Pacific Northwest.[49]

Whig penitence was further reflected in the reception accorded the Oregon Treaty in England. On the last day of the Peel government news of the Senate ratification arrived dramatically in London, and the prime minister in his valedictory address was able to announce to Parliament the terms of the settlement. As compared with the terms for which previous British governments had held out, or the terms of the Maine boundary settlement, they represented a surrender. Yet no vials of party wrath were poured on this treaty. On the contrary, Parliament and the press received it with universal satisfaction. Lord Palmerston himself was able to say of it in responding to Sir Robert Peel:

> I should be sorry to allow one of the latter topics of the right hon. baronet's speech to pass, without noticing the general and deep pleasure which the announcement he has made respecting the United States must excite in the remotest corners of the Empire. In every quarter it will be learned with entire satisfaction that the unfortunate differences between this country and the United States have been brought to a termination which, as far as we can at present judge, seem equally favourable to both parties.[50]

It was of this settlement that Lord Palmerston had written privately to Lord John Russell in February, 1846, when it was proposed by Edward Everett, that it was of the same nature "as if the gentleman on the road after taking the traveller's purse should keep the sovereigns to satisfy his own claims and give back a shilling or two to save the wounded honor of the person with whom he was thus making *an equitable distribution* of the matter in dispute."[51]

---

[49] For a discussion of other influences making for peace in the Oregon negotiation, see Essay 8.

[50] London *Times*, June 30, 1846. The speech was slightly revised in phraseology for *Hansard's*, but the concluding portion is identical in both reports. See *Hansard's*, LXXXVII, 1057.

[51] See *ante*, pp. 260–261.

British party politics have woven their thread into the texture of American history in strange patterns, some of them as yet but faintly visible. They have woven discord more often than harmony and twice they have helped to produce the tangle of war. They came near to producing war in the Oregon controversy, for the dread of party clamor was what induced the British government to postpone a settlement until passions had been aroused in the United States almost to the point of explosion. Because of a distorted Opposition charge of capitulation as applied to a treaty in the American Northeast the British government was restrained from agreeing to a capitulation that was real and necessary in the Pacific Northwest. But partisanship consisting of intransigence in external matters proved to have been unprofitable by December, 1845, and the result was that in the following spring, on the Oregon question, the lion and the lamb of British foreign politics were able to lie down in peace together.

ESSAY 10 · BRITISH GOVERNMENT PROPAGANDA AND THE OREGON TREATY*

A FLURRY of war excitement swept over the British Isles in the spring of 1845. It was occasioned by the Inaugural Address of the President of the United States. Discussing the Oregon question, then under peaceful negotiation with the British government, President Polk declared, "Our title to the country of the Oregon is 'clear and unquestionable,' and already are our people preparing to perfect that title by occupying it with their wives and children . . . our people, increasing to many millions . . . are already engaged in establishing the blessings of self-government in valleys of which the rivers flow to the Pacific. . . . The jurisdiction of our laws and the benefits of our republican institutions should be extended over them in the distant regions which they have selected for their homes."[1]

The Inaugural was typical of the Jacksonian period, a republican manifesto intended for the edification of the sovereign people of the United States. Its assertion that American title to the Oregon country is "clear and unquestionable" was a clipping from the Democratic campaign platform of 1844. In America such a declaration was adequately discounted; it produced little comment and no public excitement. In Washington negotiations went forward peacefully as before for the partition of Oregon.

But in England its reception was less calm. The modes of American politics were not so well understood there, and presidential inaugurals were conceived of as formal state papers. In earlier negotiations the American government had recognized that Great Britain had some rights to Oregon by offering to partition it and by agreeing twice to conventions of joint occupation. In the face of this record, for President Polk to declare that American title to the country is "clear and unquestionable" seemed an aggression;

* Reprinted from the *American Historical Review*, XL (October 1934).

[1] James D. Richardson, *Messages and Papers of the Presidents, 1789–1897* (Washington, 1907), IV, 381.

that he should do so in the midst of a new negotiation for partition seemed a gross impropriety. The Oregon paragraph came in the address in an irritating association. Preceding it was a triumphant announcement of the joint congressional resolution inviting Texas to enter the American Union. In old England as in New England the occupation, revolt, and annexation of Texas seemed a slave-holders' conspiracy against the Mexican Republic, and its methods were those which the Inaugural seemed to project against territory claimed by Britain. In the British press the address was everywhere regarded as a challenge, and was everywhere responded to with denunciation and defiance.

The menace of the address seemed so grave that the British ministry and the Opposition united to stage in Parliament a demonstration of national unity. In the Commons Lord John Russell, in an aggressive speech, upheld British claims to Oregon and pledged the Whig party to defend them, while Sir Robert Peel in ringing words declared that Great Britain had rights in Oregon that were "clear and unquestionable" and was prepared to maintain them. In the Lords, Clarendon moved for information, which gave Lord Aberdeen an opportunity to deliver an impressive warning to the American government.[2] In order that news of these discussions might the more promptly be brought to the United States the outgoing mail steamer was for a day detained. Blast and counter-blast succeeding each other thus brought on the Oregon storm of 1845–1846.

The Oregon area over which the storm raged was a relatively restricted one. It was a mere fragment of the great domain stretching from California to Alaska and from the Rocky Mountains to the sea over which politicians and diplomats argued. It was an area lying between the offers repeatedly made to each other by the two governments during a quarter of a century of diplomacy, a triangle bounded on the north by the 49th parallel and on the south and east by the Columbia River. Not even the entirety of this triangle was in controversy, for in 1826 the British government had offered the American a detached headland lying north of the Columbia River between Admiralty Inlet and the Pacific Ocean, a concession intended to meet the American demand for a share in the harbors that lie inside the Strait of Juan de Fuca.

[2] *Hansard's Parliamentary Debates,* vol. LXXIX, cols. 115–123, 178–199.

Lord Aberdeen, Peel's secretary for foreign affairs, was personally willing to yield the whole triangle to the United States. Conciliatory and peace loving, he saw nothing in it worth the risks of war. He conceived of its soil as a pine swamp; he knew that the great river flowing at its base, which previous British negotiators had clung to under the mistaken impression that it was the future outlet of western Canada to the sea, was for the most part unnavigable; and he recognized the reasonableness of the American demand for a share in the harbors lying inside Juan de Fuca Strait. As early as December, 1843, he was willing to agree to a line of partition repeatedly proposed by the American government—the line of the 49th parallel—stopping it short only at the coast so as not to sever Vancouver Island.[3]

But the cabinet was less pliant. It feared the political consequences of a surrender so complete. Its extensive program of domestic reform was threatened by the Opposition charge repeatedly made by Lord Palmerston that Aberdeen's foreign policy was weak and nerveless, consisting of truckling to France and America, and that the Ashburton Treaty in particular was a shameful "capitulation." Under any circumstances, to concede to the United States what previous British governments had declined to yield for over a quarter of a century was a grave political risk; to concede it after the menace of the Polk Inaugural was to expose the government to the charge of having abandoned national pride and honor. This political fear was the chief barrier in 1845–1846 to an Oregon peace.[4]

To remove this barrier was in the last analysis Lord Aberdeen's Oregon problem. It was a task of winning a nation by propaganda to views of concession, of disarming the Whig Opposition in advance of a treaty. It meant teaching the British people that the Oregon question was one of mixed right which ought to be settled in accordance with the doctrine of convenience. It meant correcting national misconceptions as to the resources and the values of the Oregon country, making clear that the fur trade, the main economic interest in it, was a dying industry; that the Columbia River, the ultimatum of earlier British governments, was of little utility

---

[3] Aberdeen to Pakenham, Mar. 4, 1844 and Pakenham to Aberdeen, March 28, 1844. Aberdeen MSS., British Museum.
[4] See Essay 9.

for a heavy commerce on account of its broken course; that, on the other hand, on all the coast between Vancouver Island and the Mexican province of California there were no safe harbors; that it was reasonable, therefore, for the American government to insist on sharing those inside Juan de Fuca Strait, and that to make a division of them on a basis insuring future tranquillity required adoption of the line of the 49th parallel to the straits.

The times were propitious for the spread of such propaganda. The period was one of "little Englanders." Colonial possessions of all sorts were regarded in England in influential circles as a burden. In particular British North America was so regarded. The Canadas exhausted British patience by their internal disorders and their constant bickering with colonial administrators. From Hudson Bay to the Rocky Mountains extended the hunting preserve of an unpopular fur-trading corporation. Beyond the Rockies lay the remote wilderness of Oregon closed to individual British enterprise by Parliament's monopoly grant in 1821 of its British trade rights to the Hudson's Bay Company.

Favorable to the spread of concession propaganda also was the spirit created by the contemporary British crusade for free trade. The free trade argument postulated international good will and fostered a generous conception of the relations between nations. British intellectuals enlisted in the crusade were nearly all conspicuous internationalists. They were friendly in particular toward the United States. They believed that repeal would improve Anglo-American relations by developing between the two countries mutually advantageous commercial relations—America would feed England and England would clothe America. Politically the free trade movement was disarming; it militated against the narrowness of faction quite as much as of nation. It released a spirit of independence of party, making less certain the rewards of factional attack on a government that made sacrifices in the interests of peace.

British business interests fostered a spirit of international conciliation. British business in 1845–1846 was only recently recovered from the economic collapse of 1837–1841. Quiet was required as a restorative of confidence and as a quickener of the flow of overseas trade. For special reasons London banking and financial classes wished Anglo-American comity. They had sold American securities, more especially the bonds of American state governments, to

British investors in large quantity. These bonds had fallen on evil days following the crash of 1837–1841. In nearly half the American states, including such well-established ones as Pennsylvania and Maryland, interest payments had been suspended; some states had gone to the length of repudiation. The state legislatures were attempting, as trade revived, to restore their fallen credit, but it was a difficult and painful process of levying new taxes on burdened communities. Politicians took refuge from it in the plausible argument that hostilities were likely to develop over the Oregon question with the nation that harbored a goodly percentage of the bond-holders.

One London banking house that had been prominent as a purveyor of American bonds and stocks to British investors and was therefore deeply committed to Anglo-American comity was the great firm of Baring Brothers. It was a power ranking in the field of international finance with the Rothschilds in Paris and wielding an influence similar to that of present day American princes of credit. It was committed by personal as well as business ties to Anglo-American friendship. The head of the house until 1831—Lord Ashburton—had established friendly connections in America by long residence and marriage there; in 1814 he had been Gallatin's counselor in the peace negotiations at Ghent, and in 1842 his conciliatory spirit had made possible the adjustment of the Maine boundary dispute. This spirit was carried on by his successors in the leadership of the house, by Joshua Bates and Thomas Baring. Joshua Bates was an American, born and reared in New England. He was a trusted adviser to successive American ministers at the Court of St. James, especially to Edward Everett and Louis McLane. He was in close touch with London diplomatic and court circles through his son-in-law, Jean Sylvain van de Weyer, minister of Belgium, whose name appears at a later point in this narrative.

Lord Aberdeen labored on the other hand under some heavy handicaps in preparing the British public for concession. He had to reckon in certain British circles with a confirmed ill will against America, a sentiment Palmerston played upon for party purposes in unleashing his thundering attack on the Ashburton Treaty. The disarming of an Opposition required access to Opposition journals which was difficult to gain since the latter were desirous of embarrassing rather than aiding the government. Cabinet colleagues had to be reconciled, a task not accomplished until January, 1846. Concession propaganda had to be guided at a distance and in secrecy lest knowledge of the conciliatory attitude of the foreign office become public property and encourage American extremists to press anew upon President Polk the demand for the whole of Oregon.

Prior to January, 1846, for these reasons Lord Aberdeen permitted others to take the lead in disseminating propaganda of concession. He contented himself with giving friendly countenance to disciples who spread the gospel for him. Nassau W. Senior was the first of these. He was a notable British economist ranking until 1848 even above John Stuart Mill. In politics he was a Whig, high in the councils of his party, and a frequent contributor on political subjects to the chief Whig quarterly, the *Edinburgh Review*. He was, however, no ordinary party man. Politically he was unshackled, and his outlook, like that of free traders in general, was international. For his party's opposition tactics during Peel's last government he had little sympathy.

Writing to the editor of the *Edinburgh Review* on October 30, 1845, Senior observed:

An Opposition . . . which opposes indiscriminately is generally wrong. The Tories did this most wickedly. But we are not without similar defects. Witness the opposition to the Factory Bill. The foreign relations of a country are, however, the points on which an Opposition is generally most unscrupulous and most mischievous. Such is the case with France now, and probably with America. Such was the case with us in the opposition to the Ashburton treaty. I hope we shall behave better in future; but I own that my principal fears for the peace of the world arise from my fears of the misconduct of the French, American, and English Oppositions. The three Governments will behave well, if they are allowed.[5]

Senior's first Oregon article was undertaken when England was feverish with war excitement over the Polk Inaugural, when a plea for concession was a voice crying in the wilderness. It was suggested either by Edward Everett, American minister at the Court of St. James or by Joshua Bates, the American partner in the house of Baring.[6] In its preparation Edward Everett took a considerable part.

[5] Macvey Napier, ed., *Selections from the Correspondence of the Late Macvey Napier* (London, 1879), pp. 501–502.
[6] McLane to Polk, Aug. 4, 1845, Buchanan MSS., Historical Society of Pennsylvania.

Lord Aberdeen gave it such countenance as he dared. The London *Examiner*, a widely read Whig weekly, was the vehicle chosen to present it to the public. A curious literary enterprise! A British publicist and the minister of the United States joining to educate the British public to a spirit of concession on a grave diplomatic issue in the columns of an Opposition newspaper with the British secretary for foreign affairs smiling his approval! It is an anomaly that strikingly illustrates the nature of the Oregon problem in its last critical year.

Edward Everett's correspondence traces from day to day the part he played in the drama. "If," he wrote Senior on March 31, 1845, "you will keep the Examiner from committing itself next Saturday, I will let you have some notes in season for next week."[7]

On April 4 he reported to the American Secretary of State:

I may state in entire confidence to you that the ground of the belief expressed by me in my number 288 that an influential Liberal journal would take a fair and candid view of the Oregon question is this, that Mr. Senior, a gentleman well known to you by reputation, has assured me that he thought our often repeated proposal to run the 49th parallel of latitude to the sea was a reasonable offer and that if I would furnish him the requisite facts and data, he would take that ground in the columns of the *Examiner*.

Having rigidly abstained on principle since I have been here from all communication with the public press, I do not feel inclined in a matter of so much delicacy to depart from this course; but I shall take care to furnish Mr. Senior with such documentary evidence as will enable him to learn the true merits of the question.[8]

On April 5 in alarm at the gravity which the demonstration in Parliament had given the Oregon question, Everett wrote Senior a letter more circumspect than he had intended, though not so guarded as to prevent imparting some helpful views.

After the grave character given to the subject of Oregon by the discussions in Parliament last evening, I feel that it would be indiscreet in me to furnish you, at any length, even in the most confidential manner, with my views on the subject. I send you, however, two pamphlets which will give you in a brief space, a more accurate knowledge of the nature and foundations of the American claim than can be derived from the statements made last evening. Mr. Sturgis (the author

[7] Everett to Senior, Mar. 31, 1845, Everett MSS., Massachusetts Historical Society.
[8] Everett to Buchanan, Apr. 4, 1845, Everett MSS.

of one of them) now a wealthy merchant in Boston, was originally a shipmaster and passed several years in that capacity on the coast of the debateable territory.

I perceive with regret that the liberal party in England has, since the accession of the present ministry, assumed the character of unfriendliness towards us. It is, I think, a false position. Not to say anything of the course pursued by some of the Leaders of the party in reference to the treaty of Washington . . . they are now urging the government to extreme counsels in asserting your claims to Oregon. . . .[9]

With respect to the present state of the question, I am of course restrained from saying anything which does not appear from public documents; but it appears from them that three times, and perhaps four, vizt in 1818, in 1824, and in 1826, we have offered to run the 49th degree of latitude (which bounds us for nearly 1500 miles east of the rocky mountains) to the Pacific. . . . You saw the line at my office the other day and exclaimed spontaneously that it was the natural and fair boundary. This fair and moderate proposal was rejected three times by the government of Lord Liverpool and Mr. Canning, chiefly I am inclined to think under the influence of the fur companies, who wish to retain the opportunity which their position gives them of taking annually perhaps £10,000 worth of beaver. What is there in such a measure as the rejection of this liberal and moderate proposal that should endear it to Lord Lansdowne, or Lord Clarendon or Lord John Russell?

I have not the least doubt that the present government would willingly embrace it did they not feel bound by the acts of their predecessors, but the liberal party is not so bound.

I do not mean to imply that this question ought to be viewed under party aspects, but I think its antecedents are such as well deserve a little scrutiny before you pledge yourself to sustain them even at the risk of the peace of the world.[10]

On April 18 the article, in the form of printer's proof, was privately submitted for approval to two high authorities. It was submitted to Lord Aberdeen who cautiously gave only the facts his sanction.[11] It was sent in proof also to Edward Everett, and a week before it appeared in the *Examiner* it was on its way to the American Department of State.

In forwarding it to Washington, Everett wrote:

It is scarcely necessary for me to disclaim an approval of every suggestion in this article, such for instance as that of the unconstitutionality of our settling Oregon. The whole is to be viewed as the produc-

[9] The omitted portion is a brief discussion of claims.
[10] Everett to Senior, Apr. 5, 1845, Everett MSS.
[11] See *post*, pp. 294–295.

tion of a candid Englishman; and the leading idea, that of running the 49th parallel to the Sound between the main land and Quadra and Vancouver's island, thus giving to England the whole of that island and community of entrance by the Straits of Fuca, and securing to us all the main land south of 49 has ever been the mode of settling the controversy which I have deemed most likely to succeed and most advantageous to the U. States.[12]

On April 26 the article was offered to British readers as the *Examiner's* leading editorial. It opened with a warm tribute to Lord Aberdeen, "a man who has the wisdom to detect and the courage to despise the vanity and want of real pride, which at present, much more than ambition or rapacity, lead nations to become instruments of mutual destruction. We congratulate the country that our minister prefers justice, moderation, and common sense to obstinacy or magniloquence, and 'keeping up a high tone.' " The Oregon country is valueless to England and similarly to America.

The only use of it to England is as a hunting ground, which enables the Hudson's Bay Company to keep up its monopoly against the English people—a monopoly which occasions many species of furs to be twice, and sometimes three times as dear in London as in Leipsic. The only use of it to America would be to make it an addition to territories already far too large for good government or even for civilization. . . . The only real point in dispute, therefore, is a point of honor; the only real question is, what is the *maximum* which either party can concede, or, which is the same, the minimum which either party can honorably accept. . . . From the Rocky mountains eastward, for more than 1000 miles, the 49th parallel of latitude divides the English possessions from those of the United States. So that the Oregon district above 49 is contiguous to the English territory and below 49 to the American. . . . South of the Straits of St. Juan de Fuca . . . there are no tolerable harbors; the only places of shelter are Port Bulfinch and the Columbia; but both are bar harbors, and at all times dangerous, and for the greater part of the year inaccessible. Above that Strait, and communicating with it, the harbors are numerous and excellent. . . . The soil is generally mountainous, rocky, and uncultivable, though there are some fertile alluvial bottoms. Of that portion which is south of the Straits of Fuca, not more than one-eighth or one-tenth is supposed to be reclaimable; and to the north of them the cultivable proportion is still less.

As for title to this inhospitable country, the writer concludes, after examining the question from the standpoint of discovery,

[12] Everett to Buchanan, Apr. 18, 1845, Everett MSS.

contiguity, treaty, and settlement, neither country has one that is perfect. Arbitration is the mode of settlement eminently suited to the character of the dispute. Failing that the next best solution is to partition the country by the line of the 49th parallel to the coast.

This would give us the whole of Vancouvers Island, and an abundance of good harbors. It would also give us the country which is best for the purposes for which we use it, the fur trade. The furs to the north of the 49th parallel are better and more abundant than those to the south. All balancing, however, of the positive advantages to be obtained by the one nation or by the other on a partition is mere childishness. The interruption of confidence for a single week costs more than the whole country is worth. A mere armament, though followed by accommodation, would cost more than a thousand times its value. . . . Whatever be Lord Aberdeen's policy, the opposition will, we trust, not add to its difficulties.[13]

The article in this form seems to have produced in England relatively little stir. When it appeared popular excitement on the Oregon question had somewhat abated and the newspapers gave it slight notice. Edward Everett called it to the attention of the American consul at Paris with the suggestion that it be employed to strengthen the Oregon case of the United States in the French press.[14] In the United States the Washington *Daily Union*, the administration organ, reprinted it and gave it a nation-wide circulation.[15] Perhaps its chief usefulness was to lead Senior to take up his pen on the Oregon question again, and on a more ambitious scale.

For the new effort the forum chosen was the *Edinburgh Review*, the principal organ of the Whig party, and in Senior's opinion, "the most important political journal, except *The Times*, that now exists."[16] With Macvey Napier, the editor of the *Review*, Senior was in active correspondence in the spring of 1845. On April 18 he wrote:

I have read nearly all the facts and shall look into the public law. It [the public law] is as to title to unoccupied lands by discovery, by contiguity, by settlement, and by cession very vague. And this will be a good opportunity to try to settle it. Indeed even if the immediate matter of Oregon be settled by July it will still remain a matter of interest both historically and as a question of the law of nations. . . .

13 London *Examiner*, Apr. 26, 1845.
14 Everett to Walsh, May 1, 1845, Everett MSS.
15 Washington *Daily Union*, May 23, 1845.
16 Senior to Napier, Jan. 26, 1844, Napier MSS., British Museum.

I assuredly shall not let out that I am writing on Oregon except to those who must give me some material such as Everett and Van de Weyer, and them I can rely on.[17]

Seven weeks later Senior wrote Napier:

Pray send me 4 proofs, two for use, and one to shew to Lord Aberdeen, the other to shew to Mr. Everett. I shall return the proofs by return of post, but during the five days that must elapse before I receive a revise I shall get the criticisms of the two ministers and strike out anything which either of them may reasonably object to in the revise. I think I have made some good international law. You know that it is we, the text writers, who make that law.[18]

Macvey Napier responded with objections to Senior's request for proofs to be sent to Lord Aberdeen and Edward Everett. Well he might, for to admit into the chief organ of the Whig Opposition an article on an important issue in foreign relations, which had secretly been submitted for approval to the foreign secretary of the government and to the minister of the American government, was to court a journalistic disaster.

Senior was obliged to yield to the objections of the editor. "Lord Aberdeen and Mr. Everett," he explained, "are my personal acquaintances, perhaps I might say friends, and writing on a subject very difficult and intricate, and on which they have great knowledge, *and opposite interests*, I have naturally consulted them. From each of them I have had valuable hints and might have more if they saw the proofs. Since, however, you see objections to it I will not shew them. I must confess that I attached little importance to it."[19]

The article thus prepared appeared anonymously in the July, 1845, number of the *Edinburgh Review*. It was in form a review of earlier controversial Oregon treatises, those notably of Thomas Falconer, John Dunn, and Robert Greenhow. In reality it was the earlier *Examiner* article elaborated. It emphasized again the unattractiveness of Oregon, representing the whole country, with the exception of a few fertile valleys, to be a waste of mountain and desert. Oregon rivers were described as too much broken to be of value for trade; Oregon harbors were described as abundant north of the 49th parallel, "but down the whole coast of the Pacific, from

[17] Apr. 18, 1845, Napier MSS.
[18] June 9, 1845, Napier MSS.
[19] June 14, 1845, Napier MSS.

latitude 48° to Port San Francisco, far within the Mexican frontier, there is no refuge except Bulfinch harbor and the Columbia—the former of which can be entered only by small vessels, and the latter is inaccessible for eight months of the year, and dangerous at all times." The fur trade, the mainstay of all that country, was shown to be a dying industry which the Hudson's Bay Company, even though enjoying a practical monopoly of it, found unprofitable.

"There are many single manufacturing establishments in England —such as the Great Western Cotton Factory in Bristol, or Mr. Marshall's in Leeds—which keep in activity a much larger capital, employ a much greater number of persons, and give a much larger annual produce." "All that any prudent Englishman or American can wish is that the controversy should be speedily and honorably settled. A week's interruption of confidence—such, for instance, as followed the reception of Mr. Polk's inaugural speech—costs each party twenty times the value of the matter in dispute." Title to this unpromising country neither state can establish on the basis of discovery, treaty, or settlement. Each state has an imperfect title by contiguity to that part of it which lies adjacent to its own territories. The line of the 49th parallel to the straits is therefore from every point of view the best solution of the controversy.[20]

The publication of such an article in the chief Whig review a few months after Lord John Russell's aggressive speech replying to Polk was a party coup d'état. It had the immediate effect of bringing down a storm of Whig condemnation upon the heads of its author and editor.

Macaulay wrote to Napier:

You have had some very good articles in the Review lately. If I were to offer any suggestion, it would be that you would be on your guard against Senior's views of our relations with America, particularly when his views are directly opposed to those of all the Tory and all the Whig statesmen in the Kingdom. The truth is that he is too deeply interested in the credit of the American States to be impartial. At all events nobody gives him credit for impartiality; and it a little derogates from the character of the Review to have it universally known, as it is, that the office of pronouncing judgment on a grave international question is confided to a person who cannot be unbiassed. If this were the feeling of Palmerston only, I should not mention it. For he is thought, justly or unjustly, by many of our own friends, to be too pugnacious on all

[20] *Edinburgh Review*, LXXXII, 238–265.

points of controversy with Foreign Powers. But Clarendon, who has always been on the pacific and conceding side, Charles Greville, who is an excellent representative of good Conservative society, and others, have made the remark which I mention to you.[21]

Napier received letters of similar objection from other Whigs. Lord John Russell, Lord Monteagle, Lord Jeffrey (former editor of the *Review*), William Empson, soon to be the editor, Andrew Doyle, editor of the *Morning Chronicle*, and Thomas Falconer, the pamphleteer, all voiced their disapproval. They buzzed for months like disturbed hornets about the ears of the venerable editor. As for Senior, the judgment passed on him by his party, according to William Empson, was "that to preserve a better dividend on his trans-Atlantic stock he wd. not only give up the Colombia [*sic*] but the Clyde."[22]

Senior wrote to Napier in reply to such critics:

I have £1500 in the New York Trust Company producing me about £90 a year, less than a fortieth part of my income. That is my whole interest in America. I had in 1839 £10,000 in the American Trust Company, but it became bankrupt in that year and it is utterly impossible, and indeed has been so for the last 4 years, that I shd ever receive a farthing for it. I shd sell it for five pounds. That is all my special interest in America, and as they have in fact robbed me of £10,000 you may easily suppose that I have no very friendly feelings towards them.

But I own that I do feel a most strong interest pecuniary and moral, in keeping the two countries at peace. I believe that a war with America would produce a war with France, and that commercial ruin, national bankruptcy and revolution might be the consequences. I believe that a war with America wd. produce worse consequences than pestilence or famine. In short I hope to die before I see the results. Under such circumstances you may believe that I heard with great alarm the discussion on Lord Clarendon's motion. That alarm was increased when I talked the matter over with him and Lord Ashburton. The Whig party seemed to me to be ready to sacrifice peace to the wish to embarrass their opponents, and the whole country seemed so totally to misunderstand the case that I feared they wd. entertain prejudices and advance pretensions from which there wd. be no receding. As there was no time to be lost I wrote a paragraph for the Examiner, of which I send you the slip. But, being very anxious not to be wrong in any of my facts, I sent the proof to Lord Aberdeen. I send you in great

[21] Napier, ed., *Selections*, p. 500.
[22] Empson to Napier, Sept. 2, 1845, Napier MSS.

confidence his answer. You will see that he sanctions *all* my facts. On comparing the article with that in the Edinburg you will of course see the coincidence which must occur when the same person writes twice on the same subject. . . .

You know that I was so anxious to be accurate that I wished to submit the proofs to Lord Aberdeen. This is a sufficient proof that I was convinced of the accuracy of my statements. I regretted then, and I regret now, that you thought it not advisable. I was also anxious, as you know, to submit them to Mr. Everett. In short I wrote that paper with the most anxious desire to be accurate in every detail. . . .

Of course it is attacked. Every impartial discussion, every decision on complicated questions which does not flatter national prejudices and national vanity will be attacked. Of course base and unworthy motives will be assigned. But I have lived too long in the political world to care about such attacks or such imputations. . . .

P. S. On looking at your letter again I see that you tell Mr. Falconer that you *will send to me his letter*. Now if *his first letter*, talking of a fear for American investments came before me regularly, the only answer must be a challenge, or a criminal information for libel. Now I have no wish to put myself on a level with Mr. Falconer, or to waste money in prosecuting him. I wish therefore that he shd not understand that you have *sent to me his letters*, but that you have merely communicated their general contents. . . . Of course you will not mention Lord Aberdeen's note—pray return it.[23]

As late as the autumn of 1845 the hapless Napier was still defending, explaining, and apologizing for the Senior article. On October 7, in accepting a proposal from Lord John Russell to write for the *Review* an appreciation of earls Grey and Spencer, he went on:

Will your Lordship allow me to avail myself of this opportunity to say a few words about a late article, which occasioned, as many of my friends, amongst others Mr. Macaulay have told me, a good deal of surprise that it shd have appeared in the Ed. Rev. on what has been called the "Oregon Question"? The surprise, as I understood the matter, was mainly owing to its having advocated a view of that Question decidedly at variance with that expressed by your Lordship and the Party generally; but there was also a separate ground, namely, that I should have committed such an article to one who was represented as having strong American interests as a sharer of American stocks, and therefore unlikely to write impartially on the subject. With respect to the first ground, I confess that I was not at the time so well acquainted with what had passed in Parliament upon the subject, as I ought perhaps to have been, before committing the Review to the side taken; and as I was impressed, ignorantly it may be, with an idea of the worthless-

[23] Senior to Napier, Aug. 27, 1845, Napier MSS.

ness of the possession, and of the tremendous evils that would result from a war with America, I certainly thought that I was doing a service to the country and the world in employing the Review, as far as possible, to avert such a calamity. Nevertheless, I would have paused had I known at the time the strong opinion that had been expressed by your Lordship; and had I supposed that Mr. Senior's views might be warped by personal interests, nothing could have induced me to commit the discussion to him. But I did not know that he then, or at any time, had invested a large sum (£ 10,000) in the New York Trust Company; and in point of fact, and in justice to him, who was greatly misrepresented in this particular, it is right to add, that four or five years *before*, he had lost the whole of that sum by the failure of that concern, and could not therefore have had any kind side to America. . . .[24]

Lord John Russell replied:

I think the appearance of the Oregon article was unfortunate. Not because, in a party view, it was at all necessary that the Edinburgh Review should write in accordance with my sentiments on such a subject, but the premature exhibition of a difference in treating the question, when all parties in Parliament had been unanimous, was likely to prejudice our negotiations at Washington. I am glad to be assured that Mr. Senior has no pecuniary interest in the abandonment of British rights.[25]

Senior's comment to Napier on being shown this letter was an amplification of his purposes in writing his article.

On the Oregon question I think Lord John wrong. Both Lord Aberdeen and Everett, each most anxious for peace, were also anxious that the case shd be fairly stated, thinking it much easier to come to an accommodation when the British public had been informed of the true state of the question than when they were blindly fancying that America was bullying them out of their rights. While we demanded the Columbia, to which we have not a shadow of claim, America naturally extended her demands to the 54th parallel, with equal but not greater absurdity. And adjustment seemed impossible. On matters of this importance I always wish the whole truth to be told, holding that the country has no more mischievous enemies than those who encourage its arrogance and impertinence by *suggestio falsi* or *suppressio veri*.

The real objection to the article among the thorough going party men is that it deprives them of a weapon against Lord Aberdeen. I never was one of those men, or you either, and I have no sympathy with them—nor shall I ever hesitate to oppose them.[26]

[24] Napier to Russell, Oct. 7, 1845, Russell MSS., Public Record Office.
[25] Napier, ed., *Selections*, p. 501.
[26] Senior to Napier, Oct. 17, 1845, Napier MSS.

But to deprive thoroughgoing party men of a weapon against Lord Aberdeen required an arm more potent even than the *Edinburgh Review*. It required the London *Times*. The *Times* had an influence over public opinion in England that was proverbial. Its readers were of all political parties, attracted to it by the brilliance of its editorial page, the enterprise of its newsgathering under John Walter, and the tradition it had established during its long history, of freedom from outside control, of independence from the dictation of party or government. Other London dailies were known to be committed on major political issues: the *Globe* and the *Morning Chronicle* to Whiggism, the latter particularly to Lord Palmerston; the *Standard* and the *Morning Herald* to the Conservative government; and the *Morning Post* to ultra Toryism and particularly to protectionism. The *Times* alone, among all London dailies, was uncontrolled; it alone was capable of attacking simultaneously and with the same vigor ministers of the government and leaders of the Opposition—for instance Sir James Graham of Peel's cabinet at the same time as Lord Palmerston.

But in the period under review the *Times* made one exception to such independence—it gave its allegiance to Lord Aberdeen. It constituted itself his special champion, defending without deviation his foreign policies, and thundering incessantly against his great Opposition critic, Lord Palmerston. It was to Lord Aberdeen what the *Morning Chronicle* was to the Whig viscount. At Lord Aberdeen's feet it laid the magnificent reputation it had built up of political independence. To the public it appeared quite free; but its columns in foreign matters were in fact pledged. On every important issue of external policy its editor was secretly taking his cues from the foreign office.

To Lord Aberdeen it was bound by various ties. At first, they were impersonal—a common interest in a peace policy that was deemed essential to the recovery of British trade. The *Times* had championed Lord Aberdeen and savagely denounced Palmerston on this score even before the fall of the Whigs in 1841. With Lord Aberdeen's advent to office a more personal relationship was established. The editor of the *Times* was John Delane, newly appointed, an untried youth of the age of twenty-three. Lord Aberdeen was a world figure, a favorite of the queen, respected and trusted by politicians of both British parties. The earl took the young man promptly into his confidence. For an ambitious editor this was a relationship of great professional advantage. It led to a personal friendship and by the end of 1842 Delane was able to invoke his patron's influence with Sir Robert Peel for the promotion of a brother in the customs.

"I enclose," Aberdeen wrote Peel in December, 1842, "an application from Mr. Delane of the 'Times' who appears to have already been a suitor at the Treasury. He seems to be perfectly well disposed and ready to make his paper of as much use to us as possible."[27] Promotion at this time in the customs was wholly in the hands of a board of customs commissioners from which Peel was reluctant to ask favors. He wrote Aberdeen that he had never before interfered with the board in a question of advancement, but that in this case he would so far depart from his rule as to intimate to the chairman that he would be personally gratified if the promotion could, consistently with justice, be made; and this turned out ultimately to be sufficient.[28]

But for a *Times* editor greater value lay in another form of patronage—the receiving from a minister advance news of important government happenings. Such news Lord Aberdeen gave Delane on frequent occasions. He gave it even occasionally in matters outside his own sphere, taking care in such cases to gain the previous approval of Sir Robert Peel. In the spring of 1844, for instance, Aberdeen asked Peel's permission to send Delane advance information of the sensational developments in the recall of Lord Ellenborough by the directors of the East India Company. "The *Times*," he wrote, "is disposed to act a very friendly part in our dispute with the Directors. This disposition it may be important to encourage. I have just received the inclosed note from the Editor, which I should be glad to be able to answer in such a manner as to give him earlier information than any of his brethren of the fact which he desires to know. I suppose anything at present would be premature, but if you can let me communicate the intelligence at the first moment it may be practicable, I think it would be of much use."[29]

So close were the relations of the foreign office and the *Times*

---

[27] Aberdeen to Peel, Dec. 24, 1842, Peel MSS., British Museum.
[28] Peel to Aberdeen, Dec. 28, 1842, Peel MSS.
[29] Aberdeen to Peel, May 3, 1844, Peel MSS.

that Peel found it necessary more than once to intervene in the interest of newspapers more wholly supporting the government. The *Standard* and the *Morning Herald* made complaint to the prime minister in the spring of 1844 that they received so little favor at the British embassy in Paris compared with the *Times* as to create the impression that they had lost the confidence of the British administration, which affected adversely their communications with the French government. Peel felt it necessary to bring the matter to the notice of his foreign secretary, and the latter had to write the British ambassador in Paris that it would be unwise, in the effort to gain the powerful support of the *Times*, "really to injure that portion of the daily press upon which we can rely."[30]

Again a few months later Peel was obliged to interfere. He wrote Aberdeen:

I think you should seriously consider whether it is fitting that any sort of friendly connection should be continued between the *Times* and the Foreign Office. It is hardly fair towards the newspapers that support the Government, and all the departments of the Government that the *Times* should appear to the world to receive information from the F.O. or to stand in any sort of amicable relation to the foreign office. For myself I care very little about the *Times* or its abuse, but the language of the *Times*, inspired by personal enemies in the House of Commons, is scandalous towards Graham. I think the discontinuance of all communications from the F.O. with the *Times* and the transference of the existing relation with that Paper to some other would do more to keep the *Times* in order than the showing to it any favor.[31]

But Lord Aberdeen thought otherwise and quietly continued his partiality to Delane. He gave Delane in December, 1845, the opportunity to win the greatest newspaper scoop of the day. The incident grew out of the Corn Law crisis. The Irish potato crop had failed and the harvest seemed short in other parts of the United Kingdom. The prospect of famine seemed so grave that Peel's cabinet considered opening British ports to foreign food by suspending the Corn Laws. The chief advocate of such a course was the prime minister himself, but in view of the fact that his government rested on Protectionist support he felt unable to venture it in Parliament without the unanimous approval of his colleagues. This he could not command. While the discussions were secretly proceeding, on

[30] Aberdeen to Cowley, May 7, 1844, Aberdeen MSS.
[31] Peel to Aberdeen, July 6, 1844, Peel MSS.

December 3, Lord Aberdeen sent for the editor of the *Times* and informed him that Peel was determined to abolish the Corn Laws, that he had threatened to resign unless his will were obeyed, and that the chief objectors in the cabinet had submitted. On the following day the *Times* announced with an air of certainty and authority to an astonished world that the discussions in the cabinet had terminated in a resolution to call Parliament together early in January for the purpose of proposing a total repeal of the Corn Laws, and that the Duke of Wellington had not only given his consent but was to bring forward the measure in the House of Lords. Such an announcement went beyond the facts disclosed, as became apparent two days later when the Peel cabinet dissolved, but there was sufficient truth in it to make it a tremendous journalistic triumph, one that set the whole of England agog and British society for years to gossiping as to the *Times'* sources of information.[32]

The Corn Law crisis followed. It reacted on the Oregon question significantly if indirectly. Peel's cabinet in the crisis dissolved. The formation of a Whig government was undertaken by Lord John Russell. To the foreign office was named Lord Palmerston. Lord Palmerston while foreign secretary in Melbourne's government and as Opposition leader in the attack on Lord Aberdeen had established a reputation for belligerence and recklessness in external affairs. Even in his own party he was regarded with apprehension. Earl Grey refused to enter a ministry in which he held the seals of the foreign office.[33] On this rock the Whig attempt at government wrecked. Sir Robert Peel had to be recalled. He reorganized his cabinet and with the aid of free trade Whigs proceeded to the repeal of the Corn Laws. To Lord Aberdeen in the new ministry a freer hand could be given than in the old. The revolt against Palmerston in the Whig party had reduced the hazards of a foreign policy of conciliation. Freedom to convert the British public to such concessions as might be necessary for an Oregon treaty seems to have been given Lord Aberdeen at the beginning of 1846.

In the meantime events occurring in Washington had emphasized the urgency of an Oregon settlement. An offer had been made by

[32] For gossip concerning the episode that found its way into fiction, see George Meredith, *Diana of the Crossways* (London, 1885); S. V. Makower, *Some Notes upon The Times* (Edinburgh, 1904), pp. 21–23.

[33] See Essay 9.

the American government to partition Oregon by the line of the 49th parallel to the sea. This the British minister, Richard Pakenham, had summarily rejected without so much as referring it to his government. By the American government it had been immediately withdrawn and no renewal of it could be extracted from President Polk though the summary rejection was by the British government promptly disavowed. By the close of 1845 the Oregon issue had thus relapsed into a dangerous state of diplomatic deadlock.

Such was the political and international weather in which Lord Aberdeen garnered the fruits of his favors to the *Times*. On January 3 the *Times* printed a leading editorial on the Oregon question. It was marked by more than ordinary penetration and information, and its tone was that of responsibility and authority. It opened with a recognition that joint occupation of Oregon by the settlers of the two countries was no longer expedient; that the territory ought to be partitioned. The two states were asserted to have equal rights there arising from an occupation that was nearly identical in time and similar in purpose. Any partition ought, therefore, to be one of even advantage. If a greater share was to be accorded to the United States than to England it must be in recognition, not of right, but of those considerations which the proximity, numbers, and past labors of the American settlers introduced as necessary elements into the question, considerations which in all such important matters it was impossible to merge in the technicalities of law or the minutiae of title. But care must be taken in such a division not to deprive British settlers of those advantages which are indispensable to the prosecution of their trade, such as the great water privilege of the Columbia and the harbor at its mouth. An important element in any partition was the fact that the boundary of the two states east of the Rocky Mountains was the 49th parallel. The editorial continued:

We think, then, that every purpose both of honour and interest would be answered, if the British Minister, on whom now devolves the duty of making fresh proposals to the Government of the United States, were to renew on his part the offer made to England by Mr. Gallatin in the presidency and under the direction of Mr. Adams. That proposal was to take the 49th degree of north latitude as far as the sea as the boundary line, reserving to Great Britain Vancouver's Island, the harbour of St. Juan de Fuca, and the free navigation of the Columbia. This would be a concession as far as superficial area of ground is concerned. It would leave the United States masters of the greater part of Oregon. But it would secure the principal advantage of the country, the free navigation of the Columbia, to the servants of the Hudson's Bay Company, as well as harbourage, anchorage, and settlements for English vessels trading with China and our possessions in Australia and New Zealand. . . .

We hope that no rules of diplomatic etiquette will prevent our representative at Washington from making some proposal of this kind. We hope, also, that no false pride, or more ignoble sentiment, will preclude the Ministry of Washington from accepting it. And if they do reject it as coming from us, we do not see how, after such a rejection, they can refuse to submit the question of miles still left in dispute to the arbitration of some neutral Power. . . .

That there are men in America who long for a war with Great Britain is, we fear, no less true than that there are men in this country to whom a war with the United States would be by no means unwelcome. But we would fain express a hope that the statesmen of the Republic are no more amenable than the Ministers of England to the influence of the most violent or the most thoughtless among their countrymen. And, more than this, we firmly believe that in both countries, the real strength of public opinion is arrayed against a belligerent policy. The relations of commerce—the affections of kindred—identity of origin, of language, and laws—the common pursuit of similar objects, the common prevalence of similar sentiments, and the common deference to the same principles of moral action—bind the two nations together by ties which it would be atrocious to sever by the sword. We are two people, but we are of one family. We have fought, but we have been reconciled. Let us hope that neither the memory of ancient feuds, nor the jealousy of present power, survive the recorded amity which ended a sanguinary struggle. . . .[34]

Such an appeal in the *Times* was impressive. It was especially so in view of the extraordinary conversion which it represented. For years the *Times* had been a savage critic of America and on the Oregon question particularly it had been uncompromisingly hostile. It had replied to the Inaugural statement of Polk concerning the movement of American pioneers into Oregon with the words: "in spite of his marauders, and what he terms his constitutional rights, the territory of Oregon will never be wrested from the British Crown, to which it belongs, but by war."[35] It had denounced the Senior article in the *Edinburgh Review* as "mischievous." "The writer," it observed, "evidently belongs to that class of speculative

[34] London *Times*, Jan. 3, 1846.
[35] *Ibid.*, Mar. 28, 1845.

politicians who affect to scorn the maritime power and colonial empire of their country."[36] As late as December 2, 1845, in commenting on the rejection by the British minister in Washington of the American offer of the 49th parallel, it had declared: "To accept under existing circumstances an offer which we deliberately rejected on three former occasions, and which involves the actual abandonment of the most important settlements of the Hudson's Bay Company and of the whole valley of the Columbia, is altogether out of the question." Hardly more than a month separated this editorial from the appeal of January 3 for peace.

That the conversion of the *Times* was an inspired one was whispered in high places. "In the highest diplomatic circle in London," Daniel Webster informed a friend on February 2, 1846, "it is *asserted* that the article in the Times of Jan. 3rd speaks the sentiments of the Foreign Office."[37] Proof of such connection was, of course, absent. Lord Aberdeen was too experienced a diplomat to commit himself in any transaction of that kind to paper. But in reply to a personal appeal from Edward Everett for an Oregon treaty on the basis of the line of the 49th parallel to the straits he called Everett's attention particularly to the *Times* editorial and commended it as being "temperately written."[38]

"If," Everett replied, "it [the editorial] is an indication of the course you are willing to pursue, it is all we can reasonably expect. It is only to be regretted that so much importance is attached to the navigation of the river which as I have already said is not navigable up to the 49th degree."[39]

Edward Everett promptly relayed Lord Aberdeen's hint as to the editorial to George Bancroft, a member of the Polk Cabinet. "The article in *The Times* of 3d January," he said, "was evidently

---

[36] *Ibid.*, July 19, 1845.

[37] Webster to Curtis, Feb. 2, 1846, Webster MSS., Library of Congress.

[38] Aberdeen to Everett, Jan. 3, 1846, Aberdeen MSS.

[39] Everett to Aberdeen, Jan. 28, 1846, Aberdeen MSS. Everett went on in this letter to say, "The *Times* commits the error, almost universal with those who discuss the subject, of speaking of the territory to be divided between us as lying between the 42^d degree and the 54° 40', and consequently as being equally divisible by the 48th parallel. The territory to be divided is bounded on the north by the Arctic Sea. This is a very important point by way of reconciling your people to the 49th." The view that the claims of the United States to Oregon extended to the Arctic Sea was a pet one of Edward Everett. He had developed it as an aid to Lord Aberdeen "by way of reconciling your people to the 49th." That he should have done this while he was American minister in England is a commentary on the nature of the Oregon problem.

written under the inspiration of the Foreign office. That Journal is very far from being an organ of the ministry. It keeps no terms with Sir R. Peel or Sir James Graham, but it always treats Lord Aberdeen with respect and occasionally receives suggestions from the Foreign office."[40]

The conversion of the *Times* was a signal triumph for peace. The January 3 editorial was followed by others of like tenor. The weight and drive of the monarch of British journalism was brought in the most crucial months of the Oregon negotiation to the service of peace. Respectability and standing were given to the policy of concession. A rallying point for the scattered forces of peace in the kingdom was established, one around which Liberal and independent journals in particular gathered—weeklies like the London *Spectator* and *Examiner*, and influential provincial papers such as the *Manchester Guardian*, the Liverpool *Times*, and the *Leeds Mercury*. A whole segment of British political thought was thus mobilized for peace, a segment that under less auspicious circumstances might have been a recruiting ground for the Opposition.

Preparation of the divergent ranks of the Conservative party for a treaty of renunciation was also necessary. This was undertaken by Lord Aberdeen relatively late, for it was the part of wisdom that other than organs of the ministry should take the lead in urging Oregon concession. Indeed the *Quarterly Review*, the Conservative journal, was employed only after it had practically ceased to be in the ministry's service. Lord Aberdeen's essayist in the *Quarterly* was J. W. Croker, a well-known Tory politician, an ex-secretary of the admiralty, a privy councilor, a founder of the *Quarterly*, and for many years an anonymous defender there of the policies of Sir Robert Peel. In January, 1846, he had ceased to be either the defender or the friend of the prime minister. The Corn Laws, which Peel was abolishing, he regarded as the very bulwark of the British constitution, and in defense of them he had gone into a despondent opposition. He remained loyal, however, to Lord Aberdeen, and his influence with the *Quarterly* was valuable as a pledge that the paper would not be used by embittered Tories to turn a rebel gunfire on the foreign office.

---

[40] Everett to Bancroft, Feb. 2, 1846, Everett MSS. In the Washington *Daily Union*, the administration organ, the hand of the foreign office in the *Times* editorial of January 3 was recognized as early as February 2, 1846.

"Though I am miserably disheartened at our political prospects at home and *therefore* abroad," Croker wrote Lord Aberdeen on January 27, "yet having formerly looked a little at this Oregon question, and now believing that it will lead to a war in which England has all to lose and nothing to gain, I should like to follow its progress and record my opinion about it, and I therefore shall be very glad to see the private memorandum you mention, and if you will send it next door to Mr. Barrow at the Colonial office, he will bring it to me."[41]

A correspondence of two months ensued devoted to the preparation of the proposed article. Croker requested and received from Lord Aberdeen constant aid, explanations of obscure points, influence in obtaining information from the Hudson's Bay Company, and the loan from the foreign office of confidential documents. A study of three weeks was, however, all the author needed to arrive at his conclusions. "My own opinion," he wrote Lord Aberdeen, "from my slight inspection of the books, maps, and negociations, is that the American offer of 49° with a *free Columbia* ought to have been accepted, and would now be the best arrangement. I hardly think the right bank of the Columbia worth holding out for, with so good harbourage in our own division. If you are at liberty, give me a hint how you, not Mr. Secretary of State, but *Lord Aberdeen,* feel on that point. . . ."[42] Lord Aberdeen's response to this request does not appear in the correspondence. If he sent any it was probably promptly committed by request to the fire. On March 20 Croker wrote: "I am expecting your commands on my article which now only waits the return of my proof."[43] On the next day, "Thank you for your notes, which shall be gratefully adopted, and I shall afterwards return them to you to be put into your own fire, though heaven knows there is no need of secret about them, but that it would be too *Yankee* to have it supposed that a Secretary of State sanctions the speculations of a Reviewer."[44] By March 26 the article was ready for the press. "I return you," Croker wrote, "the two cahiers of dispatches which you lent me and desired to have returned. I hope you will think that considering

[41] Croker to Aberdeen, Jan. 27, 1846, Aberdeen MSS.
[42] Feb. 17, 1846, Aberdeen MSS.
[43] Mar. 20, 1846, Aberdeen MSS.
[44] Mar. 21, 1846, Aberdeen MSS.

that the Q. R. has (*not* gone into but) been placed in *opposition*, I have handled the Foreign portion of the affair satisfactorily. I am satisfied that there is *now* no other solution possible. . . ."[45]

The solution thus evolved appeared in the guise of an anonymous review in the March number. It bore a striking resemblance to the solutions of the other essayists who had been in communication with Lord Aberdeen. Introducing it was the same type of argument. Neither the United States nor England has a good title to the entirety of Oregon. The question is one of mixed right, and the solution ought therefore to be one based on the doctrine of convenience. The United States on that basis is entitled to its share of the harbors lying inside the Strait of Juan de Fuca, the only safe harbors on the coast as far south as the Mexican port of San Francisco. This involves giving up the Columbia, which is, however, a slight sacrifice as the river is unnavigable throughout its middle reaches and, at its mouth, inaccessible for nine months of the year. "We may regret the loss of the agricultural establishments on the Cowlitz, at Fort Vancouver, and in Puget's Sound; of which, however, the last only is, we believe, of any importance; as to the original object of the posts on the Lower Columbia—the fur trade —it is diminishing so rapidly that the loss will be inconsiderable; and we cannot doubt that our traders will find in Fraser's River and the extensive shores to be appropriated to them, various opportunities of internal communication where they will be safe from rivalry and interruption." It is to be hoped, therefore, that the British government will propose to the American a partition of the disputed country by the line of the 49th parallel to the straits.

For fear Tory readers of the *Quarterly* might suspect that the article was a reflection of the wishes of the government there was inserted in it this amiable assurance: "There have been heretofore occasions, not a few, on which we have been able to advise our readers on authority higher than that of a mere literary fraternity— but it is needless to disclaim any ministerial influence or responsibility for our present opinions."[46] The Tory orthodoxy of the article was further guaranteed by the fact that in a lengthy postscript, the repeal of the Corn Laws was bitterly bewailed.

In London diplomatic circles the authorship of the article, despite

[45] Mar. 26, 1846, Aberdeen MSS.
[46] *Quarterly Review*, LXXVII, 599.

its anonymity, was soon known and its source of inspiration suspected. "It is quite possible," wrote Louis McLane in a private letter to the American Secretary of State, forwarding the article, "that the disposition now manifested by this Government to gain time may in part proceed from a desire to prepare the public in various ways for a basis of partition which Ministers have made up their minds to offer; and I rather think the article in the Quarterly is one of the means employed for that purpose."[47]

Another means of preparing the British public for concession was to discourage contentious literature regarding Oregon. That was done in the case of Thomas Falconer. Falconer was editor nominally of the *Westminster Review*, though better known to posterity for his pamphlet on the Oregon question, published in 1845, in which he reviewed the claims of the United States to Oregon in a polemical spirit. In the spring of 1846 he called the attention of the foreign office, as a matter of patriotic zeal, to a pamphlet published shortly before in New York defending British rights to Oregon and rebuking the American State Department for its stand in the controversy.[48] Falconer suggested that the pamphlet be republished in England at the cost of the government, offering to enhance its value by a foreword. The dry response which Lord Aberdeen directed to be sent to him was "that he considers the value of such a pamphlet . . . to be great in influencing the public mind in America, and he looks therefore on its publication in the U. States as likely to produce excellent results. But he does not believe that its republication in England would be of much utility, especially after Dr. Twiss's work and the various other treatises on Oregon which have appeared of late, and which have pretty well exhausted the subject."[49]

Such preparation of the British public for a treaty of concession was effective. The various sects of British politics were converted, each from its own pulpit, to the gospel of conciliation. The poisons left by the Polk Inaugural were removed, the tension of controversy was relaxed, the forces of the Opposition were disarmed. In the spring of 1846, when the Oregon negotiations were reopened in London, Lord Aberdeen was able to offer the American govern-

[47] McLane to Buchanan, Apr. 3, 1846, Buchanan MSS.
[48] The pamphlet was published anonymously under the title, *Tracts on the Oregon Question*. It is described in the London *Times* of April 11, 1846.
[49] Addington to Falconer, Apr. 15, 1846, F.O. 5/460.

ment a treaty project that upon its arrival in Washington was accepted without alteration by the American Senate. By the British public the ratified treaty was accepted with the same good will. Though the settlement was a capitulation, compared with the terms insisted upon by earlier British governments or compared with the Ashburton Treaty, it was hailed even by Opposition spokesmen as satisfactory. In the sigh of relief which greeted the news of the treaty in the whole British press, in the sigh of party envy that escaped Whig politicians,[50] in the instantaneous disappearance of the Oregon question thereafter from the horizon of British politics was proof of the effectiveness of Lord Aberdeen's propaganda.

In the crises of Anglo-American diplomacy government recourse to propaganda has been common. It has increased with the democratization of the suffrage. In England it increased with the Reform Act of 1832 and culminated in the intensive campaign of international proselytizing that marked the period 1914–1918. Of this development a comprehensive history, vital to an understanding of Anglo-American diplomacy, has yet to be written. Lord Aberdeen's Oregon effort can therefore be measured in perspective only tentatively. It was the effort of a none too aggressive craftsman. Lord Aberdeen, as a Conservative, had little taste for the task of adjusting the technique of diplomacy to the advance of democracy. His great Whig rival, Lord Palmerston, was the master of propaganda in the foreign affairs of the period, with a proficiency in the art that helps to explain the hold he had on the British public and the terror he inspired when he was in Opposition. Yet Lord Aberdeen was not wholly a novice in the art as appears from the evidence, fragmentary and elusive though it is, presented in this paper. His objectives rather than his skill distinguished him from his rival. In the Oregon crisis he used the art to guide the British public toward a treaty of renunciation, to win through the columns of the British press the peace of 1846.

[50] Lord Fitzwilliam wrote concerning Peel's valedictory to the Duke of Bedford on June 30, 1846, "I have now heard the whole—good—full of clap-trap—and what a Godsend for him from America!" Russell MSS.

ESSAY 11 · THE BRITISH CORN CRISIS OF 1845–46 AND THE OREGON TREATY*

THREE MAJOR crises confronted the British government in the autumn of 1845: a harvest shortage of seemingly famine proportions; a Corn Law conflict revolutionary in intensity; and a controversy over the Oregon Country that imperilled Anglo-American peace. By the spring of 1846 all three had passed out of the crisis stage: the harvest reports proved overdrawn; the anti-Corn Law crusade triumphed in Peel's famous measure; and by Aberdeen's treaty *projet* of May, ratified by the American Senate in June, the Oregon controversy was brought to a peaceful close. In recent American historical writing the thesis has gained currency that these problems stood to each other in more than a mere temporal relationship, that the harvest shortage and the Corn Law repeal were actually important causative factors in the Oregon settlement.[1] This thesis it is my purpose to examine.

The harvest shortage took on the appearance of a national catastrophe in the autumn of 1845. By all reports the two most necessary British crops, potatoes and wheat, were appalling failures. Of potatoes the report was but too true. Throughout the United Kingdom and especially in Ireland the tuber lay in the fields stricken by a mysterious and uncontrollable fungus which caused a rot in the harvest. The ravages of the disease were widespread on the continent of Europe; they extended even to distant North America. The wheat harvest was reported failed both in the United Kingdom and in the Baltic provinces from which England was accustomed to supply her deficiencies of bread. In the free-trade press the extent of the losses and the danger of famine were magnified as part of the campaign against the Corn Laws. A panic swept the public. The government was caught in it, and England passed through a political and social upheaval which was one of the gravest in her history.

* Reprinted from *Agricultural History*, VIII (July 1934).
1 See the references cited in footnotes 2 and 39.

The international effect of the shortage, according to the newer writings, was to bring Great Britain and Ireland to dependence for food on the United States. From this, it is believed, flowed in part the pacific and conciliatory attitude of the British government in the Oregon negotiations which made possible the treaty of 1846.[2]

This view is conservatively formulated by one writer as follows:

In October 1845, there had come the disheartening news of the destruction, by the potato blight, of one-half of the whole Irish crop of that year, which threatened famine for the winter, and no seed for the spring planting. Already, Peel has written, he had before this resolved to take the unusual step of purchasing on account of the Government a large quantity of Indian corn in the United States. The purchase was conducted by the Barings firm, who acted for the British Treasury. . . .

It is too much to conclude that under no conditions would England have gone to war with the United States [over Oregon], but it is certainly to be regarded as highly unlikely that with French relations in a delicate situation, with the abandonment of protectionism in mind, and with England buying sorely needed grain from the United States to meet a threatened famine, Sir Robert Peel would have risked a war with this country if it could be avoided in any honourable way.[3]

By another student the famine threat is described in its international aspects in more vivid terms.

During the summer [1845] came the terrible blight which destroyed the potato crops of western Europe as well as those of Great Britain and Ireland; and it became certain by the middle of October that the United States was the only considerable and dependable source for plentiful supplies of food. Indeed it seemed that the British Isles had suddenly been pushed off the continental shelf and anchored in the middle of the Atlantic, as dependent upon the United States for food supplies as they had ever been for raw cotton.[4]

[2] For this view see St. George Leakin Sioussat, "James Buchanan," in Samuel Flagg Bemis, ed., *The American Secretaries of State and Their Diplomacy*, 5:260-261, 398-400 (New York, 1928); Thomas P. Martin, "Free Trade and the Oregon Question, 1842-1846," in *Facts and Factors in Economic History; Articles by Former Students of Edwin Francis Gay*, 470-491 (Cambridge, Mass., 1932); and "Influence of Trade on Anglo-American Relations," ch. 10 (MS., Ph.D. Thesis, Harvard University, 1922); Henry Commager, "England and Oregon Treaty of 1846," in the *Oregon Historical Quarterly*, 28:32-38 (March, 1927). See for a variant theory, Randolph G. Adams, *A History of the Foreign Policy of the United States*, 228 (New York, 1924).

[3] Sioussat, "James Buchanan," in *American Secretaries of State*, 5:260.

[4] Martin, "Free Trade and the Oregon Question, 1842-1846," in *Facts and Factors in Economic History*, 485.

The chief constituent of this dependence thesis is the Irish short-age. It is accordingly examined first. The shortage was of un-questioned gravity, producing misery on a wide scale in Ireland. Yet it led strangely enough to no net food imports into the island. The Irish flow of food, on the contrary, in the winter and spring of 1845–46 was the usual one of export. Ireland at this time exempli-fied a cruel economic paradox—a land chronically in a state of starvation yet always sending quantities of food abroad. Of high-grade foods Ireland raised wheat, barley, and livestock. These she sent to England; from their sale she paid her rents. She even sent a portion of her plebeian potatoes and oats. Year after year that export went on impelled by the iron laws of supply and demand and the inexorable requirements of rent. It went on whether the Irish peasantry starved or survived. In the twelvemonth ending July 5, 1846, Ireland exported to England, of wheat, 354,058 quarters; of wheat flour, 1,166,111 cwts.; of oats, 1,202,854 quar-ters; of oatmeal, 845,162 cwts.; of barley, 116,270 quarters; and of sheep, lambs, swine, and beeves, numbers correspondingly large.[5]

Potatoes were Ireland's humble fare. According to Lord Devon's *Report* of 1845 they were in some areas practically her only fare.[6] They were varied in districts more prosperous by oatmeal, milk from the unsold produce of a family cow, and on holidays a slice of bacon. A failure of potatoes in any locality was followed promptly by starvation. That was not because of absence of other food. It was because the destitution of cottiers and laborers made the purchase of other food or even the holding of their own impossible.

In 1845 the failure of the potato was dramatic and widespread. In the early autumn, when the crop was nearly mature, the blight, a disease hitherto almost unknown, appeared. Its work was done with fearful swiftness. Fields which it found green were left black and decayed in a week. Potatoes on which its minute spores were washed became hills of putrefaction. The infection, favored by a wet autumn, spread throughout Ireland, ravaging especially the unhappy southern and eastern counties. Its total damage was diffi-

[5] *Parliamentary Papers* (1846), 44 (16); *ibid.* (1847), 59 (32). The British imperial quarter equals 8¼ bushels. The hundredweight is 112 lbs.
[6] *Parliamentary Papers* (1845), 11, Report of the Commissioners, 35.

cult to estimate. Half the crop was the loss estimated to Peel.[7] Probably that was an exaggeration. Early maturing potatoes came through the harvest unscathed. The losses of the later varieties differed from district to district, but the yield, except for the blight, would have been everywhere exceptional, a third over the average, and this was reflected in the amounts saved. There were compensations for potato losses in the abundance of other crops. Wheat, oats, and barley were a full average. Hay was plentiful, and there was a good yield of turnips and carrots.[8] The harvest as a whole was not a tragic failure such as that of 1846 when nature made a general sweep of Irish fields. The 1845 crops would have sufficed for Ireland if only they could have been kept at home. Of scarcity in any national sense there was none; only poverty which forced the export of foods saved from the blight.

The British government took this view of the crisis. It directed all its energies of relief to the problem of a blight-deepened poverty. Its relief measures, in order of importance, were public works designed to provide employment for the destitute, coördination of the activities of local relief committees, and the prevention of profiteering. As a check to profiteering it accumulated in Ireland a quantity of cheap food of undisclosed amount which it held during the winter suspended over the produce markets. The food thus used was Indian corn meal purchased, to the amount of £100,000, through the house of Baring in the United States. This has been cited as proof of Irish national scarcity and British dependence on the United States. But proof of Irish national scarcity it is not. A government does not provide against scarcity in a population of eight million by one purchase to the amount of £100,000. The purchase was accounted for to Parliament by Sir James Graham, speaking for the ministry as follows:

They did not so order it for the purpose of meeting the entire wants of the Irish people, but for the purpose of checking the markets, of preventing the holding back of corn [grain] to enhance the price, and of arresting the progress of the very evil of which the hon. Gentleman

[7] *Memoirs by the Right Honourable Sir Robert Peel,* 2:171–172 (London, 1858); see also London *Times,* Feb. 5, 1846.
[8] *Parliamentary Papers* (1846), 37 (735), *passim* (Correspondence explanatory of the measures adopted by Her Majesty's Government for the Relief of Distress arising from the failure of the Potato Crop in Ireland); W. P. O'Brien, *The Great Famine in Ireland,* 66 (London, 1896). Potato prices fell in Ireland in the spring of 1846.

complained—that, in midst of plenty, when the crops of oats had been unusually large, the supply of oatmeal was so limited that the price was raised one-third.[9]

The choice of American Indian corn meal as the medium of this control was made for reasons none of which support the theory that Britain was dependent on the United States. Peel preferred not to make government food purchases in British markets, more particularly purchases of ordinary European foods, lest the result be a raising of British prices. This objection was met by the purchase of corn meal in the United States. Corn meal was the cheapest of cereals; a government supply of it could be sold to Irish relief committees at less cost than oatmeal without burdening the British treasury. Peel hoped the purchase might result in the permanent addition to Irish diet of a cheap and wholesome food, correcting thus a dangerous dependence on potatoes.[10]

The experiment was a partial success. The purchase order placed in November was gradually and quietly filled, months incidentally before the Oregon negotiations of 1846 began. The meal was kept stored in Ireland; it was held in reserve until May, serving in the meantime as a curb on potato and oats speculators. In May when supplies of potatoes were nearly exhausted it was gradually sold in small lots to local relief committees at a price of £10 to £11 per ton. As a price regulator its purpose was achieved.[11]

But Ireland did not readily use corn meal. At first fear militated against its use. In Irish workhouses the meal was thought to be a poison; the serving of it led to riots.[12] In the credulous countryside women spread the dread news that to eat it was to have offspring that were yellow like mulattos, or more terrifying still, that to feed it to the men was to render them impotent.[13] If objections of this kind were ultimately overcome, one other could not be. Corn meal is a food the taste for which has to be acquired. It has never been acquired in Ireland or anywhere else in Europe. The consumption of it was therefore limited to about what the government pur-

[9] *Hansard's Parliamentary Debates* (3d series), 85:712.
[10] *Parliamentary Papers* (1846), 37 (735), *passim*.
[11] *Ibid.*, p. 223, 247.
[12] *Ibid.*, p. 84, 89; *Manchester Guardian*, Apr. 15, 1846; London *Spectator*, May 23, 1846. The government corn meal was referred to in Ireland as "Peel's Brimstone."
[13] *Manchester Guardian*, Apr. 15, 1846; *Parliamentary Papers* (1846) 37 (735): 187; see also Monteagle to Peel, Sept. 27, 1845. Peel MSS., British Museum.

chased. In the twelvemonth ending June 30, 1846, imports of corn and corn meal into Ireland from the United States amounted, according to the *Report* of the United States Secretary of the Treasury, to 425,960 bushels of the one and 33,750 barrels of the other,[14] truly not an impressive support for a dependence theory.

One considerable source of famine alarm in the autumn of 1845 was the reputed failure of the British and the European wheat harvest. This is the second constituent of the dependence thesis. The United Kingdom consumed of wheat, according to an 1846 estimate of J. R. McCulloch, the greatest of contemporary British statisticians, about 15,000,000 quarters a year.[15] Of this the bulk, in any year of normal harvest, was raised at home;[16] less than an eighth was imported. The average annual import of wheat and wheat flour for the five-year period prior to 1846 amounted to but 1,879,000 quarters.[17] Even in such a year of harvest calamity as 1847 no more than an eighth of the nation's total grain requirements, according to McCulloch, came from overseas.[18]

In 1845 the domestic wheat crop, notwithstanding early alarms, turned out to be little below the average in quantity. It was deficient in quality, but mixed with the carry-over of the excellent crop of 1844 it made satisfactory flour.[19] The United Kingdom was obliged to draw on the outside world for wheat and wheat flour in the year ending May 31, 1846 to the extent of only 1,932,000 quarters, which is but 53,000 quarters more than the average of the five years prior to 1846.[20] England had in bond in February, 1846, waiting for the repeal of the Corn Laws, the extraordinary accumulation of 1,117,000 quarters of imported wheat and 703,961 cwts. of imported flour,[21] which in itself was little short of a year's importation.

---

[14] *Sen Docs.*, 29 Cong., 2 Sess. (Serial 494), No. 7, p. 16. Exports to the whole of the United Kingdom amounted to 1,192,000 bushels corn and 50,164 barrels corn meal.

[15] J. R. McCulloch, *A Dictionary, Practical, Theoretical, and Historical, of Commerce and Commercial Navigation*, 425–449 (London, 1850).

[16] Thomas Tooke, *A History of Prices*, 2:225–345 (London, 1838).

[17] *Statistical Abstract for the United Kingdom*, 12 (1854).

[18] McCulloch, *Dictionary of Commerce*, 427, note.

[19] London *Times*, Jan. 3, 1846 (Brown and Co's. Circular); Apr. 8, 1846 (Letter of "A mealman" to the editor).

[20] *Parliamentary Papers* (1846), 44 (130):4; *ibid.* (1847), 59 (259):4.

[21] *Ibid.* (1846), 44 (114):8.

A barometer of food scarcity is price. Price would have registered scarcity had any existed in England in the spring of 1846. When scarcity did exist in June, 1847, the price of wheat rose to a peak of 102s. 5d. per quarter and the average for the year was 69s. 9d. per quarter.[22] For the first six months of 1846 the average was 54s. 9d., which is exactly the average of the preceding five years. A height of 60s. was reached in the panic months of the autumn of 1845 but by March, 1846, the price had fallen to a low of 54s. 3d.,[23] a drop that meant ruin to many an unwary grain factor who had made heavy commitments abroad in the autumn in anticipation of famine prices in the spring. An epidemic of bankruptcies among grain factors gave evidence that the autumn wheat alarms had been groundless.[24]

Even in free trade circles the groundlessness of those alarms had to be admitted. It was acknowledged by Lord John Russell on January 22, 1846, when the government bill for the repeal of the Corn Laws was introduced into Parliament.[25] Free trade journals had to follow suit. The London *Economist* for instance, which had been a leader in spreading apprehension in the autumn, confessed in March, 1846, that British wheat losses had been overstated and that insufficient account had been taken of the heavy stocks held over from the preceding year.[26]

The ministry felt the same reassurance. It abandoned the famine argument in the debate on the Corn Laws, the Protectionist Opposition in the meantime questioning the sincerity of even the autumn fears and greeting references made to them with jeers.[27] Reassurance was evident in the weary length to which the debate on Corn Law repeal was allowed to run. Not until the end of June, 1846,

[22] *Statistical Abstract for the United Kingdom*, 22 (1854); T. Tooke and W. Newmarch, *A History of Prices*, 5:142–148 (London, 1857).

[23] *Statistical Abstract for the United Kingdom*, 30 (1854); see also Hunt's *Merchants' Magazine*, 15:88–89.

[24] London *Economist*, Feb. 21, 1846, p. 231; Feb. 28, 1846, p. 261, 271; Baring Brothers & Co. to Prime, Ward and King, Mar. 18, 1846. Baring MSS., Dominion Archives, Ottawa.

[25] *Hansard's* (3d series), 83:108.

[26] London *Economist*, Feb. 28, 1846 (Body & Co's. Circular); and Mar. 14, 1846, p. 359.

[27] *Hansard's* (3d series), 83:281 (Peel); *ibid.*, 551 (Milnes); London *Times*, Jan. 17, 1846 (Speech of Sir J. Trollope); Jan. 19, 1846 (Speech of J. Bailey); Jan. 21, 1846 (Speech of Earl of Carnarvon).

was repeal enacted and not until February, 1849, did protective duties on grain altogether disappear.

If, however, the wheat harvest had been as calamitous as free traders at first reported, Britain would not have turned to America for rescue. From America she was accustomed to receive only a morsel of bread. Such imported wheat as she needed was bought in the basins of the Baltic and the Mediterranean. In the five-year period prior to 1846 she obtained there 80 percent of her wheat imports—from the Baltic 61 percent, from the Mediterranean 19 percent. From the whole of North America she obtained 15 ½ percent or less than 3 percent of her consumption.[28] In the year ending June 30, 1846, the year of supposed dependence, she obtained from the United States 975,000 bushels of wheat and 1,005,000 barrels of flour.[29]

Such facts were common knowledge in the markets, ministry, and press. They were pointed out by government spokesmen in Parliament again and again during the debates on the repeal of the Corn Laws.[30] The London *Times* at the height of the November famine scare made a detailed survey of the world's surplus wheat areas, in which it observed as to the United States: "The growth of the population in the manufacturing and non-corn [non-grain]-growing districts is sufficiently rapid to consume all the additional corn-produce of the country, supposing 130,000 acres of new land per annum to be put under wheat culture alone, and three times that quantity under other crops and pasturage. The extension of agriculture barely keeps pace with the population; and the whole supply of wheat is hardly more than one month's consumption ahead of the demand in the Union."[31]

Thus dissolves the thesis that in the period of the Oregon crisis Britain felt herself dependent on the United States for food. No informed person in England so much as conceived of such a relation. The thesis is, in truth, an historical anachronism, an anticipation of conditions later, if ever, realized.

[28] *Statistical Abstract for the United Kingdom*, 12 (1854).
[29] *Sen. Docs.*, 29 Cong., 2 Sess. (Serial 494), No. 7, pp. 14, 16.
[30] *Hansard's* (3d series), 83:629 (Sydney Herbert); *ibid.*, 606 (Lord John Russell); *ibid.*, 86:640–641. See *post*, pp. 319–320. The inability of American wheat growers to compete in the British market even under conditions of special favor is pointed out in the London *Economist*, Dec. 13, 1845.
[31] London *Times*, Nov. 11, 1845.

Another food question did, however, in British discussion relate itself to the Oregon crisis, the question of the repeal of the Corn Laws. British free traders stated the relationship in the form of the following argument. The American trans-Allegheny West is a center of surplus wheat production. It is also a center of ancient grudges against England and in particular of belligerence on the subject of Oregon. If the West by the repeal of the Corn Laws could be given a free entrance for its grain to the British market, its belligerence would yield to enlightened sectional interest. President Polk would be induced to bring the Oregon controversy to a prompt and amicable close, and Anglo-American relations would be permanently improved. Western wheat would intertwine with the Southern cotton and Eastern commerce to render forever secure the bonds of Anglo-American peace.[32]

This free-trade formula was a useful if incidental argument in the campaign against the Corn Laws. It was employed for a month or two while the Oregon crisis was acute on the hustings, in the free-trade press, and in Parliament. It was sanctioned by the ministry and by Whigs who were temporarily allied with the ministry in abolishing the Corn Laws. Lord John Russell stated it to a receptive audience in Glasgow on January 12, 1846, as follows:

There is another advantage which I think would arise from the total abolition of the duties on the importation of grain—it would bind this country much more closely in the bonds of peace and amity with foreign states, and more especially with one—I mean the United States of America [cheers]. I think nothing of the questions which are at present in dispute [loud cheering]—questions of territory, in which, as they now stand, the honour of neither country is engaged [cheers] and, regarding which I think calm men representing the government of Her Majesty and the United States, might, by a calm and fair discussion come to an amicable agreement. I see no prospect of war or serious difference arising out of the circumstance. If we are determined on this side to import the products of the United States, and if the United States are equally satisfied to do the same with the manufactures of this kingdom, that they should feed us, and that we should clothe them, if no unhallowed legislation should stand in the way of these desirable results, then we should see two nations of the same race and speaking the same language united in the bonds of amity and peace.[33]

[32] See *post*, pp. 317–319.
[33] London *Chronicle*, Jan. 15, 1846.

317

Lord Morpeth, a Liberal, linked the two issues in the same way in a public speech on his election to Parliament.

They may talk of a black cloud in the West, but the harvest sun has a ray warm enough to scatter it. [Renewed and enthusiastic cheering.] I know that on the other side of the Atlantic they are uttering big words about Oregon and we hear that the inhabitants of the Western States of the American Republic talk particularly loud on that subject, and that they are anxious to have a brush with us, while it seems that the inhabitants of the Eastern States are more pacific in their disposition. Why is this, gentlemen? . . . They [the Westerners] produce nothing but agricultural produce, and they know that if besides living five or six thousand miles away from us, the quarter of wheat which they might be inclined to send over shall have to pay a duty of 20s. when it arrives, they would not be able to get rid of a single bushel of it, and therefore they fling up their caps for war. But give them the same motives for peace which the inhabitants of the Eastern States have, and being sprung from the same stock as their brethren of Boston, New York and Philadelphia, being the sons of Puritans and broad brims themselves, they will be actuated by the same motives as their more sedate and sober fellow-citizens, and instead of wishing themselves to go a thousand miles further, where they would meet more new tribes of red Indians to contend against than draughts of water by the way, and when they arrived there, to go to war with us for a number of uninhabited pine swamps, they might think it were desirable to bestow a little more skill on their own rich clay bottoms if you would only give them the means of taking your cottons, your woolens, your worsted, your hardware, in exchange for what they can send us whether it be wheat or Indian corn.[34]

The same argument appeared repeatedly in the free-trade press. The leading Whig daily of London, the *Morning Chronicle*, presented it to the British public on January 17, 1846, as follows:

We must strengthen the bonds of the peace party in the American republic by reënforcing their pacific and patriotic counsels with the argument of commercial interest. We must disarm or neutralize the passions of the war party by presenting to it that which interests it as a free-trade party. We must subdue the hostility of the bellicose and ambitious Western States by addressing them in their other character of corn-growing States. And we must do this *soon*, at once, for time presses.[35]

---

[34] *Ibid.*, Feb. 5, 1846. John Bright advanced the same argument in repeated speeches attacking the Corn Laws. See London *Times*, Dec. 6, 8, 10, 1845; Jan. 7, 1846; and *Louisville Democrat*, Mar. 12, 1846.

[35] London *Chronicle*, Jan. 17, 1846.

Punch, a paper free-trade in sympathy, presented the argument in pictorial form. Sir Robert Peel was shown pelting a warlike Polk, who stood across the Atlantic, with a billet labeled "Free Corn," and knocking him off his legs. This British caricature needed considerable explanation. The explanation was as follows: "Peel's Free Trade must be victorious against Polk's firebrands. America may, if it pleases, pelt us with its corn, while we return the compliment by pitching into the United States some of our manufactured articles. This will be much better for both parties than an exchange of lead."[36]

The argument was used in Parliament as seasoning for the debate on Corn Law repeal. It appeared in the speeches of Lord John Russell, Lord Morpeth, Lord Clarendon, Sir James Graham, Charles Buller, and other free-trade notables. Granville Vernon's statement of it is a good sample:

Throughout America he had found but one feeling among the friends of peace, who said that if we would only interest, by prosperity, the Western States of America, which were invulnerable to our arms, and inaccessible to our commerce (for we had already the interests of the Eastern States in our favour) we should do more to promote the peace of America than all the concessions we should make in the Oregon or elsewhere.[37]

Protectionists replied to this formula by questioning the premise that repeal of the Corn Laws would benefit the American West. The only beneficiary of repeal, they maintained, would be continental Europe, which would inundate, with serf-produced grain, a British market made free. Such was the opinion of Lord Ashburton, who spoke out of the experience of many years in the international produce trade as former head of the house of Baring. Replying on January 19, 1846, to Lord John Russell's Glasgow speech Lord Ashburton observed that continental Europe currently supplied 90 percent of the grain imports of Britain. Cheap labor

---

[36] *Punch,* 10:155.

[37] *Hansard's* (3d series), 84:1466. Lord Aberdeen, foreign secretary under Peel, made the same argument as applied however to maize. He concluded a letter written on December 3, 1845 to the British minister in Washington on the Oregon question by observing: "The access of Indian corn to our markets would go far to pacify the warriors of the Western States." Aberdeen to Pakenham, Dec. 3, 1845. Aberdeen MSS., British Museum. See also C. C. F. Greville, *A Journal of the Reign of Queen Victoria* (London, 1885), II: 312, 313.

rendered this possible, and would continue to do so in a free British market. Against such a handicap the American West could not hope to compete.[38]

These opposing views, developed in the heat of political controversy, ought to be subjected to rigid testing before they are adopted for historical purposes. Yet without any testing the free-trade view has been adopted by historians who relate the Corn Law question to the Oregon question. A change in tense alone is made. Free-trade propagandists predicted that a repeal of the Corn Laws would mollify the American West. Historians of the problem assert that repeal, or rather the promise of it, did mollify the West.[39]

An analysis of this view is best begun by examining the record of the American wheat trade. The United States produced in the half-decade 1841–45 an annual average of from 90,000,000 to 105,000,000 bushels of wheat.[40] All of it, with the exception of seven or eight percent,[41] was consumed at home. The West was its own wheat market to a considerable extent, its incoming pioneers being in the first year or two of settlement chiefly grain consumers.

Exports were not only small but, relative to population, declining. In the first half-decade of the nation's life, when population was about 4,000,000, wheat exports averaged per year, reducing wheat flour to wheat, 5,118,000 bushels. In the quarter-century 1790–1814 the average was 4,642,000 bushels; in the next quarter-century 4,850,000 bushels; in the half-decade 1841–45 (when population was over 17,000,000), 7,165,000 bushels.[42] Of this 7,165,000 bushels, 73 percent went to areas adjacent to or near the United States, to Canada, to the Caribbean, and to Brazil, in the order of importance named.[43]

[38] London *Times*, Jan. 21, 1846.

[39] Sioussat, "James Buchanan," in *American Secretaries of State*, 5:256–264; R. C. Clark, "British and American Tariff Policies and Their Influence on the Oregon Boundary Treaty," in the American Historical Association, Pacific Coast Branch, *Proceedings*, 1926, 32–49; Martin, "Free Trade and the Oregon Question, 1842–1846," in *Facts and Factors in Economic History*, 470–491; Henry Commager, "England and Oregon Treaty of 1846," in the *Oregon Historical Quarterly*, 28:32–38 (March, 1927).

[40] Crop estimates of each year are to be found for this period in the annual report of the United States Commissioner of Patents in the *Congressional Documents*.

[41] See the statistics in the next paragraph.

[42] *Hazard's Commercial and Statistical Register*, 4:242; see also the reference in the succeeding footnote.

[43] 45 Congress, 3 session, *House Executive Document 15*, p. 106, 107.

American wheat was exported to Europe in any quantity only in abnormal times. The European market was unprofitable to the American farmer except when crises such as the Napoleonic Wars, the famine of 1847, or the Crimean War lifted grain prices to exceptional heights. As Henry Clay pointed out in 1824,[44] Europe was an accidental market to the American grain grower. It was not more than that on account of the competitive handicaps of the United States. Farm labor in the United States was too costly as compared with tenant labor in the United Kingdom or serf labor in Prussia or Russia. American inland transport was too expensive whether by the roundabout highway of the Mississippi or by the Great Lakes and Erie Canal which necessitated transshipments. Cheap carriage, such as the Vistula, the Bug, or the Elbe gave grain growers in northern Europe, interior America did not provide. The ocean voyage from New York or New Orleans to England was too long compared with that from Hamburg or Danzig or other north European ports. These were the disabilities, not the Corn Laws, which had been restricting the American farmer's participation in the grain markets of Great Britain. Not until after the Civil War, when prairie labor costs had been reduced by the invention and wide-scale use of agricultural machinery, when costs of grain handling had been minimized by great economies in elevator operation such as the standardization of grades, and when handicaps of distance had been lessened by revolutionary changes in lake and rail and ocean transport could the United States export wheat successfully to European markets and make felt there the full weight of its cheap and fertile land.

Repeal of the Corn Laws in the meantime proved of little advantage to the American West. Britain imported after 1846 a considerably larger proportion of her bread than before. For the five-year period 1848–53, which avoids the famine year 1847, the annual average of imports of wheat and wheat flour into the United Kingdom was 4,442,000 quarters. Of this amount the Baltic provinces gave 45½ percent, the Mediterranean 30½ percent, and North America 19 percent.[45] North America gave about the same percentage in this period as in the period 1841–45, 19 percent as against 15½ percent. Repeal merely made clear that in a free

[44] 18 Congress, 1 session, *Annals of Congress*, 2:1962–1970.
[45] *Statistical Abstract for the United Kingdom*, 12 (1854).

British market the American farmer could not offer effective competition.

In one important respect repeal actually injured the wheat grower of the American West. He lost as a result of it a favored status in the British market as a participator in Canada's privileges of colonial preference. Canada enjoyed colonial preference in the British market under an imperial law of 1828, which was based on the ancient principles of the Navigation System. Whenever British wheat prices reached a point that indicated crop shortage in the United Kingdom colonial wheat and wheat flour were admitted at a purely nominal rate of duty. The colonial duty was only half a shilling a quarter at a price of 67s. or more. At less than 67s. the duty rose to 5s. On foreign wheat the duty at the price of 67s. was 18s. 8d. If prices declined below 67s., for every shilling of fall the duty on foreign wheat advanced a shilling until at a price of 40s. the duty reached the extravagant height of 46s. 8d. At a price of 40s. the colonial duty was less than a ninth of the foreign; at a price of 67s. the colonial duty was one thirty-seventh of the foreign.[46]

In 1842 this preference was somewhat reduced. Under the new law, whenever the price per quarter was 58s. or more, the duty on colonial wheat was one shilling. When the price fell below 58s., for every shilling of fall the duty advanced a shilling until it was 5s. at prices under 55s. On foreign wheat the shilling duty applied only when the price was as high as 73s. or above. When the price declined below 73s., for every shilling of fall the duty advanced a shilling until it was 20s. at a price under 51s. The colonial duty when the price was under 51s. was but one-fourth of the foreign; it was one-twelfth of the foreign at a price of 60s.[47]

In the year after this act was passed Canada was singled out for special Parliamentary favor. As an encouragement to her forwarding and milling interests, and as a concession to a growing anti-Corn Law sentiment in Britain, Parliament, by the Canada Corn Act of 1843, permitted Canadian wheat and wheat flour to be admitted into the United Kingdom after October, 1843, at the nominal duty of a shilling a quarter, regardless of British prices.[48]

In these Canadian privileges the United States shared. Wheat

[46] 9 Geo. IV, c. 60.
[47] 5 and 6 Vict., c. 14.
[48] 6 and 7 Vict., c. 29.

from the United States entered Canada free of duty under an imperial act of 1831[49] which remained in force until October, 1843. After October, 1843, under a provincial act complementary to the Canada Corn Act, American wheat paid a duty at the Canadian border of 3s. a quarter.[50] Accordingly, American wheat, ground into Canadian flour, entered Britain after October, 1843, at the combined colonial and imperial duty of 4s. a quarter. That gave American wheat a preference as against other foreign wheat of from 10s. to 16s. a quarter, dependent on the state of British prices. Between October, 1843, and June, 1846, the actual preference was much of the time 16s. and seldom as little as 10s.[51]

Some part of this advantage was offset by the shortcomings of the St. Lawrence as an export route. Its channel was closed to commerce by ice for a considerable part of the year, some of its main improvements were completed only in 1848; the Gulf of St. Lawrence was beset by a number of perils which made insurance rates relatively high; the British navigation acts were a considerable restriction; and the varied means of assorting cargo and the assurance of return freights which New York and other American ports offered were lacking at Montreal. Gladstone in 1842 estimated these transit handicaps as equivalent to an added freight on wheat of 2s. a quarter[52] as compared with the route of the Erie Canal. But that canceled only a fraction of the legislative advantage which Canadian preference gave American wheat moving into Britain.

The Corn Laws thus constituted a protection rather than a barrier to the West.[53] Western grain growers penetrated the barrier by

[49] 1 William IV, c. 24.
[50] *Provincial Statutes of Canada*, 6 Vict., c. 31. The terms of the measure are recited in the preamble to the Canada Corn Act.
[51] *Statistical Abstract for the United Kingdom*, 22 (1854).
[52] Gladstone Memorandum, Feb. 17, 1842, Peel MSS.; *Parliamentary Papers* (1843), 53 (218); *New York Journal of Commerce*, Feb. 17, 1846. The benefits of colonial preference to Canada are minimized—unduly in my opinion—in D. L. Burn, "Canada and the Repeal of the Corn Laws," in the *Cambridge Historical Journal*, 2:252–272 (1928).
[53] Edward Everett, American minister to London, wrote to his government in 1844: "It is a matter of doubt whether the interest of the United States as a grain-growing region does not stand better under the present law with the Canada Corn bill as part of it than it would under a change either for a fixed duty or entire freedom of trade. Either of these measures would subject our corn to a competition with those ports in the North of Europe, from which it can generally be imported cheaper than from America, whereas under the present state of the law, although the transportation is monopolized by English bottoms, it would seem

means of the Canadian back door. Inside it they found protection against Prussian and Russian competitors. By the repeal of the Corn Laws the barrier and the back door were both leveled. The competition of Europe had to be met in the open British market.

The loss thus suffered by the American West is measured in the shrinkage of the "back door trade." In the period just prior to repeal this trade had been growing rapidly. From October, 1843, to June, 1846, wheat and wheat flour flowed from Canada to Britain at the annual rate of 2,030,000 bushels.[54] A large part was American grain, for Canada had little surplus of her own to export.[55] The trade was cut in half by the Corn Law repeal; it fell in the years 1848–53 to an annual average of 1,036,000 bushels.[56] In irritation over the loss Canada talked secession from the Empire and annexation to the United States.[57] Canada's partner in the trade was her partner in its fall.

Of these facts the West was not ignorant. Whig politicians kept it informed. They had an interest in proving that a British market, even open at the back door, was to the West unimportant and unattractive. That was the Whig protective tariff argument; it was the complement to the home-market argument. Statistics showing the relative decline of American wheat exports to Europe during the preceding half-century supported it and were therefore perennially spread before the West. In 1839 Samuel Hazard compiled and published them with appropriate protectionist comments in his *United States Commercial and Statistical Register.*[58] In 1841 he republished them with new data concerning the Canada back-door

---

as if all the corn imported from abroad must come from the United States through Canada." Everett to Upshur, Mar. 2, 1844, no. 93, Everett MSS., Massachusetts Historical Society.

[54] *Parliamentary Papers* (1847), 59 (259):9.

[55] *Ibid.* (1843), 53 (218):4, 5. See also *Hansard's* (3d series), 60:1235–1236 (Gladstone); Gillespie to Stanley, Jan. 10, 1842, C.O. 42:500; Stanley to Worsley, Apr. 17, 1843, Peel MSS., British Museum. The figures given by Mr. Burn in the *Cambridge Historical Journal*, 2:255, should be compared with those in *Statistical Abstract for the United Kingdom*, 12 (1854); 45 Congress, 3 session, *House Executive Document 15*, p. 106, 107. *Hazard's Commercial and Statistical Register*, 4:242.

[56] *Statistical Abstract for the United Kingdom*, 12 (1854).

[57] W. P. Morrell, *British Colonial Policy in the Age of Peel and Russell* (Oxford, 1930), 197–198; Theodore Walrond, ed., *Letters and Journals of James, Eighth Earl of Elgin*, 99ff. (London, 1872). Adam Shortt and A. G. Doughty, eds., *Canada and its Provinces* (Toronto, 1914–1917), 5:214–227. The loss to Canada was chiefly the flour milling and the transit trade.

[58] *Hazard's Commercial and Statistical Register* (1839), 1:251–253.

trade, taken from the *Detroit Daily Advertiser*.[59] Joshua Leavitt in the same year presented an elaborate grain-trade memorial to Congress, and the next year another, supported by serried rows of figures, both of which a Whig Senate ordered to be printed.[60] C. G. Child, editor of the *Philadelphia Price Current and Commercial List*, in January, 1842, published in his paper a careful historical grain-trade review, which won wide notice, and in the succeeding autumn *Niles' Register* gave the statistics yet another airing.[61] Once more when Peel's bill appeared Whigs paraded the figures before the West and this time supported the argument by dwelling on the prospective loss to the West of even the back-door trade.[62]

In America Peel's bill was awaited with intense interest. The outcome of the cabinet crisis in December had made clear that the Corn Laws would be changed, but the actual repeal measure was not published until January when Parliament reassembled, and it did not reach the United States until the 19th of February. So keen was public interest in it that a group of Eastern newspaper proprietors, to hasten its publication a few hours in New York, arranged to intercept the British mail steamer at Halifax and run the press despatches southward by special overland express.[63]

The measure chanced to arrive at the beginning of a heated American controversy over the Democratic low-tariff measure framed by Secretary Walker. To Walker's measure Peel's lent aid. It was received therefore by Democrats with delight, by Whigs with dismay. The two measures became identified in American tariff politics. Together they were gnawed and fought over as one bone of party and sectional contention.[64] This was a

---

[59] *Ibid.*, 4:242.

[60] 26 Congress, 2 session, *Senate Document 222;* 27 Congress, 2 session, *Senate Document 339.*

[61] *Niles' Register*, 63:25.

[62] See Edwin Williams, *The Wheat Trade of the United States* (New York, 1846); see also J. R. Williams, "Production of Wheat in the United States," in Hunt's *Merchants' Magazine*, 12:307–323; Charles Hudson, "Corn Trade of the United States," *ibid.*, 12:421–432.

[63] *New York Journal of Commerce*, Feb. 19, 1846.

[64] Pakenham, the British minister at Washington, described the American reception of Peel's bill as follows:

"A great, and I think I may say, a very gratifying sensation has been produced in this Country by the news received by the last Packet of the intended alterations in the Commercial Policy of England. In the midst of a general expression of satisfaction some dissenting voices are of course to be heard. Amongst these may be classed that of the Manufacturing Interests who foresee in the example thus

development which British free-trade propagandists had not taken sufficiently into account in predicting that the repeal of the Corn Laws would mollify the belligerent West.

In the East the bill had a favorable initial reception. The powerful commercial classes in the cities welcomed its promise of freer trade. Party Democrats and professional internationalists were delighted with it. Word was sent to Gladstone, who relayed it at once to Peel, that the bill had created "an immense sensation" and that there had been "illuminations."[65] Eastern Whigs and protectionists were consoled by the thought that the bill might appease the "Western Warriors" and facilitate a pacific adjustment of the Oregon controversy. Whig editors professed to discern British friendliness toward the United States in the bill though contending in the same breath that the measure could not benefit American agriculture. Whig tolerance lessened as the bill became drawn into the Walker tariff controversy. Some editors of ultra-protectionist views reacted against it then by raising their tone on the Oregon question, which led William Cullen Bryant, the editor of the Democratic New York *Evening Post*, on March 3, 1846 to observe in an article entitled "War Rather Than Free Trade," that "the loudest cry for war with Great Britain seems just at present to come from the owners of the spindles."

The bill was received in the South with enthusiasm. It was a free-trade measure which was enough to commend it to a free-trade community. It was likely to hasten reform of the domestic tariff. It was conceived of in the South as in the East as an olive branch regarding Oregon and no section more earnestly desired the preservation of Anglo-American peace than the cotton South.

The bill seemed to offer least to the West. In Western produce markets its benefits were discouragingly appraised. In Baltic mar-

---

set by England the downfall of the protective system in this country, and those also of a mischievous and ungracious class of Politicians, who trade upon the agitation of questions of an anti-English tendency, and who cannot but perceive how much the measures now under discussion in England must tend to narrow the field of their operations.

"On the other hand the anti-tariff party seem to be in the highest degree elated by the adoption of a policy so much in consonance with their views, and to consider the success of the bill lately sent to Congress by the Secretary of the Treasury for the reduction in the existing scale of import duties, to be now almost certain." Pakenham to Aberdeen, Feb. 26, 1846. F.O. 5:446.

[65] C. S. Parker, *Sir Robert Peel*, 3:374 (London, 1899).

kets wheat prices advanced promptly two to three shillings a quarter on the publication of the bill.[66] In the West prices advanced not at all.[67] They declined, on the contrary, in harmony with British prices. Cincinnati markets tell the story for the whole section. Wheat in Cincinnati in the early winter of 1845 moved sharply upward in response to reports of harvest failure in Britain and northern Europe. The price was eighty-five cents a bushel on December 18, 1845.[68] Thereafter it declined as correct accounts arrived of the state of the British harvest. The decline continued throughout the spring of 1846. On July 17, 1846, wheat sold in Cincinnati at forty cents a bushel, which was its lowest level since the year 1830.[69] Flour in Cincinnati on December 18, 1845, was $4.85 to $5.00 a barrel.[70] From this peak it declined to $2.10 or $2.15 by September 18, 1846,[71] which was its lowest level since 1822. Mess pork on October 16, 1845, was $14.50 to $15.00 per barrel.[72] From this height it fell by September 18, 1846 to $7 a barrel,[73] its lowest level, except for the disastrous period 1841–43, since 1827. A descent so general and so steep could hardly have seemed a happy augury to the West of benefits to be derived from the repeal of the Corn Laws.

An intensification of party warfare over the protective tariff was the chief political effect of the bill in the West. Soon after the bill's appearance Whig editors throughout the section broadcast in excerpt or editorially a notable congressional speech by

[66] London *Times*, Feb. 7, 14, 1846, citing Body & Co's. Circular. Baltic prices later declined, however, in sympathy with British prices. For detailed statistics of wheat prices for the years 1844–49 in European and American ports, see *Parliamentary Papers* (1850), 52 (206).

[67] J. E. Boyle, *Chicago Wheat Prices for Eighty-One Years*, 5, 6, 13 (Ithaca, N.Y., 1922); Hunt's *Merchants' Magazine*, 15:87, 214, 215, 411. See also the daily newspapers of the period.

[68] *Cincinnati Atlas*, Dec. 18, 1845. For this and the succeeding Cincinnati citations I am indebted to the kindness of Mr. T. S. Berry of Cambridge, Massachusetts.

[69] *Cincinnati Chronicle*, July 17, 1846.

[70] *Cincinnati Atlas*, Dec. 18, 1845.

[71] *Cincinnati Chronicle*, Sept. 18, 1846.

[72] *Cincinnati Atlas*, Oct. 16, 1845.

[73] *Cincinnati Chronicle*, Sept. 18, 1846. See also G. F. Warren and F. A. Pearson, "Wholesale Prices in the United States . . . 1797 to 1932," in *Wholesale Prices for 213 Years, 1720 to 1932*, 113 (Ithaca, N.Y., 1932). Wholesale prices of farm foods in the United States as measured by an index number established in this volume rose to a height of 68 in December, 1845, from which they precipitously declined by September, 1846, to 48, the lowest level, except for the period August, 1842, to September, 1844, to which they had sunk since 1821.

Charles Hudson, a Massachusetts protectionist, on "The Wheat Trade of the Country," in which the theory that a repeal of the Corn Laws could benefit Western agriculture was demolished.[74] A few weeks later the party press widely disseminated a public letter of Congressman E. D. Baker of the seventh Illinois congressional district to his constituents in which appeared an ordered demonstration of the following eight propositions:

1st. That the British wheat market has not required more than fourteen millions of bushels of wheat from abroad upon an average of any long series of years.

2nd. That a reduction of the duties will not materially diminish the amount produced by their own agriculture.

3rd. That the quantity consumed will not be largely increased.

4th. That the market, both as to quantity and price must be an unsteady, and therefore a poor one.

5th. That a reduction of the duty destroys the monopoly which we have enjoyed in consequence of the trade through Canada.

6th. That the reduction of duties gives a great advantage to the wheat-growing countries on the Mediterranean and in the North of Europe, beyond what they have previously enjoyed in competition with us.

7th. That as, notwithstanding the advantages in our favor, these countries have supplied Great Britain with the larger portion of wheat imported, so they will furnish a still larger proportion when the duties are reduced.

8th. That the market created by our domestic consumption is steadier, broader, and in every sense more profitable than any other.[75]

A discord of argument and counter-argument followed such Whig blasts.[76] Democratic editors sought to prove that on a basis

[74] 29 Congress, 1 session, *Congressional Globe*, App. 459–464. For a reply to this speech by a Virginia congressman, see *ibid.*, 402–411.

[75] See *Rochester Daily American*, Mar. 11, 1846; Alton *Telegraph and Democratic Review*, Mar. 21, 1846. The *Chicago Daily Journal* (w. ed.) of Mar. 24, 1846 commented as follows on Peel's bill: "It is too well known that we cannot supply England with wheat so cheap as can the merchants of Dantzic and the grain growing regions of the southeast of Europe. It is true Sir R. Peel proposes to admit our corn meal and buckwheat duty free. But are we assured that the shipments of such articles will prove sources of permanent traffic? It is hard to change the diet of thirty millions of people—to uproot the prejudice even in favor of rotten potatoes; and even if we do break down these walls of brass, cannot all these things be secured with the tariff as it is? . . ."

[76] This account rests on an examination of the following newspapers for the first half of 1846. Democratic: New York *Evening Post*, New York *Globe*, Buffalo *Courier*, Washington *Union*, Charleston *Mercury*, Pittsburgh *Democratic Union*, Columbus *Ohio Statesman*, Cincinnati *Enquirer*, Cincinnati *Herald*, In-

of current costs of production and distribution the West could compete successfully in the markets of England.[77] Whigs in answer pointed to the insignificance of American exports to England even via Canada and the difference between Baltic and American price reactions to Peel's measure.[78] The Democratic press appealed to national pride, maintaining with feeling that the manly and enlightened freeman of the American Republic could hold his own in any competition with European serfs. The reply of *Niles' Register* was that the American freeman could indeed compete provided he was willing to reduce his wants to the serf level.[79] Some few Democratic editors of weak faith confessed that Western wheat could not sell to advantage in the open British market, but argued that maize could, if only prejudices in the British Isles could be overcome.

However disunited and unpersuasive the Western Democratic press was on the tariff issue, it was unanimous on one score—that Peel's measure could have no effect on the Oregon question. A careful search has revealed not one Democratic journal in the whole section that had been aggressive on the Oregon question prior to the arrival of Peel's bill which subsequently changed its tone. Least mollified were the editorial "Western Warriors." Though some of them were pleased with Peel's measure they were loud in maintaining that the nation's birthright to the line of 54:40 must not be sold for a mess of pottage. Thus the editor of the *Illinois State Register*, though convinced that Peel's bill would benefit the West, warned all those who contemplated a partition of Oregon:

They may yet call upon the rocks and mountains to cover them from the wrath of an indignant people whose cherished Liberties will have received so terrible a blow: for what is it but a last final decision between those great principles of Monarchy and Democracy, as to

diana *State Sentinel*, Springfield *Illinois State Register*, *Chicago Democrat*, *Louisville Daily Democrat*, *Nashville Union*, *Jefferson Inquirer*, St. Louis *Missourian*, St. Louis *Missouri Reporter*. Whig: New York *Courier and Enquirer*, *New York Tribune*, Buffalo *Commercial Advertiser*, *Rochester Daily American*, Philadelphia *North American*, *Baltimore American*, *Baltimore Patriot*, *National Intelligencer*, *Cincinnati Chronicle*, *Cincinnati Gazette*, Chillicothe *Scioto Gazette*, *Chicago Daily Journal*, Alton *Telegraph and Democratic Review*, *New Orleans Commercial Bulletin*. Independent: *New York Journal of Commerce*, New York *Commercial Advertiser*.

[77] See in addition to the above DeBow's *Commercial Review*, 1:33–44.

[78] *National Intelligencer*, Mar. 10, 1846. See also London *Economist* for February and March, 1846.

[79] *Niles' Register*, 68:162 (May 17, 1845).

which shall take the firmest, deepest, widest foothold on the long coast of the Pacific? Divide by 49, and Democracy must crouch before Monarchy forever, on the western side of this mighty continent because the despotic flag of the latter will hold sway over two degrees, while the glorious ensign of Freedom can float over but one. Will posterity—the sons of Freedom—ever forgive a policy leading to such terrible results as this? They never will.[80]

The editor of the *Ohio Statesman*, a free-trade Democrat rejoicing in repeal, was unreconciled as late as June 15, 1846, to any partition of Oregon. He wrote:

Withered be the hand that dismembers Oregon, and palsied the tongue that consents to an act so treasonable, foul and unnatural. Let Freedom's holy banner be planted upon the farthest ice-bound cliff, to which our title is clear and unquestionable, and our answer to our arrogant foe be given in the words of Vasa—'Here will we take our stand.'[81]

Similarly unappeased by Peel's bill were the "Western Warriors" in Congress. One of their leaders was Senator Hannegan, an Indiana free-trade Democrat, an ardent expansionist, and an aspirant to the mantle of President Polk. On March 5, 1846, in a speech which attracted national notice, he assailed with impartial violence Whigs who defended, on the ground of Peel's bill, a compromise solution of the Oregon question, and a Southern Senator, Haywood, a personal friend of Polk, who had caustically described Oregon extremists as small men seeking high places and had asserted that the President was in no way committed to the extravagant policy of 54:40 Hannegan declared:

Let me tell the Senator from North Carolina, that, ... I would much sooner be found a small man seeking a high place, than the subservient, pliant, supple tool—the cringing flatterer, the fawning sycophant, who crouches before power, and hurries from its back stairs to bring before the Senate its becks, and nods, and wreathed smiles. The last steamer from Europe, it is said, puts this question in such a position, that for Oregon we can get free trade. Free trade I love dearly; but never will it be bought by me by the territory of my country. He who would entertain such an idea is a traitor to his country. I speak for myself, and my own section of the country. Free trade for a surrender of the ports and harbors on the Pacific? Never, sir; never. Whence this movement

[80] Springfield *Illinois State Register*, May 15, 1846.
[81] Columbus *Ohio Statesman*, June 15, 1846.

for free trade on the part of England? Does not every one know that she has been driven into this course by the outcries of starving millions? That she has been forced into this policy by the landowners, to save their lives from the knife of the midnight assassin, and their palaces from the torch of the prowling incendiary? But the West is to be provided for; it is to have a new and most profitable market. True it is, we in the west are born in the woods, but there are some among us who know a little, and, among other things, know that, long before our supplies could reach the British market, the granaries of the Baltic and the Black sea and the Mediterranean would have been poured into it to overflowing . . . . I have only to add, that so far as the whole tone, spirit, and meaning of the remarks of the Senator from North Carolina are concerned, if they speak the language of James K. Polk, James K. Polk has spoken words of falsehood, and with the tongue of a serpent.[82]

Such intransigeance was voiced despite Peel's bill by the whole group of "Western Warriors" in Congress. A week after the arrival of the bill the Washington correspondent of the *Manchester Guardian* wrote home:

The news of Sir Robert Peel's great economical scheme has not tended to allay the zeal of the western members for war as much as might have been expected. The constituents of these gentlemen, it must be remembered, are about the most reckless and dangerous population under the sun, just civilized enough to read the paltry village newspaper, which panders to their vanity. . . . This very day . . . Mr. Breese, senator from Illinois, Cass, from Michigan, Allen, from Ohio, and Hannegan, from Indiana, have addressed the senate in their usual strain, and endeavoured, as much as possible, to oppose the pacific views of the majority of that body. It would be impossible to name four states so likely to be benefited by Sir Robert Peel's measure as those which these persons represent; indeed, that measure seems to be framed expressly for them.[83]

When the Senate voted on June 18, 1846, to ratify the Oregon Treaty, the "Western Warriors" were still unrelenting. Though the country was then deep in the Mexican War, fourteen senators, all Democrats, reaffirmed their loyalty to 54:40 by voting against the Oregon Treaty. In the group were Allen of Ohio, Breese and

---

[82] 29 Congress, 1 session, *Congressional Globe*, 458–460. I have restored to the speech the sentence, "True it is, we in the west are born in the woods . . . ," which does not appear in the revised statement published in the *Congressional Globe*, but was reported in press accounts. See *Niles' Register*, 70:23, Mar. 14, 1846.

[83] *Manchester Guardian*, Mar. 18, 1846. The letter is dated Feb. 26, 1846.

Semple of Illinois, Hannegan and Bright of Indiana, Cass of Michigan, Dickinson of western New York, Cameron and Sturgeon of Pennsylvania, and Atchison of Missouri.[84] Allen was so outraged by the Oregon Treaty that in protest against it he resigned his chairmanship of the Senate committee on foreign relations.[85]

Thus the British free-trade prediction that American belligerence on the Oregon question would be calmed by a repeal of the Corn Laws was belied. The repeal bill failed as an American soothing syrup. It was swallowed by the East and by the South, with relish even, but they did not need the medicine. The West, where the Oregon fever raged, rejected it and fumed and sputtered as before. The thesis of the beneficent intervention of the bill in the American crisis thus dissolves. It is, in truth, the serving up of contemporary propaganda as history.

But the free-trade movement did contribute, within the British Isles, to the quieting of the Oregon crisis. It did so by removing political obstacles to a policy of concession. In earlier negotiations British governments had rejected again and again the proposal made by the American government to divide Oregon by a line drawn along the 49th parallel to the sea. Lord Aberdeen, Peel's foreign secretary, regarded this line as a reasonable basis of partition. As early as December, 1843, he was personally willing to accept it, stopping it short only at the coast so as not to sever Vancouver Island.[86] The cabinet, however, was less pliant. The territory between the 49th parallel and the Columbia River, which British governments had held out for, had become steadily more British since the first negotiations, as a result of Hudson's Bay Company occupation. A government surrendering it to the United States under such circumstances exposed itself to the Opposition charge of having abandoned British pride and honor. The chief obstacle to an amicable adjustment of the Oregon controversy during the critical years 1845–46 was this political hazard.[87]

The anti-Corn Law crusade served to lessen this hazard. It did so by releasing in England a spirit of international conciliation. The

[84] 29 Congress, 1 session, *Senate Journal*, 555.

[85] 29 Congress, 1 session, *Congressional Globe*, 972; see also Columbus *Ohio Statesman*, June 19, 1846.

[86] Aberdeen to Pakenham, Mar. 4, 1844. Aberdeen MSS, British Museum. See also Essays 8 and 9.

[87] *Hansard's* (3d series), 84:1466.

free-trade doctrine was a gospel of peace. Its postulates were international good will and the dependence of nations on each other. The anti-Corn Law League was a peace society potent in England beyond any of the professional peace societies of the period.[88] Its leaders were conspicuous internationalists, friendly in particular toward the United States. They contended, as illustrated elsewhere in this essay, that if the Corn Laws were repealed, the resulting trade would unite England and America in permanent bonds of concord—America would feed England, and England would clothe America. In the Oregon crisis the anti-Corn Law League turned the militant fervor of a triumphant crusade into channels of Anglo-American conciliation.

Louis McLane, American minister in London, wrote to his government early in February, 1846,

It is very obvious that the leading men of all parties uniting in favor of the [repeal] measure, regard it as destined to have great influence upon the intercourse with the United States; and in preserving and perpetuating amicable relations between the two countries. They do not hesitate to speak of it, and on all occasions to advocate it, as the

[88] New York *Evening Post*, Feb. 20, 1846. William Cullen Bryant commented in this issue on the League as follows:

"We have already spoken of the prodigious strength of the League in England, and the very strong support it received from public opinion. The League is not merely a combination of the hungry against the full-fed; it is the wealth of the manufacturers organized against the wealth of the landholders; but the people are on the side of the manufacturers, or rather the manufacturers are on the side of the people. . . .

"The influence which has wrought this great change [the bill abolishing the Corn Laws] is altogether an influence favorable to peace. The powerful association of which we have spoken is, in its tendencies and feelings, a kind of peace society, without peace its favorite theory cannot be put into practice; without peace it can make no perfect experiment of the benefits of free trade. Its object is to give the laboring classes of Britain the cheapest and most abundant sustenance, by drawing it directly from those parts of the world where the articles which form the food of mankind are produced in the greatest plenty and with the least cost. A war with the United States, to which the League looked for the principal supplies which are to feed the population of the United Kingdom, would wholly frustrate this object. We may trace in the language of Lord John Russell, who has so recently become a champion of free trade in corn, a def[er]ence to the views of the League on this very question of peace. He is no longer the belligerent Lord John Russell, inveighing against the weakness of the ministry in yielding to the claims of the United States. He finds, as he tells the House of Commons, that the state of the question has greatly changed, and reproves the haste with which the British minister rejected Mr. Polk's proposal for settling the boundary of Oregon by the forty-ninth parallel of latitude. He disapproves of putting by so unceremoniously the opportunity of peacefully adjusting the difference." See also J. C. Calhoun to G. Wilson, Mar. 24, 1845, in London *League*, May 3, 1845.

means of extending the interests of peace, and of making it more difficult to produce war; and, certainly, if the statesmen of England desire that the experiment of Free Trade should be successful, the surest, if not the only means of accomplishing that end, will be to cultivate peace with the United States. They would adopt the proposed scheme to very little purpose, if, for the sake of a degree of latitude on the Pacific, they should destroy the commercial intercourse of Great Britain with all the Atlantic States.[89]

But a more direct contribution of the anti-Corn Law crusade to the peaceful adjustment of the Oregon question was the realignment of British political parties it produced in the winter of 1845–46. The potato shortage and the famine scare lent to this change the drive of urgency. The shortage and the scare produced a crisis in the cabinet over the suspension of the Corn Laws, followed by the resignation of Peel. The formation of a Whig government was attempted by Lord John Russell. It failed as a result of dissension within the party over the nomination of Lord Palmerston to the Foreign Office. Sir Robert Peel was recalled. He reorganized his cabinet, and with the countenance of Lord John Russell proceeded to the abolition of the Corn Laws. Peelites and Whigs, neither strong enough to effect repeal alone, were thus brought, in the winter of 1845–46, into a temporary alliance against the embittered protectionists of the Conservative Party.

That alliance rendered possible an Oregon treaty of renunciation. It assured the ministry of Whig protection, at least until the issue of the Corn Laws could be settled. In the cabinet crisis Whigs had themselves been won over to a policy of Oregon concession. Their failure to form a government had grown out of Lord Palmerston's belligerence, as a member of the Opposition, in matters of foreign policy, which had produced the impression that the party was in the hands of a war faction. It was necessary for the party leaders to erase that impression if they were to be successful in taking over the government on Peel's impending fall. Lord John Russell, therefore, in two speeches delivered in Glasgow on January 12, 1846, warmly advocated a settlement of the Oregon question by concession.[90] In these speeches he made of the free-trade issue a bridge over which to transport himself and party from earlier belligerence

---

[89] McLane to Buchanan, Feb. 3, 1846, no. 34. Department of State, Despatches, England, v. 56, National Archives.
[90] *Manchester Guardian,* Jan. 17, 1846.

on the Oregon question to the new policy of peace. In response to an appeal from Edward Everett, former minister at the Court of St. James, for a party truce on the Oregon question, he gave Lord Aberdeen private assurance that he would make no objection to the ministry's surrendering to the United States the lower valley of the Columbia.[91] Lord John Russell bound his Whig associates by such a pledge, for they could not, without a party rift, publicly attack what he had privately approved.

As a result of these developments a settlement of the Oregon question became politically feasible. Early in January, 1846, Lord Aberdeen was actively preparing his public for a treaty of renunciation. By May the work was completed and the draft of the treaty was ready. Delay was occasioned by the difficulty of reopening negotiations which the American government had closed the preceding year. Lord Aberdeen chose to regard the reopening as accomplished by a notice from the American government announcing its decision to terminate the convention of joint occupation of Oregon at the end of a year. He despatched the completed draft of the treaty to Washington at once, which, without a single alteration, the American Senate accepted. Sir Robert Peel in his valedictory address to Parliament at the end of June, 1846, was able to announce triumphantly that the menacing Oregon problem had been solved.

By one of the accidents of history the crisis of the Oregon question was reached when England was in the midst of virtual revolution. The driving forces of the revolution were the anti-Corn Law crusade, the Irish potato failure, and the threat of famine. The Corn Laws were denounced by British urban workers in the panic months of 1845–46 as a brutal exploitation of poor by rich, a generator of famine in the interests of a landed aristocracy. The landed aristocracy, on the other hand, conceived of the Corn Laws as the bulwark of the British constitution, the removal of which meant the overturn of whatever was conservative in the British government. The free-trade agitation, the mass propaganda, the electioneering catchwords and phrases, the giant extra-legal organization of the League, the crusading temper of Leaguers and Radicals, the aligning of class against class, of city against country,

[91] Russell to Palmerston, Feb. 3, 1846. Palmerston MSS., Broadlands; see also Essay 9.

of proletariat and bourgeoisie against aristocracy, seemed to British Tories the beginning of the end of orderly government. And the Corn Law repeal seemed actual revolution. A revolution, in truth, it was, but a revolution of peace. To England it brought quietly a changed order of society; to America it helped to bring, though only as a British political by-product, the Oregon Treaty of 1846.

ESSAY 12 · SEA POWER AND THE OREGON BOUNDARY SETTLEMENT

AN EVER present element in the long Anglo-American controversy over the Oregon Country was British mastery of the seas. It was present in the wartime seizure of Astoria in 1813 which changed a nebulous rivalry of the fur trade into a problem in diplomacy. It reappeared as background in all the problem's subsequent negotiations. It is credited in some writings with having been a decisive element in solving the problem in 1845–46.

In the early nineteenth century when the Oregon problem emerged, British mastery of the seas had become not only an established fact but also a deeply embedded tradition. When, in 1798, the British admiral, Lord Nelson, reported home, after the Battle of the Nile: "Britannia still rules the waves," he was describing the tradition as well as his own destruction of the fleet of Napoleon which was to have been used in the conquest of India. When Napoleon came aboard a British naval vessel in 1815 as a prisoner of war to be taken to St. Helena, the tradition was strengthened.

By 1845 strategists in the British Admiralty were accustomed to reckoning British naval strength in terms, not of a single opponent, but of any combination of two in the world. The two most frequently so associated were France and the United States, which together had fought Great Britain during the American Revolution and during the War of 1812. In the crisis of the Oregon issue these two were thought of as probable allies again.

The sphere of the British navy in the event of such a war would have been the Atlantic Ocean and also the Pacific. On the Atlantic, British war vessels were expected to lay siege to American seaboard ports, and to ports on the Gulf of Mexico. They were expected to drive the commerce of the United States from every sea lane of the world. They were counted on to ferry British regulars to the interior of Canada and to keep them supplied. On the Great Lakes, merchant craft, converted to steam war vessels, and aided by Canadian auxiliaries, were expected to hold off American attacks. On the Pacific, three units of the Pacific squadron were kept, during the years 1845–1846, either in the waters of the Columbia River opposite Fort Vancouver or in Puget Sound. They were expected to inspire and rally British and Canadian settlers in the Oregon Country.

In the Oregon Country the Hudson's Bay Company had its own defense resources. It had a large contingent of Canadians employed at its posts and farms north of the Columbia, and it held the loyalty of others south of the river. Its retainers south of the river were a minority. But gunpowder supplies for all the Columbia River settlements were controlled by the Company, and could easily be replenished in case of war by sea, whereas American supplies would necessarily have come overland, and would have been difficult to transport. The Hudson's Bay Company had close relations with the Indians in the whole area. As for the American settlers south of the Columbia, though part were hostile to the Hudson's Bay Company, others were less so, and whether all would serve against the British, in case of a war, was uncertain. Some settlers would have been conditioned in their loyalties by the realization that reinforcements must come an immense distance, across a country of deserts, soaring mountains, and Indians.

In a boundary dispute a government possessing great naval strength can put it to peaceful use simply by exhibiting it. It can do so to overawe an aggressor. In the Oregon dispute the British government is said to have exhibited its strength pointedly to Polk, deterring him from aggression and inducing him to agree to a compromise settlement. Such a thesis has had currency in American historical writing for many years, and it is simpler than the multiple explanations of the settlement offered in these essays.[1]

The thesis rests on the premise that in 1844–1846 a "serious" claim to All Oregon from 42° to 54° 40′ was made by the "United States" for the first time. The claim is said to have been pressed aggressively until British sea power was brandished, when the

[1] Julius W. Pratt, "James Knox Polk and John Bull," *Canadian Historical Review*, XXIV (1943), 341–349, and *History of United States Foreign Policy* (New York, 1955), ch. 14, and *Ibid.* (1965), ch. 11.

pressure subsided, and a compromise was accepted. A question is raised by this thesis as to how "serious" the claim was that Polk and others made to All Oregon in the years 1844–1846.

In 1844 as a candidate for the Democratic vice-presidential nomination Polk pronounced in a public letter in favor of the annexation of Texas and the maintenance of the authority of the United States in the whole Oregon Territory. He declared that the fixed policy of the United States should be against permitting Great Britain "to plant a colony or hold dominion over any portion of the people or territory of either."[2] This pronouncement served the Democratic convention in framing an All Oregon platform and in nominating Polk, and it was a factor in Polk's election to the presidency. In his Inaugural Address he gave an impression of favoring All Oregon. He quoted the very language of the platform.[3] Whether this was a "serious" claim by the "United States" depends upon the definition given to the words "serious" and "United States." The language could have been a continuation in the Inaugural of party politics or it could have been a tactic, used against the British, in an Oregon negotiation then under way in Washington, a negotiation passed on by Tyler, as the new administration began.

Several months after the Inaugural, Polk, through his Secretary of State, James Buchanan, offered the British a settlement which had been offered again and again by American presidents in preceding negotiations—the line of parallel 49° from the Rocky Mountains to the sea. He did not offer a right to the free navigation of the Columbia River south of 49°, which earlier American negotiators had offered. Free navigation was needed by the Hudson's Bay Company to supply interior posts in the region now British Columbia. The offer was rejected by the British negotiator at once, though it could have been taken for reference to his government. It was withdrawn by Polk. Subsequently he refused to resubmit it, though asked by the British government to do so. The negotiation ended.

In his first annual message to Congress of December 2, 1845, the President used language that could have been construed as a demand

---

[2] John S. Jenkins, *James Knox Polk* (Auburn, 1851), 122.
[3] J. D. Richardson, ed., *Messages and Papers of the Presidents, 1789–1897* (Washington, 1907), IV, 381.

for All Oregon. But it could also have been construed as merely a routine assertion that the American claim to All Oregon was better than that of the British. He said, concerning the scuttled negotiation: "Our title to the whole Oregon territory was asserted and, as is believed, maintained by irrefragable facts and arguments." He recommended that Congress give a "notice" of termination of the joint occupation agreement of 1827. He declared that when this agreement had ended "we shall have reached a period when the national rights in Oregon must either be abandoned or firmly maintained. That they cannot be abandoned without a sacrifice of both national honor and interest is too clear to admit of doubt."[4] He asked Congress to offer donations of land to American citizens who would migrate to the Oregon Country, or who had already done so. His message was followed by a Congressional debate over giving "notice," destined to run to nearly the end of April 1846. At the same time the President rejected British proposals for arbitration, gave hope to the 54° 40′ elements, and frowned on compromise. Early in January 1846 he remarked to a Southern Democrat, who asked him to restrain extremists in his party, "the only way to treat John Bull was to look him straight in the eye," and that "if Congress faultered or hesitated in their course, John Bull would immediately become arrogant and more grasping. . . . Such had been the history of the Brittish nation in all their contests . . . for the last two hundred years."[5]

The debate in Congress on "notice" was marked by demands for All Oregon from extremists and this created anxiety in circles desiring peace. But it was regarded in other circles as just a forensic display. In view of the presence in the Senate of a large majority opposed to a war over All Oregon, of the overwhelming majorities by which Congress ultimately passed a form of "notice" phrased as an invitation to the British to reopen negotiations, and of Polk's vacillations on the issue, any premise that All Oregon to 54° 40′ was "seriously claimed by the United States" in the years 1844–1846 seems not a safe one from which to proceed.

During the years 1844–1846 the British government virtually ignored agitations in Congress for All Oregon. It seems to have agreed with the views of members of Congress who pronounced

[4] *Ibid.*, 397.
[5] Milo M. Quaife, ed., *Diary of James K. Polk,* (Chicago, 1910), I, 155.

them mere politics.[6] A flurry of back-talk did come from Parliament in response to the Inaugural. Sir Robert Peel, the Prime Minister, and Lord Aberdeen, his Secretary for Foreign Affairs, declared that Great Britain also had rights in the Oregon Country which were "clear and unquestionable" and was prepared to maintain them. Lord John Russell, speaking for the Opposition, expressed similar views and declared the Inaugural a "blustering pronouncement."[7] The London *Times* did, however, shrewdly observe on December 2, 1845, in anticipation of Polk's recommendation to terminate the joint occupation: "President Polk looks to the conservative and pacific check of the Senate as the means of stopping his own headlong career of excitement at home and aggression abroad."[8] And Lord Aberdeen, two days later, wrote the King of the Belgians, by way of the British minister, a quieting note: "We must make great allowance for the situation of the President, and the difficulties with which he has to contend from the excited feelings of his own friends and the American public."[9] However, the British ministry, as an insurance against any emergencies, increased its navy. It added 8 per cent to a force already overpowering.

On February 21, 1846, Polk received from Louis McLane, American minister in London, a despatch written on February 3. This is said to have been a shock to him, restoring reason.[10] The despatch referred to extensive naval preparations being made by the British. It reported Aberdeen as sorrowfully admitting that he could no longer successfully withstand preparations for hostilities, and as confessing that the enlarged British armament might have to be used not only defensively but offensively against the United States. McLane believed Aberdeen had been alarmed by Polk's abrupt ending of the negotiation, the rejection of arbitration, and the temper of the debate in Congress. McLane's despatch is said to have so shaken Polk that his Secretary of State was directed "to rush

---

[6] *Cong. Globe*, 29 Cong., 1 Sess., 245 (Jan. 26, 1846).

[7] See Essay, 9, pp. 273–274.

[8] London *Times*, Dec. 2, 1845. Proposals to serve notice of termination of the joint occupation had been under discussion in Congress in the Tyler administration.

[9] Aberdeen to Sir Hamilton Seymour, Dec. 4, 1845, Aberdeen Papers, British Museum.

[10] McLane to Buchanan, Feb. 3, 1846, No. 34, Department of State, Despatches, England, Vol. 56, National Archives.

off a note to McLane in which the Secretary almost begged for a compromise settlement."[11]

If Polk's demand for All Oregon was truly "serious," and if a decision to forego it in favor of a much more modest settlement followed McLane's warning, the thesis of the persuasiveness of naval power could be tentatively accepted. It was indeed accepted during the Mexican War by critics of Polk, who charged that he had shown himself pliable when faced by Great Britain but adamant when facing Mexico.[12] But before it is finally accepted, an inquiry must be made as to whether Polk really did reverse a "serious" stand in 1846.

A calendar of events is useful in developing this inquiry. On the calendar the initial entry would relate to the naming of McLane as minister to England on June 16, 1845, three and a half months after the famous Inaugural. McLane was privately known to be a believer in the settlement of the Oregon dispute by a line based on the 49th parallel. He accepted the London assignment with reluctance, for he had a good post as president of the Baltimore and Ohio Railroad. He took the appointment for only the time needed to bring an Oregon negotiation to a close.[13] The negotiation,

[11] Pratt, *History of United States Foreign Policy* (1955) 215. In the 1965 edition of this work a less emphatic phrase is used (p. 110).

[12] Charges of this sort were made in Congress and abroad throughout the Mexican War.

[13] The following letter from John P. Kennedy, a nationally known Whig Congressman from Baltimore, to a fellow Whig, Robert C. Winthrop, casts light on Polk's Oregon intentions. Kennedy was an important figure in the Board of Directors of the Baltimore and Ohio Railroad, of which McLane was president, and he gives inside information as to the terms on which McLane was given leave of absence to accept his appointment to London:

Polk has done a very wise and a very odd thing in the appointment of McLane. No man from this country has a better standing with the present British Cabinet than he, and I am sure he will be received with great favor. He is personally on the best terms of intimate acquaintance with the leaders of this ministry. So far the appointment is wise. The odd part is, and this is a matter not to be quoted as from me: McLane is against Polk's Oregon, is the least possible in the world of a Locofoco; a friend to *a* Bank; in favor of the distribution of the Proceeds . . . all queer enough to bring him into favor with this very rigidly Locofocoish admn. He is favorable to Texas, and that is the only point I know him to have in common with Polk. Notwithstanding the attempt to conceal it, he goes on a *special* mission for the Oregon affair—to leave England as soon as the chief business is concluded, or to remain as the permanent minister. He has already expressed his option to retire when that *chief concern* is settled, and upon this intimation we have made merely a *pro tem* President of the Rail Road in his place. He hopes to be back to resume his duties next winter, or in the spring following. He goes with a view *to make an effort to preserve the peace of the two nations.* You may gather from this

already under way in Washington as he was leaving, was expected to continue, with mere assists from London, in case of obstructions. The McLane understanding with Polk was that a settlement on the basis of partition at the 49th parallel would be accepted by the American government, and this understanding was written out in the initial instructions: "The President," Buchanan wrote, "doubts whether the judgment of the civilized world would be in favor of a war waged for a comparatively worthless territory north of 49 degrees, which his predecessors had over and over again offered to surrender to Great Britain, provided she would yield her pretensions to the country south of that latitude." Indeed a concession might be made even of the small "cap" of Vancouver Island, south of this latitude, which was of special value to Great Britain. But no right to the free navigation of the Columbia south of 49° which previous Presidents would have conceded would be yielded.[14] This continued to be McLane's understanding of the President's wishes throughout his stay in England, as he made clear in an important public address on his return to New York from his mission in August 1846.[15]

On November 5, 1845, after negotiations in Washington had ended in failure, Buchanan wrote McLane that if the British should desire a new negotiation and should submit an offer, it would be respectfully received. If it was found to contain the basis for a

---

what the chief object committed to him is. He had a long interview with Polk some days ago, told him how very indiscreet and absurd the Legislation of the H.R. was last session on the bill to occupy Oregon, repelled the notion that our claim was not one of very fair dispute; is in favor of the 49th degree, and, if need be, of arbitration. If he goes out with such a chart as this, whatever may be said of Polk's equivocation or his magnanimity, as the case may be, there will be very little risk of a quarrel. The reluctance to acknowledge the *special* mission is but a clumsy homage to the Locofoco Convention of May 27th [1844], whilst the actual design to treat on the question is a visible contempt of the principles of the party—and the whole matter is so shabbily contrived as to gain the administration no applause from either side.
John P. Kennedy to Robert C. Winthrop, June 27, 1845, Winthrop Papers, M.H.S. Kennedy represented the state of Maryland on the Board of Directors of the railroad company for two terms from 1837 to 1847. Information as to the Company's arrangement with McLane and his personal views on the Oregon issue leaked out to the Whig press in New York City and elsewhere. It produced increased scepticism as to the honesty of Polk's Oregon pronouncements. New York *Commercial Advertiser*, Oct. 29, 1845; Buffalo *Commercial Advertiser*, Oct. 31, 1845; *New York Courier and Enquirer*, Nov. 19, 1845.
[14] Buchanan to Louis McLane, July 12, 1845, in John B. Moore, ed., *Works of James Buchanan* (Philadelphia, 1908-11), VI, 186-94.
[15] *Niles' Register*, LXXI (1846), 44-45 (Sept. 19, 1846).

negotiation, it would be sent to the Senate for "previous advice." If the Senate, by a two-thirds vote, should advise the President to go forward with it to a negotiation, he would go forward. By himself, he would agree to accept nothing but the whole of Oregon. He would conform his views to those of the Senate, however.[16] This was by no means an adamant 54° 40′ position.

On December 24, 1845, the President discussed the Oregon question with Senator William Allen, a leader of the 54° 40′ element in Congress. A suggestion was made by Allen that Polk submit any proposal the British might make based on the line of 49° to the Senate for "previous advice."[17] The hope of Allen apparently was that such a proposal would serve as a target for 54° 40′ oratory. The President agreed only to the propriety of taking Senate advice.

On January 29, 1846, Buchanan wrote McLane that though the President would not of himself accept from the British any proposal short of surrender of All Oregon, he would submit to the Senate for advice the same proposal of partition he had made to the British in the summer of 1845. The President was clearly preparing to share responsibility for accepting less than 54° 40′ with the Senate, which was already then known to be dominated by elements wishing the issue to be settled by a compromise at 49°.

On February 24, 1846, Allen, at a conference with Polk, urged him to reject summarily any British offer which might be made short of a surrender of All Oregon. Polk reminded the Senator of their earlier conversation, in which he had agreed to submit to the Senate for advice any proposal based on 49°. The President thereafter, throughout the notice debate, resisted the efforts of 54° 40′ extremists to drive him into publicly coming out for 54° 40′.[18]

On February 26, five days after the arrival of the McLane despatch which is alleged to have shaken the President out of his course, Buchanan made reply to it in a despatch differing little from the course Polk had been pursuing. He outlined the terms of a British offer which the President would feel free to ask advice on from the Senate. He gave McLane discretion as to informing the

[16] Buchanan to McLane, Nov. 5, 1845, in Moore, ed., *Works of Buchanan*, VI, 289–290.

[17] Quaife, ed., *Diary of Polk*, I, 139.

[18] *Ibid.*, 248–249; Moore, ed., *Works of Buchanan*, VI, 289–290, 341–342, 366–368; see also Essay 13.

British of these terms. The President's terms were: the line of 49° as a basis from the Rocky Mountains to the sea, and no reservation by the British of a right to navigate the Columbia River south of 49°. The same despatch gave McLane information of the President's rejection of the latest British proposal to submit the Oregon issue to an arbitration. The despatch differs from preceding ones only in that it authorized McLane to make known to the British the terms the President would agree to send to the Senate for advice, an authorization not exercised by McLane for months.[19]

In appraising the effect on Polk of the February 3 despatch it is useful to remember that as early as September 1845 McLane had been sending warnings of British naval preparations to the President.[20] The newspapers of the United States, England, and France were full of the subject in the fall and winter of 1845–46. The only uncertainty was whether the preparations were intended for use against France or the United States. On December 13, 1845, Buchanan wrote McLane that the President had information as to these preparations from a variety of sources which he could not disregard. McLane was to inquire of Aberdeen as to their meaning.[21] In reply McLane reported on January 3 that Aberdeen had frankly said the preparations had been begun before relations with the United States had become as disturbing as they then were, but that they now looked to the possibility of a rupture over the Oregon issue.[22] This was a month prior to the despatch of February 3, which is credited with having abruptly reversed the President's course.

Logic as well as the calendar is useful in appraising the effect on Polk of McLane's February 3 despatch. The enormous superiority of British naval power over American was known to the world. Even an attempt to meet it did not seem feasible to Polk. In the annual message of December 1845, he recommended no increases in appropriations for the Navy. Indeed the Navy estimates were actually lowered. It is inconceivable that an 8 per cent British

---

[19] Moore, ed., *Works of Buchanan*, VI, 377–383.

[20] McLane to Buchanan, Sept. 18, 1845, No. 5, Department of State, Despatches, England, Vol. 56, National Archives.

[21] Buchanan to McLane, Dec. 13, 1845, No. 20, in Moore, ed., *Works of Buchanan*, VI, 341–342.

[22] McLane to Buchanan, Jan. 3, 1846, No. 30, Department of State, Despatches, England, Vol. 56, National Archives. McLane's warnings in this despatch were quite as impressive as those in his despatch of a month later.

increase piled upon an already overwhelming strength could have upset Polk so much as to have induced him to reverse a predetermined course. If it should be said that the naval building of the British revealed a determination not to be intimidated by the United States, the answer would be that Peel, Aberdeen, and Russell had already made that clear at the time of the Polk Inaugural.

On March 17, 1846, an inquiry was sent the President by the Senate, whether in his opinion increases in the naval and military forces of the United States were necessary in view of foreign problems. It was sent at the instance of the Whigs who were puzzled by the President's course. The President replied that increases were necessary. He took advantage of the occasion to say that American purposes would be defensive if the British made war over Oregon.[23] Shortly afterwards he wrote to his brother, to whom he had given a consular post at Naples: "That power [Great Britain] for the last two centuries never was known to do justice to any country with which she had a controversy when that country assumed a supplicatory attitude, or was on her knees before her. The only way to treat John Bull is to treat him firmly and look him straight in the eye."[24]

Late in April a weary Congress deflated the All Oregon orators. It adopted, under Senate leadership, by overwhelming majorities, a form of notice couched in conciliatory terms—terms which could be regarded by the British government as an invitation to initiate a new negotiation. This notice Polk elected to send to London,

[23] Richardson, ed., *Messages and Papers*, IV, 426–428. The London *Times* noted on March 9, 1846, that the United States had a total army strength of 9847 men, exclusive of 781 officers. It considered this a small force with which to defend home territories and invade a country 2000 miles off. However, quoting the American *Army Register* for 1843, it noted that the militia forces of the United States might have excited the envy of Xerxes or Bonaparte:

> This multitudinous host is commanded by 627 generals, 2670 general staff officers, 13,813 field officers, 44,938 company officers, being in all 62,205 officers. Nor are these numbers at all excessive, when we learn that the forces under their command consist of 1,385,645 men! For the purposes of defence against a foreign invasion we have no doubt that these American citizens would exert themselves creditably . . . But we have no hesitation in saying that to bring an efficient army of even 30,000 men into the field, prepared to march beyond their own frontiers, is the most arduous task which has ever devolved upon the Federal Government of the United States.

[24] Polk to William H. Polk, March 27, 1846, Polk Letter Press Book, Polk Papers, Library of Congress.

though he had been given discretion to withhold it. It drew from the British ministry a proposal in the formulation of which McLane cooperated. The proposal was to partition the Oregon Country by the 49th parallel to Admiralty Inlet, the line then to follow the Strait of Juan de Fuca to the sea. The right to navigate the Columbia south of 49° was to be reserved to the Hudson's Bay Company.

The President decided, on receiving the proposal early in June, to refer it to the Senate for "advice" as to whether it formed a basis for a negotiation. He first took the precaution of extracting from the Cabinet unanimous approval for this course. Next he took care to preserve his front of boldness when submitting the proposal by declaring that if the Senate should withhold its advice, he would reject the proposal.[25] He seemed confident that the advice of the Senate would be to accept it, which would absolve him of any charge of having betrayed his 54° 40′ friends. In view of all this it is very likely that, first and last, when he wrote about looking John Bull "straight in the eye," he was thinking, not of 54° 40′, but of the line he had proposed at the outset—49°.

Among other theses advanced to explain the Oregon settlement, one is antithetical to that of British mastery of the seas. It is the thesis of a French challenge to British sea power at just the time of the Oregon crisis. It proceeds from the premise that an armaments race between France and Britain was on, that steam-propelled warships had revolutionized old concepts of naval power, that a cross-channel invasion of England, in the event of an Anglo-French rupture, might occur, and that an alliance of France and the United States would follow. All this is said to have created great alarm in England and to have induced the British government to send the United States terms of an Oregon settlement "just short of an obvious surrender."[26] The very oppositeness of this thesis to the one just reviewed is intriguing. But before it is accepted the process of testing premises must be renewed.

The premise that British sea power was seriously challenged by the French in this era is best examined in terms of statistics gathered

[25] Quaife, ed., *Diary of Polk*, I, 461–462; Richardson, ed., *Messages and Papers*, IV, 449–450.
[26] John S. Galbraith, "France as a Factor in the Oregon Negotiations," *Pacific Northwest Quarterly*, XLIV (1953), 69–73, and *The Hudson's Bay Company as an Imperial Factor, 1821–1869* (Berkeley, 1957), 233, 246–247.

in 1846 for the Senate by George Bancroft, American Secretary of the Navy. In the statistics Great Britain, France, and the United States are compared in their over-all naval strength, and also in the single category of steam-propelled warships.

NAVAL ARMAMENTS—SAIL AND STEAM—1845–46[27]

	Vessels commissioned		Vessels bldg. or under repair		Totals		
	Vessels	Guns	Vessels	Guns	Vessels	Guns	Men
Britain	332	4,583	304	13,098	636	17,681	40,000
France	215	4,293	131	4,635	346	8,928	27,554
U.S.A.	47	1,155	30	1,190	77	2,345	8,724

STEAM WAR VESSELS 1845–46[28]

	Vessels commissioned		Building or under repair		Totals	
	Vessels	Guns	Vessels	Guns	Vessels	Guns
Britain	90	390	51	308	141 +58	698
France	54	349	14	81	68 +32	430
U.S.A.	3	23	2	4	5	39

The superiority of the British navy over the combined French and American navies stands out in these statistics. The same is true in the single category of steam-propelled warships. But the figures understate British superiority inasmuch as they exhibit only quantities of vessels. Qualitatively the British navy was still more superior, in percentages of large and newer steam craft and in heavier ordnance.[29] On the other hand, the British navy was more widely dis-

[27] *Sen. Docs.*, 29 Cong., 1 Sess. (Serial 473), No. 187.

[28] The supplementary figure, 58, in the British column includes steam vessels in the Indian navy and "contract mail steamers" under the control of the Admiralty in wartime. The comparable French figure, 32, is the number of Mediterranean and trans-Atlantic packets of like category. The foreign sources used by Bancroft were the monthly British *United Service Magazine* which showed the world-wide distribution of the British navy and army, and the French *Annales Maritimes et Coloniales*. The latter was partly official and partly unofficial and was voluminous. The official portion for 1845 was one volume; the "unofficial," four. For 1846, official, one volume; "unofficial," three.

[29] An illuminating comment on Prince de Joinville's Mediterranean squadron, the élite of the French navy, was made by the *United Service Magazine* in its May 1846 number. After showing that the average age of the six larger vessels

persed than the French, having a wider empire to guard. A lesser percentage of strength was concentrated in home waters. In any one locale a momentary superiority of the French navy might have existed. As for the American steam navy, it consisted of five craft of which two only were seagoing.

In the category of merchant vessels the British were less in the lead. Great Britain had 3,007,000 tons; the United States, 2,417,000; France, 839, 600 tons. In any war a merchant marine would serve as a carrier, but would also be a burden to protect from hostile warcraft and from privateers.[30]

French building of steam warships reflected the needs of an expanding empire as well as of guarding the home front in case of war. The French empire lay chiefly in Northwest Africa (Algeria and Senegal) but it also embraced holdings on the coast of West Africa, on Madagascar, in Oceania, and remnants of former possessions in the Western Hemisphere and India.

French naval building reflected also a national aspiration to escape domination by the British, which expansionists in France complained of with special bitterness. Expansionists in France, as in the United States, believed that the British were the oppressors of the world and their navy, the whip used. In the case of the French this feeling came out of a very old background. It came out of half a millenium of wars and rumors of wars. It came out of a record of frequent defeat at British hands. What French nationalists relished were the exceptions—French victories over Britain in the War of the American Revolution, and French domination over Europe in the Napoleonic wars.

The most recent record of British domination was that of 1840–1841, when the two powers had stood in dangerous confrontation over the Eastern Question. The British had supported the Sultan of Turkey against an ambitious Egyptian viceroy, nominally a vassal, Mehemet Ali, who was threatening to overwhelm his master. The French—conquerors of Algeria—had found advantage in patron-

---

in the squadron was 29 years, it went on: "If it be true, then, as many naval persons of experience allege, that no ship of war which has been at sea upwards of 10 years is fit to be led into the line, or to withstand the stormy elements, we may conclude, from this specimen of the *élite* of the French navy, that the whole is not of a very formidable character. . . ." *United Service Magazine*, 1846, part 2, 106.

[30] *Sen. Docs.*, 29 Cong., 1 Sess. (Serial 473), No. 187, p. 19.

izing Ali. The British Foreign Minister, Lord Palmerston, had pressed the confrontation zestfully. So had, on the other side, Louis Adolphe Thiers. These two would have turned Europe into a cockpit over the issue. The British had found allies among the northern powers of Europe. In the end the French king, Louis Philippe, dismissed Thiers and replaced him by the peace-loving François P. G. Guizot. In England, the Melbourne ministry, which had backed Palmerston, was replaced by the Peel ministry, in which Lord Aberdeen was Foreign Minister.

The aim of these two was to transform Anglo-French relations. It was to build an *entente cordiale,* to replace ancient antagonisms by relations of neighborliness and mutual support in external affairs. This coincided with the long-run interests and desires of the French king, who saw in it the road to French prosperity, to recovery of French prestige, and also to stability for his throne and dynasty. But the *entente cordiale* hardly got more than lip service from the restless in France. It was too sharp a break with the past. It interfered too seriously with French aspirations of overseas growth and with French concepts of grandeur. It was hardly more popular in England. In the period 1841–1846 the Opposition in both countries seized upon problems, as they arose, to challenge it and to embarrass their governments.

One problem so used was the desire of the British government to suppress the maritime slave trade. The slave trade was outlawed by virtually all governments in the western world, but was carried on clandestinely under false flags. A Quintuple Treaty was provisionally approved in 1841 by five European states under the leadership of the British, granting mutual rights of peacetime visit and search in the case of vessels suspected of being slavers, and seizure of those found carrying cargoes of slaves. It was agreed to by the French in negotiation, and was submitted to the French Chamber of Deputies early in 1842 for ratification. It was attacked by the Opposition as granting rights to the British to supervise French commerce in peacetime, as capitulating to British supremacy at sea, and as humiliating to France. The treaty was overwhelmingly defeated amid reproaches to Guizot for having even considered it. The reproaches were continued thereafter to the end of Guizot's political career.

In the same period strains were produced in the fabric of the *entente cordiale* by the reawakened French interest in expanding its overseas empire. One nearly tore the fabric apart. This was the Tahiti affair. Tahiti was one of the Society Islands in the South Pacific. In the 1830's it was the scene of a rivalry between French and British missionaries. The native Queen, Pomare, influenced by a British missionary, George Pritchard (who was also a British consul), denied entrance in 1836 to French priests wishing to get into the field. This led to controversy and in 1842 to the establishment of a French protectorate over Tahiti. In the following year a French admiral, Du Petit Thouars, without instructions from home, annexed the island and deposed the Queen. Soon afterward the British consul was seized, on the ground of encouraging disaffection, and was deported. Intense excitement was roused in British missionary circles by these happenings. More oratory and national feeling flowed in Parliament and in the press over the Tahiti issue than had flowed on the Oregon issue for a quarter century. Aberdeen was obliged to demand from the French government an apology and an indemnity for Pritchard. Guizot made concessions. He disavowed annexation, reinstated the Queen, recalled Thouars, and paid an indemnity out of executive funds to the deported missionary. This in turn led to furious assaults on him by the Opposition as a betrayer of French dignity.

In North Africa, Algeria was another scene of friction. In the 1830's an occupation of the seaboard region was achieved by the French. In the 1840's this was extended inland. It was desperately resisted by an emir of ability, Abd-el-Kader. In 1843 the emir suffered defeat and took refuge with the Sultan of Morocco. The Sultan, in response to feeling among his subjects, gave him support. This led to war between Morocco and France, and to the bombardment of Tangier and Mogador by a French fleet, led by a younger son of Louis Philippe, the ambitious Prince de Joinville. On land a brilliant victory was won over the Moroccans by General Bugeaud at Isly, which drew forth joys in France reminiscent of those of the Napoleonic era.

But Morocco was a sphere of British interest, and a French campaign into it caused anxiety in London. Under British influence the Sultan was brought to cease his support of Abd-el-Kader, and the war came to an end. In the ensuing settlement the French retained their hold on Algeria, but left Morocco intact. The settlement seemed to the Opposition in France to be another case of subservience to the British. Guizot barely survived a hostile motion, triggered by these issues, in the Chamber of Deputies early in 1845.[31]

A notable pamphlet was injected into these controversies. It was a discussion of the state of the naval forces of France. It appeared in Paris in the spring of 1844. It was anonymous but its anonymity was easily penetrated. It was from the pen of the Prince de Joinville. It emphasized the revolution which had occurred in preceding decades in the fighting ships of the world as a result of the advent of steam-propelled warships. The revolution gave France the opportunity, the Prince observed, to reach, without too great a strain, her old respectability as a naval power. Taken for granted by the Prince was that the new navy would be employed in future wars chiefly against the British. The low state of the French steam navy was deplored. As compared with that of the British, the Prince wrote, that of France was merely nominal. As a matter of strategy, the Prince believed new French units should be concentrated in home waters. This would open opportunities for invasion of the British Isles in case of war, as Napoleon had planned.

The distinguished authorship and challenging content of the pamphlet produced a sensation in Europe and in America. The piece was reprinted immediately in the *Revue des Deux Mondes* for May 1844,[32] and it appeared in various translated forms in England and in the United States.[33]

The effect of the pamphlet was to heighten in France and in England pressures already existing for new, steam-propelled warships, especially of largest size and efficiency. This is the normal effect of navalist propaganda. It would doubtless have followed even a less distinguished pen. Side effects were increased tensions in the two countries and increased fears in each of attack from

[31] For an amplification of this account see Frederick Merk, *Monroe Doctrine and American Expansionism, 1843–1849* (New York, 1966), ch. 3. See *ibid.*, p. 90, for Guizot's assurance to the Deputies on January 21, 1846, that in any Anglo-American war over the Oregon Country France would remain neutral.

[32] "Note sur L'État des Forces Navales de La France," *Revue des Deux Mondes*, VI (1844), 708–746. Joinville was the butt of ridicule for years in *Punch* following the appearance of this article. As late as January, 1848, he was the hero of its version of the Bayeux Tapestry on "Crossynge ye Brytyshe Channele," with pages of pictures accompanied by appropriate verse. *Punch*, 1848, pp. 33–38.

[33] The American edition was Prince de Joinville, *Remarks on the State of the Naval Forces of France* (Boston, 1844).

the other. The pamphlet was savagely reviewed in England, which in turn called forth savage replies in France, and comments hardly less savage on the policies of the British government. In each country a virtual panic followed, as Aberdeen and Guizot observed in discouragement.

Palmerston, however, stimulated the panic as much as possible. In a speech in the Commons on July 30, 1845, he pointed out that France had a standing army of 340,000 men and a national guard of a million men. This would, he thought, be a matter of no great concern to England, if France were separated from her by an impassable barrier, by a channel that could not be crossed, or if France were without a navy, but none of these was any longer the case:

In the first place, France has a fleet equal to ours. I do not speak of the number of vessels actually in existence, but of the fleet in commission, and half-commission, in both of which respects, the fleet of France is equal to that of this country. But again the Channel is no longer a barrier. Steam navigation has rendered that which was before impassable by a military force nothing more than a river passable by a steam bridge. France has steamers capable of transporting 30,000 men, and she has harbours inaccessible to any attack, in which these steamers may collect, and around which, on the land side large bodies of men are constantly quartered. Those harbours are directly opposite to our coast, and within a few hours voyage of the different landing places on the coast of England.

Palmerston also emphasized that the regular army of England was less than 50,000 men, of which 20,000 were permanently stationed in Ireland. Immediate reforms in the training of the militia seemed to him essential. "I venture to state that no country in Europe is in such a state of defenselessness as England is at the present moment."[34]

These assertions caught Peel on the floor of the Commons unarmed with statistics. He answered as best he could that England was in better shape to repel aggression than when Palmerston had been in office. He thought "the demonstration which we could make of our steam navy was one which would surprise the world; and, as the noble Lord had spoken of steam bridges, he would remind him that there were two parties who could play at making them." He did favor special precautions, however, which had

[34] *Hansard's Parliamentary Debates*, LXXXII, 1223–1228 (July 30, 1845).

already been taken, for the defense of naval arsenals and dockyards. He believed England would be unwilling to maintain, on any permanent footing, a standing army of 100,000 or 200,000 men.[35]

The confidence in England's security expressed by Peel was, in part, a pose. It was intended to neutralize Palmerston's irresponsible assertions that England was in a defenseless state which might suggest adventures to equally irresponsible elements in France. Privately Peel was disturbed by the idea that England might be invaded or at least that a hit-run attack by the French on British dockyards and naval arsenals might be undertaken. His rejoinder in the Commons drew confidential criticism from no less a quarter in the ministry than the Duke of Wellington. The Duke was a firm believer in massive preparations for defense, a reflection of his fighting career. He wished such preparations made for the entire British empire regardless of cost, but especially for the homeland. He let Peel know that he thought Palmerston's warnings were not without merit.[36] Suspicions as to the good faith and peaceful purposes of England's partner in the *entente cordiale* were entertained by him as well as by Peel. Both were troubled by the ill will of the public in France, by the lax rein which the government kept on its aggressive subordinates in the armed services in Oceania and in Algeria, by the possibility that the French king, who was seventy-three years of age, would die and be succeeded by an aggressive heir disposed to yield to the nationalist impulses of his public, and especially by the uproar, never subsiding, over the Tahiti affair. Both overestimated the actual naval construction occurring in France in response to Joinville's agitations. Peel was joined in these suspicions and fears by his Home Secretary, Sir James R. Graham, a close friend, who had once been First Lord of the Admiralty.[37]

[35] *Ibid.*, 1228–1233 (July 30, 1845).

[36] The Duke's letter and memorandum, together with Peel's reply, appear in Charles S. Parker, ed., *Sir Robert Peel* (London, 1891–99), III, 201–219. See also Wellington to Peel, Aug. 12, 1845, Peel Papers, British Museum; and Wellington memorandum, Sept. 10, 1845, Lord John Russell Papers, Public Record Office, London.

[37] Charles S. Parker, ed., *Life and Letters of Sir James Graham* (London, 1907), II, 17. Graham had been First Lord of the Admiralty in the Grey ministry in the early 1830's. For an illuminating exchange of letters between Aberdeen and Lord Cowley, British ambassador to Paris, as to alarmist reports the latter had sent to the Duke of Wellington (his brother) and to Graham, concerning French preparations, see Aberdeen to Lord Cowley, Sept. 30, 1845, and Lord Cowley to Aberdeen, Oct. 3, 1845, Aberdeen Papers, British Museum.

As the excitement in France accelerated, so did naval preparations in England. The naval supplies voted by Parliament early in 1845 rose to £7,304,000, an increase of over £700,000. Expenditures beyond even these were authorized by Peel on an emergency basis.[38] Block ships at naval dockyards were heavily armed to repel invasion. Increased land protection was given to naval arsenals. One of the heaviest of Britain's war steamers, the *Penelope*, was ordered home from overseas service. Peel seems to have taken the barrage of propaganda, coming and going, hard.

Aberdeen, in the meantime, remained calm. He was trustful of Guizot, and believed with him that the doctrine "prepare for war to preserve peace" as applied to powerful states was dangerous and self-defeating.[39] During a state visit to France with Queen Victoria in the summer of 1845, he gathered information quietly which confirmed his belief that the current naval preparations by both states were sheer panic.[40] On his return he wrote Guizot lamenting the stir created over the "wretched island" of Tahiti: "Is it not deplorable that you and I, two ministers of peace, should be condemned to quarrel about a set of half naked savages at the other end of the world; but your enemies well know that this must be an inexhaustible and ever-springing source of discord between us; and although they would readily abandon it [the island] themselves they will take good care, if possible, to prevent you from doing so."[41]

[38] Useful statistical tables relating to the growth of British naval forces are in Christopher J. Bartlett, *Great Britain and Sea Power* (Oxford, 1963), Appendices 1–4.

[39] The words of Aberdeen were: "There is no more false maxim, as applied to great states, than that we ought to prepare for war in order to preserve peace. A small state may perhaps arm for its defense, and to prevent war. A great state can only prepare for war, in order to make war." Aberdeen to Peel, Aug. 21, 1844, Peel Papers, British Museum.

[40] Aberdeen to Peel, Sept. 8, 1845, Aberdeen Papers, British Museum. In 1862 a pamphlet was published by Richard Cobden in London, entitled *The Three Panics*. Its theme was that navalist agitations in England and France had induced cross-channel panics in 1847–1848, 1851–1853, and 1859–1861. It opened with an account of the panic of 1845. The whole was an eloquent appeal for the limitation of naval armaments. Richard Cobden, *The Three Panics* (London, 1862).

[41] Aberdeen to Guizot, Sept. 16, 1845, Aberdeen Papers, British Museum. For a valuable expression of Aberdeen's view of British expansion over the islands of the central Pacific, see Edward Everett to Hugh S. Legaré, June 1, 1843, No. 40, Everett Papers, M.H.S.

The despatch related to an unauthorized occupation of the Sandwich Islands by a British naval officer, Lord George Paulet, which the British government at once disavowed and countermanded.

In reply Guizot wrote wearily that he was being assailed in France for lack of defense, just as was the ministry in England. Major preparations for war were being made in England, he had been told; France, he was told, had little means of resistance—her marine, coasts, and forts were in a pitiable state. Guizot insisted that the expenditures being made by his government were primarily for public works. They were for roads, canals, port improvements. To be sure, these were potentially useful in war, but they were essentially pacific. Some works of fortification, especially those around Paris, were purely defensive. Increased expenditures on steam vessels merely made up for the deficiencies of the past. Guizot agreed with Aberdeen that the maxim, "In time of peace, prepare for war" was absurd. He deplored the existing state of panic in England. His letter was promptly sent by Aberdeen to Peel.[42]

Aberdeen was so disturbed by Peel's concessions to navalist propaganda that he proposed in a letter to withdraw from the cabinet. He was weary of the burdens of office in any case, he wrote, and he felt unable to remain in a post where all his ambitions for peace seemed to be coming to naught.[43] Peel refused to accept the resignation. He believed its consequences would be disastrous, that Aberdeen could not be replaced as Foreign Minister and that the loss of such a colleague, even on personal grounds, would be irreparable. Graham expressed like sentiments.[44] Aberdeen, having made his point, stayed on, and continued to labor for peace in the cabinet to the end of the ministry.

In the autumn of 1845 a panic of a different sort assailed the governments of England and France. It was a panic produced by the potato blight. The blight had destroyed a major part of the potato crop of Ireland, Scotland, and England. It also ravaged the continent, robbing the poor of the food on which they most relied. The grain harvest in England and in the western part of Europe was likewise seriously deficient. Famine seemed ahead. By the middle of October, just at the time of Guizot's letter to Aberdeen, the disaster reports from Ireland were so alarming that summonses were sent out for a special cabinet council to consider temporarily

---

[42] Guizot to Aberdeen, Oct. 2, 1845, Peel Papers, British Museum.
[43] Aberdeen to Peel, Sept. 18, 1845, in Parker, ed., *Peel*, III, 401–402.
[44] *Ibid.*, 402–403, 407–408.

opening British ports duty free to foreign grain, by an order in council. The meeting was held at the end of October, and there Peel proposed suspension of the Corn Laws. His proposal met vehement objection from protectionists. On December 6, after a long and bitter dissension in the cabinet, Peel sent his resignation to the Queen.[45] The Queen summoned Lord John Russell to form a Whig government. Russell agreed, but failed in the attempt, owing to objection among some of the Whigs to serving with Palmerston as Foreign Minister. Palmerston had frightened even staunch Whigs by his aggressiveness toward France and the United States—by his talk especially while out of office. Russell was obliged to abandon the effort to form a government.[46] A Whig government would have been based, in any case, on a minority, and without unanimous Whig support, would have been helpless. Peel was recalled. He reorganized the cabinet, retaining the ministers willing to discard the Corn Laws. One of these was Aberdeen.

Late in January 1846, on the assembling of Parliament, Peel, in the "Address from the Throne," announced his program for dealing with the food crisis. It was the immediate reduction and early extinction of all duties on foreign grain, in other words, immediate relaxation and early Parliamentary repeal of the Corn Laws.[47] This was a revolutionary step, as revolutionary in Britain's internal policy as Aberdeen's step of an *entente cordiale* had been in external policy. It was a step also toward world peace. Removal of the barriers to the free flow of food in the world would render war less likely, as the Anti-Corn Law League was proclaiming. This was a view which Lord John Russell, the leader of the Whigs, and Richard Cobden were urging, and Peel agreed with them.

An early indication of Peel's agreement with them was a series of letters by him arranging for the ceremony to follow the "Address from the Throne." The ceremony was to include speeches from party members moving the Address and seconding it. Peel informed the chosen speakers of his own ideas. He wrote that he hoped repeal of the Corn Laws would promote the peaceful settlement of the Oregon dispute by offering free admission to British markets

[45] *Ibid.*, ch. 8.
[46] *Ibid.*, ch. 10.
[47] *Hansard's*, LXXXIII, 1–5 (Jan. 22, 1846).

of American maize. He also wrote incidentally: "Our relations with France are very friendly, and with every European power."[48] His views had become more relaxed than they had been. He believed his projected free trade measure, though originating in affliction, would end in strengthening the peace crusaders, whether across the Atlantic or across the Channel.

In reconstructing his cabinet, after the break with the Protectionists, Peel gave special thought to revitalizing its membership. He enlisted ministers who had standing in Parliament and in the nation, who had debating skill, and who were known to have aptitude in administration. He especially needed ministers with debating skill. The Earl of Haddington, who had served as First Lord of the Admiralty in the old cabinet, was sensible and right-minded and was respected for fairness and courtesy toward naval personnel. But he was lacking as a speaker and as an administrator. A new and abler man was available, Lord Ellenborough. He was without employment. He had been removed by the directors of the East India Company as Viceroy of India, despite great services in expanding Britain's hold there, because he was cantankerous and insubordinate. He was a powerful debater, and possessed great energy as an administrator. His gifts were especially needed in the House of Lords. Aberdeen did not speak easily or well. So Ellenborough was named First Lord of the Admiralty, and Haddington was promoted to Lord Privy Seal. Some consideration had been given to sending Ellenborough to Canada as governor-general. He would have liked that appointment, if, as Peel wrote the Queen, "there was the probability of war [over the Oregon issue] and [he] seemed fired with the memory of his exploits in India." But Peel assured him that in case of war there would be "ample field for his martial genius at the Admiralty."[49]

Ellenborough and his patron and defender, Wellington, were destined to become, as Aberdeen and the Queen feared at the time,

---

[48] Peel to Lord Francis Egerton, Jan. 6, 1846, in Parker, ed., *Peel*, III, 323-324; Peel to Edmund B. Denison, Jan. 7, 1846, Peel Papers, British Museum. In the Denison letter Peel also wrote: "We shall not *reciprocate* (to use an American phrase) swaggering language with Mr. Polk, but we shall quietly, and without express reference to the United States, propose an increase in our naval and military estimates."

[49] Peel to the Queen, Dec. 25, 1845, in Parker, ed., *Peel*, III, 288.

the "duo fulmina belli" of the new cabinet.[50] What is significant here, however, is that the "duo" directed their energies mostly to the New World and to Polk's aggressiveness. The massive preparations which they pressed on Peel were for Canada and the Oregon Country. Peel was less excited than they about those dangers. He did not take too seriously the noises continuing to come from the American Congress in the notice debate. He made this evident in a revealing letter to Ellenborough, dated March 17, 1846, replying to a request for special naval appropriations to guard against surprise attack. The reply came twelve days late, with an apology from Peel that he had been too busy to write sooner:

I do not feel it to be consistent with my duty to sanction the incurring by the Admiralty of expenses for naval preparation not sanctioned by the estimates laid before Parliament. I agree with you that it is very disastrous in war to be taken by surprise. But looking to the amount of our naval estimates—to the progressive increase in those estimates—to the relative state of preparation for naval hostilities in this country and [in] the United States—I cannot understand the apprehension of being taken by surprise.

For the service of the year 1845–46, the China War having terminated and all prospect of hostilities with France having passed away, we made an increase of 4,000 seamen to our naval force. We added to the naval estimates of last year £700,000. We have made another addition to the naval estimate of this year of £540,000 . . . .

Between increased expenditure on the one hand. and reduced taxation on the other, we are about to incur the serious evil of deficit in time of peace. We really had better have war at once than incur many of the evils of it by making constantly increasing preparation for it.

It is a very good thing, no doubt, to be prepared at all points, to have twice the naval force of any other country—to have every colony in a state of complete defense, well garrisoned and the fortifications in good order, to have nothing to fear in the event of hostilities, all this is very desirable if you can afford it, but if you cannot, if in order to secure these advantages you must incur debt in the time of peace, you are crippling your resources (for money and credit are resources) in the event of war. . . .

<hr />

[50] Aberdeen to Peel, Dec. 29, 1845, Aberdeen Papers, British Museum. The Queen wrote to Peel more circumspectly: "The only fear the Queen has about Ld. Ellenborough is that if he & the Duke of Wellington get together, the warlike preparations by sea and land may be urged a little too strongly." The Queen to Peel, Dec. 27, 1845, Peel Papers, British Museum. For a perceptive account of preparations by Ellenborough for Oregon troubles, see Albert H. Imlah, *Lord Ellenborough* (Cambridge, Mass., 1929), ch. 9.

Every speech made in the American Congress—every letter which I see from the United States—contains an admission that our state of preparation for naval hostilities is far more advanced than theirs.

I think it probable that a deep conviction on the part of the Executive of the United States that such is the case will facilitate a settlement of our present differences with that country, but at any rate, I see no such danger of hostilities as would justify the Treasury in sanctioning expenditures on the part of the Admiralty or in any branch of the naval service beyond that which, after very mature consideration, we ourselves proposed to Parliament to provide for . . . .[51]

From this letter it is clear that the naval panic, arising from opposition tactics in England and in France and heightened by agitations of Joinville and Palmerston, had subsided in Peel's mind long before the Oregon offer to the United States was made. "All prospect," as he wrote, of hostilities with France had "passed away."

On Peel's mind, instead, was a panic arising from the prospect of famine in Ireland. Out of this had come a new alignment of political parties and a virtual coalition of Peel's personal followers with the Whig followers of Russell. Both groups wished repeal of the Corn Laws. Neither was strong enough alone to effect it against the embittered opposition of the Tory Protectionists. They joined forces to achieve it. The Whigs under Russell extended their collaboration into the field of foreign affairs. They gave Peel's government assurances that no opposition to extensive concessions to the United States on the Oregon issue would be made.

Aberdeen had for years wished to settle the Oregon problem by extensive concessions. As early as September 25, 1844, he had proposed to Peel to offer the United States a partition line at the 49th parallel, stopped short at Admiralty Inlet. He recognized the reasonableness of the American demand for a harbor at the Straits. He realized also that the lower Columbia was not a highway to the sea, present or future, for western British North America, obstructed as it was by the bar at its mouth and by formidable waterfalls in the interior. He had found Peel unreceptive to these views in 1844. Peel would have had to bear the burden of defending such

---

[51] Peel to Lord Ellenborough, March 17, 1846, Peel Papers, British Museum. The letter to which this was an answer is Ellenborough to Peel, March 5, 1846, Peel Papers, British Museum. The sentences challenged by Peel were: "The most disgraceful as well as the most disastrous event in war is to be taken by surprise. I do not think the Country would hold us to be justified were we to be blind to the signs before us of coming dangers. . . ."

a concession. It was sure to be attacked by Palmerston for conceding what British governments had for more than a quarter of a century refused to concede. Peel would have been charged with deserting British nationals and interests in Oregon, and, even worse, with abandoning British prestige and honor. Palmerston had been trumpeting charges of this nature against the Webster-Ashburton boundary settlement for years.[52]

The immediate effect of the Peel-Russell coalition was the removal of this obstacle to an Oregon settlement. In the debate over the Address from the Throne, in January 1846, Russell expressed disapproval of the off-hand rejection of Polk's partition proposal, of which the British minister in Washington had been guilty. Privately he assured Aberdeen early in February 1846 that he would offer no opposition to an Oregon settlement based on the line of 49°, and, at the same time, pointedly informed Palmerston of this assurance. The latter was effectually muzzled and the danger of a Whig attack on any major Oregon concession was removed.[53]

An opportunity to propose the concession had to be awaited. Polk's ostentatious slamming of the door on the old negotiation, and his assurance to Congress afterwards that the door would remain closed, so far as he was concerned, had prevented the opening of any new negotiation by the British.[54] A hint as to a means of overcoming this embarrassment was given to Congress in a speech in Parliament by a Whig leader and friend of Aberdeen, Lord Clarendon. It was that Congress phrase the notice so as to make it seem an invitation to the British to proceed to a new negotiation. The hint was taken by Congress. In its joint resolution it expressed the amiable sentiment that whereas it had now become desirable to definitely settle the respective claims to the Oregon Country so "that said Territory may, no longer than need be, remain subject to the evil consequences of the divided allegiance of its American and British population, and of the confusion and conflict of national jurisdictions, dangerous to the cherished peace and good understanding of the two countries," and with the view that "the attention of the governments of both countries may be the more

[52] See Essay 8, n. 53, and Essay 9.
[53] Ibid.
[54] See Essay 13.

earnestly directed to the adoption of all proper measures for a speedy and amicable adjustment of the differences and disputes in regard to the said Territory," notice be given of the abrogation of the treaty of joint occupation.[55]

This resolution, forwarded by the President, looked to the British government like an invitation to submit a new proposal of partition to the American government. A new proposal was the result, the one already described: the line of parallel 49° from the Rocky Mountains to Admiralty Inlet and from thence to the sea by Juan de Fuca Strait, reserving to the Hudson's Bay Company (but not to British nationals generally) the right to navigate the Columbia River south of parallel 49°. The offer was much like the plan sketched by Aberdeen to Peel on September 25, 1844.

It was this offer which Polk, with the unanimous approval of the cabinet, submitted to the Senate for "advice" on June 10, 1846. It was promptly returned, by a vote of more than the necessary two-thirds, with the advice to accept it. In deference to his constitutional advisers, the President gave up the preference which he was thought to have for All Oregon and ordered the proposal to be at once converted into a treaty. This the Senate, without a change of word, ratified.

Alfred T. Mahan's *Influence of Seapower upon History* has cast a spell over the writing of peacetime, as well as of wartime history.[56] It seems to be reflected in the seapower explanations of the peacetime settlement of the Oregon question. If so, it is misapplied. The view that the Polk administration made "serious claim" to All Oregon and abandoned it because the President quailed before the seapower of the British is in conflict with the evidence of Polk's own instructions and actions. The opposite view, that Peel did the quailing in the presence of a French steam-navy challenge to British seapower and that he agreed, on this score, to an Oregon settlement "just short of an obvious surrender" is equally untenable. It conflicts with chronology. It crumbles when the discrepancy in time between the naval panic of 1845 and the British Oregon offer of 1846 is called to mind. It rests upon an obliteration of half a

---

[55] The text of the notice appears in *Senate Journal*, 29 Cong., 1 Sess. (Serial 469), 260–61 (April 23, 1846).

[56] Alfred T. Mahan, *The Influence of Sea Power upon History* (Boston, 1890), and later editions.

year's time and an ignoring of Peel's correspondence and that of his cabinet associates during this half year.

In truth, forces more potent than navies—governments directing navies and themselves directed by peace coalitions—took charge of Oregon diplomacy in the end. In England a coalition of Peelites and Russellites, seeking the abolition of the Corn Laws, and doing it in the name of peace, disarmed the ultra-nationalists of the Palmerston school and gave nonparty clearance to the conciliatory Oregon program which Aberdeen had long desired. In the United States a coalition of peace Whigs and Southern Democrats in Congress overwhelmed the wild expansionists of the 54° 40′ school whom Polk pretended to be leading and sent to England a form of notice calculated to open a new negotiation—a new road to the "cherished peace and good understanding of the two countries," referred to by Congress in its notice. These were the forces which propelled the Oregon dispute to its peaceful conclusion.

ESSAY 13 · PRESIDENTIAL FEVERS*

IN MAY, 1844, three presidential nominating conventions arrived in turn in the quiet city of Baltimore, Maryland. They arrived in the order of Whigs, Tylerites, and Democrats. The Whigs established headquarters in a church, where amid religious surroundings they did their work with decorum, harmony, and speed. They ratified decisions the party bosses had made. They named Henry Clay candidate by acclamation, without even the formality of nominating speeches. They were able to adjourn in a day. The Tylerites were similarly docile. The Democrats alone authentically registered the political turbulence of the day. Their convention was wide open, virile, and discordant. It met, as the Whig press maliciously pointed out, in the Odd Fellows Hall. The hall was large, but not large enough. The weather turned hot; the place became, in the language of a reporter, a Black Hole of Calcutta.[1] It echoed for four days to leather-lunged oratory and to interminable roll calls. The nights buzzed with intrigue in smoke-filled hotel rooms. This was the first of the modernized party conventions, and it was the first to have modernized reporting. It was reported by the sensational new Morse magnetic telegraph.

Its most divisive issues, presented in the form of contending candidacies, were the annexation of Texas, the occupation of the whole of Oregon, and the protective tariff. Another troublesome issue, involving amendment to the Constitution, was the single term for the presidency. The followers of Andrew Jackson had raised this issue after the famous "bargain and corruption" election of 1825, and Jackson, as President, had repeatedly urged Congress to act on it. He had proposed to set an example himself by serving

---

* Reprinted from the *Mississippi Valley Historical Review*, XLVII (June 1960). This paper was presented as the presidential address at the Fifty-third Annual Meeting of the Mississippi Valley Historical Association in Louisville, Kentucky, on April 28, 1960.

[1] A full account of the convention is in *Niles' Register* (Baltimore), June 1, 8, 1844. See also John R. Dickinson (ed.), *Speeches, Correspondence, etc., of the Late Daniel S. Dickinson* (2 vols., New York, 1867), II, 369.

only a single term. He had been overruled by his followers, and had then relented further by favoring Van Buren for a second term. Whigs had embraced the betrayed cause. They, and their candidates in 1840 and 1844, had pledged themselves to it, and had sought to fasten on Van Buren the stigma of desertion from a great principle.

Differences at conventions are adjusted, if possible, by compromises of viewpoint, balances of interest, ambiguities of phrasing, or discreet silences that disarm contentions. Adjustment is the law of survival of parties in a nation as large and diverse as the United States. Candidates are nominated who will attract the biggest electoral vote even if not representing the highest distinction in the party; vice-presidential candidates balance the presidential. All these expedients the Democrats resorted to in 1844. They adopted an expansionist platform balancing Texas and Oregon. They pushed aside Van Buren and nominated Polk, who had offended no section. They framed a tariff plank which meant everything to everybody, and they named George M. Dallas, a protectionist and expansionist of Pennsylvania, as vice-presidential candidate.[2] They maintained a judicious silence on the issue of the single term. They relied on Polk personally to set that matter straight, as he did. In accepting the nomination he declared that if elected he would retire at the end of one term.[3]

This declaration served a number of purposes. It poured balm on wounds inflicted on Van Buren and on his delegates, who had at one time commanded a majority of the convention. It gave hope to runners-up, such as Lewis Cass and James Buchanan, of better luck at the next convention in 1848. It restored the party to an old and honored principle, entirely out of range of Whig gunfire. It exhibited Polk to the public in the attractive democratic posture of self-denial and self-restraint. It also served Polk's personal preference. His pledge was the one specific commitment he made to the public in his letter of acceptance.

These tactics were not individually new. They were new in the perfection of their combination. They established a model that has served to the present day and that may serve the future. What is more, the tactics paid off. The party won the election. Polk became

[2] Polk's interpretation of the tariff plank is in *Niles' Register*, July 6, 1844.
[3] *Ibid.*

President. He implemented the platform, straying a little from what the convention had in mind. He did not stray from his personal pledge. He completely honored it, the only one of a number of presidents committed to the single term who did so. He gave the principle its first real testing and in so doing revealed its dangers.

A president pledging himself to a single term in effect signals the party chiefs to give thought to the succession. He invites those having ambitions in that direction to begin their preparations. The preparations consist, in a democracy, of courting the electorate. They can consist of advocating measures at variance with or even in conflict with those of the president. A president who has a second term open to him and commands eight years of actual or prospective patronage is able to restrain wide deviations from his program. A president who has cut himself off from a second term has the patronage for only four. He has, by taking the pledge, reduced by half his means of maintaining discipline in his administration.

Polk was aware of these dangers, and, in his cabinet, tried to forestall them. Whomever he invited to enter his cabinet he asked to agree to promote no candidacy for the 1848 election by any use of patronage, and, if becoming himself a candidate, to withdraw from the family. One of the persons invited upon these terms was Buchanan, who had been an aspirant to the presidency in 1844. He was invited to be secretary of state. He cheerfully accepted, with some reservations, however, as to the conditions.[4]

Party chiefs with thoughts turned to the succession are less easily restrained in the Senate than in the cabinet. As senators they have to some extent protection against patronage withholding because of their power of confirming appointments. They have abundant opportunities, moreover, of courting the electorate by reason of the Senate's established tradition of untrammeled debate and its special authority in the field of foreign affairs. Already in Polk's day the Senate was a nursery for favorite sons.

In 1845 a foreign issue well suited to president making was before the Senate. It was the Oregon issue. It had voter appeal, as the Baltimore convention had recognized. In some respects it was more attractive than the Texas issue ever had been. It was not marred by the slavery blemish; it did not align the sections so bitterly

---

[4] John B. Moore (ed.), *The Works of James Buchanan* (12 vols., Philadelphia, 1908–1911), VI, 110, 111.

against each other. It was directed only against the British. It promised to hold the stage a number of years, for the thesis that all Oregon was American was not likely to be soon accepted by the British. Senators from expansionist communities in championing that cause might hope to win not only immediate laurels but attentive consideration at a future convention for the highest prize a convention can bestow.[5]

At Baltimore the issue had been adroitly phrased. American title to all Oregon had been pronounced "clear and unquestionable." The territory was not to be "ceded" in any portion to England or to any other power. But the resolution had trailed off into an anticlimax. The "reoccupation" of Oregon was merely recommended to the cordial support of the Democracy of the Union.[6] In that form it had satisfied western Democrats and had seemed harmless to the southern.

Polk seemed committed to the full implications of the Oregon plank. He had declared in a pre-convention letter for the whole of Oregon.[7] In his Inaugural Address he unreservedly pronounced American title to the country of Oregon to be "clear and unquestionable," using quotation marks to indicate his source. He did, however, suggest no program of action. He left the door of exit from the platform open a little.

Several months later he offered the British a compromise. In a Washington negotiation, inherited from the Tyler administration, he offered what his predecessors had offered—a line at the fortyninth parallel. He withheld only one item his predecessors would have allowed—the free navigation of the lower Columbia. The proposal was at once rejected, and in terms verging on the rude. It was not even taken for reference to the British government. It was, thereupon, withdrawn and the negotiation ended. The British government at once disavowed its representative. It directed him to seek a resubmission of the offer. He humbly obeyed, but Polk would not move. Polk felt that a resubmission would show too

[5] The Nashville *Union*, a Polk organ, on January 15, 1846, referred to aspirants "who believe that Texas has made one President and that Oregon may make another."

[6] Edward Stanwood, *A History of the Presidency* (4th ed., 2 vols., Boston, 1928), I, 215. The platform was submitted to the delegates on the last day of the convention, when many had already departed for home. It was adopted without discussion.

[7] John S. Jenkins, *James Knox Polk* (Auburn, 1851), 122.

much willingness for further compromise. He doubtless realized, also, that a resubmission would infuriate the 54° 40′ element in his party.

Polk next carried the issue to Congress. In his first annual message he publicly confessed his proposal and described its rude rejection. He explained, for the benefit of those who might wonder at his having made it at all, that he had felt committed by his predecessors. He assured Congress he would not make it again. Indeed, he would make no proposal. He urged Congress to serve notice of the abrogation of the treaty of joint occupation. He gravely declared that when, a year after notice, the treaty had expired, "we shall have reached a period when the national rights in Oregon must either be abandoned or firmly maintained. That they can not be abandoned without a sacrifice of both national honor and interest is too clear to admit of doubt." He asked Congress to promise donations of land to citizens of the United States who would migrate to the Oregon Country or who had already done so.[8]

This ominous message was read with unexpected calm in England. It created less excitement than the earlier Inaugural. The British public observed that the Inaugural, also ominous, had been followed by a compromise proposal and felt comforted. It cherished the hope that arbitration would be used and would save the peace. Arbitration was, in fact, twice proposed and pressed with earnestness on Polk. It was rejected with a finality that was unmistakable. Only then did the British awake to the fact that the President had ceased to waver, that his moves were now all in the same direction, and each more threatening—the cutting off of the negotiation, the proposal to abrogate the joint occupation, the recommendation of an induced migration such as was believed to have settled the fate of Texas, the rejection of arbitration. The President was evidently preparing for a showdown. When this was realized the crisis of the Oregon issue was at hand.

Polk was indeed preparing for a showdown. He had proposed a compromise. It had been spurned. The only way to treat John Bull, he believed, "was to look him straight in the eye."[9] If John

---

[8] James D. Richardson (comp.), *A Compilation of the Messages and Papers of the Presidents, 1789–1897* (10 vols., Washington, 1896–1899), IV, 385.

[9] Milo M. Quaife (ed.), *The Diary of James K. Polk during His Presidency, 1845 to 1849* (4 vols., Chicago, 1910), I, 155; Polk to Gideon J. Pillow, February 4, 1846; and Polk to William H. Polk, March 27, 1846, Polk Letter Press Copy Book, Papers of James K. Polk (Manuscript Division, Library of Congress).

Bull desired a new negotiation he must initiate it. He had wrecked the old, let him open the new. Polk sent the Foreign Office word that a new proposal would be respectfully received. It would not in itself open a negotiation. It would be examined to see whether it contained the basis for a settlement. If it seemed to him to do so it would be sent for examination to the Senate. If two thirds of the Senate decided that it contained a basis, then a negotiation could begin. The American minister in London, Louis McLane, was directed to offer no encouragement to the making of any new proposal. He might indicate to Lord Aberdeen, the British foreign secretary, if asked, merely what kind of proposal was likely to pass the screening tests of the two branches of the American govern-ment.[10]

This unusual procedure was not, as Lord Aberdeen momentarily thought it might be, a scheme to make him "eat dirt." It was a pressure device, a wringer, by use of which Polk expected to squeeze from the British a settlement satisfactory to the United States. In such a settlement the partition line must be far enough north to give the United States harbors at the Straits. The lower Columbia must be given up to the United States. It must be given up without reservation. The right of navigation which the British had enjoyed must be given up. These were terms the British had rejected for a quarter of a century. They must now propose them, themselves, and as a mere bid for a negotiation. They were unlikely to do so except under pressure.

Pressure must be initiated by abrogating the treaty of joint occu-pation. The treaty was a hindrance to a pressure program. It was an American recognition of British rights of presence in the Oregon Country. It obligated the United States to refrain from the exercise of any exclusive sovereignty there. It could not be ignored, as some Oregon extremists proposed.[11] It must be observed until abrogated. Such a course would demonstrate American fidelity to treaty

---

[10] John Y. Mason to Louis McLane, August 12, 1845; James Buchanan to McLane, September 13, 1845; McLane to Polk, January 17, 1846, Polk Papers, Vols. 73, 74; Quaife (ed.), *Polk Diary*, I, 76; *Senate Exec. Docs.*, 29 Cong., 1 Sess. (1845–1846), No. 489 (Serial 478), 39–44; McLane to John C. Calhoun, January 3, 1846, in Chauncey S. Boucher and Robert P. Brooks (eds.), "Correspondence Addressed to John C. Calhoun, 1837–1849," American Historical Association, *Annual Report for the Year 1929* (Washington, 1930), 311.

[11] Polk was committed to this view. See a speech on it by him in *Register of Debates*, 20 Cong., 2 Sess., 129–34 (December 29, 1828), 143 (December 30, 1828), 144 (December 31, 1828).

obligations and at the same time give warning of the storm which would break over Oregon once the peace shelter was down, unless in the meantime an agreement had been reached.

Abrogation was permitted by the treaty and the method of doing it was described. A year's notice was to be given. But what authority in government would serve the notice was a detail untouched on. It was left for each side to determine for itself. By the American side it had never been determined. The Constitution was silent on it and the government had never abrogated a treaty which in its terms provided for its abrogation. The serving of notice could have been done by the chief executive in the manner of European governments. Or, it could have been done by the Senate acting in secret session, or publicly by the two houses of Congress.[12] Each of these authorities, since the days of Polk, has acted in this capacity.[13] The authority preferred by Polk was Congress. He preferred to have Congress publicly turn the screws of his pressure device. If Congress would act he could confront the British with evidence of a solid American will, legislative and executive, for a proper Oregon settlement.

Congress would act, Polk believed. In both houses it was Democratic. Its Democrats would be governed in their votes by the Baltimore platform. Even some Whigs might vote for notice in view of the summary rejection by the British of the compromise offer. Polk expected that a stout and uncompromising defense would be made in Congress of American title to Oregon, and that individuals who had reservations would withhold them so as not to damage the American case in the presence of a hostile claimant. He hoped especially that the debate would be brief, that it would end in a few weeks, and that by the close of December, 1845, the notice would be on its way to England.[14]

This was a major miscalculation. It overestimated some of the forces acting on Congress, underestimated others. One of the forces much overestimated was the zeal of the nation for expansion. This was measured in terms of the electoral vote of 1844 rather than the

[12] In the Tyler administration a measure serving notice was passed by the House, but it stopped there. *House Journal*, 28 Cong., 2 Sess. (Serial 462), 321.

[13] A good brief account of treaty termination under the Constitution is John M. Mathews, *American Foreign Relations: Conduct and Policies* (Rev. ed., New York, 1938), 596ff.

[14] Quaife (ed.), *Polk Diary*, I, 338–45; *Senate Exec. Docs.*, 29 Cong., 1 Sess., No. 489, p. 46.

popular vote. The electoral vote had been clear enough—170 for the Democrats, 105 for the opposition. But the popular vote, a better gauge of public feeling, had been far from clear. Polk had carried the South, though narrowly. He had trailed the opposition in the North and even in the Northwest.[15] Other forces which were overrated were the unity to be counted on from the Democrats in Congress and the anti-British feeling to be traded on in the nation.

What were the forces underrated by Polk? They were the recently formed, the emerging, the unclear. One of them was of his own making. It was the epidemic of presidential fevers he had released in the Senate and elsewhere by his single-term pledge. Another was the expansion of New England population into the West and its effects on sectional antagonisms. A third was the bitterness created in the North by the fight over the admission of Texas and the triumph of the South in it. A fourth was the powerful current of the world peace movement. A fifth was misgiving felt by many Democrats in Congress after the 1844 election regarding some of the agreements made at Baltimore by the party delegates. Such misgiving is one of the norms of congressional behavior. On the floor of Congress an agreement, attractively packaged, as the Oregon and Texas one had been,[16] is opened. Its items are individually inspected. The price tags on them are read with dismay, especially those still to be paid; mislabelings and confused labelings such as "reannexation" and "reoccupation" are detected and denounced. Members of the party begin throwing epithets and charges at each other—"Western warriors," "slavocracy," "Punic faith." The victory celebration ends; the fight over measures begins. The debate in Congress over the notice issue was destined to be of this nature.

In the debate Democrats from the Middle West were ardent supporters of the President. They were the ones who had spearheaded the drive for Oregon in the Baltimore convention. They represented a party constituency that was intensely expansionist, men who regarded the Oregon Country in a special sense as their own, their land of the future. They thought of it also as a land to be saved

[15] Stanwood, *History of the Presidency*, I, 223. A considerable error appears here in the addition of the Birney vote.

[16] Polk had set the pattern of linking the two issues in his campaign letter of April 22, 1844. Jenkins, *James Knox Polk*, 120.

from the British, by war if necessary.[17] They were more anti-British than the Democrats of any other section of the Union. They nursed against the British bitter memories of Indian atrocities in two wars, atrocities believed to be continuing in the Far West. They had other grounds of antipathy to the British—the alleged greed of imperialism of that people, the arrogance of its governing aristocracy, and the oppressions practiced by them on the helpless of the world, especially on the Irish. Their spokesmen professed to believe that Britain had become paralyzed in a military sense by the distresses and rebelliousness of Ireland. They found allies in such beliefs among Democrats of the border states of the South, parts of the Middle Atlantic states, and much of northern New England.

Southern Democrats on the other hand were opponents of the President's program for the most part. Cotton Democrats were especially so. They were expansionists, to be sure, but they had little interest in a crusade to acquire the frozen latitudes of the north. They were inclined to construe narrowly the Oregon plank of the party platform. They wished a partition of Oregon to be made by an amicable negotiation, and certainly not by a war. They were far from hostile to England. They were fearful of the notice proposal, and especially of its overtones in the President's message. They were apprehensive of what might happen when the peace shelter of the joint occupation treaty had come down. Allied with them in holding such views were Democrats from the commercialized and industrialized Atlantic seaboard.

Whigs were more unified than Democrats. They were hesitant about expansionism. What they saw in expansionism was the problems it would create rather than the territory it would add. They discounted the value of the Oregon Country because of its remoteness. Many of them believed, with Daniel Webster, that it would some day develop into an independent republic.[18] Others believed that it could and should be amicably divided between the United States and England. They were opposed to notice, at least to notice

17 Middle Western Whigs were skeptical of the military determination of their Democratic neighbors. Thus a state convention of Indiana Whigs on January 9, 1846, resolved that while "we will have our own at all hazards" we will not, like "some of the windy democratic orators of yesterday . . . prove *soldiers in peace—citizens in war*." The Chicago *Daily Journal*, a Whig organ, reprinted these resolutions with approval on January 23, 1846.

18 Tyler toyed with that idea as President. Richardson (comp.), *Messages and Papers of the Presidents*, IV, 258.

couched in aggressive terms. Reflecting the interests of the mercantile, the banking, and the business community they wanted peace. Some, including Webster, were Anglophiles. Others, such as Charles Sumner and Horace Greeley, were deeply influenced by the world peace movement. Nearly all objected to arming Polk with any sort of pressure weapon.

Whigs were a minority, but a strong one in Congress. They were especially strong in the Senate. They were within eight votes of equaling the Democrats in the Senate. They sympathized with Democratic conservatives of the South on a number of economic issues and were, on occasion, collaborators with them. Then, as now, conservatives in the two parties and sections were eager, and were able when joined, to shackle the wild radicals of the West. All they had to do was to cross party lines. On the Oregon issue they were especially disposed to do so.

Men of that generation, regardless of party or section, were vehemently partisan. If they crossed party lines on occasion they clung all the more blindly on others to their political brethren. Partisanship in politics was the almost universal spirit of the age. The President was no exception to it. He was, if anything, more narrowly partisan than his period. Any Whig seemed to him probably depraved, personally as well as politically. In his *Diary* he noted two exceptions to this rule—Senator Willie P. Mangum of North Carolina and the urbane Senator John J. Crittenden of Kentucky. These two he included, even if Whigs, in the ranks of honorable men. But to do this was an extraordinary feat of tolerance on his part and it occurred only in the later years of his presidency. Such intensity of party feeling was an important force among those shaping debate on notice.

Personalities were a considerable factor in the debate. On the President's side the ones of most prominence were western Democrats. At their head was Senator William Allen of Ohio. He was a young attorney, limited in education, but endowed with some of the qualifications for frontier politics, good presence, a ready tongue, a voice that won him the name of the "Ohio fog horn," and an abundance of self-assurance and ambition.[19] He was in his second Senate term. In the Senate of that era he was in a brilliant

[19] A good characterization of Allen, by a Washington correspondent of the New York *Commercial Advertiser*, appears in the issue of January 29, 1846.

assembly and there he shone less brightly than on the hustings. He was considered a demagogue, a ranter in debate, an advocate of rash and unsound measures. He was assigned to only the minor standing committees and even on these he always brought up the rear. In 1839 he obtained assignment to the important Foreign Relations Committee, but to the tail end of it. In the Whig Senate of 1843–1845 he had no standing committee assignments at all, though others of his party held minority berths.

In 1845, in the Twenty-ninth Congress, he rocketed suddenly to the heights. He became chairman of the Foreign Relations Committee. This was the premier Senate assignment, given normally to a distinguished Senate leader. In 1845, with foreign issues of expansionism critical in the program of the administration, it was a special prize. Its allotment to Allen under these circumstances was a sensation, indeed, something of a mystery. It is still a mystery, which the most patient investigation does not altogether solve.

A key to solving it is Senate usage. Whenever a new party succeeded to the control of the Senate and the White House, as it did in 1845, the Senate met in two sessions in the same year. One was an extra session, convened in March, for the installation of the president; the other, the regular session, convened in December. The March session lasted only a few days. It concerned itself chiefly with cabinet nominations and other executive business. It did no legislating. It could do none in the absence of the House. It dispensed, therefore, with standing committees.

The December session was the one which set up the standing committees. It acted through a president pro tempore who was the elected choice of the majority party. The vice-president was allowed no part in such proceedings. He was regarded as an outsider. Only twice in the Senate's history, and then under unusual circumstances, had he been allowed to make committee appointments.[20]

In 1845, however, all these traditions were cast to the winds. At the March session the majority leaders arrived at a decision to have standing committees even for a matter of days. Also, they arranged to keep the vice-president always in the chair, so that no president pro tempore could be chosen.[21] Dallas, as vice-president, a 54° 40′

[20] *Senate Journal*, 19 Cong., 1 Sess. (Serial 124), 31, 246; *ibid.*, 25 Cong., 1 Sess. (Serial 308), 27, 28.
[21] George M. Dallas to Sophia Dallas, March 14, 1845, Dallas Papers (Historical Society of Pennsylvania). On December 1, 1845, Dallas wrote Philip N. Dallas:

man, thus named the standing committees. He named a full slate of them. To the Foreign Relations Committee he named Allen as chairman, and as associates, Cass of Michigan, and Charles G. Atherton of New Hampshire, all 54° 40′ men. He named three extremists to a five-man committee, a representation out of all proportion to their strength in the Senate. This was of no immediate consequence.[22] It was of great future consequence. It anointed the extremists with the magic oil of committee seniority for the regular session.

At the regular session the Democratic leaders undertook to repeat the March procedures. They kept Dallas in the chair. A motion to allow him to name the standing committees was made by an Oregon extremist.[23] The southern Democrats, now fully aware of their danger, rebelled, kicked over the traces, joined the Whigs, and defeated the motion.[24] By way of reply the western Democrats summoned a caucus. The caucus instituted a wholly new system of setting up the standing committees—the caucus system. Allen insisted, in the ensuing distribution of places, on his right to the chairmanship of the Foreign Relations Committee on the ground of seniority gained in March. He was upheld by the other March appointed committeemen. A fourth 54° 40′ man, Ambrose H. Sevier, of Arkansas, was added. The Whigs, in their absence, were allowed one place out of five on committees. These slates were pushed through the Senate. In that way preparation was made, in the golden age of Senate history, for crises ahead in foreign affairs.

Each stage in Allen's appointment, the March and the December stage, was greeted by dismayed outcries from the Whig press. The outcries came from the East and from the West.[25] Some of the

---

"There are reasons of a peculiar nature, growing out of the weakness comparatively of the friends of the administration on the floor of the Senate, which may exact more exertion from me than would otherwise fall to my share."

[22] These standing committees served for ten days only. A full report of the proceedings is in *Journal of the Executive Proceedings of the Senate*, Vol. VI, 1841–1845 (Washington, 1887), 423, 427–28. Cass was said to have been offered the chairmanship of the committee and to have declined it. The report is of questionable authenticity.

[23] *Senate Journal*, 29 Cong., 1 Sess. (Serial 469), 7.

[24] *Ibid.*, 36.

[25] Baltimore *American*, March 14, 1845; Philadelphia *North American*, March 13, 1845; New York *Express*, March 13, 1845 *New York Tribune*, March 13, 1845. See also Allan Nevins (ed.), *The Diary of Philip Hone, 1828–1851* (2 vols., New York, 1927), II, 750.

most embittered came from Allen's own state.[26] Charles Sumner, after seeing the Senator in action and hearing Senate gossip regarding his selection, wrote: "Allen, the Chairman of the Committee on Foreign Affairs, is a tall, tobacco chewing spitting loud voiced ferocious blackguard. From this [Committee] he is running for the Presidency. . . . His position . . . gives him an importance that does not belong to him naturally. He obtained this through a caucus fizzle. Many of his own Party regret it very much."[27]

One of his own party who regretted it very much was Lewis Cass, the second on the Committee. He would have liked the chairmanship himself. He had far better claims to it than Allen except that he was a newcomer to the Senate. He was an elder statesman of the party, with a record behind him of military, executive, and diplomatic service. He was an ardent expansionist and a bitter Anglophobe—a "pestilential" one, Sumner thought—and he had lost no opportunity to let this be known to his section and to the world.[28] He had been an active candidate for the 1844 nomination of the party, and he was regarded by other Senate Democrats as the leading contender for 1848—the man in front to beat. He maintained throughout the notice debate an ill-concealed rivalry with Allen for the public ear.

Another conspicuous supporter of the President was Edward A. Hannegan of Indiana. He was of Irish extraction and of better than average education. Endowed with a gift of oratory he entered the Senate in his middle thirties, in 1843. He was an intense expansionist and upheld northern and southern projects indiscriminately, but was distrustful of southern good faith toward northern. He had heard enough at the Baltimore convention to be convinced that if the South were to win Texas first, it would be content to have the whole of Texas and half of Oregon. He was to inject into the notice debate the charge of Punic faith when the South faltered in its

[26] Cincinnati *Daily Gazette*, March 19, 1845.

[27] Charles Sumner to [Richard Rathbone], May 14, 1846, Palmerston Papers (Broadlands, England).

[28] Van Buren wrote the following shrewd judgment of Cass in his *Autobiography:* "Long a resident of the far West, where ancient antipathies between the two Countries have not equally felt the subduing influences of increasing commerce and intercourse . . . he allowed his sense of the injuries we have received from Great Britain and his consequent denunciation of her to be inflamed in the ratio of the improvement of his chances for the Presidency." John C. Fitzpatrick (ed.), *The Autobiography of Martin Van Buren*, American Historical Association, *Annual Report for the Year 1918*, Vol. II (Washington, 1920), 495.

support of Polk. He was of fiery disposition and of extravagant language. He resembled John Randolph, the Virginia orator, in these respects, and also, in his addiction to drink. Already in his Senate career his insobriety was a problem and in his later years it led to tragedy. He was the man responsible for some of the most violent scenes of the notice debate.

Lesser party champions of Polk's program came also from the West. From Illinois came Sidney Breese to the Senate and Stephen A. Douglas to the House. Both were in early stages of important careers. Breese was a tireless builder of an Illinois machine and one of the most persistent of the patronage pests pursuing the harassed Polk. Douglas was an ultra expansionist.[29] Other conspicuous party champions of the President's program came from the border states, notably David R. Atchison of Missouri and Sevier of Arkansas.

Opponents within the party to the President's program came principally from the South. They were led in the Senate by the most illustrious of southern intellects—John C. Calhoun. He was at the height of his national influence. He was remembered with gratitude in the North for having rallied southern opinion to the ratification of the Webster-Ashburton Treaty, for having enunciated a newly expanded program of nationalism at the Memphis Convention, and for having indicated a will to save the peace in the Oregon Country. Northern conservatives, even of antislavery views, were inclined to overlook his Texas and slavery transgressions on these accounts. Some of them joined in importuning him to return to public life in 1845 from which he had withdrawn on the accession of Polk. He had come to believe, himself, that he should return to save the nation from the Oregon folly of the President.[30] He had been at once returned to the Senate by his state legislature.

[29] As chairman of the House Committee on Territories Douglas reported out a bill, in defiance of his committee, calling for immediate exercise of American sovereignty over all Oregon, a bill which his committee supplanted by another conforming to the joint occupation treaty. The Douglas bill is summarized in *Niles' Register*, January 10, 1846, p. 290; the committee bill appears in *Cong. Globe*, 29 Cong., 1 Sess., 661 (April 13, 1846).

[30] See J. Franklin Jameson (ed.), *Correspondence of John C. Calhoun*, American Historical Association, *Annual Report for the Year 1899*, Vol. II (Washington, 1900), 647ff.; Boucher and Brooks (eds.), "Correspondence Addressed to John C. Calhoun," *ibid., 1929*, pp. 125ff.; also New York *Journal of Commerce*, November 3, 1845.

Thomas H. Benton was another Democrat of national stature opposing a radical Oregon program. He had been an expansionist for years, though never a wholly consistent one. He had advocated Texas annexation, yet at the end had opposed the treaty authorizing it. He had been a quixotic Oregon crusader, but in 1845–1846 was known to have deserted the 54° 40′ cause. He opposed militant expansionist pressures on Mexico. Sturdily independent, he was pompous, vain of his learning, and opinionated, all qualities to be exhibited in the Oregon debate. Another Democratic maverick was William H. Haywood of North Carolina, a friend and former college companion of the President.

Among Whig opponents of the President's program Webster was the leader. The opposite number to Calhoun in his party, he had recently, like Calhoun, served as secretary of state and had recent knowledge of the Oregon issue. He was suspected of being partial to the British, and this lessened the weight of his influence in the Senate. But it added to the weight of it in England. Another Whig prominent in the debate was Crittenden, the honorable Kentuckian, holder of Henry Clay's seat in the Senate.

A prompt opening of the debate on the convening of Congress was expected by Polk. In neither house was the expectation realized. In the lower a notice resolution was bottled up in committee for a month by a contest between its expansionists and a combination of southern Democrats and Whigs. A resolution was finally voted out only in the absence of part of the committee. The resolution was "naked," which meant uncovered by a peace preamble. In this form it was debated five weeks, to a total of ninety speeches, each mercifully limited to an hour.[31] At the end a notice resolution, transformed by a conciliatory amendment, was accepted and sent to the Senate.

In the Senate, Allen and his committee were promptness itself. On December 18, 1845, they voted out a resolution, also naked. But it was hastily put to bed by southern Democrats and Whigs. It reappeared on the floor on January 12, only to be whisked under cover for another month, until February 10. The votes by which this was done were a clear evidence that a majority of the Senate did not regard the early appearance of the resolution as essential.

[31] *Cong. Globe*, 29 Cong., 1 Sess., 343–50 (February 9, 1846).

But the 54° 40′ men were determined to appear themselves on the floor. On December 9 Cass appeared there with resolutions instructing the three standing committees on military affairs to examine at once into the state of readiness of their services for war. None of those standing committees had yet been organized or was to be for another week. But the resolutions set the stage for a resounding speech in the course of which Cass assured the Senate that a war would soon come. The British would take the notice, which he assumed would pass, as an occasion for declaring war. In such a case, Cass thought, nothing was ever gained by pusillanimity. It was always better to fight for the first inch of the national territory than for the last. California was also in his mind. Any administration, he said, which would crown its labors of expansion by a peaceful acquisition of California, would win for itself imperishable honor. At the end of the speech an annoyed southern Whig asked what the emergency was which necessitated running ahead of the formation of the standing committees to make such an exhibit of "sublimated patriotism" and such a "splutter of patriotic emotion." Allen came to the support of Cass. He believed war was, indeed, likely, for no American government could ever honorably accept a settlement short of 54° 40′. War could be avoided only if adequate preparation was made for it, and in the United States the most effective preparation was the "preparation of the hearts of the people."[32] The themes of these two speeches—the "inevitability of war," and the "preparation of the hearts of the people"—were picked up by the Whigs and used ironically as echoes to expansionist speeches for the remaining months of the debate.

In competition with Cass, Allen sought to set up a sounding board for himself while debate on notice was held up. He brought to the Senate a resolution on European interference in the affairs of the independent states of the two Americas. The subject was before his Committee yet he undertook to score a personal triumph by submitting a resolution of his own. Calhoun objected to this as a breach of Senate rules and a beginning of premature debate on the Oregon issue. He was supported by other southern Democrats and by Whigs, and leave to introduce was denied. Later the leave was

[32] *Ibid.*, 30 (December 9, 1845), 45–50 (December 15, 1845), 58 (December 16, 1845).

given, but the Senate at the same time ordered the resolution to be returned to the Committee, where it was thereafter kept bottled up.[33]

The time for the opening of the notice debate at length arrived. It was signaled by an extraordinary two-day speech by Allen. Sixty-three years had passed, he began, since Great Britain had acknowledged American independence. Yet the British still maintained their law, handed down judgments, carried out executions, in a vast American territory, 640,000 square miles in extent, in the Pacific Northwest. No question remained any longer as to American title to all that country. Even discussion of it was out of order. British pretensions were baseless; they were "absolute frivolity." They were, however, in character with other British aggressions on the United States—inciting savages to hack women and children to pieces, impressing American seamen, seizure of half of Maine by chicanery. One question alone remained to be answered: whether the American government had the nerve to maintain its rights, or whether it would cringe, quail, and cower before the British. If the government would stand firm, the British would not dare fight. Surrounded by embittered rivals, threatened by domestic convulsion, crippled by a parliamentary system of instability, exhausted by efforts to keep 128,000,000 colonists in subjection, they were helpless. The American people were strong. They needed only to be told that Oregon was theirs. Ask them if they are willing to surrender this large part of their country because of mere dread of invasion by a rabble of armed paupers. Ask them this "and they will give you an answer which will make the British empire tremble throughout its whole frame and foundation."[34] This was the performance of the chairman of the Committee on Foreign Relations. From its specious beginning to its melodramatic end it was the ranting of a demagogue.

Subsequent speeches were in a pattern earlier established in the House, with western Democrats demanding all Oregon, war or no war, and southern Democrats and Whigs insisting on further negotiation and peace. Hannegan early undertook to establish three theses: first, that all Oregon to 54° 40′ is the property of the United States; second, that the American government has no power to

---

[33] *Ibid.*, 197 (January 14, 1846), 239–48 (January 26, 1846).
[34] *Ibid.*, Appendix, 834–42 (February 10–11, 1846).

transfer its soil to any foreign state; third, that the surrender of any of Oregon would be an abandonment of honor and character. Challenged by a southerner as to his own Texas record he replied that already in 1844 he had foreseen Punic faith from the South.[35] Cass returned to the theme of inevitable war.[36] Breese insisted that England did not dare fight, that she had never been in a more precarious state. As for his own community, its honor was involved, and rather than submit to dishonor it would endure anything war would bring.[37] In reply southern Democrats and Whigs scoffed at the thesis of the unquestionable American title to all Oregon. They reminded the western Democrats of the repeated American offers in the past to partition Oregon.[38]

But a principal anxiety of southern Democrats and Whigs was uncertainty as to the use which would be made of notice by the President. The use he had suggested in the message, and especially in its overtones, was belligerent. The message had breathed war. Yet the portion on the national defenses had breathed peace. The President had asked for no enlargement of military appropriations; indeed, the estimates had been lowered.[39] The President could by a word have removed this uncertainty. But the word was precisely the one he would not utter. It was sure to reach the British. Yet the South and the Whigs were insistent on knowing what they were voting for in voting for notice.

Over this issue the Democrats fell into a bitter internal quarrel early in March. The quarrel was set off by Haywood, the President's North Carolina friend. In a major speech he confidently predicted that the use the President would make of notice would be a reopening of the suspended negotiation. In that negotiation the President would surely accept a partition line at 49° if offered by the British. The clamor of the 54° 40′ men Haywood pronounced the noise of "selfish demagogues," interested only in "exalting little

---

[35] *Cong. Globe*, 29 Cong., 1 Sess., 351 (February 10, 1846), 372 (February 16, 1846), 379 (February 17, 1846). The same charge was made by Douglas in the House. *Ibid.*, 125, 126 (January 2, 1846).

[36] *Ibid.*, 425, 426 (February 25, 1846).

[37] *Ibid.*, Appendix, 378ff. (March 2, 1846).

[38] The constitutionality of congressional notice was challenged by Whig opponents of Polk and by others, who maintained that the treaty making power is the treaty terminating power. A minority report of the House Committee on Foreign Affairs set forth this thesis. *Cong. Globe*, 29 Cong., 1 Sess., 138, 139 (January 5, 1846); *ibid.*, Appendix, 363 (February 7, 1846).

[39] *Ibid.*, Appendix, 369ff. (March 4, 1846). See also Note 46, below.

men to high places." The tactic of these men was to create a public impression that "the administration is with us."[40] The charge of Punic faith was analyzed and pronounced false.[41] The thesis of the extremists was examined point by point and its hollowness exposed. Haywood disclaimed any White House authority for these views. He relied, he said, solely on the public record.

The potency of this speech was indicated by the fury of the replies made to it. The speech was hardly ended before Hannegan was assailing it in a tirade that became more violent as it progressed. The President was unquestionably committed, Hannegan maintained, to 54° 40'. A denial of this was merely new evidence of southern treachery. If the President were to take the course just laid out for him the truth would come to light, and he would be in "irretrievable disgrace."

So long as one human eye remains to linger on the page of history, the story of his abasement will be read, sending him and his name together to an infamy so profound, a damnation so deep, that the hand of resurrection will never be able to drag him forth. He who is a traitor to his country, can never have forgiveness of God, and cannot ask mercy of man. . . . I have only to add, that so far as the whole tone, spirit and meaning of the remarks of the Senator . . . are concerned if they speak the language of James K. Polk, James K. Polk has spoken words of falsehood, and with the tongue of a serpent.[42]

As Hannegan closed Allen jumped to his feet scarcely able to resist an impulse of his own to hew Haywood down. He was recognized, but the Senate was exhausted by the carnage it had witnessed and voted to adjourn.

The battle was reopened on another front. The western warriors gathered in caucus. They named a delegation, consisting of Hannegan and Atchison to visit the President and compel him to define his stand. The delegation found the President prepared; he had been warned by a southern Democrat of its coming. Hannegan, after a gingerly opening, propounded the big question. "Do you go for the whole of Oregon to 54° 40', or do you intend to settle

[40] The administration organ, the Washington *Union*, helped to produce such an impression. It seconded Polk's pressure tactics too heartily. Its editor, Thomas Ritchie, was never admitted to the inner recesses of Polk's mind.

[41] The charge was also analyzed and refuted by Calhoun. See *Cong. Globe*, 29 Cong., 1 Sess., Appendix, 475, 476 (March 16, 1846).

[42] *Cong. Globe*, 29 Cong., 1 Sess., 460 (March 5, 1846).

for 49°?" The President bristled. He would answer that question, he said, to no man. The foreign relations of the country were his charge, and it was unheard of for a President to say outside his cabinet what his foreign policy of the future would be. That was the end of the conference except for a little conversation to remove the chill from the air. As the interviewers departed Allen arrived. He proved more persistent than they; he came twice. The second time he drew from his hat a statement he wished the President to authorize him to read to the Senate: a statement that the speech of Haywood was without White House sanction; that the President had, indeed, asserted American title to 54° 40′; and that he had not changed his mind. Such a statement the President flatly refused to authorize. Allen, too, had to leave no wiser than he came.[43]

The Senate was refreshed soon after by a speech of Calhoun. In penetration of analysis and lucidity of statement it was the intellectual climax of the debate, and one of the greatest of Calhoun's career. It was critical of Polk. It began with a cold examination of the setting of Polk's request for authorization to give notice. He had expressed the conviction that no Oregon compromise acceptable to the nation was to be looked for from the British; the only course open was notice; after notice the nation must be ready either to uphold its rights or to abandon them. Notice, Calhoun said, had thus been equated virtually with war. This view of notice had been taken by western expansionists, by the community at large, and by those in the Senate, who, like himself, had for that reason opposed notice. Some moderates had, it was true, placed confidence in a general statement made elsewhere in the message, of hope for a peaceful settlement, and had therefore favored notice. This confidence, Calhoun believed, had been misplaced. Some moderates had believed notice was intended only as a moral weapon for obtaining an acceptable compromise. A moral weapon, Calhoun thought, could mean only intimidation, and intimidation even of a feeble nation was a hazardous tactic. Turned against a nation as great and powerful as the British it would be self-defeating. Since the message a transformation had occurred, Calhoun thought, in the state of the question. Public opinion had found time to develop on the two sides of the ocean. It had audibly and clearly demanded a compromise of the issue. It had won a favorable response from the British

[43] Quaife (ed.), *Polk Diary*, I, 270–79.

ministry. A large majority of the Senate favored compromise. The only question remaining was which side would take the first step in resuming negotiations. The Senate should do so by adopting a friendly form of notice. It should do so soon. Such a notice was being awaited by the British as a signal for the resumption of negotiations. In the United States it would, if adopted, end agitation and consolidate peace. Calhoun closed with a moving description of the horrors and costs of an Anglo-American war and, likewise, of the blessings of peace in a world that was being transformed in its potentialities for the happiness of mankind by the magic powers of steam and electricity.[44]

A seconding speech was made soon afterward, by Webster. It restated Calhoun's thesis in large part, but in terms more bluntly critical of Polk. It expressed uncertainty as to the wisdom of notice. It recommended simply a new negotiation without more ado. It proposed the forty-ninth parallel as the basis of a settlement. It gave friendly warning to the British that nothing more could be conceded by any party in the United States.[45]

Whigs fired challenges other than speeches at Polk. With the aid of southern Democrats they sent him repeated embarrassing requests for documents. They first called for recent correspondence exchanged between the two governments on the Oregon issue; also for correspondence exchanged between the State Department and its minister in London. The resolution was framed by Webster. It drew from Polk documents revealing his rejection of arbitration and also information concerning British naval armament. Another resolution was directed to the question whether foreign affairs necessitated increases in American naval and military forces. This brought the prompt reply that increases were necessitated by the Oregon crisis.[46] The last resolution requested the latest Oregon correspondence. It did not specifically include, as the first had done,

---

[44] *Cong. Globe,* 29 Cong., 1 Sess., Appendix, 471–76 (March 16, 1846). The House of Representatives was deserted during the speech. The Philadelphia *North American,* March 26, 1846, developing a theme in the speech, criticized a demand of the extremists that the nation rally around the President. "What for? For 49°, or 54.40? For peace or war? . . . We are asked to embrace a mist—to reconcile a bundle of contradictions."

[45] *Cong. Globe,* 29 Cong., 1 Sess., 567ff. (March 30, 1846).

[46] Congress voted no increases prior to the Mexican War. Benton was opposed to increases. For an illuminating speech by him on this issue, see *ibid.,* 253 (January 27, 1846).

correspondence between the American government and its London representative, McLane, of which a considerable quantity was in Polk's possession, containing reports of highly pacific Oregon conversations between McLane and Lord Aberdeen. This drew the bland reply from Polk that no correspondence between the two governments had taken place since the last transmission to Congress. Whig press reporters were aware, from information confidentially supplied by the British minister in Washington, of the McLane-Aberdeen conversations, and at once branded the President's reply as deliberately misleading.[47]

As the debate drew to a close Cass undertook to repair a serious breach made by Whigs in the line of 54° 40'. He hoped, doubtless, to hold also the leadership he had tried to maintain of his side. The breach had been made chiefly with the explosive ammunition that a succession of Democratic statesmen had tendered the British the line of 49°, which indicated that to them the 54° 40' claim of the United States was not at all perfect. What could be treasonable if a line, so often offered by these distinguished Americans, were taken now as the boundary? In refuting this argument Cass asserted that the line of 49° had been offered under a misconception—an early belief, founded in the error that the line had already been established in the eighteenth century under the Treaty of Utrecht by an Anglo-French commission. This error had only recently been laid bare by a historian, Robert Greenhow, who had shown that no such line had ever been drawn. Offers made in error were legal and moral nullities. Other claims to the Oregon Country the British had none. Nor did they have the power to impose a baseless claim on the United States. They were an enfeebled state.[48]

---

[47] The correspondent of the Philadelphia *North American* in Washington, who was the first to make this charge, was the best informed of any of the press correspondents in Washington in this period. Philadelphia *North American*, April 16, 1846. The requests to Polk are in *Cong. Globe*, 29 Cong., 1 Sess., 274–75 (January 29, 1846), 303, 304 (February 3, 1846), 510 (March 17, 1846), 656 (April 11, 1846), and for the replies see *ibid.*, 332ff. (February 7, 1846), 540ff. (March 24, 1846), 660 (April 13, 1846). See also, Quaife (ed.), *Polk Diary*, I, 208, 209, 213, 294, 296, 329. Calhoun, in supporting the request of April 11, exposed the contradictions inherent in Polk's concept that a notice could be voted by the Senate without knowledge of the state of the negotiation. *Cong. Globe*, 29 Cong., 1 Sess., 634 (April 9, 1846).

[48] *Cong. Globe*, 29 Cong., 1 Sess., Appendix, 422 (March 30, 1846); Robert Greenhow, *History of Oregon and California* (Boston, 1844). The Greenhow view was upheld later by historians.

This speech roused Benton, relatively quiet till now. He could not silently permit the furthering of a presidential candidacy by a falsification of history. Himself a historian and teacher of the Senate, he believed he had a duty to set Cass straight. In a full-length address he maintained that the line of 49° had indeed been drawn under the Utrecht settlement, and that Greenhow's researches were not to be relied on. He, himself, did not appraise the claim north of 49° until after the close of the notice debate. Then he pronounced it unfounded, the exact opposite of what he had said in the Senate four years earlier. His duel with Cass, which continued, was inconclusive, but the net result of it was that the great Missouri Senator became aligned against the ultras on the Oregon issue.[49]

The debate had now run well over four months and the end was not in sight. Even the Senate had become a little breathless. One of its members observed ruefully that a debate lasting twelve nights in the British Parliament was considered a "monstrous debate." He begged that this one be closed. In London, McLane despaired. He lamented that the notice issue had ever been sent for public discussion to Congress. He believed that the Peel government was ready for major concessions to the United States, but its tenure was precarious and might end before the debate ended. He was pressing Lord Aberdeen, despite his instructions, to begin negotiations informally at once. But Aberdeen and Peel felt unable to move.[50] Even Polk was troubled. He had expected a brief debate, one that would show American unity and a sturdy faith in American claims. But the debate had loosed an avalanche of oratory, proof of sectional disunity, doubts as to the validity of the full American claim, and a disposition to challenge his own direction of foreign affairs. It had undercut his Mexican as well as his Oregon policy. It had encouraged the Mexicans to hold out against his efforts to settle American grievances by keeping alive a hope for an Anglo-American embroilment.

---

[49] *Cong. Globe*, 29 Cong., 1 Sess., 913 (May 28, 1846); *ibid.*, 27 Cong., 3 Sess., Appendix, 18 (August 18, 1842); Quaife (ed.), *Polk Diary*, I, 117.

[50] McLane to Buchanan, April 18, May 4, 1846, Buchanan Papers (Historical Society of Pennsylvania); McLane to Buchanan, No. 43, May 3, 1846, Despatches, England, 56, State Department Records (National Archives); McLane to Polk, May 8, 1846, Polk Papers, Vol. 74; Aberdeen to Pakenham, May 4, 1846, Aberdeen Papers (British Museum).

The Senate finally consented to a vote in April. The vote was to be on the question of the form of notice, if notice were sent. The form Allen now wanted was the one of the House. He had given up his own Senate form as unattainable. The House form relieved the President of responsibility for serving notice. It directed him to act. Another form, proposed by Crittenden, placed full responsibility for serving on the President. The Crittenden form was more conciliatory in its language, also, than the House form. It won in a preliminary test of strength by a large majority in the Senate.[51]

This moved Allen to make a speech berating the majority. He reminded them that the President had asked Congress to serve the notice. The Senate, instead of complying, had "divided, faltering, paltering, manacled, hampered by a frightful unwillingness to meet responsibility—saying, oh! we leave it all to your discretion." The Senate, Allen thought, had showed hostility to the President in foisting this responsibility on him. But the President would not shirk. He would "go behind no bush."[52] This was a reprimand questionable in taste for any senator. From one of Allen's years, in such terms, to a majority it was unbearable. It was, moreover, of a piece with the bad manners he and his associates had exhibited throughout the debate. They had resorted to browbeating. Whoever was unwilling to fight for 54° 40′ was lacking in nerve, in patriotism, must be pro-British, or even treasonable. The opponents had protested these tactics and had replied to them as they could.[53] Now at the end of the debate, Crittenden boiled over. For half an hour he administered to Allen a tongue lashing such as is seldom heard in the decorous precincts of the Senate.[54] The Senate listened in silent approval. Allen felt impelled, in reply, to refer to the "grotesque faces" Crittenden made in speaking. Whereupon Crittenden answered that he would be content to learn manners from anybody, even from a blackguard. On this note the monster debate ended.[55]

But the Senate still had its own rebuke to give Allen and his methods. By an overwhelming vote of 40 to 14 it rejected his proposed notice and approved Crittenden's. And by a like vote it

[51] *Cong. Globe*, 29 Cong., 1 Sess., 198 (January 14, 1846), 680 (April 16, 1846).
[52] *Ibid.*, 681 (April 16, 1846).
[53] *Ibid.*, Appendix, 370ff. (March 4, 1846); 521 (March 18, 1846).
[54] *Cong. Globe*, 29 Cong., 1 Sess., 681–83 (April 16, 1846).
[55] *Ibid.*, 682–83 (April 16, 1846).

rejected him as a member of the conference committee which was to iron out differences between the Senate and House forms, though the House had named its foreign affairs committee chairman to head its conferees.[56]

The conference committee quickly reached agreement on a resolution of notice which left the President discretion to serve and was conciliatory to the British. The resolution was overwhelmingly approved by both houses and was at once dispatched by the President to the British government.[57] It effected the desired object of reopening the negotiation.

The reopened negotiation took the form of a series of cabinet deliberations at which Lord Aberdeen pressed for concessions to the United States and was prompted from outside by McLane. Aberdeen had been personally willing to agree to a line at 49° as a basis for a boundary two and a half years before. He had failed to win over Peel and the cabinet. Now he succeeded. He got permission to propose that line, stopped short, however, at the Straits so as not to sever Vancouver Island. He was less successful with the Columbia River issue. Navigation of the river had been enjoyed by the British for half a century. Vested interests in it had become established. Yet the President had declared publicly he would agree to no continuation, and he had sent insistent warnings to McLane that any proposal continuing it would be rejected offhand. This was the sticking point in the deliberations. It was finally resolved by a compromise wherein navigation rights were retained for the Hudson's Bay Company but not for British subjects generally. Possessory rights to occupied land of the Company south of 49° were also given protection. These were the main items of a proposal, highly conciliatory, agreed to by the cabinet.[58]

What were the forces, British and American, producing these concessions? Was Polk's program of pressure among them? One

[56] *Ibid.*, 683 (April 16, 1846), 703 (April 21, 1846). The rebuke of the Senate to Allen was unprecedented, according to the press.

[57] *Ibid.*, 717, 720, 721 (April 23, 1846).

[58] These terms were under discussion with the Governor of the Hudson's Bay Company well before the treaty project was drawn. In Sir John H. Pelly to Aberdeen, March 13, 1846, Aberdeen Papers, the Governor submitted a list of Hudson's Bay Company properties south of 49°. See also London *Times*, January 17, 1846. The navigation right of the Hudson's Bay Company was reluctantly proposed by McLane to Aberdeen as a lesser evil than a general British right. McLane to Buchanan, No. 58, July 3, 1846, Despatches, England, 56, State Department Records; McLane to Polk, May 28, 1846, Polk Papers, Vol. 74.

force was Peel's eagerness to clear away the last of the conflicts with the United States inherited from Palmerston's days. Another was his wish to give peace protection to the great free trade experiment for which he had become responsible. A third was cabinet confidence in Aberdeen. A fourth was apprehension over the consequences of allowing the Oregon issue to slide, in the United States, into the autumn elections, and in England, into the hands of Palmerston on his expected return to the Foreign Office.[59] Another was Webster's warning that no party in the United States could accept less than the forty-ninth parallel as the basis of a settlement. Insignificant was the pressure program of Polk, and still less the fulminations of the war hawks. Peel was not a man to yield easily to intimidation.

The British proposal reached Polk on June 6. It did not meet his minimum. Its Columbia River provision was short of his public prescription. Yet a rejection, without a counter offer, would lead, he believed, to war,[60] and the nation was already deep in the Mexican War. The proposal was referred to the cabinet. If the cabinet would unanimously decide that it should be sent to the Senate he would yield. The cabinet decided it should be sent, with Buchanan alone opposed. Buchanan declared he would not commit himself before knowing the nature of the President's letter of transmission. He declared that the 54° 40′ men "were the true friends of the administration and he wished no backing out on the subject." The cabinet was astounded. Buchanan had been an exponent of the line of 49° throughout the preceding year. His dispatches to McLane had even been in need of stiffening. His turning to the 54° 40′ men augured trouble and his remark that he wished "no backing out" was adding insult to injury. The President kept his temper and outlined what he would say in a letter of transmission. His own views, he would say, remained as they had been, but he would "conform" them to those of the Senate if that body, by a two-thirds vote, would advise him to accept the British proposal—with or without modification. If the Senate should decline to advise

[59] Aberdeen to Pakenham, May 18, 1846, "Precis," p. 125, Aberdeen Papers. News of the outbreak of the Mexican War had not reached England by May 18.

[60] The cabinet also believed the British would make use of American involvement in the Mexican War to declare their offer an ultimatum and its rejection a ground for war. McLane likewise had such fears. Quaife (ed.), *Polk Diary*, I, 445, 453; McLane to Polk, undated [May 29 to June 1, 1846], Polk Papers, Vol. 74.

him, he would reject the proposal. He wished Buchanan to draft such a letter. Buchanan refused. His refusal seemed to the President designed to avoid responsibility for a compromise with a view, if compromise proved unpopular, of standing well with the 54° 40' men. At a private meeting the next day the President again asked the Secretary to draft the letter, adding that he intended to send also the correspondence Buchanan had been having with McLane. He was giving warning, perhaps, that any private reversing of gears by the Secretary would be difficult. Buchanan refused again, and objected to the sending in of the correspondence. Heated words were exchanged. A break in the relations of the two men seemed imminent.

At a subsequent cabinet meeting the President read a draft of a letter to the Senate he had himself written. It was approved by all except Buchanan. The cabinet then took the wayward Secretary in hand. It reminded him pointedly of the views he had so long been expressing. It referred, also, to his compromising dispatches. It all but suggested that this was a case of presidential fever. He responded finally to this treatment, and, in the end himself re-drafted the President's letter. The letter, as agreed to, cited George Washington as having begun the practice of referring treaty issues for previous advice to the Senate. It emphasized the special appropriateness of this course on an issue so publicly and recently debated by the Senate. Then it repeated the President's formula that his own convictions were unchanged, but that he would conform his actions to those of the Senate.[61]

The Senate took up the letter and its accompanying offer in executive session. It would, under ordinary circumstances, have referred them to the Committee on Foreign Relations, and this Allen moved should be done. His motion was defeated by the overwhelming and humiliating margin of 37 to 9. Then Haywood moved to give advice to accept the offer. A hostile amendment was beaten off, following which, by a vote of 38 to 12, well above the two-thirds majority needed, the motion of Haywood was adopted.

This vote the President had expected. It corresponded with the sentiment of the Senate in the debate and with the overwhelming

---

[61] Quaife (ed.), *Polk Diary*, I, 451–62; Richardson (comp.), *Messages and Papers of the Presidents*, IV, 449. Buchanan had been a 54° 40' exponent prior to the Baltimore convention.

majority given the Crittenden notice.[62] It was not only expected, it was desired by him. The advice of the Senate was a convenient bush behind which to withdraw from the several Oregon positions he had taken.

But why did he want to withdraw? The answer is compound. He was under new pressures. One of them was the pressure of public opinion. Public opinion had undergone, during the debate, a marked change, as Calhoun had pointed out. In 1844 it could have been considered expansionist. By April, 1846, it was frowning on expansionism, at least of the war hawk variety. In February, 1846, Sumner was writing an English friend: "The war spirit has talked itself hoarse and feeble; and the conscience of the nation is awakening."[63] A New York correspondent of an English journal observed: "The rampant patriots in Congress, who threw themselves upon their war-horses and charged upon St. George with the certainty of the American people following them, have to their confusion found themselves riding all alone in their glory, whilst the nation has either forgotten them in their profound contempt or made merry at their ludicrous pranks."[64]

The President was powerfully influenced also by anxiety concerning his party. The party was breaking up over the 54° 40' issue. Its southern and eastern wings were separating themselves from the western and falling into the arms of the Whigs. Disruption of party seemed to Polk irretrievable disaster. It had happened to the Whigs at the beginning of the preceding administration and had reduced that whole administration to impotence. This apprehension is reflected in increasingly anxious references to party dissensions in the *Diary* in the spring of 1846, in a new impatience with the 54° 40' men whom he had earlier favored, and in a conviction that what they were primarily interested in was not 54° 40' or 49° but '48.[65] Still another pressure on Polk, which was recent, was the war with Mexico which had come early in May. One war at a time was enough.

[62] Moore (ed.), *Works of Buchanan*, VII, 3.
[63] Edward L. Pierce, *Memoir and Letters of Charles Sumner* (4 vols., Boston, 1877–1893), II, 378.
[64] London *Morning Post*, February 19, 1846.
[65] Quaife (ed.), *Polk Diary*, I, 261–65, 278–80, 285–88, 289, 295–300, 344, 345, 351, 352, 359–62; Roger Wolcott (ed.), *The Correspondence of William H. Prescott, 1833–1847* (Cambridge, 1925), 585; William Sturgis to George Bancroft, June 15, 1846, Bancroft Papers (Massachusetts Historical Society).

The advice of the Senate was promptly translated therefore into a formalized treaty which Buchanan and the British minister signed. The treaty was a copy of the British offer. It contained defects as well as virtues of the offer—technical defects destined to plague Anglo-American relations for many years.[66] Correction of these seemed less important in the spring of 1846 than speed of completing the treaty.[67] The Peel government was tottering to a fall and a return of the treaty quickly to London for final approval was essential. In short order the treaty was ratified. The vote of ratification gave striking evidence of the weakness of the 54° 40′ sentiment in the nation. It was 41 to 14. The ratified treaty was hurried to London where it arrived none too soon; indeed, after the Peel government had fallen though before it had given up office. Peel was able in his valedictory to hail the treaty as one of the triumphs of his administration in the cause of Anglo-American peace.

In the meantime a valedictory of another sort was delivered before the Senate. It was the resignation of Allen from the Committee on Foreign Relations. It reflected his feeling, after the crucial vote of advice to the President, that his defeats and humiliations at the hands of the Senate had made his further service on the Committee impossible. But it was by no means an admission of failure. It was meant to spark off a revolt against those in the administration responsible for the collapse of the 54° 40′ cause. Allen had sought vainly to induce his Democratic colleagues on the Committee to join him in a mass resignation of protest. He referred to the treaty privately as treason and predicted an outcry against it.[68]

[66] The technical defects, all recognized in 1846, were inexact definition of the water boundary circling the tip of Vancouver Island, uncertainty as to the duration of the rights of navigation of the Hudson's Bay Company on the Columbia, and indefiniteness as to the kind and extent of possessory rights guaranteed to that Company. Moore (ed.), *Works of Buchanan*, VII, 3, 11; Pakenham to Aberdeen, June 13, 1846, Aberdeen Papers; McLane to Buchanan, April 18, 1846, Buchanan Papers.

[67] The Washington *Union* on May 7, 1846, published under the caption "Momentous" an extract of a letter from London clandestinely supplied to it by Buchanan, discussing the probable unpleasant results for the United States of the expected return of Palmerston to the Foreign Office. The identity of the writer was withheld. The writer was A. Dudley Mann, special agent of the State Department, who was passing through London on his way to diplomatic service in the states of Germany. Mann to Buchanan, April 18, 1846, Buchanan Papers.

[68] Allen to Effie Allen, June 28, 1846, William Allen Papers (Manuscript Division, Library of Congress), Vol. 14. A discriminating biography of Allen is Reginald C. McGrane, *William Allen: A Study in Western Democracy* (Columbus, 1925). It is less satisfactory on Allen's chairmanship than elsewhere.

No outcry occurred. The Mexican War and its issues crowded the treaty out of public sight. Even the colleagues of Allen on the Committee deserted him. Cass hastened to the White House to let the President know of the attempt at a collective resignation and of his own refusal to countenance it. He assured the President that though he would vote against the treaty he would never thereafter make an issue of it.[69] Sevier actually voted for ratification. Other 54° 40′ crusaders, including Dallas, abandoned the cause. Allen was defeated for re-election when his term ended and sank into an obscurity from which he emerged only briefly after the Civil War as a leader of the Ohio Greenback movement.

The debate eventuating in the treaty was of more than passing significance. It exerted for years an influence on American politics. It gave politicians warning that a pledge to the electorate of a single term is unsafe.[70] After 1848 such a pledge was never again given by a presidential candidate or a president. That relic of Jacksonian democracy disappeared. Also, the debate was significant in sowing distrust between western and southern Democrats.[71] The distrust was destined to harden as the slavery controversy deepened, and to disrupt the party on the eve of the Civil War. The debate was significant, also, for the judgment it called down on Polk. It drew public attention to his shifting Oregon positions, his disingenuous tactics, and his final dodging of responsibility for the result. It projected a portrait of him on the screen as a man of short and narrow vision, of deviousness in thought and action, and of aggressiveness in dealing with other states to the point of recklessness. That portrait was by critics, to be sure, but by critics of both parties, Whigs and disenchanted Democrats. It figured in the politics of the later years of the administration and in the judgment of historians. The judgment of historians was ultimately modified, perhaps too much, by the publication of the famous *Diary*, which revealed the problems faced by the President.

But the primary impact of the debate was on its own day. The

---

[69] Quaife (ed.), *Polk Diary*, I, 471, 475–77.

[70] In the Nashville *Union* of March 31, 1846, Polk's Oregon troubles were explicitly ascribed to the single-term pledge. See also New York *Journal of Commerce*, April 11, 1846.

[71] The "double dealing" of Polk and its divisive effect on his party was the theme of much Whig press comment in the spring of 1846. See especially a series of penetrating articles in the Philadelphia *North American* by its Washington correspondent, March 20, 24, 28, and June 15, 1846.

debate spread knowledge of the Oregon issue. It revealed the intrinsic weakness of the American claim to the whole of Oregon, the likelihood of a ruinous war if it were pressed to a showdown, and the irresponsibility and numerical inferiority of those pressing it. The debate gave, likewise, precious months of time to the public to reflect on this information—a major service. The magnitude of that service was dramatically shown, even as the debate closed, when a Texan boundary issue, inflamed by an order of the President to the American army to occupy the disputed region, flared into an incident, which swept Congress and the public off their feet and into the Mexican War. By giving time, by very reason of being a monster debate, this one on Oregon allowed a public opinion to form which was calm and enlightened, and which, despite presidential fevers, saved the peace in the crisis.

RÉSUMÉ

A FIXED idea pervaded the initial Oregon boundary negotiations held in the spring and summer of 1818 in London. It was that a boundary line at the 49th parallel already existed between British Rupert's Land and French Louisiana west of the Lake of the Woods. The line was believed to have been agreed upon by Anglo-French commissioners under the terms of the Treaty of Utrecht of 1713. It was thought to have been run at least to the Rocky Mountains. The existence of the line was attested to in maps and atlases published in Europe and in America. The line became of increasing importance after Louisiana passed in 1803 into American possession.

In 1807 the line's reality seemed to be confirmed by an agreement made in London. Two American plenipotentiaries, James Monroe and William Pinkney, had been sent there to compose controversies arising out of British interferences with American neutral rights at sea and, especially, with the impressment of American seamen. The plenipotentiaries were able to obtain two agreements, one relating to neutral rights, and a second, relating to the boundary westward of the Lake of the Woods. The second specified that the boundary "westward of the said lake as far as the territories of the respective powers extend in that quarter" should be the 49th parallel.[1] This bore the distinct impress of the Utrecht line. But neither agreement was ever ratified. The Americans had violated their instructions on the sore issue of impressment and Jefferson refused to submit either agreement for ratification to the Senate, much to the chagrin of Monroe.

The 1807 approval by the British of a line identical with that of Utrecht was still in Monroe's mind when, in 1814, as Secretary of State he drew up instructions for the American peace delegation at Ghent.[2] Assuming that Astoria had fallen during the war, an assumption which proved correct, he directed the delegation not

[1] *American State Papers, Foreign Relations* (Washington, 1832–59), VII, 164–165.
[2] See Essay 1.

to permit, in any arrangement for partitioning the Oregon Country, a line that would run south of 49°. A line at 49° already was the boundary east of the mountains, he believed, and the delegates were to be careful in regard to the Oregon Country not to "countenance in any manner, or in any quarter, a pretension in the British government to territory south of the line." John Quincy Adams, the leader of the Ghent delegation, was thus alerted to the line of 49° east of the mountains, and later, when he became Secretary of State under Monroe, he wrote into the instructions for the first Oregon negotiation of 1818 the fixed idea of Monroe regarding a Utrecht line.

In the negotiation of 1818 Albert Gallatin and Richard Rush were the American plenipotentiaries. They were, like their chief, under the influence of the idea of a Utrecht line. They made this evident in a report at the close of the negotiation. They had been instructed to settle the boundary issues on both sides of the mountains, and also other issues. In summing up what they had accomplished they referred to a boundary east of the mountains as though it had been long established and to the "Columbia River" issue as one still to be settled. They wrote:

This subject [Columbia River issue] was, during the whole negotiation, connected by the British plenipotentiaries with that of the boundary line [east of the mountains]. They appeared altogether unwilling to agree to this [east of the mountains line] in any shape, unless some arrangement was made with respect to the country westward of the Stony mountains. This induced us to propose an extension of the boundary line, due west, to the Pacific ocean. We did not assert that the United States had a perfect right to that country, but insisted that their claim was at least good against Great Britain. The forty-ninth degree of north latitude had, in pursuance of the treaty of Utrecht, been fixed, indefinitely, as the line between the northern British possessions and those of France, including Louisiana, now a part of our territories. There was no reason why, if the two countries extended their claims westward, the same line should not be continued to the Pacific ocean. So far as discovery gave a claim, ours to the whole country on the waters of the Columbia was indisputable. . . .[3]

Of special interest in this account is the immediate appearance of the 49th parallel as the American offer of partition. It emerges

[3] Albert Gallatin and Richard Rush to John Quincy Adams, Oct. 20, 1818, in *A.S.P., F.R.,* IV, 381.

at the opening of the negotiation, and for a reason the American plenipotentiaries thought conclusive: That line was already the boundary separating British and American possessions for a great distance east of the Stony Mountains. "There was no reason why . . . the same line should not be continued to the Pacific ocean." The east line had been fixed, so Gallatin and Rush said, "indefinitely, as the line" between the possessions of the British and those of the French, including Louisiana "now part of our territories." Here was the *idée fixe* at work. Its truth was not challenged by the British plenipotentiaries, both alert persons, Frederick J. Robinson and Henry Goulburn.

A quarter of a century later, Robert Greenhow, an American scholar, challenged the Utrecht line in the closing stages of the Oregon controversy. He maintained that the Utrecht idea was a myth perpetuated by incompetent cartographers.[4] He was upheld in the Senate by Lewis Cass, who spoke for American expansionists eager for a 54° 40′ settlement, and who argued that the offer the American government had made of the line of 49° was, because based on a false myth, a moral nullity. He was answered by a Southern Democrat, Thomas Hart Benton, who was widely thought to be a great scholar, and who favored a compromise settlement on the basis of 49°. Benton insisted that Greenhow's history was wrong, that the Utrecht line had assuredly been drawn at 49°, and, indeed, that it had been drawn even across the Oregon Country. In this case the researches of Greenhow and Cass were subsequently upheld by the researches of later American scholars.[5]

In the course of the 1818 negotiation the eastern line finally was fastened down. Between the possessions of the United States and those of Great Britain the 49th parallel became the boundary for the entire distance from the Lake of the Woods to the crest of the Stony Mountains. The myth of Utrecht was converted into reality. Support was provided for the contention in all later American negotiations that a line reaching as far as the Rocky Mountains should be extended beyond the mountains to the Pacific.

The negotiation of 1818 is of significance, in spite of its not

---

[4] Robert Greenhow, *History of Oregon and California* (Boston, 1844), 281–283.
[5] See Essay 13, pp. 385–386. See also C. O. Paullin, "The Forty Ninth Parallel," in *Canadian Historical Review*, IV (1923), 127–131 and J. S. Reeves, *American Diplomacy under Tyler and Polk* (Baltimore, 1907), 194–198.

having achieved a partition of the Oregon Country. It laid out a case for each side and established a pattern destined to become fixed and to be a major factor in generating the crisis of 1845–46. Each side during the negotiation was willing to recognize that the other had meritorious claims in the Oregon Country. The American plenipotentiaries admitted at the outset that the United States had no perfect claim to All Oregon. The British took a like stand. Their government had taken it already in the preliminaries to the negotiation in agreeing to a restoration of the Astoria post under the terms of the Ghent Treaty.

In the negotiation a very persuasive case was made by the Americans for the thesis that the Oregon line should be the 49th parallel. The case might almost be described as excessively persuasive, should a demand ever arise for a partition line farther north. It began with the Utrecht line thesis, and thus brought to bear the concept in international law known as contiguity. This, moreover, was reinforced by equity and convenience, also much cited in international law. Equity was the thesis that where both sides in a controversy had strong claims, partition should be resorted to and should be as nearly as possible on a basis of parity. The 49th parallel would be the answer. No exact division of values could be laid out, to be sure. The Oregon Country is mountainous, much is semi-arid, or even arid. But parity could be arrived at by an approximate halving of Oregon's square mileage and the 49th parallel did that. As for convenience, harbors in any big area are needed for intercourse with the outside world, and 49° would provide them. The United States would have a harbor at the mouth of the Columbia and others inside the Strait of Juan de Fuca. The British would have harbors at Nootka, inside the Straits, and on Oregon's northern shoreline.

But rivers of importance would be severed if harbors were to be so divided. Rivers in a severed state are notorious breeders of dissension. Unfortunately the most important of all Oregon rivers would be cut if the 49th parallel were to be the line of partition. The Columbia sprawls across the whole of the Oregon Country, either in its main stem or in its branches. The problem was how to share the harbors and at the same time reduce to a minimum the evil of severing a needed river.

The Columbia, by its very nature, suggested the solution. Its flow is turbulent, reflecting its mountainous origins. It is so broken by waterfalls and rapids that it is useless for a heavy commerce. It is obstructed by a dangerous sandbar, moreover, at its mouth. It was used by British fur traders only for special services. They used it for canoe transportation to interior trading posts and for carrying off the annual catch of furs. Since it seemed to the British government, despite all its limitations, indispensable as a connection with the interior, the American government offered to share navigation rights on it in that part of the river which would come to the United States if the partition line should be at 49°.

The case made by the Americans took account of exploration as a factor in determining the line of partition. Exploration seemed to give force to the contention that the 49th parallel be the line. An American mariner, Captain Robert Gray, had discovered the mouth of the Columbia River and the Lewis and Clark expedition had explored the valley in the interior, all south of the 49th parallel. British exploration had its locale principally north of that parallel, as the names of such explorers as Mackenzie, Vancouver, Fraser, and Thompson bore witness. Settlement made after exploration is important in tying down claims and here again much could be said for the 49th parallel, though the British had rather the edge there. The line of 49° thus conformed with Utrecht, with contiguity, with exploration, and in general with settlement.

On the British side arbitration was the earliest proposal made in 1818. It was made by Castlereagh for both the boundary issues —east and west of the mountains. It was rejected at once by John Quincy Adams in Washington and the direct negotiation followed.[6] In that negotiation the American offer of 49° attracted no British counter offer, but merely an intimation that if the line were offered to the Columbia, with the river to be followed thereafter to the sea, it might be accepted. The intimation was hardly an offer but at least it was the basis for subsequent British offers.

The core of territory lying between the two basic offers was not considered of major consequence in itself. It seemed to experts on both sides to be of inferior quality. A reputed American expert, Ramsay Crooks, who knew the Columbia, sent Albert Gallatin the amazing testimony that it was "extremely worthless"—deficient in soil, timber, and furs.[7] To British experts, also, it seemed of little consequence, judged in purely territorial terms. What did seem of

[6] See Essay 2.
[7] See Essay 3, pp. 65–66.

consequence to them was the trade flowing up and down the Columbia, not only the trade as it was, but what it might become in the future.

The trade, as it was in the opening years of the Oregon negotiations, was of no great dimension. Indeed, it was surprisingly slight. Yet it seemed worth fighting for to the North West Company, and the Company was a fighting organization. It did not hesitate to engage in armed conflict, either on the Columbia against Americans, or in the interior of Rupert's Land against a great British organization, the Hudson's Bay Company. On the Columbia, prior to the War of 1812, it fought John Jacob Astor. In Rupert's Land it challenged its older rival, even though the latter held from the Crown an exclusive charter to the trade and soil of the province. In 1813, in cooperation with the navy of England, the North West Company sought out Astor's post at Astoria. One of its craft piloted a war vessel into the Columbia to seize the establishment. Seizure proved unnecessary. The North West Company's local agents had decided it would be better to buy the post and its fur contents than to let them become the prize of the warcraft's crew. The purchase had taken place to forestall a seizure. But a seizure of the establishment, pro forma, was effected by the naval captain in hauling down the American flag and raising the British in its place.

The North West Company's London agent in dealings with the British government was Simon M'Gillivray, one of the Company's leading partners. He was the Company's specialist in boundary and charter clashes and its spokesman before the Colonial Office and the Foreign Office. He had represented the Company's interests there during the Ghent negotiations. He had been unable to prevent a provision in the treaty for mutual restoration of conquests made during the war. But he promptly developed the thesis that this provision did not cover Astoria because the post had passed into British hands by purchase, not by capture.

In 1818 M'Gillivray published a pamphlet in London entitled *Notice Respecting the Boundary*. In it he developed the thesis that the aggressive American government had designs on the Pacific Northwest even above the line of 49°. He offered as evidence a copy of a recently published American map, on which the line of 49° 40′ had been drawn. He accompanied it by a second map of his own on which two great streams, the Columbia and another to the north of it, named "Caledonia," appeared, both of which would be severed by a line drawn at 49°. The "Caledonia" was a fabricated, an apocryphal stream. But it was accepted by diplomats and map-makers alike for years, since the North West Company was a cartographic authority on the wilderness of the Pacific Northwest. The map became a force militating against any British acceptance of a partition line at the 49th parallel.[8] In the 1818 negotiation a partition proved unattainable and an agreement of joint occupation of the disputed region was adopted instead.

By the time of the 1823–24 negotiation a new defender of British interests in the Oregon Country had appeared. It was the Hudson's Bay Company, old in years, but new to the Pacific Northwest. Its advent was the outcome of a merger with the North West Company in 1821. It had received, as a reward for the merger, a monopoly of all British trade rights in the Oregon Country.

In the 1823–24 negotiation, after the Adams-Onís Treaty had been won, Adams momentarily lifted his sights. He instructed Richard Rush to start off with a proposal of a line at 51°. But he did not press the idea with his accustomed vigor, and Rush was almost perfunctory in asking for 51° and then dropping back to 49°. He extracted nothing in the way of countervailing concessions in his descent, which is a commentary on the effectiveness in Oregon matters of the Adams-Onís Treaty.

For a number of years the Hudson's Bay Company derived little profit on the lower Columbia from its monopoly of British trade rights. It actually considered withdrawing from the lower river to what is now British Columbia. Late in 1825 it applied to the Foreign Office for guidance as to its course. It was aware of the approach of the expiration date of the joint occupation agreement. It wished to know whether, in a new Oregon negotiation, it could count on retaining the north side of the Columbia.[9] Its communication came before George Canning, the Secretary for Foreign Affairs in the Liverpool government. Canning was an intense nationalist who had been Foreign Secretary during the years in which the United States was being driven into war with England in defense of its rights as a neutral at sea. He had been one of the most relent-

[8] See Essay 3.
[9] Frederick Merk, ed., *Fur Trade and Empire: George Simpson's Journal* (Cambridge, Mass., 1931), 257–259.

less of the elements in England in blows at the American merchant marine in an effort to curb it and Napoleon.[10]

Canning responded to the suggestion that a new negotiation be instituted by asking questions of the Company as to the extent of its trade in Oregon, the agricultural value of the area, and the degree of dependence of the area on the Columbia River. To these questions George Simpson, the field governor of the Company, made answer during a visit to London. Asked to distinguish between the districts at the north and south of the Columbia, he wrote that those to the north and south "produce about an equal quantity of Furs amounting together in value to between 30 and £40,000 p. Annum." These were not impressive figures. They were less than the gross of many a textile factory in England. Prefacing the figures was an observation, however, that the trade of the Columbia was still "in its infancy," which was a matter of opinion and proved of questionable truth.[11] Simpson reported enthusiastically on the agricultural possibilities of the lower Columbia and on its timber resources. He made a positive assertion that if the navigation of the Columbia River was not kept free to the Company and if the territory on its northern side was not secured to them, "they must abandon and curtail their trade in some parts, and probably be constrained to relinquish it on the West side of the Rocky Mountains altogether."[12] This was just the information Canning wanted, and he stored it for use in the new negotiation.

He further directed the Under Secretary for Foreign Affairs, Henry U. Addington, to draw up a memorandum appraising the claims of the two powers to the disputed country. Addington was a protégé of Canning and knew what his chief desired. His memorandum was less an appraisal than a combative defense of British

[10] The contemporary American view of Canning as a relentless foe of the United States is challenged by Bradford Perkins in *Prologue to War* (Berkeley, 1961), 221–222; and in *Castlereagh and Adams* (Berkeley, 1964), *passim*.

[11] Merk, ed., *Fur Trade and Empire*, 260–266. Statistics of profit and loss of the various districts of the Columbia Department are published for the years 1838–1845 in Edwin E. Rich, ed., *Letters of John McLoughlin, Second Series, 1839–44, Publications of the Champlain Society, Hudson's Bay Company Series*, VI (Toronto, 1943), 235; and in Robert C. Clark, *History of the Willamette Valley Oregon* (Chicago, 1927), I, 865–870. The profits varied from £11,203 for the Outfit of 1838 to £9,613 for the Outfit of 1845. They rose after 1845, somewhat, chiefly from increased trade at the Fort Vancouver Sale Shop with American pioneers.

[12] Merk, ed., *Fur Trade and Empire*, 261–266.

claims to Oregon. It asserted that Francis Drake had explored the whole Oregon coast from latitude 37° to 48°, though the scholarly world believed even then that the voyage had gone no farther north than 42° or 43°. It questioned Gray's discovery of the Columbia and dismissed the Lewis and Clark expedition with a mere mention. It developed the thesis, originally propounded by Canning, that the American acquisition of Spain's claims to the Oregon Country had weakened, not strengthened, the case of the United States. It resurrected the M'Gillivray thesis that Astoria should not have been ordered restored to the United States because it had been purchased by the British, not captured.[13]

Shortly before the opening of the negotiation Canning sent this appraisal to Lord Liverpool, the Prime Minister. He added comments of his own and in them outdid his subordinate. What Addington had merely questioned—that Gray had discovered the Columbia—Canning forthrightly denied. He concluded with the sentiment that in view of those facts he did not know how to contemplate surrendering Britain's claims.[14]

The Prime Minister was unconvinced. He still wished dispassionate consideration to be given to the old American proposal of the 49th parallel. He thought the cabinet should know the value of the trade carried on in the Oregon region. Also, he thought the cabinet should know whether the American proposal of 49° would leave the British adequate outlets to the sea "by Nootka and other ports," and how far such communications would be less advantageous than those through the Columbia. These were pointed questions.

Canning remembered now that he had not sent the cabinet Simpson's testimony of the preceding January showing the slightness of the trade in the Oregon Country. He had forgotten it, so he wrote. Before sending it in he lessened the impact of its figures for the benefit of Liverpool:

But it is not from what our trade is now, that the question is to be estimated. It is when China shall be open to English as well as American commerce that the real value of settlements on the Northwest coast of America will become apparent.[15]

[13] E. J. Stapleton, ed., *Some Official Correspondence of George Canning* (London, 1887), II, 110–115.
[14] *Ibid.*, 55.
[15] *Ibid.*, 62.

He further commented, when finally submitting the Hudson's Bay Company materials:

We cannot yet enter this [China] trade, on account of the monopoly of the East India Company. But ten years hence that monopoly will cease; and though at that period neither you nor I shall be where we are to answer for our deeds, I should not like to leave my name affixed to an instrument by which England would have foregone the advantages of an immense direct intercourse between China, and what may be, if we resolve not to yield them up, her boundless establishments on the N. W. Coast of America.[16]

The negotiation of 1826–27, so initiated, was meager of outcome. Its only progress was a British offer of an isolated area north of the Columbia fronting on the Strait of Juan de Fuca—an offer apparently made in response to pressures applied to Canning in the cabinet. The area would have been an *enclave*, surrounded by territory and waters that were British. It was rejected by Gallatin at once. It was not even taken for reference to his government. The negotiation ended in a renewal of the joint occupation agreement, which meant postponement of a settlement of the issue once again. A kind of groove had by now been established at 49° along which flowed American ambitions to reach the Pacific.

Between the first negotiation in the London series and the first in Washington a quarter of a century elapsed. This was an era of revolutionary changes in the world's modes of transportation. The railroad age came into its own. In 1829 the first locomotive was set going on American tracks. By 1840 locomotives operated on 2800 miles of rail tracks in the United States. Imagination outraced construction. It carried railroads to the shores of the Pacific. In the 1840's Congress was being besieged by the American public to give aid to the construction of a railroad from the Great Lakes to the Pacific. Concepts of national growth expanded with the new modes of travel and communication. The Jeffersonian concept that prohibitions of distance and mountains precluded an extension of the government of the Union to the trans-Rocky Mountain area was discarded. Instead the concept of Manifest Destiny—that the American Republic would yet acquire continental proportions— became an article of faith among American expansionists.

[16] *Ibid.,* 71–75.

Dreams of connection by rail altered the character and location of specific stakes of Oregon diplomacy. They gave new value to the harbors inside the Straits. Prior to the railroad age those harbors seemed hopelessly circumscribed by lack of natural connection with the interior such as was enjoyed by the harbor at the mouth of the Columbia. They were cut off from the interior by range after range of mountains. Their only river, the Fraser, was utterly unnavigable.[17] Now they were viewed as connected with the interior by the railroads of the future. What nature had denied, man would provide. The intrinsic excellence of those harbors—their deep waters, their capaciousness, their inland position, safety from the winds and sands of the ocean, and convenient lanes to the sea— won recognition. Those harbors became the major commercial prizes of the Oregon Country.

The harbor at the mouth of the Columbia declined by comparison. It did so in the estimation of American and British governments alike. Its perilous barred entrance and its broken interior course were given increasing notice in public discussion in both countries. The report of the Charles Wilkes Exploring Expedition (which described the loss of one of its vessels on the Columbia bar, and lauded the beauties of the harbors at the Straits) enforced the contrast. It made clear that the Straits harbors were the only safe ones on the entire Pacific shore to which the United States had any claim.

But the area embracing those harbors (the whole area south of the Straits to the north bank of the lower Columbia) was a British sphere. It had become virtually a possession of the Hudson's Bay Company. It was British in trade and in farming and grazing. Its inhabitants were British—servants of the Hudson's Bay Company and of the Puget Sound Agricultural Company. Its status as a British sphere had been upheld in repeated negotiations for a quarter century. If the British were to concede the Straits harbors to the Americans, they must surrender the whole of the area.

The first of the Washington series of Oregon negotiations was held in 1842. It was held by governments newly established in both countries. In England the Peel government had come into office in 1841, with Aberdeen as its Secretary for Foreign Affairs. In the United States the Tyler government (heir to the electoral triumph

[17] The myth of the Caledonia River had been discredited by 1824.

of Harrison) had come into office, with Daniel Webster as Secretary of State. The two governments were eager to clear away an accumulation of issues that had dogged their relations for generations. The most stubborn were the explosive Northeastern boundary dispute, the heightening dispute over Oregon, and the old controversy over British rights of search at sea in peacetime —a controversy revived as a result of Britain's efforts to suppress the African slave trade.

A special mission to deal with these problems and others subsidiary to them was proposed by the British government at the end of 1841. Washington was suggested as its seat, and Lord Ashburton, former director of an internationally known London banking house and popular in the United States, was proposed as its head. This suggestion was gladly adopted and the work of preparing instructions for the negotiation was put under way in London at the end of 1841.

Difficulties developed in the course of the work. The time allowed for it was short. The ministry wished the negotiation to begin promptly in order to take advantage of the presence of a friendly Whig majority in the Senate and to avert the dangers of the developing quarrel between Tyler and his party. Aberdeen was able to give little supervision to the Oregon portion of the instruction. He was busy mastering the manifold problems of Britain's world position and acquainting himself with the intricacies of the Northeastern boundary controversy and the right-of-search problem. He had little knowledge of the Oregon issue. Ashburton, likewise, was unacquainted with that problem—his special competence was the Northeastern problem. The Oregon portion of the Ashburton instruction was left, therefore, to be drawn by the career staff of the Foreign Office.

This was leaderless at the time. It had lost its veteran head, John Backhouse, through illness. Aberdeen was obliged to fill the post with an emergency appointment. The person he chose was Henry U. Addington, who had been in retirement for some years. Addington was widely experienced in American affairs. He had been minister to the United States in 1824–25 and Under Secretary for Foreign Affairs for Canning thereafter. He had been one of the plenipotentiaries meeting Gallatin in the negotiation of 1826–27 in London. He had been found by Gallatin "extremely difficult," in that negotiation.

The Oregon instruction he drew for Ashburton was based on his earlier experiences. Its first authorization was an offer which was a verbatim copy of a proposal received from Simpson in 1825. The proposal was to start the boundary at a point where the 49th parallel intersects the crest of the Stony Mountains. The line was to drop southward along the crest to the Snake River, and thence follow the Snake and the Columbia to the sea. This was a line Canning had seen no point in proposing. He had already offered a more favorable one to the American negotiator in 1823–24 without success. The Snake line was the one Addington in 1842 directed Ashburton to begin with in his negotiation. The second offer was to be the 49th parallel to the Columbia and the river to the sea. This had been thrice refused by the United States in previous negotiations. It was made Ashburton's final recourse. He was not authorized to repeat the *enclave* offer of 1826. The *enclave* offer was neither described nor referred to in the instruction. The fact that it had once been held out was unknown to Aberdeen or to Ashburton.

The negotiation with Webster under these circumstances ran onto shoals promptly. Ashburton informed Webster, at the outset, of the limits of his instructions. Mystified, Webster took refuge in a misty proposal. He suggested a "tri-partite" arrangement involving the harbor at San Francisco, an arrangement intended to be worked out in the future between the American, British, and Mexican governments.[18] This derailed the negotiation, which was never, thereafter, resumed. Ashburton could doubtless have obtained a liberalization of his Oregon instructions had he realized in time their restrictive character and the vagueness and difficulty of Webster's response to them. But he realized this only when his mission had virtually come to an end. He had found the mission in its Northeastern boundary phases strenuous. He labored under the infirmities of age. He was tortured at the end of the mission by the heat and humidity of the Washington summer, and was eager to return home. He did not see the signs of a new storm in Anglo-American relations rising in the West and was satisfied with what he had accomplished.

The failure of Ashburton to settle the Oregon dispute was a disappointment to Aberdeen and to Peel. They had hoped for a clean sweep of Anglo-American controversies. They were uneasy over

[18] See Essay 6.

the marked increase in agitation on the Oregon issue in the United States. In 1843 Aberdeen moved, in response to nudging from Edward Everett, the American minister in London, whom he trusted, toward a new negotiation in Washington. He had in mind for it a new minister to the United States, Richard Pakenham, who had won his spurs as a minister to Mexico.

Aberdeen canvassed with Everett the question of Pakenham's instructions. He learned from Everett of Canning's *enclave* offer of 1826. He was astounded to hear of it. He had to have it verified by a reference to the published record of the 1826 negotiation, which Everett sent him. In chagrin he turned to Addington, who insisted he had no recollection of such an offer ever having been made. When Aberdeen reported this to Everett the latter was "staggered," as he wrote home. Addington was the plenipotentiary who had submitted the offer to Gallatin.

Aberdeen took a very direct hand, thereafter, in preparing Pakenham's instructions. He sought to make them sufficiently elastic. He repeated every concession previously offered the American government, including the *enclave* offer of 1826. In trying to meet the American demand for safe harbors on the coast he offered to convert any which the American government might desire between the 49th parallel and the Columbia River, whether on the mainland or on Vancouver Island, into free ports. He specifically mentioned harbors in Puget Sound among those which could become free ports. He had no authority by himself to go further in the formal instructions. He believed the cabinet would oppose anything more. He directed Pakenham to propose arbitration to the American government if the negotiation should not prosper.

Candidly he told Pakenham on the latter's departure for Washington that he was not very sanguine of an agreement on the basis of these instructions. Should such apprehensions prove well founded Pakenham was told to draw out from the American negotiator, without committing himself or his government, a proposal that the 49th parallel, to the water's edge, be the boundary, with the proviso that all Oregon harbors south of it, including the one at the Columbia's mouth, be free ports to Great Britain. The American negotiator might be given reason to hope, Pakenham was told, that such a proposal would be viewed by the British cabinet with favor. But he was warned that the cabinet had not been consulted and would need to be won over. Early in 1844 Pakenham was sent a private letter for his guidance embodying these conversations. The letter was a record of the effect on Aberdeen of the revelation made by Everett of Canning's *enclave* offer of 1826 and, also, of a growing understanding of the Oregon problem.

In Washington the chief interest of the Tyler government at the time of Pakenham's arrival was the annexation of Texas. This was being energetically pressed by Abel P. Upshur as Secretary of State, and, after his death, by John C. Calhoun. In American politics in this period the annexation issue and the Oregon issue were being joined in preparation for the oncoming presidential election of 1844. Expansionist Democrats were hoping to profit from such expansionist sentiment as existed in each section of the Union, by combining the "immediate" annexation of Texas with the acquisition of "All Oregon." Whigs, on the other hand, were hesitating on both counts. They considered the immediate annexation of Texas a danger to the harmony of the sections and an American claim to All Oregon to be not only extravagant but a menace to peace if pressed to a showdown.

In this climate of opinion Calhoun moved gingerly in the Oregon negotiation with Pakenham. He had, in the Senate, served as a brake on aggressive Oregon proposals. He had advocated a policy of "masterly inactivity." He now made clear to Pakenham that any British proposal short of the line of the 49th parallel would run foul of the Senate. Also, he declined repeatedly, on the same ground, Pakenham's pleas for an arbitration. He could not be drawn into proposing terms of a settlement such as Pakenham had been directed to extract. The negotiation hardly more than drifted as the Tyler administration, in impotence, moved to its close.[19]

A decided change came with the advent of Polk. Polk was committed, or at least he seemed to be, to an All Oregon program. He had pledged himself to it in a public letter prior to the Democratic nominating convention of May 1844. Even more, he seemed committed by the party's platform, which declared that no portion of the Oregon territory was to be "ceded" to England or to any other power. On entering the White House he declared in his Inaugural Address that American title to the country of the Oregon was

[19] St. George L. Sioussat, "John Caldwell Calhoun," in S. F. Bemis, ed., *American Secretaries of State and Their Diplomacy* (New York, 1928), V, 191-197.

"clear and unquestionable." He won applause in these ways from expansionists in the Middle West and elsewhere.

Yet several months after delivering the Inaugural he proposed to Pakenham—through his Secretary of State, James Buchanan—to divide the Oregon Country by the old American offer—the line of the 49th parallel. He withheld one offer his predecessors had proposed—British rights to navigate the Columbia south of 49°. To Pakenham this seemed so far short of his government's requirements that he peremptorily rejected the offer. Imitating Gallatin's action of 1826 he did not even take it for reference to his government. Polk promptly ordered it withdrawn, and refused to resubmit it when Pakenham requested resubmission on orders from Aberdeen. The negotiation came to an end.

Polk carried the problem now to Congress. In his first annual message of December 2, 1845, he reported what had happened. He explained that he had made a compromise offer out of deference to his predecessors. He assured Congress he would not make it again. He would make no offer to the British. He recommended to Congress that it adopt a resolution serving "notice" on the British of termination of the convention of joint occupation. He declared that when the convention had expired after the notice "we shall have reached a period when the national rights in Oregon must either be abandoned or firmly maintained. That they can not be abandoned without a sacrifice of both national honor and interest is too clear to admit of doubt."

The tone of the message was decidedly martial. It cheered those among the Democrats who believed the British had no rights in Oregon, were mere intruders there, and were, by their presence, violating the principles announced by Monroe in 1823 against new colonization of America by European states.[20] In Congress the "notice" debate, in which such views were persistently aired by Democrats, ran to nearly the end of April 1846.

Polk gave encouragement as far as he could to those views. He calculated that a show of belligerence, combined with the "notice" which would follow, would induce the British to come to terms. He was a believer in tactics of pressure in diplomacy. Yet, in correspondence with Louis McLane, the new American minister in

---

[20] Frederick Merk, *Monroe Doctrine and American Expansionism, 1843–1849* (New York, 1966), ch. 4.

London, he remained moderate in his objectives. He wished merely that the British government repeat the offer he had submitted to it and which Pakenham had rudely declined—the old offer of the line of 49°. He let McLane know, however, that a British proposal in which a right to the free navigation of the Columbia south of 49° was reserved to British subjects would not be entertained by him. He thought free navigation had been improvidently offered by his predecessors in the hope of a settlement. In general he differed from his predecessors less in the matter of his goals than in the manner of reaching them. He believed in forcing things to a decision. His tactics were those of confrontation. His 54° 40' tone and his notice proposal to Congress were part of the forcing idea.

The implementation of this idea was attended by difficulties. One was that Congress remained uncertain whether all this belligerence was really meant or was just a pose. Congress could not be enlightened since even a confidential word would leak out, the British would get wind of it, and the act would be spoiled. Yet those members wishing a peaceful settlement of the issue were reluctant to vote on the notice without knowing whether it meant peace or war.

Congress was Democratic in its majorities in both houses. But its Democrats were divided on the Oregon issue. A small but vocal minority, chiefly from the Middle West, was attracted by the lure of All Oregon even if it should lead to war with the British. But the great majority wished a peaceful settlement of the dispute and thought one based on a partition at the line of the 49th parallel was attainable. This feeling was especially strong among cotton Democrats in the South. They were not interested in vast territorial additions to the northward, and they wished British markets to remain available for their surplus cotton. An Alabama congressman, Edmund S. Dargan, voiced this feeling in the House in a speech and in a resolution that attracted wide national attention. He declared the Anglo-American differences over the Oregon Country were still subject to honorable negotiation and compromise. He proposed: "That the line [49°] separating the British provinces of Canada from the United States should be extended due west to the coast . . . and from thence through the centre of the Straits of Fuca to the Pacific ocean. . . ."[21] He actually would have

[21] Cong. Globe, 29 Cong., 1 Sess., 346 (Feb. 9, 1846).

attached this idea to the resolution of notice. In its rationalizations and in its form the Dargan proposal was reminiscent of the Gallatin and Rush proposal of 1818. In the Senate similar sentiment was set forth by Calhoun, who had returned there late in 1845. Among Northern Democrats in Congress, many, representing the Van Buren wing of the party, were of like views and were suspicious of Polk and his tactics.

Whigs were a minority, though a strong one in both houses. They were nearly unanimous in wishing a peaceful settlement of the Oregon dispute on the basis of a partition at the line of 49°. None of them liked the idea of arming Polk with a pressure weapon against the British in view of the belligerence of his tone. Whigs and Southern Democrats of like feeling controlled Senate voting whenever they joined forces. They were the real center of authority in the American government on the Oregon issue.

As the debate in Congress dragged on into the spring of 1846, these elements came to regard the notice resolution in a new light. They came to believe that, couched in conciliatory terms, it might seem to the British government to be an opportunity to reopen negotiations on the closed issue. They had learned from reading the British newspapers, from observing the debates in Parliament on the Corn Laws and the conciliatory Oregon views of opposition leaders, especially the broad hint thrown out by Lord Clarendon—Aberdeen's friend—that a notice resolution might actually be welcomed in London. Some of them appear to have been in touch with Pakenham. They were hopeful that the notice would be followed by a British proposal of real concession to the United States. Consequently, the form of notice became an important issue in the Senate discussion. Under the leadership of a Southern Whig, Senator John J. Crittenden, a form that was conciliatory was adopted by a large majority, despite the agonized opposition of the All Oregon leader, William Allen. A conference committee of the two houses, from which Allen was pointedly excluded, also agreed to a notice which was conciliatory. This was overwhelmingly adopted by both houses and was sent to London by Polk.

In London it was promptly accepted as an invitation to a new negotiation. It led to the framing of a highly conciliatory offer by the cabinet under the inspiration of Aberdeen, with discreet McLane guidance from the outside. The offer was to partition

Oregon by a line which would follow the 49th parallel from the Rocky Mountains to the water's edge, then go out to sea via the Strait of Juan de Fuca so as not to sever Vancouver Island. Regarding the Columbia River, it reserved navigation rights south of 49° to the Hudson's Bay Company, though not generally to British subjects. It furthermore extended protection to the posts and lands of the Company actually in the latter's possession south of the line.

The offer reached Polk on June 6. It did not meet all his requirements, but it met the essential ones. The Mexican War was then under way. Polk thought the offer worthy of being sent to the Senate for previous advice. He did not wish to do this on his own responsibility, however, for it meant betraying his 54° 40' followers. He believed he should have cabinet unanimity even for a decision to refer it to the Senate. Buchanan, who suddenly exhibited 54° 40' symptoms, was bludgeoned into changing his mind and the offer went to the Senate. It was at once approved there without a change. It was formalized by Buchanan and Pakenham into a treaty which the Senate ratified by more than the needed two-thirds majority. It was sent by Polk at once to London to be proclaimed. The treaty was basically the proposal Gallatin and Rush had made in London twenty-eight years before.[22]

*　　*　　*　　*

It is an axiom of diplomacy that a boundary dispute dragged across numerous negotiations and many years picks up added difficulties in the process. The Oregon dispute did this for both contestants, and for the British especially. The British government, at the end of a quarter century's diplomacy, was committed to rejection of American partition proposals at the 49th parallel. It had become committed despite the uneasiness of Liverpool in the negotiation of 1826–27 and that of Aberdeen later. Aberdeen would have been willing as early as December 1843 to ignore the commitment. But Peel, responsible for a domestic program drawing fire from his own ranks, was fearful of doing so. Such action would have meant abandoning British nationals resident in the disputed area. Worse yet, it would have meant abandoning British prestige, and even honor—at least so the opposition would charge—and doing it under the menaces of an American President. Peel had been

[22] See Essay 13.

under fire of that kind from Palmerston for years, especially with regard to the settlement of the Northeastern boundary dispute.

In Peel's early life a challenge to British honor, not unlike that from Polk, had come from the Spanish government. Spain had claims to sovereignty in the Oregon Country of old date which were being intruded upon by adventurers—British, Russian, and American—in the 1780's. In 1789 a Spanish navy captain, in enforcement of his country's claim, had seized British fur traders establishing themselves at Nootka, dispossessed them of their property, and imprisoned them. Intense excitement had followed in England. A general European war—with Great Britain and her allies ranged on one side and Spain and her allies on the other—seemed ahead. But in the end Spain, abandoned by France, backed down in the face of British power. She agreed in 1790 to a restoration of the property and site seized, paid an indemnity to the injured traders, and renounced her claims to exclusive sovereignty on the Northwest Coast.[23]

Peel realized that so resounding a diplomatic victory would be recalled and used against his government if he were to back down before the pressures being applied by Polk. Aberdeen knew it also, and was aware of the obstacle it formed to a peaceful settlement. This is what he meant when he replied again and again to Everett's urging of a settlement on the basis of a partition at the line of the 49th parallel that his government could not concede everything it had so often and so long refused.

That roadblock to peace was removed as a result of disaster in Ireland in 1845, the effect of which in England was disruption of the ministry and reorganization of the government. A blight in Ireland in the summer of 1845 destroyed the potato crop. The harvest was otherwise meager in Ireland and in England. Peel saw famine ahead. He sent out summonses in the autumn for a special cabinet council to consider opening British ports free of duty to foreign grain. He proposed to the council a plan to suspend the Corn Laws. This was bitterly opposed by the protectionists in the party and it led, early in December, to dissolution of the cabinet. Lord John Russell

[23] A thorough account of this episode is William R. Manning, *The Nootka Sound Controversy*, in American Historical Association, *Annual Report, 1904*, 281–478.

was called to form a Whig government. He consented but failed, owing to objections among Whigs to serving with Palmerston as Foreign Minister. Peel was recalled and his cabinet was reconstituted without the protectionists, who became an angry opposition. Peel and Russell went forward, in informal coalition, to repeal the Corn Laws. They extended their cooperation to foreign affairs. The Palmerston element was effectively silenced. Peel was able to permit Aberdeen to make an Oregon offer safe from partisan charges of dishonor. He was able to win, on behalf of concession, the moral peace fervor of the Anti-Corn Law crusade.[24]

But what of Polk and his All Oregon followers? What of their impassioned argument that the rights of the United States to All Oregon were clear and unquestionable and that the rights of Great Britain were nil? Was this an extravagance of election day politics carried into the White House by Polk and there used as a tactic in diplomacy?

In answering these questions the historian looks farther than to the pronouncements and writings of Polk. These are contradictory —one thing said to the public and another privately written. The historian looks to the basic interests and sentiments of the President. Polk was a Southerner. Like Calhoun he was more interested in Southern than in Northern expansion. He deeply desired Texas. He wished to have the Californias from Mexico. He wished in addition to have much more from Mexico than he got by the Treaty of Guadalupe Hidalgo. Cuba, he desired from Spain, and moved with energy to acquire. He was the first American president to attempt acquisition of the island. He attempted it in spite of the explosion his success would have set off in sectional politics.[25] For Oregon he had no such passion. All he deeply wanted was what his predecessors had wanted when in 1818 and later they proposed the line of the 49th parallel. This he set out to get. The rest was politics and tactics. His diary and his instructions to his minister in London, sent through Buchanan, bear out such a judgment. He was not averse to merging politics with diplomatic tactics in the program of expansion which he and his party had formulated in 1844. Yet he did question the rectitude of extremists

[24] See Essay 9.
[25] Merk, *Monroe Doctrine and American Expansionism*, ch. 9.

in the final stages of the notice debate, who, in their wild course were, he thought, interested not in 54° 40′ or 49°, but in '48. The extremists, in turn, believed they had been betrayed by their leader.

In the period of the evolution of the Oregon question two courses of development occurred. One was the solidification of a pattern—a pattern of diplomatic offers and rejections of offers by the two claimants to the Oregon Country. The other was a transformation of means of travel, a transformation that changed the stakes of diplomacy in Oregon and also concepts of the extent to which a democracy could expand its boundaries without perishing. The two developments went hand in hand and their conjunction prepared the way for crisis. Domestic politics, personal and sectional, and the tactics of Polk in diplomacy—pressure and confrontation of the kind he was applying to Mexico in the Texas boundary issue—heightened the crisis, endangering Anglo-American peace.

The process by which this crisis was resolved is significant as an example of the peaceful settlement of an international dispute. It was the process of marshaling the latent peace forces in both countries. In the United States those forces were commerce in the cities; agriculture, chiefly in the Cotton Kingdom, which valued British markets; business and transportation throughout the nation faced with problems of rejuvenating an economy not yet recovered from the prostration of the early 1840's and needing the aid of British capital; above all, American common sense which considered the thesis that the British were intruders in the Oregon Country, who ought to be expelled, a form of lunacy. These forces brought the reckless and noisy expansionists, seeking political profit from the exploitation of a dangerous international issue, under control. They did it with quiet efficiency at the end of the Senate debate, acting through a coalition of peace Whigs and Southern Democrats which registered the real will of the American public.

In England the public likewise registered its will for peace in the crisis. It never had been roused by an election campaign on the Oregon issue. It was relatively uninterested in the Oregon Country. It had been made ready for concessions to the United States by propaganda quietly slipped into Conservative and Whig journals by Lord Aberdeen.[26] It was interested in the repeal of the Corn Laws. It was swayed by the peace appeal contained in the so-

[26] See Essay 10.

called "Friendly Addresses," which peace groups and the Anti-Corn Law League initiated in British cities and sent to peace groups in American cities.[27] It expressed its will, as did its counterpart in the United States, nonpartisanly through a coalition of Peelites, Russellites, and Anti-Corn Law Leaguers. It silenced the nationalists of the Palmerston school, indeed, induced Palmerston actually to applaud in the end the concessions made to the United States. The triumph of such elements and methods on opposite sides of the Atlantic was hardly less significant historically than the substance of the Oregon Treaty itself.

This treaty, ratified by the Senate on June 15, 1846, and proclaimed by Peel soon afterward, divided between the two claimants an area of approximately 500,000 square miles, an area equal in extent to that of Great Britain and Ireland, France, the two Germanies, Holland, and Belgium combined. Of this area it gave about half to each claimant and, in addition, effective outlets to the Pacific, the first Pacific outlets each had. It gave the United States and Canada windows to the Orient and interests, immediate and future, in the affairs of the Pacific world. Not least, it completed a transcontinental boundary that the United States and Canada have lived with in harmony for nearly a century and a quarter.

[27] Merle E. Curti, *The American Peace Crusade 1815–1860* (Durham, 1929), 113–117.

INDEX